Study Guide

Essentials of Managerial Finance

Principles and Practice

Study Guide

Essentials of Managerial Finance

Principles and Practice

James Buck
University of Virginia

Charles R. Idol
Idaho State University

Houghton Mifflin Company / Boston

Dallas   Geneva, Illinois   Hopewell, New Jersey   Palo Alto   London

Printed in the U.S.A.

ISBN: 0-395-30089-4

Contents

TO THE STUDENT   vii

PART I   THE NATURE AND SCOPE OF FINANCE   1
    1   Finance and the Firm   3
    2   The Operating Environment of the Firm   15
    3   Financial Statements and Ratios   36
    4   Budgeting   60
    5   The Mathematics of Finance   73

PART II   CAPITAL BUDGETING   89
    6   Capital Budgeting Under Conditions of Certainty   91
    7   Capital Budgeting and Risk   119

PART III   COST OF CAPITAL AND CAPITAL STRUCTURE   141
    8   An Introduction to the Cost of Capital   143
    9   Cost of Capital for Individual Securities   154
    10   Capital Structure and Cost of Capital   179
    11   Dividend Policy   200

PART IV   WORKING CAPITAL MANAGEMENT   213
    12   Cash and Marketable Securities   215
    13   Inventory and Accounts Receivable Management   228

PART V   SHORT AND INTERMEDIATE-TERM SOURCES OF FUNDS   243
    14   Sources and Forms of Short-Term Financing   245
    15   Sources and Forms of Intermediate-Term Financing   257

PART VI   LONG-TERM SOURCES OF FUNDS   273
    16   Marketing Long-Term Securities   275
    17   Long-Term Debt   286
    18   Preferred and Common Stock   299
    19   Convertible Securities and Warrants   314

PART VII   SPECIAL SITUATIONS IN FINANCIAL MANAGEMENT   327
    20   Mergers   329
    21   Failure and Reorganization   344
    22   Multinational Financial Management   359

CONTENTS

REVIEW TESTS   375
    For Part I   377
    For Part II   385
    For Part III   391
    For Part IV   399
    For Part V   404
    For Part VI   409
    For Part VII   414
    Answers to Review Tests   421

To The Student

This study guide is designed as a learning supplement to Bolten and Conn's Essentials of Managerial Finance. You will find the guide useful in preparing for class discussions and exams. Its ultimate objective, however, is to help you become more efficient and effective managers.

For each chapter in Essentials of Managerial Finance, this guide presents six parts:

1. Overview
2. Study Objectives
3. Chapter Outline
4. Study Problems
5. Review Questions
6. Key Definitions

The overview is a brief statement of the chapter content. You will probably use it to orient yourself to the overall subject matter of the chapter before reviewing it more intensively.

The study objectives correspond to the major questions asked at the beginning of each text chapter. They help organize the material into three or four key topics and show you exactly what you should be able to do when you have mastered the chapter.

The chapter outline is a major part of the study guide. It organizes all the points in the text and offers additional explanations and examples. You may want to concentrate on concepts that seemed difficult when first presented in the text or in class.

The study problems are a special feature of this guide. Each problem is intended to challenge you to think through and apply the concepts in the chapter. The best approach is to work out the solution yourself and then compare it with the solution in the guide. Or, if you are pressed for time, you may simply read through the problem and solution. The first option, of course, provides more opportunity for practical learning.

The review questions are multiple-choice questions that cover the entire chapter. Answers are provided to help you evaluate the extent of your learning.

Key definitions conclude each chapter in the study guide. They are in alphabetical order to provide a ready reference. When read consecutively, they provide a random review of key concepts in the chapter.

TO THE STUDENT

At the end of the study guide are seven review tests, one for each of the major parts of the text. Since each covers several chapters, they can help you prepare for major examinations. Answers are at the end of the guide.

This study guide is a "self-help" tool. By using it conscientiously along with the text, you should be able to reinforce and evaluate your learning throughout the course. We hope it will help you master the Essentials of Managerial Finance and face the future with confidence.

J. B.

C. R. I.

Part One
The Nature and Scope of Finance

The traditional view of the finance function was restricted to acquiring funds to finance projects. The contemporary view extends this responsibility to that of coordinating both financing and investment. The finance function of organizations in the future is expected to be even more expansive, dealing with mergers and acquisitions, hedging, and other activities that maintain the firm's direction toward its goals.

Part I of Essentials of Managerial Finance explains the fundamental functions of finance in varying organizational forms and economic environments/objectives (Chapter 1). Both internal and external characteristics of the firm are examined and interrelationships are outlined in Chapter 2. The analysis of the firm from a historical perspective is accomplished through the use of ratio analysis (Chapter 3), whereas forecasting, planning, and control are examined using the budget and pro forma statement approach (Chapter 4). Finally, Chapter 5 presents the mathematics of finance (time value of money) as an introduction to the area of investment decisions that must be made in the capital budgeting process, which is presented in Part II.

Chapter One
Finance and the Firm

OVERVIEW

This chapter is an introduction to the field of financial management within various forms of business organizations. The characteristics of proprietorships, partnerships, and corporations are presented. The impact of organizational structure on the finance function is discussed in terms of goals to be achieved by the firm. Profit maximization and shareholder-wealth maximization are contrasted with other company goals, including fulfillment of the firm's social responsibility.

STUDY OBJECTIVES

1. To define the characteristics of proprietorships, partnerships, and corporations.

2. To describe the position of financial officers in the managerial hierarchy and to outline their functions.

3. To compare and contrast various major goals the firm may choose and to explain how they affect financial decisions.

CHAPTER OUTLINE

I. Several forms of business organizations exist in the United States today.

   A. Proprietorships make up the largest number of business organizations.

      1. Proprietorships are typically smaller businesses that require no formal procedures to establish or dissolve.

      2. The owner's personal liability for the firm's debts is unlimited.

      3. Financing is usually provided by the owners or by government small-business loans. Loans are made to the owner, not the firm.

      4. Company earnings or losses are included in the owner's personal income for tax purposes. Certain tax-deferred retirement plans (KEOGH),

which may not be available to other business people, are available to proprietors.

5. Government regulations (licenses, employer taxes, social security, and so on) are a significant aspect of proprietorship operations. Proprietors of very small businesses may be excluded from certain overburdening regulations.

6. The proprietorship technically ceases to exist upon the death of the owner. Subsequent estate and inheritance taxes may critically impair the continuity of the organization.

B. Partnerships represent contractual (legal) arrangements among the partners. They make up about 8 percent of all the businesses in the United States.

1. Many partnerships are registered under the Uniform Partnership Act with the secretary of the state in which they are established.

2. Two basic forms of partnerships are commonly found.

    a. General partnerships are agreements whereby any partner can enter into contractual obligations on behalf of the firm. The participants usually bear the management responsibilities.

    b. Limited partnerships are created to limit the authority, as well as the benefits and liability, of a partner. General partners are personally liable for the obligations of the firm, whereas the personal liability of limited partners is subject to legal limits.

3. The financing of partnerships is similar to that of proprietorships. The partnership does not have "securities" to sell.

4. The partnership agreement specifies the distribution of earnings. Losses as well as gains are divided among the partners in accordance with the conditions of the contract, and they become part of the partners' personal income.

5. Partnerships and proprietorships are regulated and taxed by the government in the same general manner.

6. The partnership agreement can be used to indicate the disposition of a partner's interest upon that partner's death. Thus it is possible to arrange for the continuity of the partnership.

C. Although corporations make up only about 14 percent of all U.S. firms, they account for the vast majority of sales (86 percent). The corporate form is easily distinguished from other organizational structures.

1. Laws limit the liability of shareholders in a corporation to the amount of funds invested. The corporation is a separate legal entity.

2. Corporations can finance growth by creating securities to sell in the financial markets. The type of security sold can be tailored to meet investor expectations.

3. Owners of common stock are entitled to residual profits--that is, earnings remaining after all prior expenses and other claims have been satisfied.

4. Federal, state, and sometimes local governments regulate and tax corporations.

    a. A double tax occurs at the federal level, because the corporation pays taxes on earnings and the shareholder pays taxes on dividends (in excess of $100) paid from corporate earnings.

    b. Corporations usually pay an annual franchise tax in the states in which they conduct business.

5. The continuity of a corporation is independent of any single shareholder. No interruption occurs in normal operations when a shareholder dies or sells her or his ownership position. This gives the corporation a theoretically infinite life.

D. Note: The financial functions of investing and fund raising are common to all forms of enterprise. However, because the corporate form dominates the proprietorship and partnership in relative productive importance, much of our discussion will be couched in corporate terms. Nevertheless, most of the general financial principles developed in this book are applicable to all types of businesses.

II. The financial officer is a member of the corporate staff. The accompanying simplified organizational chart for a corporation illustrates his or her position.

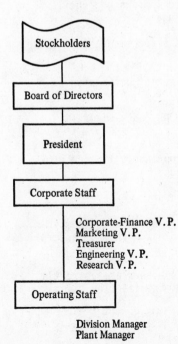

Stockholders

Board of Directors

President

Corporate Staff

Corporate-Finance V.P.
Marketing V.P.
Treasurer
Engineering V.P.
Research V.P.

Operating Staff

Division Manager
Plant Manager

A. The president is primarily responsible to the board of directors for the daily operations of the firm.

B. The corporate-finance vice president is directly responsible to the president in the areas of selecting investments and financing growth.

   1. The evaluation of investment opportunities requires that the financial officer perform several functions.

     a. Gather relevant information on each proposed project.

     b. Conduct a standardized evaluation and comparison of the project with other projects.

     c. Communicate the results of the evaluation to the firm's decision makers.

   2. The general path that investment proposals take is as follows:

     a. An idea for a new project is developed in a corporate staff office and communicated to the staff via the president.

     b. The staff vice president sends a memo to the president, requesting the project.

     c. The president requests the staff vice president to prepare a detailed forecast of the project's potential (inflows and outflows).

     d. The president requests the corporate-finance vice president to evaluate the project in terms of forecasted inflows and outflows as well as the corporation's position and goals.

     e. The corporate-finance vice president makes a recommendation to the president.

     f. The president acts on the recommendation, asking permission of the board of directors when necessary.

     g. The treasurer disburses the funds required during implementation and operation.

   3. The corporate-finance vice president must appropriately finance proposed projects. Factors in this process include:

     a. Determining the total amount of funds necessary.

     b. Determining how much of the required outlay should come from internal funds (reinvestment of earnings) and how much from external funds (security offerings).

     c. Determining what type of securities that investors are currently willing to purchase will minimize cost and maximize flexibility and investor receptiveness.

III. The tasks of the financial officer are suggested by the names given to the supporting staff in the finance area. The accompanying diagram shows a common division of the financial officer's staff.

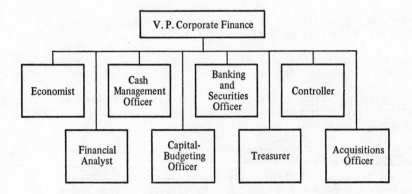

A. The staff <u>economist</u> concentrates on forecasting general economic trends and sales and costs for specific projects.

B. The <u>financial analyst</u> has the task of analyzing internally the financial and operating results of different profit centers in the firm.

C. The <u>cash management officer</u> must balance the corporate goals of maintaining liquidity and eliminating idle funds.

D. The <u>capital-budgeting officer</u> has the task of evaluating long-term investment proposals.

E. The <u>banking and securities officer</u> must maintain a strong working relationship with the suppliers of funds (banks and investment bankers) that sell the firm's securities to the public.

F. The firm's <u>acquisitions officer</u> must search for other firms that might be profitably absorbed into the firm's operation.

G. The supporting staff of the corporate-finance vice president can vary considerably from one firm to another, but they must all work together to attain the overall corporate goals.

IV. The firm's financial decisions must be compatible with the firm's general corporate goals. Many corporate goals exist.

A. <u>Profit maximization</u> is the goal of increasing the firm's dollar earnings as much as possible in the shortest period of time.

1. Its major advantage is its focus on short-run profits, which are necessary to the firm's continued existence.

2. It also has several disadvantages.

     a. Profit maximization typically overlooks the risks associated with achieving short-run profits.

     b. Short-run emphasis may ignore the long-run profitability of the firm.

     c. Management may be unwilling to endorse profit maximization because of the risks it entails to their own job security.

     d. Projects that achieve the goal of profit maximization may be too costly for the firm to finance.

B. Shareholder-wealth maximization is the goal of maximizing the price of the firm's common stock. Share prices are a function of management's performance in the following areas.

     1. Earnings achievement. Positive earnings and dividend growth create the perception of efficient management. Investors respond to this perception by purchasing additional shares, creating upward pressure on prices. Negative earnings create the opposite perception and tend to reduce share price.

     2. Risk management. Investors consider the appropriate amount of risk to be a favorable sign of managerial performance, which encourages them to purchase shares and hence increases prices. When management takes on too much or too little risk, investors change their ownership position to achieve the level of risk they desire relative to profit potential.

     3. External factors. Political events and changes in interest rates can affect investors' perceptions of the firm. These events are essentially beyond the control of the financial officer.

     4. Several drawbacks exist in the goal of maximizing shareholder wealth.

          a. Management may be frustrated and distracted when share prices do not accurately reflect their performance. The short run may become more important than long-term considerations.

          b. External factors beyond management's control may overpower management's ability to maximize shareholder wealth.

C. Behavioral goals do not emphasize the attainment of any maximization objective. Satisficing is the objective of barely satisfying both stockholder and management. This approach is often considered the only attainable operational goal of the firm. Satisficing tends to resolve conflicts among members of management as well as between management and shareholders.

     1. Severe penalties exist for unsuccessful investment and financing decisions, even when the probability of failure was communicated to others before the decision was made. However, there is often no penalty for a mediocre performance. Thus management must consider the unequal rewards and penalties associated with their decisions.

2. The satisficating approach has several drawbacks.

    a. Satisficing requires that we partially ignore factors that are critical to the maximization goals.

    b. Partial solutions may lead to a takeover by another corporation or by existing shareholders.

    c. Satisficing firms produce profits and share prices that are vulnerable to competing firms with maximization goals.

    d. Satisficing firms have stated corporate goals that emphasize the status quo.

D. Managerial-reward maximization is the goal of managers who attempt to maximize their own welfare and benefits.

1. Decisions are made largely in terms of the impact they will have on the manager's salary and/or expense account.

2. The basic drawback of this approach is that it distorts the manager's investment and financing decisions, leading to adverse changes in profits.

3. Managerial-reward maximization does not maximize profits, share prices, or anything other than the manager's benefits.

E. Corporate social responsibility is the contention that the firm should bear the costs of the negative effects it has on society.

1. Government is no longer considered responsible for detrimental industrial activities.

2. The corporation is a grant or trust from the people, which requires that it reflect the social qualities of a "good citizen."

3. The extent of the corporation's social responsibility is debatable.

    a. The firm's "moral minimum" is its responsibility not to initiate programs that would have unavoidable negative effects.

    b. At the other extreme, the firm is required to correct past and existing social injury.

    c. Most firms adopt a compromise position between the moral minimum and the other extreme.

4. The goal of social responsibility has certain drawbacks.

    a. Decreased efficiency and higher prices may result from the firm's attempts to live up to its social responsibility.

    b. Competing firms operating in areas wherein social-responsibility programs are less demanding have a competitive advantage over firms that attempt to eliminate their contributions to social injustices.

F. Conflicts between corporate activities and established goals will occur no matter which goal is selected. There are several reasons for this conflict.

   1. Some managers concentrate on internal operating goals without recognizing the larger, overall corporate goal.

   2. Some managers feel that they are not sufficiently rewarded for their performance and thereby adopt the goal of maximizing managerial rewards.

   3. Government policies and regulations can force management to accept less than maximizing strategies.

   4. Conflicts can exist between the general corporate goals themselves. For example, social responsibility may interfere with profit maximization or shareholder-wealth maximization.

G. Shareholder-wealth maximization is the goal that firms should, but do not always, strive to achieve.

REVIEW QUESTIONS

1. Proprietorships make up the _____ number of business organizations in the United States.
   a. largest
   b. smallest
   c. neither of these

2. In a proprietorship, the owner's personal liability for the firm's debt is
   a. limited to his or her investment.
   b. dependent on the asset value.
   c. unlimited.
   d. none of these.

3. Earnings from a proprietorship are taxed at
   a. the U.S. partnership tax rates.
   b. the U.S. corporate tax rates.
   c. the capital-gains tax rates.
   d. the personal-income tax rate of the owner.

4. If the owner of a proprietorship dies, the firm technically
   a. continues as usual.
   b. ceases to exist.
   c. operates on a reduced scale.
   d. none of these.

5. In a limited partnership, limited partners have _____ on their personal liability.
   a. no limits
   b. legal limits
   c. decreasing limits
   d. none of these

6. The partnership agreement can be used to
   a. declare the payment of dividends.
   b. set up the sale of securities.
   c. minimize the U.S. partnership tax.
   d. assure the continuity of the partnership.

7. Although corporations make up the smallest number of business organizations in the United States, they account for approximately _____ percent of total sales.
   a. 14
   b. 20
   c. 60
   d. 86
   e. none of these

8. Laws limit the liability of shareholders in a corporation to
   a. the expected dividends.
   b. the current market value of the stock.
   c. the amount of funds invested.
   d. none of these.

9. Owners of common stock are entitled to profit after the payment or retention of:
   a. dividends to preferred stockholders.
   b. interest charges.
   c. retained earnings.
   d. all of these.
   e. none of these.

10. If the corporation pays cash dividends, there is a _____ tax at the federal level.
    a. lower
    b. higher
    c. double
    d. new

11. The continuity of a corporation is generally _____ a single shareholder's position.
    a. dependent on
    b. independent of
    c. responsive to
    d. none of these

12. The _____ of the firm is primarily responsible to the board of directors for the financial operation of the firm.
    a. financial officer
    b. treasurer
    c. president
    d. none of these

13. In determining the type of securities to use in financing growth, the financial officer seeks to
    a. minimize cost.
    b. maximize flexibility.
    c. maximize investor receptiveness.
    d. all of these.

14. The financial analyst within the corporate-finance staff has the task of
    a. recommending projects to be implemented.
    b. maintaining liquidity and eliminating idle funds.
    c. evaluating the internal performance of divisions.
    d. all of these.

15. Profit maximization is the goal of
    a. maximizing the market price of common stock.
    b. increasing the firm's dollar earnings.
    c. satisfying both management and owners.
    d. none of these.

16. Profit maximization as a goal has the drawback(s) of
    a. overlooking risks.
    b. maximizing share prices.
    c. ignoring the long-run profitability of the firm.
    d. both a and b.
    e. both a and c.

17. Shareholder-wealth maximization is a goal that
    a. may frustrate and distract management when share prices do not reflect performance.
    b. may be offset by external factors that overshadow the performance of management.
    c. seeks to maximize stock prices.
    d. all of these.

18. Satisficing
    a. is the corporate goal of seeking to satisfy both stockholders and management.
    b. requires that some important factors be partially ignored.
    c. can result in profits and share prices that are vulnerable to firms with maximization goals.
    d. all of these.

19. The goal of managerial-reward maximization suggests that
    a. managers will attempt to maximize their own welfare and benefits.
    b. managers will seek to maximize sales.
    c. managers will seek to maximize shareholder wealth.
    d. none of these.

20. The goal of corporate social responsibility contends that
    a. government is responsible for harmful industrial activities.
    b. corporations know what is best for society.
    c. corporations should bear the costs of their detrimental effects on society.
    d. corporations should take responsibility for their employees' social lives.

21. A drawback of the goal of attaining corporate social responsibility is that
    a. most firms do not subscribe to this goal.
    b. it reduces efficiency and leads to higher prices.
    c. firms that are not required to comply can gain competitive advantages.
    d. both b and c.
    e. none of these.

KEY DEFINITIONS

Acquisitions officer: member of the financial staff who seeks other firms that might be profitably absorbed.

Banking and securities officer: member of the financial staff who maintains good relations with the financial community.

Capital-budgeting officer: member of the financial staff who evaluates long-term investment projects.

Cash management officer: member of the financial staff who forecasts and manages the firm's liquidity and excess funds.

Corporate social responsibility: the view that the firm should bear the costs of any detrimental effects it has on society.

Economist: member of the financial staff who is concerned with economic forecasting.

Finance function: financial manager's role of determining what to invest in and how to finance those investments.

Financial analyst: member of the financial staff who analyzes (internally) the financial and operating results of divisions of the firm.

General partnership: a legal association in which each partner represents the firm, may enter into contractual obligations in the firm's behalf, and has unlimited personal liability.

Investor receptiveness: investors' willingness to purchase various securities.

Limited partnership: a legal association that limits the authority and liability of each limited partner.

Managerial-reward maximization: the goal of seeking to maximize the managers' welfare and benefits.

Partnership: a legal association of two or more people as co-owners of a business.

Profit maximization: the goal of increasing the firm's dollar earnings as much as possible.

Proprietorship: a form of business organization with a single owner who bears unlimited liability for the firm's debts and who owns all the firm's profits.

Satisficing: the goal of finding the "middle ground" that pacifies owners and managers but does not maximize anyone's position.

Shareholder-wealth maximization: the goal of maximizing the price of the firm's common stock.

CHAPTER 1

ANSWERS TO REVIEW QUESTIONS

1. a	7. d	12. c	17. d
2. c	8. c	13. d	18. d
3. d	9. d	14. c	19. a
4. b	10. c	15. b	20. c
5. b	11. b	16. e	21. d
6. d			

Chapter Two
The Operating Environment of the Firm

OVERVIEW

The firm does not operate in a vacuum. Decisions are made in the context of complex internal and external forces. Every analysis must include the possible impact of such external factors as consumers, government, regulatory authorities, investors, and inflation. The internal operating characteristics of the firm also play a large part in the financial decisions that must be made. This chapter focuses on the impact of both external forces and the internal characteristics of the firm in the development of management policies and decisions.

STUDY OBJECTIVES

1. To determine what groups and forces outside the firm might affect investment and financing decisions.

2. To examine the operating characteristics of the firm and their impact on investment and financing decisions.

3. To determine how management policies and abilities can affect investment decisions.

CHAPTER OUTLINE

I. Society and government are the two major forces outside the firm that affect its investment decisions.

   A. Consumer groups are becoming a larger factor in investment decisions.

      1. National boycotts of products can influence investment decisions.

      2. Consumer lobbyists have succeeded in influencing state and federal legislation.

   B. Environmentalists seek to preserve ecological balance. Organized protests by these groups have led to court rulings affecting the firm's investment decisions.

C. Government factors can be especially important in influencing investment
    decisions.

    1. The federal budget influences investment decisions through the
        government's purchasing activities and the effects of its fiscal
        policy.

        a. Companies that supply the government with resources it needs are
            directly affected by the budget.

        b. The fiscal policy of the government affects the general level of
            economic activity, which affects the firm's investment policy.

        c. The government's efforts to raise the funds needed to support the
            budget compete with the firm in acquiring financing and thereby
            affect the firm's investment decisions.

    2. Government taxing policies are designed to stabilize the economy.
        Changes in the general economy cause changes in taxes, which affect
        the firm's investment decisions.

    3. The U.S. Treasury alters interest rates as it attempts to support
        government spending. Government debt-management operations can de-
        stabilize interest rates and the availability of funds.

    4. Federal, state, and local government agencies impose regulations that
        affect the firm's investment decisions.

        a. The Securities and Exchange Commission (SEC) plays a significant
            part in the financial officer's activities when new securites are
            offered to the public.

        b. Wage and price controls have a dramatic effect on the firm's
            investment decisions and the willingness of investors to supply
            capital.

    5. The Federal Reserve System uses monetary policy to influence financial
        markets, which subsequently affects the firm's investment and financing
        decisions.

        a. Interest rates may increase or decrease, thereby changing the
            cost of capital. Rates are negotiated, and they depend on the
            strength of the firm and the lender, market conditions at the
            time, and the particular terms of the security being offered.

        b. The availability of funds affects the firm's investment and
            financing decisions. Monetary policy is used to tighten the
            availability of funds and to increase interest rates when demand
            is increasing. The opposite occurs when monetary policy is used
            to increase the supply of funds. In extreme cases, funds may
            not be available at any interest rate.

        c. The financial officer's skill in timing the acquisition of funds
            can increase the number of acceptable projects and help the firm
            earn the highest possible return on each dollar invested.

      d. <u>The security buyer's receptiveness</u> to the purchase of the firm's securities is generally a result of macroeconomic conditions, which are beyond the firm's direct control. The financial officer must tailor the firm's security offerings to the needs and expectations of potential buyers in order to achieve the lowest possible cost of capital for the firm.

D. <u>Inflation</u> has a pervasive effect on the nation's economy. Interest rates, project costs, and the availability of funds are all a function of changes in inflation.

    1. Investors demand higher interest rates to offset the anticipated effect of inflation during the period of the investment, prompting tighter marketing policies.

    2. The original costs of a long-term project can be dramatically affected by inflation—to the point of changing a profitable project into an unprofitable one.

    3. Inflation can force operating costs higher over a project's life.

    4. Inflation affects the project's replacement cost and salvage value. Replacement cost may exceed funds available when replacement is due, but this effect may be offset by inflated salvage values.

II. The operating characteristics of the firm affect its investment decisions.

A. Some firms operate in relatively stable industries. Forecasting and planning in these industries are usually reliable. At the other extreme, some firms exist in industries that have highly volatile environments, making forecasting and planning very difficult.

B. Of primary concern in planning is the sensitivity of the firm's proposed investment projects to the <u>general business cycle</u>. Some projects fluctuate in unison with the business cycle, whereas others move in an opposite manner. This is an important consideration in the investment decision.

C. The <u>quality of sales</u> associated with a project is an important aspect of the investment decision. Some projects are more sensitive to shifts in the desires of purchasers than others.

D. The <u>cost and availability of materials</u> can affect the investment decision. Some projects require resources that are beyond the control of the firm and very volatile. The probability that a project will become inoperable because resources become unavailable or prohibitively expensive must be considered in the investment decision.

E. The firm's response to the anticipated action of competitors is part of the investment decision.

F. The impact of external groups and forces must be considered in the investment and financing decisions of the firm. The financial officer must anticipate such effects and plan contingency strategies.

III. <u>Operating leverage</u> occurs when the firm can expand its operating revenues without proportionately increasing its operating costs.

   A. Operating revenues (sales) are the dollar amount of sales generated by the firm.

   B. Total operating costs are the sum of fixed and variable costs.

      1. <u>Fixed operating costs</u> are constant even though output may change. Per-unit fixed cost decreases as output increases, but the overall fixed cost does not change.

      2. <u>Variable operating costs</u> vary directly with the number of units produced and sold. Firms with high variable costs are more flexible and can adjust faster to market changes.

      3. <u>Total operating costs</u> equal fixed costs plus variable costs, excluding interest charges and taxes.

   C. Operating profit is the difference between operating revenues and total operating costs. Net profit equals operating profit less interest and tax charges.

   <u>Example</u>: Snyder, Inc., has total operating revenues (TR) of $26,000 and total operating costs (TOC) of $20,000. Its operating profit (OP) is

   $$OP = TR - TOC$$
   $$= \$26,000 - \$20,000$$
   $$= \$6,000$$

   D. Firms with high fixed cost and low variable operating cost experience greater variability in operating profits (greater operating leverage) than firms with low fixed cost and high variable operating cost. The implication for the financial officer is that operating leverage can be used to judge the degree to which the profits actually generated by a proposed investment may vary from projected profits. Firms attempt to balance the degree of operating leverage to a point at which the associated risk is acceptable.

   E. The <u>degree of operating leverage</u> depends on the proportion of fixed and variable costs in the total costs as well as on the firm's present level of output. At a particular level of output, the degree of operating leverage is found as follows:

   $$\text{Degree of operating leverage} = \frac{\text{percentage change in operating profits}}{\text{percentage change in sales}}$$

   <u>Example</u>: RCL, Inc., has the following operating statistics.

	1980		1979
Units produced	72,000		60,000
Sales (S)	$720,000		$600,000
Fixed cost (FC)	$240,000	$240,000	
Variable cost (VC)	72,000	60,000	
Total operating costs (TOC)	$312,000		$300,000
Operating profit (OP)	$408,000		$300,000

For RCL, Inc., the percentage change in <u>operating profit</u> is

$$\frac{\$408,000 - \$300,000}{\$300,000} = 36\%$$

and the percentage change in <u>output</u> is

$$\frac{\$720,000 - \$600,000}{\$600,000} = 20\%$$

The degree of operating leverage (DOL) for the RCL Company at an output of 60,000 units is

$$DOL_{60,000} = \frac{36\%}{20\%} = 1.80$$

DOL = 1.8 indicates that any percentage increase in sales will result in an increase in operating profits that is 1.8 percent of any increase in sales. That is, a 20 percent increase in sales would result in a (20 percent * 1.8) = 36 percent increase in operating profits, as experienced between 1979 and 1980. (A DOL of 1.8 indicates relatively large fixed costs and relatively low variable costs.)

    F. An alternative method of finding the DOL is as follows:

$$DOL_X = 1 + \frac{FC}{OP_X}$$

       where

             DOL_X = degree of operating leverage at output X
             FC   = fixed operating costs
             OP_X = operating profit at output X

<u>Example:</u> For the RCL example,

$$DOL_{60,000} = 1 + \frac{\$240,000}{\$300,000}$$
$$= 1 + .8$$
$$= 1.8$$

    G. The DOL of a firm reveals several important characteristics for the financial manager to consider.

       1. The variation of future operating profits is greater when fixed costs are high in relation to current operating profits.

       2. Operating profits vary more over the business cycle for firms with a high DOL than for firms with a low DOL.

       3. Projected profits may be more inaccurately estimated by the high-DOL firm than by the low.

       4. High-DOL firms should be more sensitive to external factors in their operating environment.

5. The high-DOL firm should be careful not to rely heavily on external funding for projects, because it is more likely to be unable to meet fixed charges. High-DOL firms that borrow heavily increase their likelihood of financial difficulty.

6. Greater operating risk (DOL) makes it harder to place the firm's securities at a reasonable cost.

IV. Financial officers are especially concerned about finding that number of units sold (or dollar sales) that achieves the <u>breakeven point</u> (at which the firm does not lose money). At this point, net profit is zero.

A. <u>Net profit</u> is the difference between total revenue and all costs. Interest expense is considered a part of total fixed costs, and taxes are included in total variable cost. Therefore,

$$\text{Net profit} = \text{total revenue} - \text{total cost}$$
$$NP = TR - TC$$

B. The breakeven point occurs where the project's <u>total revenue (TR) equals its total cost (TC)</u> and net profit is zero.

C. <u>Total revenue</u> is the selling price per unit multiplied by the number of units sold. That is,

$$TR = P * X$$

where

    TR = total revenue
    P = selling price per unit
    X = total number of units sold

D. <u>Total cost</u> is the sum of the fixed and variable costs.

$$TC = FC + (V * X)$$

where

    TC = total cost
    FC = fixed cost (including interest)
    V = variable costs per unit
    X = total number of units sold

E. Three basic steps can be used to derive the breakeven point.

1. The objective of breakeven is to find the level of output X at which TR = TC.

2. Using the detailed definitions of TR and TC, we find that $P * X = FC + (V * X)$.

3. Solving for X, we define the breakeven point as

$$X_{BEP} = \frac{FC}{P - V}$$

At this point (X_{BEP}), net profit is zero.

Example: Assume that the following price and cost statistics apply to the GENTRY Company.

Price per unit of output	$ 8.00
Total fixed cost	$64,000.00
Variable cost per unit	$ 4.00

The breakeven point (X_{BEP}) is

$$X_{BEP} = \frac{FC}{P - V} = \frac{\$64,000}{\$8.00 - \$4.00} = 16,000 \text{ units}$$

If GENTRY can sell 16,000 units, it will reach the breakeven point, at which net profit is zero. Selling less than 16,000 units would result in a loss; selling more would yield a profit.

F. The breakeven-point analysis can be presented in graphical form, as shown in the accompanying figure.

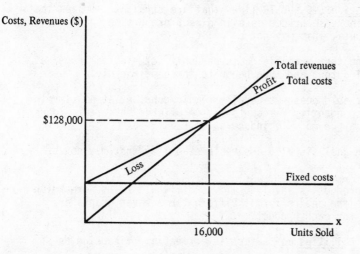

The vertical axis measures revenues and costs, whereas the horizontal axis measures the number of units sold.

Total revenue is directly related to the number of units produced. In this example, it increases $8.00 for every unit sold.

Fixed costs are represented as a horizontal line, because they do not change as the number of units sold changes.

The total-cost line starts at the fixed costs and increases by the additional variable cost as units are produced. Net profit or loss is the difference between the line representing total revenue and the line representing total costs. When TR = TC, the lines intersect and X_{BEP} is defined. X_{BEP} occurs where 16,000 units are produced and sold. Selling less than 16,000 units results in a net loss. Selling more than 16,000 units results in a profit.

G. Breakeven-point analysis can be used to quickly evaluate projects, alternative production techniques, and operating risk.

 1. To evaluate a project, the financial officer determines the breakeven point and the likelihood that the firm will achieve the required level of sales.

 2. Alternative selling prices or production methods can be easily and quickly examined via breakeven-point analysis. The sensitivity of a project to competitive pricing can also be examined using X_{BEP}.

 3. Projects with relatively high fixed costs compared to their variable costs usually reach the breakeven point at a much higher sales volume than projects with low fixed costs.

H. The linearity assumption (TC and TR lines that are straight) implies that costs and revenues increase or decrease in direct proportion to increases or decreases in output. This may not be valid.

 1. It is often found that variable costs per unit actually fall over a certain range of output and then begin to increase rapidly.

 2. Revenue per unit sold does not usually remain constant at all levels of sales, because quantity discounts may be offered on larger orders and price cuts may be made to induce sales.

 3. Linear breakeven analysis also assumes a stability that may not be attainable in practice.

I. When more than one product is involved, it is difficult to use breakeven analysis to evaluate the entire firm. Different breakeven graphs are usually constructed for each product.

V. Management policies and abilities may affect investment and financing decisions.

A. Management often adopts broad policy guidelines that affect investment and financing decisions. For example, it may automatically refuse to offer any debt securities.

B. Management may not have the ability or sufficient staff to undertake certain projects.

1. Projects are attractive when management has the ability to use the project's assets profitably.

2. Profit fluctuations are often reduced when management diversifies properly without losing control of its operations or going beyond its expertise.

3. The general operating skills of management play a significant part in reducing profit fluctuations. These skills include the ability to maintain internal control, to hire and keep valuable employees, to patent the firm's products, and to instill consumer loyalty.

C. Management's ability to respond quickly and correctly to the business cycle can make the difference between successful and unsuccessful projects. Typically, firms with large fixed costs and inflexible production schedules do not respond well to changes in the business cycle. Management's ability to reduce the negative impact of the cycle is critical to the success of most projects.

VI. The corporate financial staff must view its function as an integral part of the entire firm, not in terms of its special interests.

A. Successful financial management requires that the financial officer consider all facets of investment evaluation and financing. These facets include:

1. Providing a climate in which ideas flourish.

2. Gathering relevant information on a project's probable inflows and outflows.

3. Screening projects for initial accept-or-reject decisions.

4. Implementing the decision to accept (emphasizes the timing and financing factors).

5. Coordinating and controlling ongoing operations.

6. Providing contingency plans.

B. The integrated view of the finance function leads the corporate financial staff to base every decision on the impact it will have on the entire firm.

STUDY PROBLEMS

2.1. Greenway, Inc., produces silicone chips. Each chip sells for $30.00. Variable cost is $20.00 per chip, and fixed costs are $100,000 per year regardless of the number of chips sold.

a. Graphically determine the breakeven point of the firm.

b. What is the breakeven point in units?

c. What is the breakeven point in dollar sales?

d. Present an income statement on the basis of your answer to part c.

e. If 8,000 units were sold, what would be the net profit?

f. If 12,000 units were sold, what would be the net profit?

Solution

a.

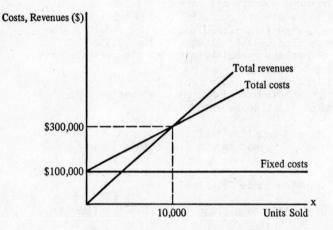

b. $X_{BEP} + \dfrac{FC}{P - V} = \dfrac{\$100,000}{\$30 - \$20} = 10,000$ units

c. $X_{BEP} = 10,000$ units, so the breakeven point in sales dollars would be $X_{BEP} * P = 10,000 * \$30 = \$300,000$.

d.
Sales	$300,000
-FC	(100,000)
-VC (10,000 * $20)	(200,000)
Net profit	0 (at breakeven point)

e. For 8,000 units, sales = 8,000 * $30 = $240,000.

Sales	$240,000
-VC (8,000 * $20)	(160,000)
-FC	(100,000)
Total net loss	(20,000)

f. For 12,000 units, sales = 12,000 * $30,00 = $360,000.

Sales	$360,000
-VC	(240,000)
-FC	(100,000)
Net profit	$20,000

24

2.2. Easyway, Inc., produces a complete line of do-it-yourself books. The books sell at $15.00 each, with an associated variable operating cost of $10.00 per unit. Fixed operating costs average $15,000 per year.

a. What would be the firm's operating profit at 3,000 units, 4,000 units, and 5,000 units?

b. Calculate the degree of operating leverage at 3,000, 4,000, and 5,000 units.

Solution

a. Operating Profit (OP):

	3,000 Units	4,000 Units	5,000 Units
Sales	$ 45,000	$ 60,000	$ 75,000
VC	(30,000)	(40,000)	(50,000)
FC	(15,000)	(15,000)	(15,000)
OP	0	$ 5,000	$ 10,000

b. Operating Leverage:

$$DOL_X = \frac{\text{percentage change in operating profits}}{\text{percentage change in output}} = 1 + \frac{FC}{OP_X}$$

$$DOL_{3,000} = 1 + \frac{15,000}{0} = 0$$

and is therefore undefined. Note that the DOL formula does not work when the initial period's OP is zero.

$$DOL_{4,000} = 1 + \frac{15,000}{5,000} = 4.00$$

$$DOL_{5,000} = 1 + \frac{15,000}{10,000} = 2.50$$

2.3. Freeman, Inc., produces oxygen equipment. Its present fixed cost is $60,000, its variable cost per unit is $10,000, and Freeman has no interest expense. The market is such that Freeman can sell each unit for $70.00.

a. Calculate the breakeven point in units and sales.

b. What would be the degree of operating leverage for sales of 3,000 units?

c. Given the degree of operating leverage that you found in part b, what would you expect operating profits to be if the firm experienced a 40 percent increase in units sold?

d. Create an income statement to verify your findings in part c.

Solution

a. $X_{BEP} = \dfrac{\$60,000}{\$70 - \$10} = \dfrac{\$60,000}{\$60} = 1,000$ units

$\$_{BEP} = X_{BEP} * P = 1,000$ units $* \$70$ per unit $= \$70,000$

b. 3,000 units:

Sales	$210,000
-VC	(30,000)
-FC	(60,000)
OP	$120,000

$DOL_X = 1 + \dfrac{FC}{OP_X}$

$\quad = 1 + \dfrac{\$60,000}{\$120,000}$

$\quad = 1.50$

c. Since

$$DOL = \frac{\text{percentage change in operating profits}}{\text{percentage change in sales}}$$

the expected change in operating profits is

OP = DOL * percentage change in sales
$\quad = 1.5 * 40\%$
$\quad = 60\%$

New operating profit would be $120,000 * 1.60 = $192,000.

d. Sales = (3,000 * 1.40) * $70 = $294,000

-VC	= 4,200 * $10	= (42,000)
-FC		(60,000)
OP		$192,000

2.4. Recent events have raised serious doubts about the quality of the oxygen equipment that Freeman, Inc., manufactures.

a. Using the original data presented in Question 2.3, find the breakeven point (in units and dollar sales) that will result if the sales price declines to $40 per unit.

b. Would this decline in sales price change the degree of operating leverage? (Assume sales of 3,000 units.) By how much?

c. How would sales have to increase to exactly offset the impact of the decline in price to $40 per unit (that is, to keep operating profit unchanged)? What is the DOL at this price?

Solution

The decline in price would change the breakeven point to

a. $X_{BEP} = \dfrac{\$60,000}{\$40 - \$10} = \dfrac{\$60,000}{\$30} = 2,000$ units

$\$_{BEP} = 2,000 * \$40 = \$80,000$

Both units sold and dollar sales must <u>increase</u> to reach the breakeven point.

b. For 3,000 units sold, the DOL would be found as follows:

```
Sales = 3,000 * $40 = $120,000
-VC   = 3,000 * $10 =  (30,000)
-FC                   (60,000)
 OP                  $ 30,000
```

$DOL = 1 + \dfrac{60,000}{30,000} = 3.0$

The degree of operating leverage is twice what it was when the sales price was $70. This occurs because fixed costs are now much larger relative to the sales price. That is, the marginal contribution has decreased by 50 percent to $30 ($40 - $10) from $60 ($70 - $10).

c. If the firm wanted to maintain the same degree of operating leverage and operating profits that occurred prior to the price decrease, sales would have to increase to 6,000 units (or $24,000).

```
Sales = 6,000 * $40 = $240,000
-VC   = 6,000 * $10 =  (60,000)
-FC                    (60,000)
 OP                  $ 120,000
```

We find this by recognizing that a $40 sales price results in a $30 contribution to fixed cost ($40 - $10). Since fixed cost is $60,000, and the desired level of operating profit is $120,000, the number of units that must be sold is

$\dfrac{\$60,000 + \$120,000}{\$30} = 6,000$ units needed

and the DOL at 6,000 units and OP of $120,000 is

$DOL = 1 + \dfrac{\$60,000}{\$120,000} = 1.50$

(This is the same DOL that we found when sales were 3,000 units and the sales price was $70 per unit.)

CHAPTER 2

Use the following information to answer Questions 2.5 through 2.9.

PH, Inc., produces chemical products. The following operating statement represents the typical characteristics of the firm. Assume that it has no interest expense.

Sales	$500,000	($50 per unit)
Variable cost	(300,000)	($30 per unit)
Fixed cost	(100,000)	
Operating profit	$100,000	

2.5. What is the breakeven point in units and in dollars?

Solution

$$X_{BEP} = \frac{\$100,000}{\$50 - \$30} = 5,000 \text{ units}$$

$$\$_{BEP} = 5,000 * \$50 = \$250,000$$

2.6. What is the degree of operating leverage at the $800,000 sales level?

Solution

Sales	$800,000 or 16,000 units
-VC	($480,000)
-FC	($100,000)
OP	$220,000

$$DOL = 1 + \frac{\$100,000}{\$220,000} = 1.455$$

2.7. On the basis of your answer to Question 2.6, determine what the operating profit would be if the units produced increased from 16,000 by 50 percent. Verify the answer you obtained using DOL by presenting an income statement.

Solution

Since

$$DOL = \frac{\text{percentage change in OP}}{\text{percentage change in sales}}$$

then

$$\begin{aligned}\text{percentage change in OP} &= DOL * \text{percentage change in sales} \\ &= 1.455 * .50 \\ &= .7275\end{aligned}$$

New operating profit would be 72.75 percent higher than before, or 172.75 percent of prior operating profit: $220,000 * 1.7275 = $380,050.

Income Statement

Sales	$1,200,000
-VC	(720,000)
-FC	(100,000)
OP	$380,000

2.8. PH, Inc., has an opportunity to increase its production capacity to 12,500 units. The expansion will increase fixed costs to $500,000 and reduce variable costs to $25 per unit. Should the firm undertake the expansion plan?

Solution

$$X_{BEP} = \frac{\$500,000}{\$50 - \$25} = 20,000 \text{ units}$$

No. The firm should forgo the expansion, because it can produce only 12,500 units. It needs to produce 20,000 just to break even.

2.9. Given the information in Question 2.8, by how much would PH have to increase its unit price to reach the breakeven output level that exhausts productive capacity of 12,500 units?

Solution

Consider that

$$12,500 = \frac{\$500,000}{P - \$25}$$

$$12,500 P - \$312,500 = \$500,000$$

$$P = \frac{\$812,500}{12,500}$$

$$P = \$65$$

Therefore, if the price increases to $65,

$$X_{BEP} = \frac{\$500,000}{\$65 - \$25} = 12,500 \text{ units (exhausting productive capacity)}$$

2.10. What is the DOL for JIMAH, Inc., with fixed costs of $80,000 and an operating profit of $240,000 in 1980?

Solution

$$DOL = 1 + \frac{FC}{OP}$$

$$= 1 + \frac{\$80,000}{\$240,000}$$

$$= 1.333$$

CHAPTER 2

REVIEW QUESTIONS

1. A project that is accepted must be financially feasible and
    a. compatible with other interested segments of society.
    b. compatible with industry restrictions and characteristics.
    c. compatible with the internal policies and abilities of management.
    d. all of these.

2. Investment decisions must include consideration of
    a. consumer groups.
    b. environmental groups.
    c. government regulations.
    d. all of these.

3. The federal budget affects corporate investment decisions, because
    a. many companies are suppliers to the government.
    b. of its impact on general economic activity.
    c. of the financing requirements it creates.
    d. all of these.

4. In periods of economic recession, the government's budget should
    a. decrease spending.
    b. increase spending.
    c. stabilize spending.
    d. none of these.

5. Government taxing policies are designed _____ the economy.
    a. not to affect
    b. to stabilize
    c. to depress
    d. to support
    e. none of these

6. The firm usually tries to avoid offering its securities at a time when the _____ is(are) engaged in debt management.
    a. Congress
    b. state government
    c. U.S. Treasury
    d. top U.S. corporations

7. Federal agencies can affect investment decisions through
    a. wage and price controls.
    b. debt restructuring.
    c. inflation.
    d. all of these.

8. Monetary policies are initiated by the
    a. U.S. Treasury.
    b. executive office of the president.
    c. Federal Reserve System.
    d. none of these.

9. Monetary policy can directly affect
    a. interest rates.
    b. product-pricing strategies

    c. the availability of funds.
    d. both a and c.
    e. none of these.

10. Interest rates can be defined as
    a. an adjustment for inflation.
    b. an adjustment for opportunity costs.
    c. the price of the credit extended to borrowers from lenders.
    d. none of these.

11. Finding the lowest-cost funds available to support corporate growth depends on such factors as
    a. timing fund raising properly.
    b. structuring the firm's security offerings to the needs of the potential buyer.
    c. decreasing the use of funds.
    d. both a and b.

12. Inflation affects
    a. interest rates.
    b. project costs.
    c. project operating costs.
    d. project operating revenues.
    e. all of these.

13. Continuing inflation forces operating costs and operating revenues _____ over the project's life.
    a. higher
    b. lower
    c. to decline in a linear manner
    d. to remain constant

14. Projects that fluctuate with the business cycle are _____ projects that do not have cyclically sensitive profits.
    a. less risky than
    b. more risky than
    c. as risky as
    d. no different from

15. The firm's operating characteristics that affect the investment decision include
    a. quality of sales.
    b. the general business cycle.
    c. cost and availability of materials.
    d. response to competition.
    e. all of these.

16. Poor quality of sales is an operating characteristic of the firm that refers to
    a. the low dollar volume of sales.
    b. the low volume of units sold.
    c. sales based on fads and fleeting fashion.
    d. all of these.
    e. none of these.

17. Since the profitability of an entire project can rest on the ability of the firm to acquire raw materials, the financial officer must
    a. obtain reliable sources.
    b. incorporate into the decision about whether to accept a project the possibility of not obtaining the resources.
    c. hire skilled production supervisors.
    d. increase operating efficiency.

18. The alert financial officer _____ in an appropriate manner.
    a. anticipates or responds quickly to external changes
    b. increases control
    c. changes managerial personnel
    d. all of these
    e. none of these

19. Operating leverage occurs when
    a. the firm uses more debt than equity.
    b. the firm can expand operating revenues without expanding operating costs.
    c. the firm increases sales relative to fixed cost.
    d. none of these.

20. Total operating costs include
    a. accounts payable.
    b. the use of plant and equipment.
    c. interest expense.
    d. both fixed and variable operating costs.
    e. none of these.

21. An alert financial officer uses the _____ as an indicator of the degree to which the profits actually generated by proposed investment projects may vary from projected profits.
    a. accounting rate of return
    b. current-assets ratio
    c. return on investment
    d. operating leverage

22. The degree of operating leverage (DOL) _____ work when the initial period's operating profit is zero, because, under these conditions, fixed cost divided by operating profit is infinite.
    a. does
    b. does not
    c. will often
    d. none of these

23. The high-DOL firm should be careful not to rely too heavily on _____ funds to finance its investments.
    a. equity
    b. preferred-stock
    c. borrowed
    d. short-term

24. The breakeven point occurs when the project's total revenues _____ its total costs.
    a. exceed

b. equal
c. are less than
d. none of these

25. When a firm has fixed costs of $200,000, variable costs of $8.00 per unit, and a sales price of $10.00 per unit, what is its breakeven point in units?
    a. 20,000
    b. 10,000
    c. 100,000
    d. 25,000
    e. none of these

26. Breakeven-point analysis can be used to
    a. evaluate proposed projects.
    b. determine the effect of alternative selling prices.
    c. evaluate changes in production costs.
    d. all of these.
    e. none of these.

27. A major problem with linear breakeven analysis is the assumption that
    a. increases or decreases in cost result in directly proportionate revenue increases or decreases.
    b. fixed costs vary.
    c. variable costs are constant over a certain range.
    d. none of these.

28. A primary operating characteristic of the firm that could affect investment and financing decisions is
    a. the number of existing employees.
    b. the cash balance of the firm.
    c. whether the firm has enough (and sufficiently skilled) management staff to undertake a project.
    d. none of these.

29. Management policies and abilities generally affect investment and financing decisions in the areas of
    a. asset utilization.
    b. diversification.
    c. general operating skills.
    d. countercyclical response.
    e. all of these.

30. Firms that have relatively little fixed investment and low fixed costs generally _____ to the business cycle.
    a. respond poorly
    b. cannot respond
    c. respond well
    d. none of these

KEY DEFINITIONS

Asset-utilization ability: management's ability to use the project's assets properly.

Breakeven analysis: determination of how many units of the product (or dollar sales) a proposed project must generate to at least break even (where net profit is zero).

Breakeven point: the point at which total revenues equal total costs.

Business-cycle sensitivity: sensitivity of the firm's investment proposals to the general business cycle.

Countercyclical response: management's ability to respond quickly and appropriately to the business cycle.

Degree of operating leverage: the relationship of the percentage change in operating profits to the percentage change in output.

Diversification policy: proper management of products and resources such that profit and production are stable.

Fiscal policy: the federal government's budget decisions.

Fixed operating costs: production costs that do not change as output changes.

Integrated view of finance: the view of investment decisions in terms of their effect on the firm as a whole.

Monetary policy: the Federal Reserve System's efforts to influence financial markets--for instance, by controlling the money supply.

Net profit: total revenue less all costs.

Operating characteristics of the firm: factors that affect investment decisions, such as general business cycle, quality of sales, availability and cost of materials, and so on.

Operating costs: production costs of each item manufactured.

Operating leverage: condition that exists when the firm's operating profits (losses) change proportionately more than its revenues.

Operating profit: total operating revenues less total operating costs.

Quality of sales: the degree of certainty about future markets.

Total operating costs: the sum of fixed operating costs and variable operating costs.

Variable operating costs: production costs that vary directly with the number of units produced.

Wage and price controls: limits on changes in wages and prices, which the federal government can impose in an effort to control the economy.

CHAPTER 2

ANSWERS TO REVIEW QUESTIONS

1.	d	9.	d	17.	b	24.	b
2.	d	10.	c	18.	a	25.	c
3.	d	11.	d	19.	b	26.	d
4.	b	12.	e	20.	d	27.	a
5.	b	13.	a	21.	d	28.	c
6.	c	14.	b	22.	b	29.	e
7.	a	15.	e	23.	c	30.	c
8.	c	16.	c				

Chapter Three
Financial Statements and Ratios

OVERVIEW

Financial statements are used as a report of the firm's past financial condition and operating results and as a tool for planning. The balance sheet is a financial statement that shows what the firm owns (assets) and owes (liabilities) at any given time. The income statement is a report of the firm's inflows, outflows, and profits over the entire accounting period. This chapter describes how we can analyze the firm by using, in ratio form, the information contained in the financial statements. The ratios presented summarize the firm's liquidity, activity, profitability and long-term solvency, and common stock position. Noting trends that these ratios exhibit over time and comparing them with industry standards enhance their usefulness as evaluative tools. Financial statements are reduced to a "common size" when each item on the income statement is expressed as a percentage of sales and each item on the balance sheet is expressed as a percentage of total assets or total liabilities and stockholders' equity. Using ratios in this manner leads to more comprehensive analyses of the firm.

STUDY OBJECTIVES

1. To define and examine the type of information contained in typical financial statements.

2. To use financial statements as a means of evaluating the firm's financial condition and operations.

3. To develop a method of comparing financial statements of different firms for different years.

CHAPTER OUTLINE

I. Three common forms of financial statements are often used in presenting the company's position to the public.

   A. The balance sheet reflects the company's financial condition at any given time, usually at the end of the accounting period. Assets, liabilities, and stockholders' equity are included.

1. <u>Assets</u> represent what the firm owns. Total assets include current and long-term asset values.

   a. Current assets typically consist of cash, marketable securities, accounts receivable, and inventory. These items normally become cash, are consumed, or are sold within a year.

   b. Long-term assets are less liquid than current assets. Examples include property, plant, and equipment. These assets are used for several years and experience gradual deterioration. The gross value of depreciable assets is reduced to reflect accumulated depreciation, leading to a net value that approximates the prevailing worth of the long-term assets (fixed assets).

2. <u>Liabilities</u>, which are found on the right side of the balance sheet, reflect what the firm owes its creditors.

   a. <u>Current liabilities</u> are those that are usually paid within a year. Examples include notes payable, accounts payable (owed to suppliers), and accruals (obligations made but not paid).

   b. <u>Long-term liabilities</u> are usually repaid in various installments over several years. An example is long-term debt.

3. <u>Stockholders' equity</u> represents owners' interest <u>and</u> the firm's asset value after liabilities have been subtracted. The total value of stockholders' equity is an indication of the owners' original investment <u>and</u> any profits that the firm has retained and reinvested.

   <u>Note</u>: Total assets must equal total liabilities and stockholders' equity.

   a. <u>Net worth</u> can be found by subtracting the firm's total liabilities from its total assets (NW = A - L). This indicates the stockholders' investment in the firm.

   b. The balance sheet is often used to evaluate the existing position of the firm and to plan for the firm's future.

Example

PUNGO INDUSTRIES, INC.
Balance Sheet
December 31, 19X0

Assets

Current assets
Cash		$ 20,000
Marketable securities		15,000
Accounts receivable		185,000
Inventories		400,000
Total current assets		$620,000

Long-term assets
Gross property, plant and equipment	$600,000	
Less accumulated depreciation	400,000	
Net property, plant and equipment		200,000
Total assets		$820,000

Liabilities and stockholders' equity

Current liabilities
Notes payable		$ 50,000
Accounts payable		200,000
Accruals		20,000
Total current liabilities		270,000
Long-term debt	$200,000	
Total long-term liabilities		200,000
Total liabilities		470,000

Stockholders' equity
Common stock	50,000	
Retained earnings	300,000	
Total stockholders' equity		350,000
Total liabilities and stockholders' equity		$820,000

B. The income statement summarizes the firm's earnings over the accounting period. Inflows (sales, other income) and outflows (operating expenses, taxes) are compared to determine net income to be retained and/or paid to shareholders in the form of dividends.

1. Sales represent the firm's revenue from operations. Net sales are gross sales less discounts given and returns/allowances.

2. Cost of goods sold includes the primary costs of raw materials and the direct labor used in the production process.

3. Gross profit summarizes the impact of operations by subtracting the costs of goods sold from net sales.

4. Operating expenses differ from the cost of goods sold in that they are not directly linked to the production process.

5. <u>Financial expenses</u> generally represent the firm's costs other than operating expenses and the cost of goods sold, such as interest expense.

6. <u>Net income before taxes</u> is profit remaining after the deduction of financial expenses.

7. <u>Net income after taxes</u> represents the money available to the firm's shareholders after deduction of federal income taxes.

8. <u>Earnings per share</u> represents net income after taxes, divided by the number of shares of common stock outstanding.

<u>Example</u>

PUNGO INDUSTRIES, INC.
Income Statement
For the Period Ended December 31, 19X0

Sales		$1,000,000
Cost of goods sold		800,000
Gross profit		200,000
Less operating expenses:		
Selling and administrative	$60,000	
Lease payments (rent)	20,000	
Depreciation	40,000	120,000
Operating profit		80,000
Less interest expense		20,000
Net income before taxes		60,000
Federal income taxes (40% rate)		24,000
Net income after taxes		$ 36,000
Earnings per share (10,000 shares outstanding)		$3.60

C. The <u>Statement of Retained Earnings</u> reports the exact amount disbursed to the stockholders as dividends and the exact amount retained in the firm.

<u>Example</u>

PUNGO INDUSTRIES, INC.
Statement of Retained Earnings
December 31, 19X0

Balance of retained earnings as of January 1, 19X0	$278,400
Add net income after taxes 19X0	36,000
	$314,400
Subtract dividends to stockholders ($1.44 per share)	14,400
Balance of retained earnings as of December 31, 19X0	$300,000

Note that the net income after taxes in 19X0 is disbursed in two directions: (1) to shareholders in terms of dividends ($1.44 per share or 40 percent of earnings) and (2) to the company in the form of retained earnings (60 percent), which will be reinvested. This increased the

retained earnings account by $21,600 to $300,000. (The prior year's retained earnings are typically not held as cash but are invested in other
assets.)

II. Ratio analysis has become a valuable tool in the evaluation and planning
   areas of finance. Key ratios are indexes of the firm's liquidity, activity,
   profitability, long-term solvency, and common stock. (Each of the following
   ratios uses data based on Pungo Industries, Inc.)

   A. Liquidity and short-term solvency ratios are used to determine the firm's
      ability to meet current liabilities with current assets.

      1. Current ratio = $\dfrac{\text{current assets}}{\text{current liabilities}} = \dfrac{\$620,000}{\$270,000} = 2.296$

         This ratio reveals that the firm's ability to meet short-term obliga-
         tions (current liabilities) using only short-term assets (current
         assets) is 2.296. This means that the firm has $2.296 dollars of
         current assets for each dollar of current liabilities. A ratio of
         2.000 is considered acceptable (though this rule may vary among in-
         dustries), so Pungo Industries is just above the minimum.

      2. Acid-test ratio = $\dfrac{\text{current assets - inventories}}{\text{current liabilities}}$

         $= \dfrac{\$620,000 - \$400,000}{\$270,000} = .815$

         This ratio recognizes the fact that, due to obsolescence or mere un-
         salability, inventory is potentially the most illiquid current asset.
         Therefore, Pungo Industries has a much lower liquidity position when
         the acid-test ratio is used rather than the current ratio. According
         to the acid-test ratio, the firm has less current assets (.815) than
         current liabilities.

      3. Average collection period = $\dfrac{\text{accounts receivable} * 360}{\text{annual credit sales}}$

         $= \dfrac{\$185,000 * 360}{\$1,000,000} = 66.6 \text{ days}$

         If Pungo Industries has a policy of extending 60-day credit to its
         customers in the regular course of trade, the 66.6 day average col-
         lection period is out of line. Thus the average collection period
         ratio reveals a problem in the area of accounts receivable collection
         policy.

      4. Accounts receivable turnover = $\dfrac{\text{annual credit sales}}{\text{accounts receivable}}$

         $= \dfrac{\$1,000,000}{\$185,000} = 5.41 \text{ times}$

         This ratio measures the liquidity of the firm's accounts receivable.
         It is assumed that accounts receivable liquidity increases as the
         ratio increases, because this indicates a more rapid collection
         policy. Note that a 60-day credit policy would result in a turnover
         of (360/60) = 6. Pungo Industries, with a turnover ratio of 5.41, is
         somewhat below the minimum we would expect.

a. A low turnover ratio is undesirable; it reflects slow and in-effective collections.

b. A very high turnover ratio could also be undesirable; it might reflect an overly restrictive credit policy.

c. Ratios must be compared to acceptable industry standards and viewed in light of the firm's credit terms.

5. Inventory turnover $= \dfrac{\text{cost of goods sold}}{\text{average inventory}}$

$$= \frac{\$800,000}{(\$400,000 + \$400,000)/2} = 2.00 \text{ times}$$

This ratio measures the liquidity of the firm's inventories. The cost of goods sold is used because it reflects the cost of inventory. Average inventory--(beginning + ending) all divided by two--is used to reflect average inventory levels.

B. Activity ratios indicate the efficiency with which management uses the firm's assets to generate sales and profits.

1. Total asset turnover $= \dfrac{\text{sales}}{\text{total assets}}$

$$= \frac{\$1,000,000}{\$820,000} = 1.22$$

This ratio indicates the sales dollars generated per dollar of invest-ment in assets. A high ratio reflects more revenue generated per dollar of assets. As with other ratios, we must compare this one with a standard to properly evaluate its meaning.

2. Return on total assets $= \dfrac{\text{net income after taxes}}{\text{total assets}}$

$$= \frac{\$36,000}{\$820,000} = .044$$

This ratio, sometimes called return on investment (ROI), indicates how effectively management has used every dollar of assets to generate net profit. To evaluate the investment success of the firm, we should compare a return on total assets ratio to that which alternative in-vestment opportunities would have yielded.

3. Return on total capitalization $= \dfrac{\text{net income after taxes}}{\text{long-term debt + stockholders' equity}}$

$$= \frac{\$36,000}{\$200,000 + \$350,000} = .065$$

The return on total capitalization ratio indicates management's effi-ciency in generating net income from funds provided by suppliers (creditors and stockholders). Current liabilities are excluded. Higher ratio values indicate increasing efficiency.

4. Return on stockholders' equity = $\dfrac{\text{net income after taxes}}{\text{stockholders' equity}}$

$$= \frac{\$36,000}{\$350,000} = .103$$

This ratio reveals how effectively the firm has worked with the stockholders' investment. Better profit management results in higher ratio values.

5. Physical ratios are often used in evaluating how efficiently management has used the firm's assets. Each industry has its own particular physical measurement of asset utilization. Examples include sales per square foot (retail industry) and load factor (airline industry).

C. Profitability ratios measure the degree of profitability that management has achieved. As profit per dollar of sales increases, management efficiency is perceived as increasing.

1. Gross profit margin = $\dfrac{\text{sales - cost of goods sold}}{\text{sales}}$

$$= \frac{\$1,000,000 - \$800,000}{\$1,000,000} = .200$$

This ratio indicates how efficiently the firm produced each unit of product. In comparison with an industry standard, we would interpret the higher gross profit margin as signaling greater manufacturing efficiency.

2. Operating profit margin = $\dfrac{\text{operating profit}}{\text{sales}}$

$$= \frac{\$80,000}{\$1,000,000} = .08$$

Operating profit represents profit after the deduction of the cost of goods sold and other operating costs. Thus a high operating profit margin ratio indicates manufacturing efficiency in manufacturing and in selling and distributing the product. Tracking the operating profit margin and the gross profit margin can reveal changes in the distributing and/or manufacturing efficiency of the firm.

3. Net profit margin = $\dfrac{\text{net income after taxes}}{\text{sales}}$

$$= \frac{\$36,000}{\$1,000,000} = .036$$

This ratio provides a useful reflection of management's overall ability to generate profits by efficient use of the manufacturing, selling, and financing areas of the firm. Comparing the net profit margin with the operating profit margin for the same period provides insights into how efficiently the firm is being financed.

D. <u>Long-term solvency</u> ratios quantify the firm's management of debt. The amount of debt used depends on such factors as the size of the cushion provided by stockholders' equity and the firm's ability to generate sufficient funds to meet interest and debt repayment schedules.

1. Debt ratio = $\dfrac{\text{current liabilities} + \text{long-term liabilities}}{\text{total assets}}$

   $= \dfrac{\$270,000 + \$200,000}{\$820,000} = .573$

   The proportion of total assets financed by creditors is expressed in the debt ratio. As the debt ratio increases, the firm increases its financing of assets with greater proportions of borrowed funds. This increase in the use of debt increases the chance of default on the firm's obligations. Lenders generally prefer a lower debt ratio.

2. Debt/equity ratio = $\dfrac{\text{total debt}}{\text{stockholders' equity}}$

   $= \dfrac{\$470,000}{\$350,000} = 1.34$

   Note that <u>total debt</u> is the sum of long-term debt and current liabilities. Increases in debt relative to stockholders' equity expose the firm to greater risks of insolvency or inability to meet fixed obligations. Low debt/equity ratios suggest greater long-term solvency and less financial risk.

3. Long-term debt/total capitalization ratio = $\dfrac{\text{long-term debt}}{\text{total capitalization}}$

   $= \dfrac{\$200,000}{\$550,000} = .364$

   This ratio emphasizes the long-term solvency of the firm, ignoring current liabilities and <u>including</u> stockholders' equity plus long-term debt in the total capitalization figure.

4. Fixed charges earned

   $= \dfrac{\text{net income before taxes} + \text{interest expense} + \text{lease payments}}{\text{interest expenses} + \text{lease payments}}$

   $= \dfrac{\$60,000 + \$20,000 + \$20,000}{\$20,000 + \$20,000} = 2.500$

   This ratio points out that the two most prominent fixed charges of the firm are interest expense and lease payments ($10,000 in this example). These expenses must be met regardless of the firm's profitability. Larger values of this ratio suggest greater ability to meet long-term obligations. To be most useful, the ratio should be compared to a reasonable industry standard <u>or</u> to its previous values in the firm.

5. Interest coverage ratio = $\dfrac{\text{net income before taxes} + \text{interest expense}}{\text{interest expense}}$

   $= \dfrac{\$60,000 + \$20,000}{\$20,000} = 4.000$

This ratio reflects the funding available to pay the interest expense during the year. Only the interest charge is used in this measurement, so the results may be misleading when significant fixed charges exist.

E. <u>Common stock ratios</u> are used to help the financial officer maximize shareholder wealth.

1. Book value per share = $\dfrac{\text{stockholders' equity}}{\text{number of shares}}$

   $= \dfrac{\$350,000}{10,000} = \$35.00$

   This measurement may be important if the firm is to be liquidated, but it does not usually reflect the market value of the assets or shares it represents.

2. Payout ratio = $\dfrac{\text{dividends per share}}{\text{earnings per share}}$

   $= \dfrac{\$1.44}{\$3.60} = .40$

   This ratio indicates the proportion of earnings that are paid to shareholders. Larger payment ratios mean smaller retention of earnings for reinvestment by the firm.

3. Price/earnings ratio = $\dfrac{\text{stock price}}{\text{earnings per share}}$

   $= \dfrac{\$36.00}{\$3.60} = 10$

   This ratio (sometimes referred to as P/E) reflects the relationship of stock price to earnings. In this example, current investors are willing to pay 10 times earnings of $3.60 per share.

III. <u>Common-size financial statements</u> express each item on the income statement as a percentage of total sales and each item on the balance sheet as a percentage of total assets or total liabilities and stockholders' equity. This method of analysis can be used to interpret financial statements between companies and over time.

A. <u>Common-size income statements</u> represent items on the income statement as a percentage of total sales. An example follows.

PUNGO INDUSTRIES, INC.
Common-Size Income Statement
December 31, 19X0

Sales		100.00%
Cost of goods sold		80.00
Gross profit		20.00
Less operating expenses:		
Selling and administrative	6.00%	
Lease payments (rent)	2.00	
Depreciation	4.00	12.00
Operating profit		8.00
Less interest expense		2.00
Net income before taxes		6.00
Federal income taxes		2.40
Net income after taxes		3.60%

Comparing several common-size statements is a good way to evaluate the firm over time. Unusual changes in expenses related to sales can be easily identified.

B. Common-size balance sheets express balance sheet items as a percentage of total assets or total liabilities and stockholders' equity. An example follows.

PUNGO INDUSTRIES, INC.
Common-Size Balance Sheet
December 31, 19X0

Assets

Current assets		
Cash		2.44%
Marketable securities		1.83
Accounts receivable		22.56
Inventories		48.78
Total current assets		75.61
Long-term assets		
Gross property	73.17%	
Less accumulated depreciation	48.78	
Net property		24.39
Total assets		100.00%

Liabilities and Stockholders' Equity

Current liabilities		
Notes payable		6.10%
Accounts payable		24.39
Accruals		2.44
Total current liabilities		32.93%
Long-term debt		
Total long-term liabilities		24.39
Stockholders' equity		57.32%
Common stock (10,000 shares)	6.10%	
Retained earnings	36.58	
Total stockholders' equity		42.68
Total liabilities and stockholders' equity		100.00%

An analysis of trends in items on several common-size balance sheets can help reveal areas of improvement as well as deterioration.

C. Trend analysis of ratios or common-size financial statements is an important method of examining the firm's progress over a number of years. Unfavorable trends alert the financial officer to the fact that further analysis of the areas involved is required.

D. Ratios are commonly used in bank loan evaluations, customer credit evaluations, stock and bond analysis, internal management control, utility regulation, and merger valuation. Unfavorable trends or significant discrepancies from industry standards call attention to areas of concern.

E. Sources of comparative industry ratios include the following:

1. Dun and Bradstreet's Key Business Ratios in 800 Lines.

2. The Quarterly Financial Report for U.S. Manufacturing Corporations, published by the Federal Trade Commission and the Securities and Exchange Commission, includes common-size financial statements.

3. Statement Studies, by Robert Morris Associates, covers 313 industries.

4. Trade associations often provide industry-wide ratios.

5. The Analysts Handbook, by Standard and Poor's Corporation, provides ratios used by investors.

6. The Almanac of Business and Industrial Financial Ratios is a comprehensive source of industry-wide ratios.

F. Problems with ratio analysis can arise when the financial officer uses ratios for planning, control, or reporting purposes.

1. Accounting comparability between firms and accounting periods can become distorted, making it impossible to make reasonable comparisons using ratios.

2. Ratio analyses must not be used in isolation, and they must not be based on superficial data. A ratio profile should be used to accurately apply ratios to the planning and control process.

3. Industry classification of a firm is important in developing meaningful comparisons. Many firms have operations that span a number of industries, leading to difficulties in comparing company ratios to industry standards.

4. Interim reports can be highly misleading as the basis of ratio analysis when the firm's sales exhibit seasonal cycles.

5. Ratios and common-size financial statements may not accurately reflect important size differences between the firm and industry standards or other firms.

6. Ratios are based on <u>historical data</u> that cannot be assumed to represent the firm's future performance.

<u>Note</u>: Ratios are only rules of thumb that alert us to the need for further, deeper investigation.

Summary of Financial Ratios

Liquidity and Short-Term Solvency

1. Current Ratio $\dfrac{\text{Current assets}}{\text{Current liabilities}}$

2. Acid Test (Quick) Ratio $\dfrac{\text{Current assets } - \text{ inventories}}{\text{Current liabilities}}$

3. Average Collection Period (days) $\dfrac{\text{Accounts receivable} * 360}{\text{Annual credit sales}}$

4. Accounts Receivable Turnover Ratio $\dfrac{\text{Annual credit sales}}{\text{Accounts receivable}}$

5. Inventory Turnover Ratio $\dfrac{\text{Cost of goods sold}}{\text{Average inventory}}$

Activity (Asset Utilization)

1. Total Asset Turnover Ratio $\dfrac{\text{Sales}}{\text{Total assets}}$

2. Return on Total Assets Ratio (%) $\dfrac{\text{Net income after taxes}}{\text{Total assets}}$

3. Return on Total Capitalization Ratio (%) $\dfrac{\text{Net income after taxes}}{\text{Long-Term debt } + \text{ stockholders' equity}}$

4. Return on Stockholders' Equity (%) $\dfrac{\text{Net income after taxes}}{\text{Stockholders' equity}}$

Profitability

1. Gross Profit Margin (%) $\dfrac{\text{Sales } - \text{ cost of goods sold}}{\text{Sales}}$

2. Operating Profit Margin (%) $\dfrac{\text{Operating profit}}{\text{Sales}}$

Summary of Financial Ratios (cont.)

3. Net Profit Margin (%)

$$\frac{\text{Net income after taxes}}{\text{Sales}}$$

Long-Term Solvency (Coverage)

1. Debt Ratio (%)

$$\frac{\text{Current liabilities} + \text{long-term liabilities}}{\text{Total assets}}$$

2. Debt/Equity Ratio

$$\frac{\text{Total debt}}{\text{Stockholders' equity}} \quad or \quad \frac{\text{Long-term debt} + \text{current liabilities}}{\text{Stockholders' equity}}$$

3. Ratio of Long-Term Debt to Total Capitalization

$$\frac{\text{Long-term debt}}{\text{Total capitalization}} \quad or \quad \frac{\text{Long-term debt}}{\text{Long-term debt} + \text{stockholders' equity}}$$

4. Fixed Charges Earned Ratio

$$\frac{\text{Net income before taxes} + \text{interest expense} + \text{lease payments}}{\text{Interest expense} + \text{lease payments}}$$

5. Interest Coverage Ratio

$$\frac{\text{Net income before taxes} + \text{interest expense}}{\text{Interest expense}}$$

Common Stock Characteristics

1. Book Value per Share ($)

$$\frac{\text{Stockholders' equity}}{\text{Number of shares}}$$

2. Payout Ratio (%)

$$\frac{\text{Dividends per share}}{\text{Earnings per share}}$$

3. Price/Earnings Ratio

$$\frac{\text{Stock price}}{\text{Earnings per share}}$$

STUDY PROBLEMS

Use the following financial statements to answer Questions 3.1 through 3.6.

EVELAR, INC.
Balance Sheet (thousands of dollars)

	December 31, 19X0	December 31, 19X9
Assets		
Current assets		
Cash	$ 60,000	$ 30,000
Marketable securities	10,000	14,000
Accounts receivable	540,000	566,000
Inventories	600,000	620,000
Total current assets	1,210,000	1,230,000
Long-term assets		
Gross property, plant 4,000,000		3,800,000
Less accumulated depreciation 2,000,000		2,100,000
Net property, plant	2,000,000	1,700,000
Total assets	$3,210,000	$2,930,000
Liabilities and Stockholders' Equity		
Current liabilities		
Notes payable	$ 150,000	$ 145,000
Accounts payable	200,000	220,000
Accurals	80,000	70,000
Total current liabilities	430,000	435,000
Long-term liabilities		
Long-term debt	800,000	700,000
Total liabilities	1,230,000	1,135,000
Stockholders' equity		
Common stock (20,000,000 shares) 400,000		400,000
Retained earnings 1,580,000		1,395,000
Total stockholders' equity	1,980,000	1,795,000
Total liabilities and stockholders' equity	$3,210,000	$2,930,000

EVELAR, INC.
Income Statement (thousands of dollars)

	19X0		19X9	
Sales		$7,000,000		$6,500,000
Cost of goods sold		6,300,000		6,000,000
Gross profit		700,000		500,000
Less operating expenses:				
Selling and administrative	80,000		70,000	
Lease payments-rent	20,000		20,000	
Depreciation	80,000	180,000	100,000	190,000
Operating profit		520,000		310,000
Less interest expense		100,000		80,000
Net income before taxes		420,000		230,000
Less federal income taxes (50%)		210,000		115,000
Net income after taxes		$ 210,000		$ 115,000
Earnings per share		$10.50		$ 5.75

EVELAR, INC.
Statement of Retained Earnings (thousands of dollars)
December 31, 19X0

Balance of retained earnings as of January 1, 19X0	$1,395,000
Add net income after taxes, 19X0	210,000
	1,605,000
Subtract dividends to stockholders ($1.25 per share)	25,000
Balance of retained earnings as of December 31, 19X0	$1,580,000

3.1. What is the liquidity position of Evelar, Inc.? (Discuss in relationship to 19X9.)

Solution

	19X0	19X9
Current ratio	2.814	2.828
Acid-test ratio	1.419	1.402
Average collection period	27.771	31.348
Accounts receivable turnover	12.963	11.484
Inventory turnover	10.500	9.677

Note that the firm is experiencing improvements over 19X9 in the areas of the acid-test ratio, average collection period, accounts receivable, and inventory turnover. These slight improvements indicate that management is maintaining the liquidity position of the firm.

3.2. What is the asset utilization (activity) position of the company? (Discuss in relationship to 19X9.)

Solution

	19X0	19X9
Total asset turnover	2.18	2.22
Return on total assets	6.54%	3.92%
Return on total capitalization	7.55%	4.61%
Return on stockholders' equity	10.61%	6.41%

Asset utilization in terms of all ratios (except the slight decline in total asset turnover) has increased dramatically. Most measures of activity increased more than 150 percent over 19X9. This provides a very favorable picture of management over the last year. Comparisons with other years or industry standards would be necessary before further evaluation would be useful.

3.3. What is the profitability position of Evelar? (Discuss in relationship to 19X9.)

Solution

	19X0	19X9
Gross profit margin	10.00%	7.69%
Operating profit margin	7.43%	4.77%
Net profit margin	3.00%	1.77%

In comparison with 19X9, the firm has improved its profitability position considerably, almost doubling the margins. Comparisons with other time periods or industry standards would more precisely reflect the current ability of management to maintain profitable operations.

3.4. What is the long-term solvency (coverage) position of the firm? (Discuss in relationship to 19X9.)

Solution

	19X0	19X9
Debt ratio	38.32%	38.74%
Debt/equity ratio	62.12%	63.23%
Long-term debt/total capitalization	28.78%	28.06%
Fixed charges earned ratio	4.50	3.30
Interest coverage ratio	5.20	3.88

The coverage position of the firm is acceptable, given the firm's 5.20 interest coverage ratio and 4.50 fixed charges earned ratio. In comparison with 19X9, the firm is improving its solvency position considerably.

3.5. What is the firm's position in terms of common stock relative to 19X9?
Note: The firm paid $1.00 in dividends in 19X9; the market price is currently
$80.00 per share; the 12/31/X9 market price was $70.00 per share.

Solution

	19X0	19X9
Book value per share	$99.00	$89.75
Payout ratio	11.90%	17.39%
Price/earnings ratio	7.62	12.17

The firm is improving its stock position in terms of higher book values and current
market price. Although earnings and dividends increased over 19X9, the percentage
of earnings paid out as dividends decreased, as did the ratio of price to earnings.

3.6. Derive a common-size balance sheet for Evelar for the year 19X0.

Solution

EVELAR, INC.
Common-Size Balance Sheet
December 31, 19X0

Assets

Current assets		
Cash	1.87%	
Marketable securities	.31	
Accounts receivable	16.82	
Inventories	18.69	
Total current assets		37.69%
Long-term assets		
Gross property, plant	124.61%	
Less accumulated depreciation	62.30	
Net property, plant		62.31%
Total assets		100.00%

Liabilities and Stockholders' Equity

Current liabilities		
Notes payable	4.67%	
Accounts payable	6.23	
Accruals	2.49	
Total current liabilities		13.40%
Long-term liabilities		
Total long-term debt		24.92
Stockholders' equity		
Common stock	12.46%	
Retained earnings	49.22	
Total stockholders' equity		61.68
Total liabilities and stockholders' equity		100.00%

Use the following financial statements and industry data to answer Questions 3.7 through 3.10.

MICRO ELECTRONICS
Balance Sheet (unaudited)
December 31, 19XX

Cash	$ 1,800	Accounts payable	$180,000
Accounts receivable	18,000	Long-term debt	-0-
Inventory	450,000	Stockholders' equity	379,800
Net fixed assets	90,000		$559,800
Total assets	$559,800		

MICRO ELECTRONICS
Income Statement (unaudited)
December 31, 19XX

Sales (net)	$450,000
Cost of goods sold	360,000
Gross profit	90,000
Operating expenses	18,000
Net income before taxes	72,000
Taxes	28,800
Net income after taxes	$ 43,200

ELECTRONICS INDUSTRY RATIOS

Current ratio	2.50
Acid-test ratio	1.50
Debt ratio	.60
Average collection period	30.6
Return on stockholders' equity	.15
Net profit margin	.12
Return on total assets	.14
Inventory turnover	2.57

3.7. What seems to be the major difference between the firm's position and that of the industry?

Solution

To solve this problem, we must calculate ratios for the firm in each of the areas of liquidity, activity, long-term solvency, profitability, and common stock.

The liquidity position of the firm is much worse than the industry average (.11 acid-test for the company versus 1.50 for the industry). The firm also has the problem of turning its inventory much less frequently than the industry (.80 versus 2.57 times) each year. A positive aspect is the firm's ability to collect its accounts receivable (this ratio is much better than the industry's by 14.4 versus 30.6 days), unless this is an indication that the credit policy of the firm is too restrictive.

<u>3.8.</u> How could you use the information provided to bring the firm in line with the industry?

Solution

First of all, it would be generally inappropriate to use data from only one period to justify drastic changes in the firm. The information provided could be based on an accounting period that does not really represent the typical position of the firm <u>or</u> the industry.

If the data <u>are</u> representative of the firm, the financial officer would be well advised to evaluate the investment in inventory and profit margins. With a very low acid-test ratio, the firm must have a <u>relatively</u> large inventory combined with a very low turnover. This set of characteristics, along with a basically low profitability position, could lead to serious problems if an economic downturn occurs.

Given the objective of attaining company ratios similar to industry norms, the financial officer would adjust the values of the variables used to calculate the desired ratios, thereby creating company characteristics in line with the industry. (An example follows.)

<u>3.9.</u> If Micro Electronics wanted an average collection period more in line with the industry, what would its average accounts receivable need to be? Explain how this change should improve the firm's acid-test ratio.

Solution

$$\text{Average collection period} = \frac{\text{accounts receivable} * 360}{\text{annual credit sales}}$$

$$30.6 = \frac{\text{accounts receivable} * 360}{\$450,000}$$

$$\$13,770,000 = \text{accounts receivable} * 360$$

$$\text{Accounts receivable} = \$38,250$$

Micro Electronics has an accounts receivable policy that lowers its average accounts receivable balance from an industry average of $38,250 on $450,000 in sales to $18,000. Relaxing the credit policy to increase accounts receivable would shift current assets from inventory to accounts receivable (and probably increase sales), thereby improving the firm's acid-test ratio.

<u>3.10.</u> How can we use the firm's ratio values to forecast the <u>change</u> in stockholders' equity that would occur if sales increased 20 percent over 19XX?

Solution

The profit margin on sales is 7.7 percent. If sales increased 20 percent over 19XX, the dollar <u>increase</u> would be .20 * $450,000 = $90,000. With a 7.7 percent net profit margin, net income after taxes would be .077 * $90,000 = $6,930.00. Assuming that no dividends would be paid, all of the $6,930 would be held in retained earnings, thereby increasing the stockholders' equity section of the balance sheet by $6,930.

REVIEW QUESTIONS

1. The financial statements that are commonly found in a firm's annual report are
   a. balance sheet.
   b. income statement.
   c. statement of retained earnings.
   d. statement of sources and uses.
   e. a, b, and c.
   f. a, b, and d.

2. The balance sheet reflects
   a. a summary of the firm's performance over the year.
   b. the firm's financial position at a given time.
   c. the market value of the firm's assets.
   d. none of these.

3. Accumulated depreciation is meant to reflect
   a. the changing market value of liabilities.
   b. the gradual increase in the value of assets.
   c. the gradual deterioration of the asset's ability to produce efficiently.
   d. decreasing values of current assets.

4. The right side of the balance sheet reflects
   a. the degree of stability of the firm.
   b. the net asset values of fixed plant and equipment.
   c. what the firm owes its creditors and what remains for the stockholders.
   d. what the firm owns without claims.

5. Net worth is the difference between
   a. current assets and current liabilities.
   b. fixed assets and fixed liabilities.
   c. total assets and total liabilities.
   d. stockholders' investment and cash.

6. Operating expenses reflect
   a. production costs.
   b. expenses not directly connected to production.
   c. the cost of goods sold.
   d. none of these.

7. Earnings per share represent
   a. the amount to be received by shareholders.
   b. net income after taxes divided by the number of shares outstanding in common stock.
   c. net income after taxes divided by the number of shares outstanding in preferred stock.
   d. none of these.

8. Key areas where ratios have been extensively applied are
   a. liquidity and activity.
   b. profitability and long-term solvency.
   c. common stock.
   d. stability.
   e. all of these.

CHAPTER 3

9. Activity ratios measure the firm's ability to
   a. meet short-term obligations.
   b. generate sales and profits from assets.
   c. turn each sales dollar into profit.
   d. all of these.

10. A current ratio of _____ to 1.0 has traditionally been considered an acceptable level for proper liquidity.
    a. 2.0
    b. 1.0
    c. .50
    d. 2.5
    e. none of these

11. A current ratio much larger than the acid-test ratio indicates
    a. a large amount of inventories in current assets.
    b. a small amount of inventories in current assets.
    c. that the firm will have high profitability.
    d. that the firm will have a high inventory turnover.

12. A very low accounts receivable turnover ratio may be undesirable, because
    a. it indicates a slow and ineffective collection policy.
    b. it indicates a rapid and overly effective (restrictive) collection policy.
    c. sales may go up.
    d. none of these.

13. The return on total assets ratio reflects
    a. management's efficiency in generating net income from funds provided by creditors and stockholders.
    b. sales dollars generated per dollar of investment in assets.
    c. returns on common stockholders' equity and current assets.
    d. how effectively management employed every dollar of assets to generate net profit.

14. The operating profit margin measures
    a. how efficiently the firm produced each unit of product.
    b. the efficiency with which management not only manufactured the product but also sold and distributed it.
    c. the efficiency with which management manufactured the product.
    d. the efficiency with which management sold and distributed the product.

15. Total capitalization is the sum of
    a. total assets and total liabilities.
    b. current assets and long-term debt.
    c. long-term debt and stockholders' equity.
    d. none of these.

16. The interest coverage ratio measures the amount of funds
    a. available to pay interest during the year.
    b. available to pay long-term debt.
    c. available to pay leases during the year.
    d. available to pay dividends during the year.

56

17. Book value per share
    a. is the firm's net worth divided by the number of common shares.
    b. represents the firm's market value.
    c. may be important if the firm stops operating and liquidates.
    d. all of these.
    e. both a and c

18. The payout ratio reflects the proportion of earnings
    a. generated by dividends.
    b. paid to shareholders.
    c. placed in retained earnings.
    d. none of these.

19. If the price/earnings ratio of the firm is 10 and earnings per share are $5.00, the stock price of the firm is
    a. $2.00.
    b. $20.00.
    c. $50.00.
    d. $25.00.

20. Common-size financial statements can express each item on the income statement as a percentage of _____ and each item on the balance sheet as a percentage of _____.
    a. total assets, total sales
    b. total sales, total assets
    c. total profit, total liabilities
    d. none of these

21. Financial ratios are commonly used in
    a. bank loan valuations.
    b. customer credit valuations.
    c. stock and bond analysis.
    d. all of these.

22. When ratio analysis is used in planning, controlling, or reporting, the user must recognize such potential problems as
    a. lack of accounting comparability.
    b. use of single ratios instead of trends or profiles.
    c. difficulty in finding reasonable industry comparisons.
    d. use of interim reports.
    e. all of these.

KEY DEFINITIONS

Accruals: current liabilities that were recently incurred and have yet to be paid.

Activity ratios: measures of the firm's ability to generate sales and profits from its assets.

Balance sheet: record of the firm's financial condition at any given time.

Common-size statements: expression of each item on the income statement as a percentage of total sales and each item on the balance sheet as a percentage of total assets or total liabilities and stockholders' equity.

Common stock ratios: measures of characteristics of the common stock of the firm rather than its operating or financial characteristics.

Cost of goods sold: the total of primary costs of raw materials and direct labor used in the production process.

Current assets: assets usually converted to cash, consumed, or sold within a year.

Current liabilities: debts generally paid within one year.

Earnings per share: net profit after taxes, divided by the number of common shares outstanding.

Financing expenses: expenses incurred through the process of obtaining the funds required to support the needs of the firm.

Historical data: past information that can be misleading in terms of ratio analysis and planning for the future.

Income statement: a record of the firm's earnings over the accounting period.

Interim reports: reports filed during the overall accounting period, which may lead to distorted ratio values when sales are subject to seasonal cycles.

Liabilities and stockholders' equity: what the firm owes its creditors and what remains for the stockholders.

Liquidity ratios: measures of the firm's ability to pay its current liabilities.

Long-term assets: fixed assets, mainly property, plant, and equipment.

Long-term liabilities: borrowings that are to be repaid in various installments over several years.

Long-term solvency ratios: measures of the firm's use of debt and its ability to meet interest charges and debt-repayment schedules.

Net worth: total assets less total liabilities.

Operating expenses: expenses that are necessary but are not a direct part of the production process.

Profitability ratios: measures of the firm's ability to turn each dollar of revenue into profits and to produce profits from each invested dollar.

Statement of retained earnings: record of the exact amount disbursed to the stockholders as dividends and the exact amount retained in the firm.

Stockholders' equity: measurement of owners' interest, reflecting the firm's asset value remaining after all liabilities have been subtracted.

Trend analysis: examination of trends in ratio values to identify deterioration or improvement in the firm's position.

ANSWERS TO REVIEW QUESTIONS

1.	e	7.	b	13.	d	18.	b
2.	b	8.	e	14.	b	19.	c
3.	c	9.	b	15.	c	20.	b
4.	c	10.	a	16.	a	21.	d
5.	c	11.	a	17.	e	22.	e
6.	b	12.	a				

Chapter Four
Budgeting

OVERVIEW

The firm uses budgets to develop its overall operating plan. Budgets are important in planning, coordinating, and controlling the overall operations of the organization. This chapter presents the sales budget, cost of goods sold budget, selling and administrative expense budget, and overall operating budget (the master plan of the firm). Cash inflows and outflows are summarized in the cash budget to forecast shortages and/or surpluses. Emphasis is placed on the role of flexible budgets as tools to be used in guiding the progress of the firm toward its objectives.

STUDY OBJECTIVES

1. To identify operating budgets that the financial officer typically encounters.

2. To outline projected cash inflows and outflows in a cash budget.

3. To summarize the use of budgets in control of the firm's operations.

CHAPTER OUTLINE

I. Budgets can be long-term or short-term methods of <u>planning</u>, <u>coordinating</u>, and <u>controlling</u> the operations of the entire firm. Major budgeting areas with which the financial officer must be familiar are <u>operations</u>, <u>cash coordination</u>, and <u>capital expenditures</u>.

   A. <u>Operating budgets</u> reflect forecasted plans for sales, production, and expenses.

   B. <u>Cash budgets</u> are designed to coordinate the firm's cash inflows and outflows to prevent unacceptable cash positions.

   C. <u>Capital expenditure budgets</u> are developed as forecasts of the firm's investments in long-term assets.

D. Primary uses of budgets include the following:

1. <u>Planning</u> both financial and operating objectives. Current costs and revenue prospects are projected in a plan that states financial and operating objectives for the budget period.

2. <u>Coordinating</u> the firm's many different and complex efforts into an organized plan to attain overall objectives. This method attempts to integrate the firm's activities.

3. <u>Controlling</u> the firm's various departments via budget targets. Deviations from budgeted amounts are immediately apparent, signaling the need for remedial action.

II. <u>Budget construction</u> involves the interchange of information and feedback from operating divisions to budget committees and back. This process includes several important steps in all organizations.

A. Step 1 is the sales budget, which the marketing department is asked to prepare for the next planning period.

B. Step 2 involves evaluation of the sales budget by the budget committee and dissemination of the final sales budget to the operating divisions, which use it in developing their production budgets.

C. Step 3 is review by the budget committee of each budget that has been developed from the sales budget to ensure consistency within the firm and compatibility with its objectives.

D. Step 4 is the process by which the budget committee coordinates all the departmental budget requests into a general operating budget to be used as the master plan for the coming period. The general operating budget is distributed to all departments and monitored throughout the period to control the direction of the firm.

III. The construction of a <u>general operating budget</u> requires coordination of all units within the firm.

A. The typical <u>sales budget</u> forecasts sales for the planning period, including estimates of the unit sales and sales revenue for each division or product for each subperiod. The resulting forecast is also used to set monthly sales quotas.

B. Using the sales budget as its base, the <u>production budget</u> projects the number of units to be produced during the next planning period. This allows for acquisition of the machinery and materials required to satisfy the forecasted demand. The proper coordination of sales and production budgets ensures that the firm will have the productive capacity to meet sales projections.

C. The production budget is used to estimate the <u>expected costs</u> associated with the units to be produced. Production expenses include the following:

1. <u>Raw materials</u> - needed to meet the production budget.

2. <u>Direct labor</u> - amount and cost required to meet the production budget.

3. <u>Purchases</u> - amount, type, and cost of necessary supplies other than raw materials.

4. <u>Manufacturing overhead</u> - plant expenses that will be incurred in meeting the production budget.

The proper coordination of these budget needs leads to the overall <u>cost of goods sold budget</u>. This process yields a single cost figure to represent the budgeted cost of achieving the production projected for the given planning period.

D. <u>Selling and administrative budgets</u> are developed by departments not directly involved with the production process. These budgets might include the following:

1. <u>Advertising</u> - budgeted advertising expenses.

2. <u>Selling expenses</u> - budgeted salaries for the sales force.

3. <u>Research and development</u> - forecasted research and development costs.

4. <u>Administrative expenses</u> - forecasted executive costs.

The general operating budget combines all the budgets into one summary of the projected revenues and expenses for the entire company for the next period. This budget is then used as a device for monitoring the performance of the firm. Significant deviations from the budgeted amounts are easily identifiable and should be investigated.

IV. Financial officers prepare a <u>cash budget</u> in addition to an operating budget. This budget focuses on the cash flow characteristics expected over the planning period.

A. The objective of the cash budget is to coordinate the timing of the firm's cash needs. This process quickly identifies shortfalls in cash resources, and necessary plans can be made. Excess cash can also be identified, and plans can be made to make use of these funds. The cash budget enhances the firm's ability to take advantage of cash discounts on accounts payable, pay debt obligations when due, formulate dividend policies, plan the financing of capital expansions, and unify the production schedule and thereby smooth out seasonal fluctuations.

B. Three basic steps are involved in developing a cash budget.

1. <u>Establishing the format</u> to set the time period and subperiods involved in the planning period (usually monthly, for twelve consecutive months).

2. <u>Identifying the cash inflows</u> to specify inflows that will occur over the planning period--that is, cash sales, collection of accounts receivable, financing inflows, and so on.

3. Identifying the cash outflows to specify outflows that will occur over the planning period--this is, purchases, payments on accounts payable, wages expense, salaries expense, manufacturing overhead, financing expenses, and so on.

C. Carefully planned cash budgets allow the alert financial officer to pre-arrange funding that may be required or investments that can be made with excess funds.

V. Budgets can be used effectively as a control mechanism and contingency plan to guide the firm toward its overall objective.

A. The control-interval technique can be used to identify significant deviations from the budgeted amount. The accompanying figure illustrates the development of control limits (both upper and lower) around which actual values are plotted. When actual values exceed the limits set, financial officers direct their attention to identifying the cause and meaning of the significant deviation from the budget.

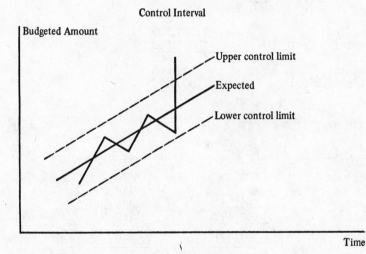

B. Because we cannot continually predict with consistent accuracy, alternative courses of action must be developed. The financial officer must prepare these contingency plans as alternatives that can be used when budget estimates are inaccurate.

1. Contingency budgets relfect alternative plans or budgets and schedules to which the firm will retreat or expand if the original estimates prove inaccurate.

2. Readily available contingency budgets make the firm more flexible and allow timely adjustments in the event that original plans must be dropped or revised.

General Operating Budget, An Example

This example reflects and summarizes the set of budgets that together make up the general operating budget of RPB, Inc., for the next accounting period. RPB produces pillows that sell for $6.00 each and require 2 pounds of cotton ($.90/pound) to produce each unit.

SALES BUDGET

	Units	Revenue
First quarter	300,000	$ 1,800,000
Second quarter	400,000	2,400,000
Third quarter	800,000	4,800,000
Fourth quarter	200,000	1,200,000
Total	1,700,000	$10,200,000

PRODUCTION BUDGET

Unit sales forecasted	1,700,000
Add desired inventory, Dec. 31	200,000
Total units required	1,900,000
Less present inventory, Jan. 1	100,000
Budgeted production (units)	1,800,000

RAW MATERIALS BUDGET

	Type of Material	Amount	Cost
First quarter	Cotton	600,000	$540,000
Second quarter	Cotton	800,000	720,000
Third quarter	Cotton	1,600,000	1,440,000
Fourth quarter	Cotton	400,000	360,000
Total		3,400,000	$3,060,000

COST OF GOODS SOLD BUDGET

Inventory, beginning of period		$ 800,000
Cost of inventory during the period:		
Raw materials	3,060,000	
Purchases	300,000	
Direct labor	2,000,000	
Manufacturing overhead	1,500,000	6,860,000
Inventory, available for sale		7,660,000
Less inventory on hand, end of period		
Raw materials	400,000	
Work in process	200,000	
Finished goods	1,200,000	1,800,000
Cost of goods sold		$ 5,860,000

GENERAL OPERATING BUDGET SUMMARY

Sales	$ 10,200,000	(from sales budget)
Cost of goods sold	5,860,000	(from COGS budget)
Gross profit	4,340,000	
Selling expenses	1,000,000	(from selling/ administrative budget)
Administrative expenses	1,000,000	(from administrative expense budget)
Operating profit (before depreciation)	$ 2,340,000	

STUDY PROBLEMS

<u>4.1.</u> The following is the sales forecast for NOTA, Inc. All sales are on credit, net 30 days. Historically, the firm has collected 60 percent of the receivables the month after sale, 20 percent the next month, and the remaining 20 percent in the third month after sale. Compute a schedule of cash inflows for the months of July, August, and September.

Forecasted Sales (Net)

January	$100,000	July	$220,000
February	$120,000	August	$240,000
March	$130,000	September	$300,000
April	$150,000	October	$100,000
May	$140,000	November	$ 80,000
June	$200,000	December	$ 60,000

<u>Solution</u>

July inflows are based on sales in April, May, and June.
August inflows are based on sales in May, June, and July.
September inflows are based on sales in June, July, and August.

July:
  .20 * April sales = .20 * $150,000 = $ 30,000
  .20 * May sales = .20 * $140,000 = $ 28,000
  .60 * June sales = .60 * $200,000 = $120,000
                        Total $178,000

August:
  .20 * May sales = .20 * $140,000 = $ 28,000
  .20 * June sales = .20 * $200,000 = $ 40,000
  .60 * July sales = .60 * $220,000 = $132,000
                        Total $200,000

September: .20 * June sales = .20 * $200,000 = $ 40,000
            .20 * July sales = .20 * $220,000 = $ 44,000
            .60 * August sales = .60 * $240,000 = $144,000
                        Total $228,000

Schedule of Cash Inflows

	July	August	September
Amount of inflow	$178,000	$200,000	$228,000

4.2. The following are the cash outflow data for NOTA, Inc. Compute a schedule of cash outflows for the months of July, August, and September.

Cash Outflow Data

The cost of goods sold is 50 percent of monthly sales. (Use the sales data supplied in Problem 4.1.)
The cost of goods sold is paid as follows: 60 percent the month following sale and 40 percent the next month.
Salary and administrative expenses are $80,000 per month.
Advertising expense is $20,000 per month.

Solution

Cost of Goods Sold Budget

```
May    = .50 * $140,000 = $ 70,000
June   = .50 * $200,000 = $100,000
July   = .50 * $220,000 = $110,000
August = .50 * $240,000 = $120,000
```

Payment Schedule for Cost of Goods Sold

May - 60 percent in June and 40 percent in July
June - 60 percent in July and 40 percent in August
July - 60 percent in August and 40 percent in September
August - 60 percent in September and 40 percent in October

Cash Outflows

	July	August	September
Cost of goods sold	$ 28,000 (May)	$ 40,000 (June)	$ 44,000 (July)
	60,000 (June)	66,000 (July)	72,000 (August)
	88,000	106,000	116,000
Salary and administrative expense	80,000	80,000	80,000
Advertising expense	20,000	20,000	20,000
Total cash outflows	$188,000	$206,000	$216,000

4.3. What would be the net cash-flow position of NOTA, Inc., for the months of July, August, and September? (Note: Combine results of Problems 4.1 and 4.2, assuming a beginning cash balance of $36,000 and a minimum cash balance desired of zero.)

Solution

	July	August	September
Inflows			
Accounts receivable (from Problem 4.1)	$178,000	$200,000	$228,000
Outflows			
Cost of operations (from Problem 4.2)	188,000	206,000	216,000
Cash excess (shortfall)	(10,000)	(6,000)	12,000
Cash beginning of month	36,000	26,000	20,000
Less minimum balance	4,000	4,000	4,000
Cash available at beginning	32,000	22,000	16,000
Cash excess (shortfall)	(10,000)	(6,000)	12,000
Cash available	26,000	16,000	28,000
Previous cash (beginning)	36,000	26,000	20,000
Less cash used	10,000	6,000	0
Plus cash excess	0	0	12,000
Cash at end of month	$ 26,000	$ 20,000	$ 32,000

4.4. Assume that NOTA, Inc., can borrow funds at an annual interest rate of 12 percent. The firm has a policy of borrowing as little as possible and repaying as soon as possible. Using the cash budget developed in Problem 4.3, develop a new cash budget. Assume that the firm's beginning cash balance in July is $4,000 rather than $36,000. Also assume that interest payments are made only after funds are repaid, and in the following month thereafter.

Solution

The firm barely had enough cash when it started with a beginning balance of $36,000. Therefore, it is obvious that borrowed funds will be required in the following budget.

	July	August	September
Inflows			
Accounts receivable	$178,000	$200,000	$228,000
Outflows			
Cost of operations	188,000	206,000	216,000
Cash excess (shortfall)	(10,000)	(6,000)	12,000
Cash beginning of month	4,000	4,000	4,000
Less minimum balance	4,000	4,000	4,000
Cash available at beginning	0	0	0
Cash excess (shortfall)	(10,000)	(6,000)	12,000
Cash available	(10,000)	(6,000)	12,000
Financing position			
Owed at beginning of month	0	10,000	16,000
Repayment	0	0	12,000
Borrowing	(10,000)	(6,000)	0
Total owed	10,000	16,000	4,000
Investment position			
Cash excess	0	0	12,000
Repayment	0	0	12,000
Cash acquired	0	0	0
Previous cash	4,000	4,000	4,000
Less cash used	0	0	0
Cash end of month	$ 4,000	$ 4,000	$ 4,000

4.5. Rolina, Inc., typically grows at a rate that reflects the general economic activity of the nation. Given the following economic forecasts and budget requests, identify those areas that seem to be out of line with historical expectations.

Economic/Marketing Forecasts

Expected economic activity index		114%
Expected inflation index (base = 100%)		118%
Year-end inventory		100,000 units
Sales		$1,000,000
Sales price per unit (average)		$5.00
Cost of goods sold:		
Raw materials	$600,000	
Labor	200,000	
Purchases	50,000	
Manufacturing overhead	50,000	
Total cost of goods sold		$900,000
Selling expenses		55,000
Administrative expenses		25,000
Total costs		$ 980,000
Operating profit		$ 20,000

Previous Year's Data

Sales		$800,000
Raw materials	$600,000	
Labor	100,000	
Purchases	25,000	
Manufacturing overhead	25,000	
Total cost of goods sold		750,000
Selling expenses		30,000
Administrative expenses		10,000
Total costs		$790,000
Operating profit before depreciation		$ 10,000

Solution

Sales: Judging by sales in the base year, where the economic activity and inflation indexes are 100 percent, we would expect new sales to increase 32 percent over the previous year's data--14 percent due to economic growth and 18 percent as a result of inflation. Therefore, new sales would be $800,000 * 1.32 = $1,056,000. The forecasted amount of $1,000,000 is conservative and probably should be adjusted upward by $56,000.

The cost of goods sold includes the costs of raw materials and labor costs.

Raw materials costs would be expected to increase by 32 percent to $600,000 * 1.32 = $792,000. The forecasted amount of $600,000 is much below that which should occur. Maintaining the raw materials costs at the same figure as the previous period completely ignores the obvious increases due to economic activity and inflation, unless offsetting factors are apparent. This budget request needs much additional information.

Labor costs would be approximately 12.5 percent of sales if the base-year relationship holds. This would lead to an expected cost of .125 * $1,000,000 = $125,000,
which is much less than the budgeted amount of $200,000. Further data are re-
quired before the $200,000 amount is accepted as a reasonable expectation.

Purchases and manufacturing overhead are forecasted to be approximately 10 percent
of sales, whereas they were 6 percent of sales in the base year. This forecasted
increase would need further explanation.

Selling and administrative costs are forecasted to become a much larger cost factor
than in the previous year, even after adjustments for economic growth and inflation.
Further justification would be required to support these forecasted amounts.

Operating profit in the previous year was 1.25 percent of sales. In the forecasted
year, operating profit will be 2.00 percent of sales. This increase is forecasted
because of a 25 percent forecasted increase in sales and a .75 percent decrease in
total costs. That is,

	Previous Year	Forecasted Year
Sales	$800,000 (100%)	$1,000,000 (100%)
Total costs	790,000 (98.75%)	980,000 (98%)
Operating profit	$ 10,000 (1.25%)	$ 20,000 (2.00%)

In summary, the forecasted values do not reflect the impact of economic activity,
inflation, or the tendency of past relationships to sales to remain relatively
stable. Although the total cost forecasted as a percentage of sales is in line
with the past, adjustments need to be made to all components of total cost to make
them reflect prior-year relationships (unless new factors have occurred to change
these historical trends).

REVIEW QUESTIONS

1. Budgets can serve as long-term or short-term methods of
   a. planning.
   b. controlling.
   c. coordinating.
   d. all of these.

2. Cash budgets are designed to
   a. reflect forecasted production and expense plans.
   b. forecast the firm's investments in long-term assets.
   c. coordinate the firm's cash inflows and outflows to prevent unacceptable
      cash positions.
   d. all of these.

3. The first step in creating a budget for the entire firm is to draw up
   a. the capital budget.
   b. the sales budget.
   c. the cash budget.
   d. the operating budget.
   e. none of these.

4. The production budget draws its base data from the _____ budget.
   a. operations
   b. sales
   c. general operating
   d. none of these

5. The cost of goods sold budget includes the
   a. manufacturing overhead budget.
   b. purchases budget.
   c. raw materials budget.
   d. direct labor budget.
   e. all of these.

6. Selling and administrative budgets are developed by departments
   a. not directly involved with the production process.
   b. directly involved with the production process.
   c. directly involved with advertising expenses.
   d. none of these.

7. Financial officers prepare a _____ budget in addition to an operating budget.
   a. sales
   b. production
   c. cost of goods sold
   d. cash
   e. none of these

8. The cash budget of the firm enhances the firm's ability to
   a. take advantage of cash discounts on accounts payable.
   b. pay debt obligations when due.
   c. formulate dividend policies.
   d. plan the financing of capital expansions.
   e. all of these.

9. The control-interval technique can be used to
   a. establish the exact amount of cash.
   b. identify small deviations from the budgeted amount.
   c. identify significant deviations from the budgeted amount.
   d. all of these.

10. Contingency budgets reflect
    a. alternative plans and schedules to be used when original estimates prove inaccurate.
    b. the limits of contingencies available during the accounting period.
    c. the failure to recognize errors in forecasting.
    d. none of these.

11. Budgets should be used to _____ employees.
    a. confuse
    b. pressure
    c. motivate
    d. reprimand

12. Contingency budgets make for _____ and _____.
    a. flexibility, timeliness
    b. rigidity, timeliness
    c. flexibility, delays
    d. none of these

13. The general operating budget includes
    a. the cost of goods sold.
    b. purchases.
    c. finished goods.
    d. all of these.

14. Forecasted amounts used in developing budgets must include adjustments for the effect of
    a. inflation.
    b. anticipated changes in economic activity.
    c. past relationships that are expected to continue.
    d. all of these.

15. Contingency plans, budgets, and schedules are necessary, because
    a. we can always predict with certainty of making no errors.
    b. we cannot continually predict with consistent accuracy.
    c. we have no confidence in the original budgets.
    d. none of these.

KEY DEFINITIONS

Capital expenditure budget: budget that forecasts the firm's investments in long-term assets.

Cash budget: budget designed to coordinate the firm's cash inflows and outflows to prevent unacceptable cash positions.

Contingency plans: alternative plans, budgets, and schedules to which the firm will retreat or expand if the original estimates prove inaccurate.

Control-interval technique: means of setting upper and lower control limits of the budget and thereby highlighting significant deviations from the budgeted amount.

Cost of goods sold budget: budget that reflects anticipated costs of raw materials, direct labor, purchases, and manufacturing overhead over the planning period, leading to a single cost figure for attaining the production budget.

General operating budget: the master plan of the firm, which combines all the individual budgets into one summary.

Operating budget: budget that reflects forecasted plans for sales, production, and expenses.

Production budget: budget that projects the number of units to be produced during the next planning period.

Sales budget: the basis of all other budgets, reflecting anticipated sales during the planning period.

<u>Selling and administrative budget</u>: budget developed by a department not directly involved with the production process.

ANSWERS TO REVIEW QUESTIONS

1.	d	5.	e	9.	c	13.	a
2.	c	6.	a	10.	a	14.	d
3.	b	7.	d	11.	c	15.	b
4.	b	8.	e	12.	a		

Chapter Five
The Mathematics of Finance

OVERVIEW

The objective of this chapter is to introduce the concept of the time value of money and its relationship to the use of capital as a limited resource. In essence, dollars received in the future are not so valuable as dollars received today, because we forgo the opportunity to invest the funds today.

STUDY OBJECTIVES

1. To examine the concepts of compound value and present value.

2. To develop an understanding of the time value of money as it relates to the use of capital as a limited resource.

3. To determine the compound sum and present value of an annuity.

4. To examine the derivation of the payments required to amortize a loan or deposits required to accumulate a desired amount, using concepts related to the time value of money.

CHAPTER OUTLINE

I. Compound value refers to the ending amount to which an original deposit grows due to the compounding process--that is, the process of earning interest on remaining principal and on previously earned interest.

   A. Compound-value formulas compound forward to the future value (P_n) an original investment (P_0) for a number of years (n) at an annual interest rate (i) on the cumulative balance. Therefore, the compound or future value of $100 invested at 10 percent annual compounded interest for 2 years would be found as follows:

$$P_n = P_0 * (1 + i)^n$$
$$= \$100 * (1 + .10)^2$$
$$= \$100 * (1.10)^2$$
$$= \$100 * 1.2100$$
$$= \$121.00$$

1. Precalculated tables exist to provide the values for $(1 + i)^n$, called CIT (compound-interest term) values. Extensive table values for CITs under different compound interest rates (i) and time periods (n) are given in Appendix A. Therefore,

$$P_n = P_0 * CIT \text{ (where CIT values are as given in Appendix A)}$$

Example: What is the compound value of $300 invested for 5 years, earning 8 percent compounded annually?

P_n = $300 * CIT (where i = 8%, n = 5 years)
   = $300 * 1.4693 (from Appendix A)
   = $440.79

2. CIT values can be used to determine growth rates (i) and time periods (n) as well as compound values (P_n). Because $P_n = P_0 * CIT$, CIT depends on the interest rate and the time period. Therefore, knowledge of P_n, P_0, and i or n allows us to determine the missing variable in the equation.

Example: How long will it take for current sales of $100,000 to grow to $459,500 if sales increase at a compound annual rate of 10 percent? Consider the following data:

Sales today = $100,000 = P_0
Future sales = $459,500 = P_n
Compound annual growth rate = 10% = i
Years of growth required = 7 = n

Because $P_n = P_0 * CIT$,

CIT = P_n/P_0
   = $459,500/$100,000
   = 4.5950 (where i = 10%, n = ?)

By reading Appendix A for i = 10 percent, we find the nearest CIT value (exactly 4.5950 in the example) in the row where n = 16. Hence, the time required will be 16 years.

3. An approximation to determine the missing number of years (n) or compound annual interest rate (i) is found through the "Rule of 72." Note that this procedure will provide approximations <u>only</u> when the change being investigated is 100 percent (double the prior amount). Two types of problems can be solved:

    a. Approximate interest rate required to double the compound value in a known number of years (where $i = 72/n$).

    b. Approximate number of years required to double the compound value when the interest rate is known (where $n = 72/i$).

<u>Example One</u>: What is the approximate annual compound-interest rate that we must earn to double our investment over an 8-year period?

Because $i = 72/n = 72/8 = 9$ percent, our investment must earn approximately 9 percent compounded annually to double in 8 years.

<u>Example Two</u>: What is the approximate number of years required to double an investment in a savings account that earns 12 percent compounded annually?

Because $n = 72/i = 72/12 = 6$ years, the investment will double in value in approximately 6 years if it earns 12 percent compounded annually.

B. Compound interest is a significant aspect of financial management. By earning interest on interest remaining in an investment, we can shorten the time required to reach a financial objective. This powerful concept increases in power as the compound interest rate and the period of the investment increase.

C. Compounding can occur over shorter periods than a year--quarterly, monthly, or daily, for example. As the number of compounding periods increases, we increase the earnings of interest on interest remaining. Nonannual compounding can be accomplished by making two important adjustments to the general compound-value formula:

1. Increase the number of periods per year ($n * m$).

2. Change the rate of compound interest paid (i/m).

Because $P_n = P_0 * (1 + i)^n$ for annual compounding, $P_n = P_0 * (1 + i/m)^{n*m}$ for nonannual compounding, where m is the number of periods in which compounding occurs in period n.

<u>Example</u>: (This example compares annual with semiannual compounding.) What will be the compound value of $100 invested in a savings account for 3 years when it will earn 6 percent compounded annually?

$P_n = P_0 * (1 + i)^n$ for annual compounding

  $= \$100 * (1 + .06)^3$

  $= \$100 *$ CIT (where i = 6%, n = 3)

  $= \$100 * 1.1910$

  $= \$119.10$

What would the compound sum be if the same investment paid interest that was compounded semiannually (twice each year)?

$$P_n = P_0 * (1 + i/m)^{n*m} \text{ for nonannual compounding,}$$
$$= \$100 * (1 + .06/2)^{3*2} \text{ for m = 2 per year,}$$
$$= \$100 * (.103)^6$$
$$= \$100 * CIT \text{ (where i = 3\%, n = 6)}$$
$$= \$100 * 1.1941$$
$$= \$119.41$$

The compound sum (P_n) increases as the number of compounding periods (m) increases, due to the higher interest paid on interest.

II. <u>Present value</u> is the inverse of compound value. This value is especially important in the selection of long-term assets (capital budgeting), because it tells us the present value of the expected future cash flows of the investment. Waiting for future value requires that we forgo the opportunity to invest the funds now. This loss is incorporated in the formulation of present value, which quantifies the fact that money received sooner is more valuable than money received later.

A. The process of determining the present value of future inflows is often called "discounting," which is the reverse of compounding:

Compound value: $P_n = P_0 * (1 + i)^n$

Present value: $P_0 = P_n * [1/(1 + i)^n]$

<u>Example</u>: (This example compares compound value with present value.)

a. What is the compound value of $100 invested today at 6 percent, compounded annually, for 1 year?

$$P_n = P_0 * (1 + i)^n$$
$$= \$100 * (1.06)^1$$
$$= \$106$$

b. What is the present value of $106 to be received in 1 year if the interest rate forgone (discount rate) is 6 percent?

$$P_0 = P_n * [1/(1 + i)^n]$$
$$= \$106 * [1/(1 + .06)^1]$$
$$= \$106 * .9434$$
$$= \$100.00$$

The $P_0 = \$100$ indicates that this amount, invested at 6 percent for 1 year would be worth $106 at the end of the year.

1. Precalculated tables exist to provide values for $1/(1 + i)^n$ discount factors, called present-value interest terms (PIT). Extensive table values for PIT under different interest rates (i) and discount periods (n) are available in Appendix B. Therefore,

$$P_0 = P_n * \text{PIT (for varying values of i and n)}$$

Example: What is the present value of receiving $400 two years from now when the discount rate (rate of forgone interest income) is 12 percent?

$P_0 = P_n *$ PIT (where i = 12%, n = 2)

   = $400 * .79719 (from Appendix B)

   = $318.88

2. The "discount rate" (i) used in present-value calculations represents the annual interest rate that we cannot earn because we must wait to receive the funds. This value often adjusts the future flows for the minimum rate of return expected on various investments.

3. The "discount period" is the number of years during which we must wait before receiving the funds.

    We discount to find the present value of an expected future amount.

B. The power of discounting expected future flows parallels that of compounding a present amount, but the direction has changed. Discounting shows that the present value of expected future flows decreases as the discount rate (i) and/or the discount period (n) increases.

III. Annuities can be represented as a series of inflows or outflows of funds that meet the following criteria: (1) flows occur at regular intervals, and (2) flows never change in amount received or paid.

A. We find the compound sum of an annuity (A_n) by summing the individual CIT values and multiplying this sum by the constant flows involved.

Example: What is the compound sum of an annuity of $1,000 invested annually for the next 4 years at 12 percent compound interest?

Consider the following data:

Annual flow = $1,000 = P_0

Compound-interest rate = 12% = i

Years involved = 4 = n

Accumulated ending sum = ? = A_0

Individual inflows approach:

$P_n = P_0 * (1 + i)^n$ for each period

Year Invested	Years of Compounding	Formula Value	Total (yearly)
1	4	$P_4 = 1,000 * (1.12)^4$	$1,573.50
2	3	$P_3 = 1,000 * (1.12)^3$	1,404.90
3	2	$P_2 = 1,000 * (1.12)^2$	1,254.40
	1	$P_1 = 1,000 * (1.12)^1$	1,120.00
		Total accumulated compound sum =	$5,352.80

Annuity approach:

$$A_n = R(1 = i)^n + R(1 + i)^{n-1} + \cdots + R(1 + i)^1$$

$$= R((1 + i)^n + (1 + i)^{n-1} + \cdots + (1 + i)^1)$$

$$= R * CAIT \text{ (from Appendix C)}$$

where

A_n = compound sum of an annuity
R = annual, equal flows
i = annual compound-interest rate
n = number of years involved
$(1 + i)^n$ = individual CIT values for each flow
CAIT = sum of individual CIT values (Appendix C)

Therefore,

$$A_n = R[(1 + i)^n + (1 + i)^{n-1} + \cdots + (1 + i)^1]$$

$$= \$1,000 * [(1.12)^4 + (1.12)^3 + (1.12)^2 + (1.12)^1]$$
$$= \$1,000 * (1.5735 + 1.4049 + 1.2544 + 1.1200)$$
$$= \$1,000 * CAIT \text{ (from Appendix C)}$$
$$= \$1,000 * 5,3528$$
$$= \$5,352.80$$

The CAIT value of 5.3528 represents the sum of the individual CIT values and can be found in Appendix C for the i and n values.

1. Precalculated tables exist for values of the compound annuity in-terest term (CAIT). Appendix C provides CAIT values for different time periods (n) and annual compound-interest rates (i).

Note: A_n must exceed the sum of R values, because interest is earned, as reflected in the CAIT values.

2. The power of the compound annuity is similar to that of the individual flows that depend on the levels of i and n. The larger the interest rate and the longer the time period, the more powerful the impact of compounding on an annuity flow.

B. The present value of an annuity is the opposite of compound sum. This value shows the current worth of a series of future equal receipts occurring at equal time intervals. Note that the present-value-of-an-annuity concept continues to recognize that present flows are worth more than future flows, because the opportunity to earn interest is forgone by waiting. We find the present value of a future annuity (A_0) by discounting the future constant flows by the sum of the individual PIT values.

Example: (This example compares determining the present value of individual flows with determining that of an annuity.) How much should we invest today (present value) in an annuity from which we will receive $1,000 at the end of each of the next 4 years, recognizing that we will forgo the opportunity to earn 12 percent (discount rate) compounded annually on the funds we must wait to receive?

Present-value-of-individual-flows approach:

We can find the present value of a series of individual flows by calculating the individual present value of each flow and adding them together.

$$P_0 = P_n * 1/(1 + i)^n = P_n * PIT \text{ for each year, } \underline{\text{summed over all years}}$$

Year Received	Years of Discounting	Formula Value: $P_0 = P_n * PIT$	Yearly Total
4	4	P_4 = $1,000 * .6355	$635.50
3	3	P_3 = $1,000 * .7118	711.80
2	2	P_2 = $1,000 * .7972	797.20
1	1	P_1 = $1,000 * .8929	892.90
		Total present value of future flows	$3,037.40

Present-value-of-an-annuity approach:

We can simplify finding the present value of individual flows by recognizing that the sum of the PIT values is provided in Appendix D in a table of PAIT values.

A_0 = R * PAIT
A_0 = R * 3.0374   (from Appendix D)
  = $1,000 * 3.0374
  = $3,037.40

Note that the sum of the PIT values (.6355 + .7118 + .7972 + .8929) is the same as the PAIT value found in Appendix D (3.0374).

C. When the streams of inflows or outflows are not equal, we must use the individual-flows approach to determine the compound or present value of the stream. When both constant and unequal streams occur during different time periods, we may combine the annuities and individual-flows methods.

Example: A bond owner expects a series of constant inflows in the form of annual interest income and a single-period inflow when the bond is sold or redeemed (at maturity). Therefore, the total present value of the series of flows is a combination of equal flows (interest income) and a single inflow at maturity (un-equal to the annual flows).

How much would you be willing to pay today (present value) for a bond that will return $120 in interest income each year for the next 20 years plus $1,000 at the end (maturity), if the discount rate (forgone interest) is 12 percent?

Consider the following data:

Annuity inflows = $120 = R
Single-period inflow = $1,000 = P_n

Time period = 20 = n
Discount rate = 12% = i

Total present value combines A_0 = R * PAIT and P_0 = P_n * PIT. Therefore, the total value of the investment today is the sum of the present value of the interest annuity and that of the single inflow at maturity.

A_0 = R * PAIT

   = $120 * 7.469 (Appendix D, i = 12%, n = 20)
   = $896.33 (present value of interest)

P_0 = P_n * PIT

   = $1,000 * .10367 (Appendix B, i = 12%, n = 20)
   = $103.67 (present value of single-period inflow)

The total present value = $896.33 + $103.67 = $1,000.00. This is the most we would be willing to pay for the bond.

In general,

$$P_0 = \sum_{t=1}^{n} \frac{I_t}{(1 + i)^t} + \frac{P_n}{(1 + i)^n}$$

where

$\sum$ = summation
t = year
n = total number of years
I_t = annual interest income from bond
P_n = future return of principal investment

Given knowledge about a bond's present value (P_0), interest inflows (i), and future return at maturity (P_n), we can determine its <u>yield to maturity</u> by a trial-and-error process.

Example:

$$P_0 = \sum_{t=1}^{n} \frac{I_t}{(1 + i)^t} + \frac{P_n}{(1 + i)^n}$$

so, using our previous example to find the yield to maturity,

$$\$1,000 = \sum_{t=1}^{n} \frac{\$120}{(1 + i)^t} + \frac{\$1,000}{(1 + i)^n}$$

we could solve for i (the yield to maturity) using different rates for i given in the appendices until we found the rate that equates the current value ($1,000) and the future inflows. The interest rate (12 percent in this example) that equates cost and benefit represents the yield to maturity on the investment.

IV. The time value of money has many uses. Concepts of compound value and present value can be extended to include the determination of many other funding and interest-rate requirements in financial analysis.

A. <u>Annual installment deposits</u> (sinking funds) can be calculated using the compound-sum-of-an-annuity method by solving the $A_0 = R * CAIT$ formula for R, because A_0 and CAIT are known. This approach reveals the annual fixed annuity required to accumulate a desired future sum.

Example: What annual installment is required if we need $60,000 in 10 years to purchase a home, when the annual installments can be placed in a savings account earning 7 percent compounded annually on the remaining balance?

Consider the following data:

R = ? = annual installment required to achieve the desired future sum
A_n = $60,000 = desired sum that the annuity should attain
n = 10 = years that the annuity will be deposited
i = 7% = annual compounding rate of interest

Because $A_n = R * CAIT$,

R = A_n/CAIT
  = $60,000/14.784 (from Appendix C, i = 7%, n = 10)
  = $4,058.44

Therefore, we must deposit $4,058.44 annually for 10 years, earning 7 percent compounded annually, to have $60,000 at the end of the period.

81

Note: We can check our answer by solving the equation $A_n = R * CAIT$ for an annuity of $4,058.44 inbested at an annual compounding interest rate of 7 percent for 10 years.

$$A_n = R * CAIT = \$4,058.44 * 14.784 \text{ (Appendix C)}$$
$$= \$60,000 \text{ (the desired accumulated total)}$$

B. We can determine the <u>payments required to amortize a loan</u> by using the present-value-of-an-annuity method. When we borrow funds, we are required to make annual payments that include principal and interest. The interest charged for the loan is usually determined by the amount of the remaining principal outstanding in a given year. To determine the fixed amount required to amortize both principal and interest over the life of the loan, we can use the present-value-of-an-annuity approach.

Example: What annual payment is required to completely pay off the principal and interest of a $20,000 loan that has a 3-year maturity and an interest charge of 10 percent on the declining principal balance?

Consider the following data:

R = ? = annual payment that amortizes a loan

A_0 = $20,000 = present value of loan amount

n = 3 = years that the payments will be made
i = 10% = interest charged on declining principal
PAIT = 2.4868 = present-value-interest term, where i = 10%, n = 3 (Appendix D)

Because

$A_0 = R * PAIT,$

$R = A_0/PAIT$

$= \$20,000/2.4868$
$= \$8,042.46$ (annual payment required to amortize the loan)

Note that we can check this answer by constructing the following amortization table.

Year	Payment	=	Principal[a]	+	Interest[b]	Declining Principal Balance[c]
1	$8,042.46		$6,042.46		$2,000.00	$13,957.54
2	$8,042.46		$6,646.71		$1,395.75	$ 7,310.83
3	$8,042.46		$7,311.38		$ 731.08	Approx. zero

[a] payment less interest charge

[b] .10 * (c) at beginning of year

[c] beginning principal balance less (a)

Formula Review Table

Type of Problem	Description of Flows	
	Individual	Annuity
Compound value	$P_n = P_0 * CIT$	$A_n = R * CAIT$
Present value	$P_0 = P_n * PIT$	$A_0 = R * PAIT$
Installment deposits	--	$R = A_n/CAIT$
Amortize a loan	--	$R = A_0/PAIT$
Value of a bond	$P_0 = P_n * PIT$	$A_0 = R * PAIT$

STUDY PROBLEMS

5.1. What would be the future (compound) value of $1,000 invested for 6 years, earning 8 percent interest compounded annually?

Solution

$$P_n = \$1,000 * CIT = \$1,000 * 1.5869 = \$1,586.90$$

5.2. What would be the compound value of the investment outlined in Problem 5.1 if the compounding effect were based on quarterly rather than annual compounding?

Solution

$$P_n = P_0 * CIT \text{ (where } i = .08/4 \text{ and } n = 6 * 4)$$
$$= \$1,000 * 1.6084 \text{ (from Appendix A)}$$
$$= \$1,608.40$$

5.3. Approximately how many years will it take us to accumulate a savings account worth $10,000 if we invest $5,000 today at 6 percent compounded annually?

Solution

Using the "Rule of 72," we find that

$$n = 72/i$$
$$= 72/6$$
$$= 12 \text{ years}$$

5.4. What is the present value of $4,000 to be received in 5 years when the investor forgoes the opportunity to earn a 10 percent return during the 5-year period?

Solution

This is a present-value problem, wherein

$$P_0 = P_n * PIT$$
$$= \$4,000 * .62092$$
$$= \$2,483.68$$

5.5. How much would you be willing to pay today for a $60,000 cash flow to be received at the end of 20 years if you were capable of earning 12 percent compounded annually on your investments?

Solution

This is a present-value problem, wherein

$$P_0 = P_n * PIT$$
$$= \$60,000 * .10367$$
$$= \$6,220.20$$

5.6. What would be the accumulated sum of a fixed annual investment of $2,000 for 10 years if the investment earned 8 percent compounded annually?

Solution

This is a compound-value-of-an-annuity problem, wherein

$$A_n = R * CAIT \text{ (where } i = 8\%, n = 10 \text{ years)}$$
$$= \$2,000 * 15.645 \quad \text{(from Appendix C)}$$
$$= \$31,290.00$$

5.7. What is the present value of a series of future cash flows ($3,000 each) to be received over the next 7 years when the forgone interest-income opportunity (discount rate) is 11 percent?

Solution

This is a present-value-of-an-annuity problem, wherein

$$A_0 = R * PAIT \quad (i = 11\%, n = 7 \text{ years})$$
$$= \$3,000 * 4.7122 \quad \text{(from Appendix D)}$$
$$= \$14,136.60$$

5.8. How much would you be willing to pay today for a project that is expected to return $6,000 annually over the next 25 years when you have the opportunity to invest in alternatives earning 15 percent?

Solution

This is a present-value-of-an-annuity problem, wherein

$$A_0 = R * PAIT$$
$$= \$6,000 * 6.4641$$
$$= \$38,784.60$$

5.9. What is the most you would pay for a corporate bond that pays $90 per year in interest and is expected to be redeemed by the company for $1,000 at maturity (20 years from now), if you had alternative opportunities that would return 10 percent annually?

Solution

This is a present-value problem that combines the annuity flows of interest income with the single-period return of $1,000 at maturity.

$$\text{Total value} = \text{present value of interest annuity} + \text{present value of the single-period return of } \$1,000$$
$$= (R * PAIT) + (P_n * PIT)$$
$$= (\$90 * 8.5136) + (\$1,000 * .14864)$$
$$= \$766.22 + \$148.64$$
$$= \$914.86$$

5.10. How much must we save annually to accumulate $100,000 over the next 10 years if we can earn 13 percent interest compounded annually on the balance remaining?

Solution

This is an installment-deposits (sinking fund) problem, wherein

$$R = A_n/CAIT$$
$$= \$100,000/20.815 \quad \text{(from Appendix C, i = 13\%, n = 10)}$$
$$= \$4,804.23$$

5.11. If we borrowed $50,000 from a bank that charged 12 percent on the loan balance outstanding, what annual fixed payment would be required to completely pay off the loan over the next 5 years?

Solution

This is an amortization-of-a-loan problem, wherein

$$R = A_0/PAIT$$
$$= \$50,000/3.6048 \quad \text{(from Appendix D, i = 12\%, n = 5 years)}$$
$$= \$13,870.40$$

5.12. You have the opportunity to receive one of the following alternatives: (a) $10,000 in cash to be invested at 10 percent, compounded annually, or (b) $20,000 in cash to be received in a lump sum 5 years from now. Which would you prefer?

Solution

This is a present-value problem in which we compare the present value of $10,000 with the calculated present value of $20,000 to be received 5 years from now.

$$P_0 = P_n * PIT \quad \text{(where i = 10\%, n = 5 years)}$$
$$= \$20,000 * .62092 \quad \text{(from Appendix B)}$$
$$= \$12,418.40$$

You would prefer alternative (b); the present value of $20,000 to be received in 5 years is greater than the present value of $10,000 received today.

REVIEW QUESTIONS

1. The compound value of $300 invested for nine years in a savings account that pays 6 percent compounded annually is
    a. $503.13.
    b. $506.85.
    c. $480.00.
    d. $177.57.

2. What is the compound value of $500 invested in a savings account that pays 12 percent compounded monthly over a 2-year period?
    a. $634.85
    b. $627.20
    c. $563.40
    d. $550.00

3. What is the approximate interest rate being earned annually on an investment that has grown from $3,000 to $6,000 over the last 10 years?
    a. 10 percent
    b. 5 percent
    c. 7 percent
    d. 9 percent

4. What is the approximate interest rate being earned on an investment that has increased in value from $1,000 to $3,105.90 over the last 10 years?
    a. 30 percent
    b. 15 percent
    c. 12 percent
    d. 10 percent

5. What is the present value of $100,000 to be received 20 years from now, discounted at the forgone-interest rate of 7 percent?
    a. $37,689.00
    b. $25,842.00
    c. $22,571.00
    d. $18,425.00

6. What would be the real purchasing power of a $20,000 gift to be received in 3 years if the compound annual rate of inflation were 10 percent during that period?
    a. $15,026.20
    b. $20,000.00
    c. $16,323.40
    d. $14,000.00

7. If we placed $9,000 in a savings account each year for the next 7 years what would be the accumulated sum if the account paid 6 percent compounded annually?
    a. $35,460.00
    b. $66,539.70
    c. $80,084.70
    d. $86,539.70

8. How much would we be willing to pay today for $4,000 to be received in each of the next 10 years if the forgone interest rate (discount rate) were 14 percent?
   a. $40,000.00
   b. $29,320.00
   c. $19,785.60
   d. $20,864.40

9. What would you pay for a corporate bond that yields interest income of $60.00 per year for 20 years and a single-period return at maturity of $1,000 if you could earn 8 percent on similar investments?
   a. $1,000.00
   b. $ 803.64
   c. $ 589.09
   d. $1,200.00

10. A company has an option to purchase a parcel of land 10 years from now at a cost of $312,900. How much must it save annually (in equal amounts) to accumulate this future cost if it can earn 8 percent on the savings account?
    a. $28,161
    b. $31,290
    c. $20,000
    d. $24,787

11. What would be the annual payment required to pay off a loan of $187,779 over the next 20 years when the interest charge on the remaining balance is 15 percent?
    a. $ 9,388.95
    b. $28,166.85
    c. $31,952.45
    d. $30,000.00

12. The "Rule of 72" provides good approximations when the value involved doubles because, when the interest rate multiplied by the time period equals the number 72, the CIT values always approximate
    a. 1.00.
    b. 3.00.
    c. 2.00.
    d. 1.50.

KEY DEFINITIONS

Amortization payments: payments required to completely pay off the principal and interest of a loan over the loan period.

Annual installment deposits (sinking funds): yearly deposits required to obtain a desired future sum.

Annuity: a series of flows that occur at regular intervals and never change in amount.

Compound sum of an annuity: total future value of an annuity.

Compound value: the ending amount to which an original deposit grows due to the compounding process of earning interest on interest.

Discounting: restating future values in present-value terms.

Discount period: years during which we must wait before receiving the funds.

Discount rate: annual interest rate that we cannot earn because we must wait to receive the funds.

Nonannual compounding: compounding that is calculated other than annually.

Present value: the present worth of future expected benefits; the inverse of compound value.

Present value of an annuity: current worth of a series of future equal flows occurring at equal time intervals.

Rule of 72: approximation of the interest rate or time period required to double an original amount.

ANSWERS TO REVIEW QUESTIONS

1. b	4. c	7. c	10. c
2. b	5. b	8. d	11. d
3. c	6. a	9. b	12. c

Part Two
Capital Budgeting

The ability of the firm to survive in highly competitive and complex environments depends on management's success in developing, analyzing, and selecting the most profitable investment opportunities. The capital budgeting process brings the firm to the point where it can select the set of projects that will attain the corporate goal within the constraints of funds available, certainty of cash flows, and the objective of minimizing the cost of capital.

Part II presents the capital budgeting process. Cash flows are defined along with the assumed cost of capital. Chapter 6 discusses project selection techniques based on discounted cash flows and internal rate of return, in addition to less favorable methods such as payback period. Chapter 7 reviews project selection methods in light of limitations on funding available and the risk associated with the cash flows.

At the completion of Part II, you should be able to develop, analyze, and select the best available investments under the constraints that apply. One such constraint is the cost of capital, which is presented in greater detail in Part III.

Chapter Six
Capital Budgeting Under Conditions of Certainty

OVERVIEW

This chapter examines the important problem of establishing criteria for selection of the firm's long-term assets. The information needed to make capital-budgeting decisions (such as expected cash flows and the cost of capital), the criteria the firm uses in selecting or rejecting a project (such as discounted cash flow and internal rate of return), and the impact of capital rationing (limited availability of funds) are examined.

STUDY OBJECTIVES

1. To outline the information required to make a capital-budgeting decision.

2. To determine the acceptance and rejection criteria of the firm.

3. To investigate the problem of disbursing limited funds among the acceptable investments (capital rationing).

4. To examine the impact of constant or changing costs of capital on the selection or rejection of projects.

5. To investigate the process of project selection for mutually exclusive projects.

CHAPTER OUTLINE

I. Three types of information are necessary in making capital-budgeting decisions.

   A. A project's cash flows are critical to the investment decision. The analysis of cash flow includes the initial-cost cash outflow (including working capital), subsequent net cash flows, the timing of net cash flows, the after-tax salvage value of the project, and the timing of project completion or abandonment.

B. Most capital projects require a significant <u>initial cash outlay</u> before they generate cash inflows. The additional <u>working capital</u> required to support the project must also be included in the estimate of the initial cash outflow. For example, it is necessary to include additional accounts receivable, additional inventory, and additional cash balance.

C. Net cash flows that occur after the initial-cost cash outflow (<u>future net cash flows</u>) indicate the difference between sales revenues and cash expenses associated with the project. Two methods of determining expected net cash flows exist.

<u>Example</u>: The estimated income statement for project X is as follows:

INCOME STATEMENT

<u>Project X</u>

1980

Net revenues		$600,000
Cost of goods sold	$300,000	
Selling, administrative costs	150,000	
Depreciation	130,000	
Total operating expenditures		580,000
Operating income		$ 20,000
Taxes (50%)		10,000
Net income after taxes (NIAT)		$ 10,000

<u>Method 1</u>: Subtracting <u>cash</u> outflows (excluding depreciation) from cash inflows. That is,

Inflows			$600,000
Outflows:	Cost of Goods Sold	$300,000	
	Selling, Administration	150,000	
	Taxes Paid	10,000	
			$460,000
Net cash inflow			$140,000

<u>Method 2</u>: Add noncash charges (depreciation) to net income after taxes. That is,

NIAT	$ 10,000
Depreciation	130,000
Net cash inflow	$140,000

Note that both methods give the same result.

D. Financial officers must be careful in estimating future net cash flows, because this is a critical part of the project's evaluation. At this point, we assume that the <u>net cash flows are certain to occur</u>, as estimated. Each year's net cash flow can also be different, as shown in the following table.

Project Life (year)	Cash Flow (net)
0	($500,000) initial outflow
1	150,000
2	180,000
3	200,000
4	250,000

E. Net cash flows may vary over the project's life. The timing of these varying flows can also vary during the year, (beginning, middle, or end). Money has time value, so timing is an important consideration in project analysis. For the purposes of this text, we assume that all net cash flows occur at the end of the year.

F. To properly analyze a project, we must first decide when the project will be terminated.

G. The final period's net cash flows must be adjusted to reflect two events.

   1. The receipt of salvage value on sale of the asset (salvage is the difference between market value and taxes paid on the sale) must be added to the inflows.

   2. The release of any working capital as a result of termination must be added to the cash flows of the final year.

Example: Project X has the following estimates for its last year or operation.

NIAT	$120,000
Depreciation	130,000
After-tax salvage value	50,000
Released working capital*	25,000
Final year's net cash flow	$325,000

   *Refers to reduction in commitment to
   supply working capital such as cash,
   inventory, accounts receivable, and
   the like.

H. The cost of capital represents the required rate of return of investors who provide funds to the firm. Expressed as a percentage, this represents the minimum rate of return a project must attain in order to be a good investment.

II. Capital-budgeting decision crietria combine appropriate project information in a format that ultimately dictates acceptance or rejection of the project.

   A. Discounted Cash Flow (DCF) is a decision criterion that reduces the relevant project information to two figures, the present value of the cash flows (PV) and the initial-cost cash outflow (C).

   DECISION CRITERION: IF THE PV OF THE PROPOSED PROJECT IS GREATER THAN OR EQUAL TO C, ACCEPT THE PROJECT. OTHERWISE, REJECT IT.

Symbolically,

If PV $\geq$ C, ACCEPT
If PV < C, REJECT

Example: Consider the following net cash flows.

Project Life (year)	Net Cash Inflows
1	$1,000
2	2,000
3	3,000
4	4,000

Find the present value of the future net cash flows by using the firm's cost of capital (k). If the cost of capital is 10 percent, the present value of Project Y's net cash flow is

$$PV = \frac{\$1,000}{(1.10)^1} + \frac{\$2,000}{(1.10)^2} + \frac{\$3,000}{(1.10)^3} + \frac{\$4,000}{(1.10)^4} = \$7,547.96$$

or, using the present-value interest factors given in Appendix B,

$$PV = (\$1,000 * .90909) + (\$2,000 * .82645) + (\$3,000 * .75131) +$$
$$(\$4,000 * .68301) = \underline{\$7547.96}$$

The present value of the project's cash flow stream discounted at the cost of capital is $7,547.96. Therefore, if the initial cost (C) of the project is <u>equal to or less than</u> $7,547.96, we will <u>accept</u> (because PV $\geq$ C). If the initial cost <u>exceeds</u> the present value of $7,547.96, we will <u>reject</u> (because PV < C).

1. The Discounted Cash Flow (DCF) formula represents the present value of future net cash flows, as follows:

$$PV = \sum_{t=1}^{n} \frac{CF_t}{(1 + k)^t} + \frac{S_n + W_n}{(1 + k)^n}$$

where

CF = project's net cash flow each year
t = year of project
n = year of termination
k = cost of capital
S_n = project's after-tax salvage value
W_n = working capital released at termination

2. When the <u>net cash flows are equal</u>, finding the PV is the same as determining the PV of an annuity (see Chapter 5).

Example: Project Z has an initial-cost cash outflow of $5,000. Subsequent net cash flows of $1,200 are expected to occur for the next 5 years (no salvage or working-capital impact). The cost of capital is 10 percent. What is the PV of the project?

PV = 1,200 (PV of an annuity, 10 percent, 5 years)
   = 1,200 * 3.7908   (from Appendix D)
   = $4,548.96

We would reject this project using the DCF criterion, because PV < C (that is, the present value of future cash flows is less than the initial outlay of $5,000).

B. Net Present Value (NPV) is a decision criterion that is a variation on the DCF approach.

NPV = PV - C

Therefore, the net present value (NPV) represents the difference between the present value (PV) of the future net cash flows and the initial-cost cash outflow (C).

DECISION CRITERION: IF THE PROPOSED PROJECT'S NPV IS ZERO OR POSITIVE, ACCEPT THE PROJECT. IF ITS NPV IS NEGATIVE, REJECT IT.

Symbolically,

If NPV $\geq$ $0, ACCEPT
If NPV < $0, REJECT

Example: Using the data for project Z, we found the PV to be $4,548.96, and the initial-cost cash outflow was $5,000. The NPV would be found as follows:

NPV = PV - C
    = $4,548.96 - $5,000
    = ($451.04)

Project Z would be rejected because its NPV is negative.

1. NPV and DCF methods always agree on accepting or rejecting a proposal.

2. NPV and DCF are both consistent with the objective of maximizing shareholder wealth. Accepting a project with a positive NPV increases the present value of the firm.

C. The Profitability Index (PI) is another variation on the DCF approach. Here capital-budgeting decisions are made by comparing the PV of net cash flows with the initial-cost cash outflow in ratio form. That is,

$$PI = \frac{PV}{C}$$

When we use this method (sometimes called the benefit/cost ratio), the accept-reject criterion is

DECISION CRITERION: IF THE PROPOSED PROJECT'S PI IS GREATER THAN OR EQUAL TO 1.0, ACCEPT THE PROJECT. OTHERWISE, REJECT IT.

Symbolically,

If PI $\geq$ 1.0, ACCEPT
If PI < 1.0, REJECT

Example: Using the data for Project Z, we find that

$$PI = \frac{\$4,548.96}{\$5,000.00} = .91$$

We reject the project, because the PI is less than 1.0.

D. The Internal Rate of Return (IRR) approach determines the discount rate that equates the expected net cash flows with the initial-cost cash outflow. Thus the IRR becomes the discount rate that gives a capital project a NPV of zero.

1. The IRR formula solves for the value of r that equates the left and right sides of the following equation:

$$C = \sum_{t=1}^{n} \frac{CF_t}{(1 + r)^t} + \frac{S_n + W_n}{(1 + r)^n}$$

Example: Consider the following data.

$$\$500,000 = \frac{\$120,000}{(1 + r)^1} + \frac{\$180,000}{(1 + r)^2} + \frac{\$300,000}{(1 + r)^3}$$

Solving for r, we find the internal rate of return that equates the initial-cost cash outflow of $500,000 with the subsequent net cash flows. The solution is based on a trial-and-error process using different r values, as shown in the following calculations.

Selecting r = 10 percent:

$$\$500,000 = \frac{\$120,000}{(1.10)^1} + \frac{\$180,000}{(1.10)^2} + \frac{\$300,000}{(1.10)^3} \qquad \text{(from Appendix B)}$$

$500,000 = (120,000 * .90909) + (180,000 * .82645) + (300,000 * .75131)

$500,000 $\neq$ $483,244.80

The PV and C are not the same, so the r value of 10 percent does not represent the IRR. The project is not earning a 10 percent return, so we try a lower return estimate.

Selecting r = 8 percent:

$500,000 = (120,000 * .92593) + (180,000 * .85734) + (300,000 * .79383)

$500,000 $\neq$ $503,581.80

From the trial-and-error process, we see that the IRR of this project (which equates the present value of the initial outlay with the present value of expected net cash flows) is somewhere between 8 percent and 10 percent.

Interpolating:

At r = 10%, PV = $483,244.80
At r = 8 %, PV = $503,581.80

Thus, for PV = $500,000,

$$r = 8\% + \left(\frac{\$503,581.80 - \$500,000}{\$503,581.80 - \$483,244.80} * 2\%\right) = 8\% + (.176 * 2\%) = 8.352\%$$

Thus 8.352 percent is the approximate rate of return that equates the initial-outlay cost with the present value of expected cash flows.

> DECISION CRITERION: IF THE IRR OF THE PROPOSED PROJECT IS EQUAL TO OR EXCEEDS THE COST OF CAPITAL (k), ACCEPT IT. OTHERWISE, REJECT IT.

Symbolically,

> If IRR (r) $\geq$ k, ACCEPT
> If IRR (r) < k, REJECT

2. The IRR approach is more computationally difficult. Nevertheless, many firms prefer this approach, because it provides a percentage value that is easily comparable to the cost of capital.

3. Many analysts believe IRR is a better approach because it separates the cost of capital calculation from the initial use of the cost of capital, thereby evaluating projects "independently" of their financing costs.

4. IRR and NPV techniques almost always give the same decisions for a single project, yet their rankings of multiple projects often differ due to differing assumptions about reinvestment rate.

    a. IRR assumes a reinvestment rate for annual net cash flows equal to the project's IRR.

    b. NPV assumes a reinvestment rate for annual net cash flows equal to the firm's cost of capital.

Appendices 6A and 6B of the text examine the NPV and IRR reinvestment assumptions in greater detail.

III. Other decision criteria are used by firms in their selection of long-term projects. However, most of these approaches ignore important factors in the asset-selection process.

A. The average net income earned on the average investment in a project is called the average rate of return (ARR). That is,

$$ARR = \frac{\text{average annual NIAT}}{\frac{\text{original cost + salvage value}}{2}}$$

Example: A 5-year project has an average annual NIAT of $6,000 and an original cost of $12,000. Salvage value is expected to be $4,000. The ARR is found as follows:

$$ARR = \frac{\$6,000}{\dfrac{\$12,000 + \$4,000}{2}} = \frac{\$6,000}{\$8,000} = 75\%$$

The ARR (75 percent) is compared to the minimum required rate of return to determine the acceptability of the project.

> DECISION CRITERION: IF THE ARR OF THE PROPOSED PROJECT IS EQUAL TO OR EXCEEDS THE COST OF CAPITAL, ACCEPT IT. OTHERWISE, REJECT IT.

Symbolically,

> If ARR $\geq$ k, ACCEPT
> If ARR $<$ k, REJECT

1. ARR does not consider depreciation as a part of the cash flow by using NIAT. This distorts the cash flows and the capital-budgeting decision.

2. ARR ignores working-capital requirements that can be a large part of the initial investment.

3. ARR ignores the time value of money.

4. ARR does not account for the timing of the cash flows. Projects can have the same ARR and average annual flows, even though one project is superior to the other because it has larger inflows in earlier years.

5. ARR ignores the number of years in the project prior to termination. Several projects can have the same ARR, even though one is better because it provides returns for a much longer time.

B. Payback (PB) is a technique that assists financial managers in making capital-budgeting decisions by indicating the time required to recover the initial-cost cash outflow.

Example: A project has an initial-cost cash outflow of $80,000. The expected net cash flows are as follows:

Year	Cash Flows
1	$20,000
2	40,000
3	20,000
4	60,000
5	90,000

Therefore PB = 3 years.

DECISION CRITERION: IF THE PB FOR A PROPOSED PROJECT IS LESS THAN OR
EQUAL TO AN ACCEPTABLE NUMBER OF YEARS DETERMINED
BY THE FIRM AS APPROPRIATE, ACCEPT THE PROJECT.
OTHERWISE, REJECT IT.

Symbolically,

If PB $\leq$ N, ACCEPT
If PB > N, REJECT

1. PB ignores cashflow timing beyond the payback period. A project
could be rejected even though its large net cash flow later in the
project's life exceeds the overall return of the accepted project
that has a faster return of investment.

2. PB ignores the time value of money.

3. PB does not consider the cost of capital.

4. PB is more appropriate when only the short-run outlook can be
reasonably estimated.

5. Firms with liquidity troubles often turn to PB as the decision criterion in selecting projects.

6. PB is useful for firms that emphasize short-run earnings. However,
this policy may cause problems for the firm in the long run.

IV. Selecting the appropriate decision criterion depends on the practices of the
firm and the particular circumstances surrounding the decision.

A. DCF, NPV, and IRR methods are considered best because they encourage
evaluation of all the important considerations in the project-selection
process.

B. Most firms use more than one decision criterion (only about 14 percent
use only one method). We must know all the decision criteria, because
more than one are often used.

V. The application of capital-budgeting methods for single projects can be expanded to include replacement projects, multiple project rankings, and
mutually exclusive projects.

A. The financial officer must often evaluate a project as the replacement
for an existing project. The analysis examines whether the new asset's
generation of additional net cash flow is worth the additional investment.

Example: A new, more efficient machine is being considered as a replacement
for an existing machine. The incremental cash flows expected after the replacement
are as follows:

Year	Cash Flow of New Machine	Cash Flow of Old Machine	Incremental Cash Flow
1	$100	$60	$40
2	80	50	30
3	60	40	20
4	30	0	30

The new machine will cost $100, with an expected salvage value of <u>zero</u>. The old machine has a salvage value of zero. The present value of the incremental cash flows is calculated as follows (k = 12 percent).

PV = ($40 * .89286) + ($30 * .79719) + ($20 * .71178) + ($30 * .63552)

= $92.93

$92.93 is the present value of the incremental cash-flow stream resulting from replacing the old machine with the new.

   <u>Decision</u>: Reject replacement of the old machine, because the PV of the incremental flows ($92.93) is <u>less than</u> the initial-cost cash outflow ($100) of the replacement machine.

   B. Companies <u>do not usually have the ability to acquire unlimited funds</u>. Therefore, after all of the unacceptable projects have been rejected, the firm may still have a set of acceptable projects the total costs of which exceed the funds available. Furthermore, the cost usually rises as additional funds are obtained, which can make previously acceptable projects unacceptable.

   1. If we assume (unrealistically) that the firm can acquire unlimited funds at a constant cost, we could rank the acceptable projects by NPV and IRR.

      a. Projects could be <u>ranked in descending order of their respective NPVs</u>. All projects with a zero or a positive NPV would be accepted. The total capital budget would be the cumulative cost of all accepted projects.

      b. Projects could also be ranked in <u>descending order of their IRRs</u>. All projects with an IRR equal to or in excess of the cost of capital would be accepted. The total capital budget would be the cumulative cost of all accepted projects (see the accompanying graph).
         As the IRR of individual projects declines and the total capital budget increases, a point is reached at which the IRR crosses the cost-of-capital line (k). Subsequent projects are rejected. Note that the rankings of NPV and IRR values can differ but that the proposed projects that are acceptable under each method are the same.

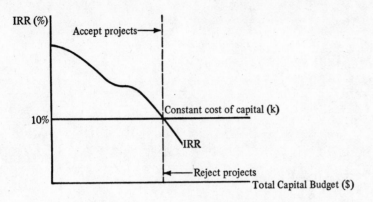

2. Other ranking techniques can be used. For example, Payback (PB) and the Average Rate of Return (ARR) are available. PB rankings are in ascending order of payback period, whereas ARR rankings are analogous to those used in the IRR procedure.

3. If we assume the more realistic condition of rising interest rates with the increasing use of debt, the cost of capital rises as shown in the accompanying figure.

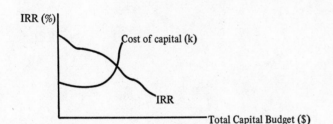

This graphical presentation of the tradeoff between IRR and k leads to a different cut-off point in the rankings than the assumption of constant capital costs (k). When the cost of capital increases with increases in the total capital budget, the IRR curve intersects the k curve at a higher point, reducing the number of acceptable projects.

4. The cost of capital (k) tends to shift because of factors beyond the firm's control. This has a direct impact on the projects accepted or rejected, as shown in the figure.

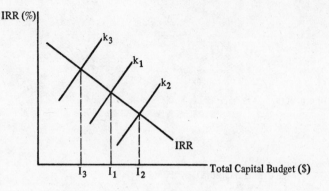

When k_1 declines to k_2, a larger number of projects become acceptable. A shift from k_1 to k_3, on the other hand, reduces the number of acceptable projects. Hence, acceptable projects can become unacceptable because of increases in the cost of capital, and unacceptable projects can become acceptable because of decreases in the cost of capital.

C. <u>Capital rationing</u> occurs when firms have more acceptable proposed projects than available funds, forcing the firm to forgo acceptable projects. Graphically,

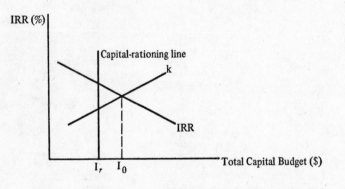

When capital rationing is in effect, the firm cannot operate at the optimal point (I_0) and is forced to operate at I_r, thereby failing to maximize the value of the firm.

Financial officers use different methods to select project sets when capital rationing is in effect.

1. IRR methods suggest that the firm should undertake as many acceptable projects as possible.

DECISION CRITERION: UNDERTAKE ACCEPTABLE PROJECTS IN ORDER OF THEIR
DESCENDING INTERNAL RATES OF RETURN UNTIL ALL CAPI-
TAL, OR AS MUCH OF IT AS POSSIBLE, IS EXHAUSTED.

Example: The firm has the following projects, ranked in descending order of
IRR. The firm's cost of capital (k) is 10 percent.

Project	Cost	IRR, %
A	$14,000	30
B	90,000	27
C	50,000	22
D	60,000	18
E	16,000	12

All projects are acceptable in that IRR $\geq$ k. If the firm had only $120,000 to in-
vest, which projects would it select?

Solution: The firm should use all, or as much as possible of, the funds
available for projects where IRR $\geq$ k. In this example, the firm would select
projects A, B, and E. The total cumulative cost would be exactly $120,000. Al-
though projects C and D have a higher IRR than project E, funds are not available
to undertake them.

2. The NPV-Aggregation Method is valuable in capital rationing. Using
    this approach, the financial officer finds that combination of
    projects that maximizes the total NPV within the constraints of the
    funds available.

DECISION CRITERION: SELECT THAT AFFORDABLE COMBINATION OF PROPOSED
PROJECTS WITH THE HIGHEST COMBINED NPV.

Example: Assume that a firm has a capital budget that limits spending on new
projects to $13,000. The following proposals are considered acceptable; that is,
NPV $\geq$ $0.

Project	Cost	NPV (descending order)
A	$8,000	$4,800
B	6,000	4,200
C	5,000	1,000
D	2,000	800
E	3,000	600

Step 1: Rank projects in descending order of cost.

Project	Cost
A	$8,000
B	6,000
C	5,000
E	3,000
D	2,000

Step 2. Find the <u>feasible combination</u> of projects within the $13,000 spending constraint.

Feasible Combinations	Total Cost	Aggregate NPV
A, C	$13,000	$5,800
A, E	11,000	5,400
A, E, D	13,000	6,200
B, C	11,000	5,200
B, C, D	13,000	6,000
B, E	9,000	4,800
B, E, D	11,000	5,600
B, D	8,000	5,000
C, E	8,000	1,600
C, E, D	10,000	2,400
C, D	7,000	1,800
E, D	5,000	1,400

<u>Solution</u>: In this problem, the combination of projects A, E, and D leads to the highest aggregate NPV of $6,200--with an aggregate cost that exactly offsets the total amount of funds available ($13,000).

D. When competing investment proposals will perform the same task, the projects are said to be <u>mutually exclusive</u>. The acceptance of one of these projects <u>automatically excludes the others</u> from consideration. When projects are mutually exclusive, choose the project with the highest IRR or NPV.

STUDY PROBLEMS

<u>6.1.</u> Selbine, Inc., is considering the purchase of a new product line. The project costs $60,000 and had a 10-year life expectancy, without salvage value. The following net cash flows are associated with the project:

Year	Net Cash Flows
1	$10,000
2	12,000
3	14,000
4	14,000
5	14,000
6	12,000
7	10,000
8	10,000
9	8,000
10	8,000

Assume that the cash inflows occur at the end of each year and that the cost of capital is 12 percent.

a. What is the DCF?

b. What is the NPV?

c. What is the PI?

d. What is the IRR?

e. What is the PB?

f. What is the ARR? (Assume straight-line depreciation.)

g. Should the firm accept or reject the project on the basis of each decision criterion investigated? (The company's required PB is 4 years.)

Solution

a. Using Appendix B, we find that

PV = ($10,000 * .89286) + ($12,000 * .79719) + ($14,000 * .71178) +

($14,000 * .63552) + ($14,000 * .56743) + ($12,000 * .50663) +

($10,000 * .45235) + ($10,000 * .40388) + ($8,000 * .36061) +

($8,000 * .32197)

PV = $65,403.60

DCF = $65,403.60

b. NPV = PV - C

= $65,043.60 - $60,000

NPV = $5,043.60

c. PI = $\frac{PV}{C}$ = $\frac{\$65,043.60}{\$60,000}$ = 1.08

d. The IRR is the discount rate that equates the initial cost with the present value of future benefits, using a trial-and-error approach. Because the NPV is positive, the rate of return is in excess of the cost of capital (k = 12 percent). Therefore, we can start the trial-and-error process with an IRR rate of something higher than 12 percent, say 15 percent.

Trial at 15 percent

$60,000 = PV of future net cash flows at 15%

= ($10,000 * .86957) + ($12,000 * .75614) + ($14,000 * .65752)

+ ($14,000 * .57175) + ($14,000 * .49718) + ($12,000 * .43233)

+ ($10,000 * .37594) + ($10,000 * .32690) + ($8,000 * .28426)

+ ($8,000 * .24718)

≠ $58,407.56

Using r = 15 percent, we find that the PV is $58,407.56, which is less than the initial cost (C = $60,000). Therefore, the IRR must be between 12 percent and 15 percent.

Trial at 14 percent

$60,000 = PV of future net cash flows at 14%

= ($10,000 * .87719) + ($12,000 * .76947) + ($14,000 * .67497)

+ ($14,000 * .59208) + ($14,000 * .51937) + ($12,000 * .45559)

+ ($10,000 * .39964) + ($10,000 * .35056) + ($8,000 * .30751)

+ ($8,000 * .26974)

= ?

Using r = 14 percent, we find that the PV is $60,602.44, which is slightly more than the $60,000 initial cost. The approximate IRR is thus between 14 and 15 percent. By interpolating we can determine a more precise estimate:

$$14\% + \frac{\$60,602.44 - \$60,000}{\$60,602.44 - \$58,407.56} = 14\% + .274\% = 14.274\%$$

Thus, the project's IRR is 14.274 percent.

e. The time required to recover the initial cost of $60,000 is about 5 years. At the end of the fifth year, the cumulative cash inflows will be about $64,000.

f. Depreciation for the project will be $6,000 per year ($60,000/10), resulting in zero salvage value. The average inflows will be the sum of the inflows divided by the number of years. That is,

($10,000 + $12,000 + $14,000 + $14,000 + $14,000 + $12,000
+ $10,000 + $10,000 + $8,000 + $8,000) / 10 = $11,200

Therefore, the ARR = $\dfrac{\$11,200}{\dfrac{\$60,000 + 0}{2}}$ = 37.33%

g. The following table summarizes the results of the methods that have been applied to this problem.

Method	Model	Model Results	Decision Criterion	Decision
DCF	$PV = \sum\limits_{t=1}^{n} \dfrac{CF_t}{(1+k)^t} + \dfrac{S_n + W_n}{(1+k)^n}$	PV = \$65,403.60	Accept if PV $\geq$ C	Accept
NPV	NPV = PV - C	NPV = \$5,403.60	Accept if NPV is positive or zero	Accept
IRR	$C = \sum\limits_{t=1}^{n} \dfrac{CF_t}{(1+r)^t} + \dfrac{S_n + W_n}{(1+r)^n}$	r = about 14.274%	Accept if IRR $\geq$ k	Accept
PI	$PI = \dfrac{PV}{C}$	PI = 1.08	Accept if PI $\geq$ 1	Accept
PB	PB = years to recover investment	PB = about 5 years	Accept if PB is less than or equal to firm PB	Reject

Answer: With every decision criterion except Payback, the decision is to accept the project. If the firm has no significant liquidity problem and is not in a situation in which short-term considerations are extremely important, the financial officer would accept the project.

6.2. Determine the net cash flow of a project with the following estimated income statement.

INCOME STATEMENT FOR 19X1 ($000)

Project X

Net revenues		$16,000
Cost of goods sold	$10,000	
Selling/Administration	2,000	
Depreciation	3,000	
Total operating expenses		$15,000
Operating income		$ 1,000
Taxes (40%)		400
Net income after taxes (NIAT)		$ 600

Solution

One approach to defining the net cash flow is to add NIAT to depreciation:

$600 + $3,000 + $3,600

Another method is to reconstruct the income statement to determine the difference between cash inflows and cash outflows:

Cash inflows		$16,000
Cash outflows		
Cost of goods sold	$10,000	
Selling/Administration	2,000	
Taxes	400	12,400
Net cash flow		$ 3,600

6.3. Consider the following investment proposals. (Assume that k = 10 percent.)

a. What are the DCF and NPV of each proposal?

b. Which would you select if they are mutually exclusive?

	Proposal A		Proposal B
Year	Net Cash Flow	Year	Net Cash Flow
0	($20,000)	0	($28,000)
1	4,000	1	10,000
2	6,000	2	9,000
3	9,000	3	6,000
4	10,000	4	4,000

Solution

a. DCF:

$$PV_A = (\$4,000 * .90909) + (\$6,000 * .82645) + (\$9,000 * .75131)$$
$$+ (\$10,000 * .68301)$$
$$= \$22,186.95$$

$$PV_B = (\$10,000 * .90909) + (\$9,000 * .82645) + (\$6,000 * .75131)$$
$$+ (\$4,000 * .68301)$$
$$= \$23,768.85$$

NPV:

$$NPV_A = \$22,186.95 - \$20,000 = \$2,186.95$$

$$NPV_B = \$23,768.85 - \$28,000 = (\$4,231.15)$$

b. Although project B has the highest PV, it has a negative NPV. You would select project A with its positive NPV of $2,186.95 and eliminate project B from further consideration.

6.4. What would be the IRR of an investment that costs $14,432.20 and is expected to produce annual net cash flows of $2,000 per year over the next 10 years? (Assume no salvage value and a cost of capital of 14 percent.)

Solution

Because the cash flows are the same as an annuity, we can simplify the trial-and-error process required to find r. The ratio of initial costs to annual inflows defines the present value of an annuity interest factor that equates initial costs with net cash flows. That is,

$$\frac{\$14,432.20}{\$2,000} = 7.2161$$

In Appendix D, we examine the interest factors that apply to the 10-year period (n) to find 7.2161. In this case, 7.2161 falls between 7.0236 (r = 7 percent) and 7.3601 (r = 6 percent). Therefore, the IRR of the investment is somewhere between 6 percent and 7 percent, which is less than the cost of capital. We would reject the proposal.

6.5. Reers, Inc., is considering four investment proposals in its 1981 capital budget. The following table outlines the characteristics of these projects.

Project	Cost	Annual Net Cash Flow	Life of Project
1	$ 4,100	$1,000	5 years
2	7,582	2,000	5 years
3	10,683	3,000	4 years
4	10,066	2,000	7 years

Projects are independent and indivisible, with each flow occurring at the end of each year. The firm's cost of capital is 8 percent.

a. Rank the projects in descending order of their IRRs.

b. What is the size of the optimal budget?

c. Rank the projects in order of their NPVs.

d. Is there any difference between the rankings in parts a and c? What would cause differences between the rankings?

Solution

a. IRR calculations (all annuities)

Project A: $\dfrac{\$4,100}{\$1,000}$, 5 years; IRR = 7%

Project B: $\dfrac{\$7,582}{\$2,000}$, 5 years; IRR = 10%

Project C: $\dfrac{\$10,638}{\$\,3,000}$, 4 years; IRR = 5%

Project D: $\dfrac{\$10,000}{\$\,2,000}$, 7 years; IRR = 9%

Ranking:

Project	IRR	
B	10%	ACCEPT
D	9%	
A	7%	REJECT
C	5%	

b. On the basis of part a, the size of the optimal budget includes the costs of projects B and D only: $7,582 + $10,066 = $17,648.

c. NPV calculations (k = 8 percent)
Project A: NPV = ($1,000 * 3.9927) - $4,100 = ($107.30)
Project B: NPV = ($2,000 * 3.9927) - $7,582 = $403.40
Project C: NPV = ($3,000 * 3.3121) -$10,638 = ($701.70)
Project D: NPV = ($2,000 * 5.2064) -$10,066 = $346.80

Ranking by NPV:

Project	NPV	
B	$403.40	ACCEPT
D	346.80	
A	($107.30)	REJECT
C	($701.70)	

d. **No.** The rankings could differ because of the timing of the cash flows; the reinvestment rate assumed; or the fact that IRR rankings are in percentages, whereas NPV rankings are based on dollar amounts.

6.6. Use the NPV-Aggregation method to determine which of the following indivisible projects should be accepted if the capital budget must be limited to $750,000. (Assume that the cost of capital is the same for each project.)

Project	Cost	NPV
1	$106,250	$ 42,500
2	425,000	127,500
3	318,750	159,375
4	637,500	212,500
5	212,500	42,500
6	200,000	63,750

<u>Solution</u>

Rankings by Cost:

Project	Cost	NPV
4	$637,500	$212,500
2	425,000	127,500
3	318,750	159,375
5	212,500	42,500
6	200,000	63,750
1	106,250	42,500

Feasible Combinations of Projects:

Project	Total Cost	Aggregate NPV
4, 1	$743,750	$255,000
2, 3	743,750	286,875
2, 5	637,500	170,000
2, 6	625,000	191,250
2, 1	531,250	170,000
2, 5, 1	743,750	212,500
2, 6, 1	731,250	233,750

Note: <u>Ten additional feasible combinations exist at this point</u> in the analysis. Projects 2 and 3 have the highest aggregate NPV of $286,875, and only remaining combinations with <u>possibly higher</u> aggregate NPVs need to be examined. Project combinations for projects 3, 5, 6, and 1 remain, but a preliminary examination shows that they would all have to be combined if they were to exceed $286,875, and this is not feasible.

<u>Answer</u>: The combination of projects 2 and 3 should be financed at a cost of $743,750 with an aggregate NPV of $286,875.

<u>6.7</u>. The following proposals are available in a firm's capital budget.

Project	Cost	Profitability Index
J	$100,000	1.30
K	180,000	1.10
L	90,000	1.80
M	60,000	1.00
N	120,000	1.25

Which set of projects should be selected if the firm's funds are rationed to $200,000?

<u>Solution</u>

$$PI = \frac{PV}{C}, \text{ so}$$

$$PV = C * PI$$

$PV_J = (\$100,000 * 1.30) = \$130,000$

$PV_K = (\$180,000 * 1.10) = \$198,000$

$PV_L = (\$ 90,000 * 1.80) = \$162,000$

$PV_M = (\$ 60,000 * 1.00) = \$ 60,000$

$PV_N = (\$120,000 * 1.25) = \$150,000$

Results also show that

$NPV = PV - C$

$NPV_J = \$130,000 - \$100,000 = \$30,000$

$NPV_K = \$198,000 - \$180,000 = \$18,000$

$NPV_L = \$162,000 - \$ 90,000 = \$72,000$

$NPV_M = \$ 60,000 - \$ 60,000 = \quad 0$

$NPV_N = \$150,000 - \$120,000 = \$30,000$

Rankings by NPV:

Project	Cost	NPV
L	$ 90,000	$72,000
J	100,000	30,000
N	120,000	30,000
K	180,000	18,000
M	60,000	0

Answer: If funds are rationed to $200,000, the combination of projects L and J should be accepted. The total cost will be $190,000 and the aggregate NPV will be $102,000.

REVIEW QUESTIONS

1. Capital-budgeting problems require knowledge of
   a. projected net cash flows.
   b. original cost outflow.
   c. cost of capital.
   d. changes in working capital requirements.
   e. all of the above.

2. The initial-cost cash outflow does not include
   a. working-capital requirements.
   b. raw materials.
   c. future changes in interest rate.
   d. additional inventory requirements.
   e. none of these.

3. A project's net cash flows after the initial outflow are
   a. cash inflows less cash outflows.
   b. NIAT plus depreciation.
   c. net revenues plus depreciation.
   d. both a and b.
   e. both b and c.

4. In considering the timing of cash flows, we make the assumption that
   a. cash flows occur quarterly.
   b. cash flows are paid at the beginning of each year.
   c. cash flows are paid at the end of each year.
   d. none of these.

5. Which of the following adjustments is(are) made to the final year's net cash flow of a project?
   a. The after-tax impact of salvage value is added.
   b. The previous year's depreciation charges are removed.
   c. The release of working capital is added.
   d. All of these.
   e. Both a and c.

6. The DCF method of capital-budgeting analysis
   a. determines the NPV of a project.

    b. determines the IRR of a project.
    c. determines the PV of a project.
    d. none of these.

7. If the PV is less than the initial-outlay cost
    a. we reject the project.
    b. we accept the project.
    c. we use another method.
    d. none of these.

8. DCF methods consider
    a. the timing of cash flows.
    b. all the information that should be considered in a capital-budgeting decision.
    c. initial tax consequences.
    d. none of these.

9. The NPV of any investment represents
    a. the firm's cost of capital.
    b. the initial cost of outflow discounted to the present.
    c. the present value of expected cash flows less the initial-cost cash outflow.
    d. both a and b.
    e. none of these.

10. We would accept a project that has a NPV that is
    a. positive.
    b. negative.
    c. greater than the cost of capital.

11. NPV and DCF methods always _____ on whether to accept or reject a proposed project.
    a. vary
    b. disagree
    c. agree
    d. none of these

12. A project with a positive NPV will
    a. decrease the value of the firm.
    b. increase the value of the firm.
    c. not change the value of the firm.

13. A Profitability Index (PI) of 1.50 indicates that
    a. the NPV is negative.
    b. the return on total assets is 150 percent.
    c. the NPV is positive.
    d. both b and c.
    e. none of these.

14. If we accept a project with a PI of .60
    a. the value of the firm will increase.
    b. the value of the firm will decrease.
    c. the value of the firm will not be affected.

15. The IRR represents the percentage rate that
    a. exceeds the cost of capital.
    b. exceeds the average rate of return.
    c. equates expected cash flows and initial cash outflows.
    d. equates expected cash flows and initial salvage value.

16. We compute the IRR by
    a. using the cost of capital.
    b. performing a trial-and-error process.
    c. using the project's life and salvage value.
    d. ignoring the time value of money.

17. We would accept a project when the IRR exceeds the
    a. profitability index.
    b. annual return to the project.
    c. accounting rate of return.
    d. cost of capital.
    e. none of these.

18. Firms often prefer the IRR process, because
    a. the outcome is expressed as a percentage.
    b. the IRR can be easily compared to the cost of capital.
    c. it separates the financing and project-selection decisions.
    d. all of these.
    e. a and b only.

19. IRR and NPV almost always yield _____ accept/reject decisions for a
    given project. Their rankings of multiple projects frequently _____.
    a. different, are identical
    b. different, change
    c. identical, differ
    d. identical, remain the same

20. IRR and NPV rankings differ due to
    a. differing assumptions about reinvestment rate.
    b. different timing factors.
    c. the use of the cost of capital.
    d. less precision in IRR calculations.

21. The Average Rate of Return (ARR) method uses the project's original cost,
    _____, in the calculations.
    a. including working-capital requirements
    b. excluding working-capital requirements
    c. including the initial-cost cash outflows
    d. none of these

22. The ARR approach has the weakness of
    a. excluding depreciation in cash flows.
    b. ignoring timing of flows.
    c. ignoring interest costs.
    d. all of these.
    e. a and b only.

23. Payback (PB) is a method that indicates the
    a. percentage return on investment.

    b. time required to recover the initial-cost cash outflow.
    c. time required to pay back the associated debt.
    d. none of these.

24. Payback has the weakness of
    a. ignoring cash flow.
    b. ignoring the cost of capital.
    c. providing an indicator of liquidity.
    d. all of these.
    e. a and b only.

25. The vast majority of firms use either _____ or _____ in their capi-
    tal-budgeting decisions.
    a. PB, ARR
    b. PB, NPV
    c. NPV, PI
    d. NPV, IRR
    e. none of these

26. In project-replacement decisions, the _____ stream of cash flows must be
    discounted to its present value.
    a. existing
    b. constant
    c. incremental
    d. none of these

27. When funds are <u>unlimited</u>, the firm will accept projects as long as the
    _____ is positive or the IRR exceeds the _____.
    a. DCF, average rate of return
    b. NPV, cost of capital
    c. NPV, DCF requirements
    d. none of these

28. Shifts in the firm's cost of capital can result in _____ in the projects
    that are accepted or rejected.
    a. favorable changes
    b. unfavorable changes
    c. both of these
    d. neither of these

29. When capital rationing exists, financial officers use _____ techniques in
    _____ to select the best set of acceptable projects.
    a. ranking, IRR and NPV
    b. DCF, IRR and NPV
    c. Payback, IRR and NPV
    d. none of these

30. When two projects are mutually exclusive
    a. selecting one project requires that the other project be selected also.
    b. rejecting one project requires that the other be rejected also.
    c. accepting one project requires that the other be rejected.
    d. none of these.

KEY DEFINITIONS

<u>Average rate of return (ARR)</u>: annualized expression of average net income earned on the average investment in a capital project.

<u>Capital rationing</u>: condition in effect when the firm has more acceptable proposed projects than available funds, forcing the rejection of acceptable projects and the need to be selective in establishing the best subset of remaining projects.

<u>Discounted cash flow (DCF)</u>: approach to capital budgeting that determines the present value of the expected net cash flows of a project.

<u>Final year's net cash flow</u>: NIAT + depreciation + after-tax salvage value + released working capital.

<u>Future net cash flows</u>: annual net cash benefits after the period of initial-cost cash outflow; the difference between cash inflows and cash outflows; also calculated as NIAT + depreciation.

<u>Initial-cost cash outflow</u>: net initial cash outlay needed to acquire a project.

<u>Internal rate of return (IRR)</u>: capital-budgeting method that indicates the discount rate (r) that equates the expected net cash flows to the initial-cost cash outflow.

<u>Mutually exclusive projects</u>: projects that perform similar tasks and therefore should not be undertaken simultaneously. Selection of one of two or more mutually exclusive projects automatically results in the rejection of all others.

<u>Net present value</u>: approach to capital budgeting that defines the difference between DCF and initial-cost cash outflow (NPV = PV - C).

<u>NPV-aggregation method</u>: in capital-rationing situations, a means of determining the subset of projects that stays within the funds available for investment and maximizes the aggregate NPV.

<u>Payback (PB)</u>: the time (in years) that will elapse before a project's initial investment has been recovered.

<u>Profitability index (PI)</u>: project-selection method that compares PV of cash flows to initial outlay (PI = PV/C).

<u>Ranking techniques</u>: means of selecting the best subset of acceptable projects from a larger set that cannot be funded in its entirety.

<u>Reinvestment-rate assumption</u>: the assumption made in IRR and NPV capital-budgeting methods about the rate at which interperiod cash inflows are reinvested over the life of the project. IRR assumes reinvestment at the IRR rate; NPV assumes reinvestment at the cost-of-capital rate.

<u>Replacement projects</u>: projects that differ from new projects in that cash flows are defined as <u>incremental</u> differences between existing and new assets.

<u>Working-capital requirements</u>: changes in current assets and liabilities that are part of the project.

CHAPTER 6

ANSWERS TO REVIEW QUESTIONS

1.	e	9.	c	17.	d	24.	e
2.	c	10.	a	18.	d	25.	d
3.	d	11.	c	19.	c	26.	c
4.	c	12.	b	20.	a	27.	b
5.	e	13.	c	21.	b	28.	c
6.	c	14.	b	22.	d	29.	a
7.	a	15.	c	23.	b	30.	c
8.	b	16.	b				

Chapter Seven
Capital Budgeting and Risk

OVERVIEW

Financial officers do not operate in an environment of complete certainty. Capital budgeting requires the ability to forecast net cash flows. This chapter addresses the issues of (a) identifying influential future events that may offset net cash flows, (b) making assumptions about the likelihood of such events actually occurring, and (c) estimating the impact of forecasted events on future cash flows. Methods of measuring and incorporating risk are discussed in light of the capital-budgeting process. The techniques of determining standard deviation, probability of acceptance error, and risk-adjusted discount rate are presented as ways of adjusting capital-budgeting decisions for uncertainty. Finally, a discussion of overall risk characteristics with respect to several projects is presented.

STUDY OBJECTIVES

1. To examine how the financial officer estimates cash flows.

2. To develop measures of risk that can be incorporated into the capital-budgeting decision.

3. To estimate the effect of overall risk when projects are evaluated as a group.

CHAPTER OUTLINE

I. A major task of financial managers is <u>estimating net cash flows</u> to be used in the capital-budgeting process.

    A. Past experience helps the financial officer identify areas and events that will probably affect the project's net cash flows.

        1. Historical events that strongly affected similar projects assist in the estimation process.

        2. Other events, which did not have a significant impact on similar projects, are not treated as serious factors in the forecasting process.

B. After identifying potentially influential events, the forecaster must make specific assumptions about each.

C. Having made these assumptions, the forecaster must estimate the impact that each assumption might have on future cash flows. This process culminates in expression of the estimate in dollar terms.

   1. The event matrix can be used to summarize the identification, assumption, and estimation phases of forecasting.

   2. Circulating the event matrix to knowledgeable colleagues in each area of the forecast can generate valuable input to the final estimate of cash flows, resulting in a completed project information form.

D. Completed project information forms are used by the financial officer in applying one or more of the capital-budgeting decision methods that we discussed in Chapter 6.

Note: Deriving accurate estimates of net cash flows is the most difficult part of capital budgeting. Inaccurate estimates cause inaccurate investment evaluations.

E. Communicating the recommendation to accept or reject a proposed project to the decision makers and to others in the firm is an important part of the capital-budgeting process. A Capital Project Reporting Sheet is often used to summarize these events and point out the variability of each project's NPV under different assumptions.

II. The concepts of uncertainty, risk, and probability are key components of the capital-budgeting problem.

A. Certainty prevails when the future contains only one possible net cash flow in any one year. Uncertainty prevails when the future contains an unknown number of possible net cash flows in any one year.

B. Risk refers to a situation that has a finite number of estimated or possible net cash flows in a given year. The financial officer assigns a risk estimate or probability of occurrence to each estimated net cash flow.

   1. If a project's lowest estimate of net cash flow has 3 chances in 10 of occurring, a 30 percent probability is assigned.

   2. Probabilities are also assigned to the low, medium, and high estimated net cash flows of any year.

   3. Assigning probabilities is really a formal quantification of estimates that we usually make in a more subjective manner.

   4. Note that the probabilities of all possible outcomes add up to 100 percent.

C. If the corporation is able to assign probabilities to the events anticipated, a risk-adjusted capital-budgeting analysis is possible.

1. A key consideration in the risk-adjusted capital-budgeting process is the <u>mean value</u> (or <u>expected value</u>) of the cash flows.

<u>Example</u>: Experts within the firm have agreed to the following event matrix for a project:

Event i	Probability of i Occurring	Associated Net Flows
Heated economy	.20	$100,000
Normal economy	.50	70,000
Recession	.30	40,000
	1.00	

This matrix indicates the consensus of expert opinion that there is a 20 percent chance of a "boom" or heated economy, a 50 percent chance of a normal economy, and a 30 percent chance of a recession next year.

The expected value represents the weighted average value of future cash flows. That is,

Expected value = sum of each estimated net cash flow times its probability of occurring

$$\overline{CF} = \sum_{i=1}^{n} CF_i * P_i$$

where

$\overline{CF}$ = expected value of annual cash flow

P_i = probability of event i

CF_i = net cash flow if event i occurs

n = number of anticipated events

In this example, the expected value would be

$\overline{CF}$ = ($100,000 * .20) + ($70,000 * .50) + ($40,000 * .30)

   = $67,000

2. The expected value of $67,000 summarizes the expectations of those who developed the event matrix. Heavier weight is given to the event of a normal economy, so $\overline{CF}$ is nearer the cash flow associated with a normal economy.

D. Expected values represent the "best guess" estimate of the range of all the anticipated possible net cash flows. This figure alone does not communicate the entire picture of the future, however. Financial officers must also indicate <u>the likelihood of realizing the $\overline{CF}$ value</u>.

1. When many net cash flows exist far above and below the expected value ($\overline{CF}$), this wide range increases the chance of not realizing $\overline{CF}$. The width of this range about the expected value (called <u>dispersion</u>) can be used to quantify risk.

CHAPTER 7

Example: The following information was provided by the financial officer for two independent projects next year.

Project A

Event i	P_i	CF_i
High growth	.2	$10,000
Normal growth	.5	46,000
Low growth	.3	70,000
	1.0	

Project B

Event i	P_i	CF_i
High growth	.2	$40,000
Normal growth	.5	46,000
Low growth	.3	50,000
	1.0	

$$\overline{CF}_A = (\$10,000 * .20) + (\$46,000 * .50) + (\$70,000 * .30)$$
$$= \$46,000$$

$$\overline{CF}_B = (\$40,000 * .20) + (\$46,000 * .50) + (\$50,000 * .30)$$
$$= \$46,000$$

Note: The expected value ($\overline{CF}$) for both projects is the same ($46,000), but the ranges (dispersions) of cash flows differ significantly.

Range of cash flows:

Project A = $60,000 (that is, from $10,000 to $70,000)
Project B = $10,000 (that is, from $40,000 to $50,000)

Note: A wider dispersion around the expected value indicates greater risk.

E. The approach typically used to quantify dispersion is the standard deviation. The most useful relative dispersion measure is the coefficient of variation.

1. A project's dispersion about the mean $\overline{CF}$ is summarized by the standard deviation (S), where

$$S = \sqrt{\sum_{i=1}^{n} (CF_i - \overline{CF})^2 * P_i}$$

Example: Using the data given in the previous example for projects A and B, we find that

$$S_A = \sqrt{[(\$10,000-\$46,000)^2*.2]+[(\$46,000-\$46,000)^2*.5]+[(\$70,000-\$46,000)^2*.3]}$$
$$= \$20,784.61$$

$$S_B = \sqrt{[(\$40,000-\$46,000)^2*.2]+[(\$46,000-\$46,000)^2*.5]+[(\$50,000-\$46,000)^2*.3]}$$
$$= \$3,464.10$$

This indicates that the risk of realizing $\overline{CF}_A$ is greater than the risk of realizing $\overline{CF}_B$, because the standard deviation of A exceeds the standard deviation of B. In general, the least risky project among projects with the same expected value has the lowest standard deviation.

    2. The coefficient of variation (V) is another measure of risk. This measure allows us to compare various projects in terms of the risk per dollar of expected value of net cash flows. The model for V is

$$V = \frac{S}{\overline{CF}}$$

Example: Using the data for projects A and B, we find that

$$V_A = \frac{\$20,784.61}{\$46,000.00} = .45$$

$$V_B = \frac{\$3,464.10}{\$46,000.00} = .08$$

The lower the value of V, the lower the relative risk. This could occur in a series of projects, even though the standard deviation of the project with the lowest relative risk (V) is not the lowest in the series.

Note: Projects with lower coefficients of variation are usually preferred over projects with higher coefficients of variation.

III. Three basic approaches are commonly used to take risk into account in the capital-budgeting process.

    A. The Expected Value - Standard Deviation approach may be used with any present-value model. This discussion concentrates on applications using NPV.

        1. Step 1 requires the analyst to calculate the expected value of the estimated annual net cash flows each year ($\overline{CF}_t$).

        2. Step 2 applies the $\overline{CF}_t$ values found for each year in the NPV model :

$$\overline{NPV}_p = \sum_{t=1}^{n} \frac{\overline{CF}_t}{(1 + k)^t} - cost$$

where

$\overline{NPV}_p$ = expected net present value

$\overline{CF}_t$ = expected value of net cash flow in t

k = cost of capital

n = number of years in project's life

The calculation of $\overline{NPV}_p$ is the same as in the previous NPV method (Chapter 6), except that CF_t values are replaced by annual $\overline{CF}_t$ values. The $\overline{NPV}_p$ found indicates the expected net dollar return from the project.

3. Step 3 evaluates the project's risk by calculating the variance around each year's expected-value net cash flow over the project's life. This results in a value of S_t^2 for each year of the project's life. That is,

$$S_t^2 = (CF_t - \overline{CF}_t)^2 * P_i$$

4. Step 4 combines the annual risk measures, S_t^2, into an overall risk measure for the project. That is,

$$S_p = \sqrt{\sum_{t=1}^{n} \frac{S_t^2}{(1 + k)^{2t}}}$$

S_p reflects the dispersion about the project's $\overline{NPV}_p$, a summary of the project's risk.

5. Step 5 extends the risk analysis to determine the relative degree of risk of each project, using the coefficient of variation.

$$V_p = \frac{S_p}{\overline{NPV}_p}$$

V_p then represents the risk per dollar of expected return, which can be used in a risk comparison among projects.

Example: The corporation has developed the following table of data on anticipated annual cash flows for a single project.

Year (t)	Anticipated Cash Flow	P_i	$\overline{CF}_t$	S_t
1	$60,000	.30		
	30,000	.40	$33,000	$19,520
	10,000	.30		
2	60,000	.30		
	30,000	.50	$35,000	$18,028
	10,000	.20		
3	60,000	.40		
	30,000	.40	$38,000	$19,391
	10,000	.20		

Step 1 requires calculation of the expected value of each year's net cash flow ($\overline{CF}$), which can be summarized as follows:

Year (t)	$\overline{CF}_t$
1	$33,000
2	35,000
3	38,000

Step 2 calculates the expected value of the project's net present value (NPV), assuming a cost of capital (k = 12 percent and cost = $50,000 for this project).

$$\overline{NPV} = \frac{\$33,000}{(1.12)^1} + \frac{\$35,000}{(1.12)^2} + \frac{\$38,000}{(1.12)^3} - \$50,000 \quad \text{(using Appendix B)}$$

$$\overline{NPV} = (\$33,000 * .89286) + (\$35,000 * .79719) + (\$38,000 * .71178) - \$50,000$$

$$= \$34,414$$

Step 3 begins the process of measuring risk by summarizing the data provided:

Year (t)	S_t
1	$19,520
2	18,028
3	19,391

Step 4 combines each year's standard deviation of the expected net cash flow over the project's estimated life:

$$S_p = \sqrt{\sum_{t=1}^{n} \frac{S_t^2}{(1 + k)^{2t}}}$$

$$= \sqrt{\frac{(\$19,520)^2}{(1.12)^{2*1}} + \frac{(\$18,028)^2}{(1.12)^{2*2}} + \frac{(\$19,391)^2}{(1.12)^{2*3}}}$$

$$= \$26,473$$

At this point in the analysis, we have a measure of the project's expected return (NPV = $34,414) and risk (Sp = $26,473). These estimates reflect all anticipated possible net cash flows and their associated risks over the project's life.

Step 5 determines the degree of relative dispersion, using the coefficient of variation.

$$V_P = \frac{\$26,473}{\$34,414} = .7693$$

Vp = .7693 can be used to compare this project with others under consideration. Projects with lower coefficients of variation (say, V = .55) would ordinarily be preferred to projects with higher coefficients of variation (say, V = 210.00).

    B.   The Probability of Acceptance Error approach determines the probability that a project's realized NPV will be negative. (If it is negative, the project was accepted in error.)

        1.   Estimated NPVs can be modeled as a probability distribution, as shown in the accompanying figure.

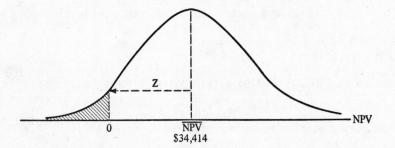

The estimated NPVs that lie to the left of NPV = 0 suggest that the project should have been rejected. In this example, the NPV of $34,414 exceeds NPV = 0 and the project is accepted. However, if the realized NPV falls within the shaded area, the project should have been rejected.

        2.   Two steps are needed to find the probability of NPV being negative. First, convert the realized NPV to the number of standard deviations (Z) that it is from the expected NPV:

$$Z = \frac{realized\ NPV - NPV}{S}$$

For our example,

$$Z = \frac{0 - \$34,414}{\$26,473} = -1.30$$

Hence an NPV of zero occurs 1.3 standard deviations to the _left_ (minus) of the project's NPV.

Second, using Appendix E (standard normal distribution), we find that 9.68 percent of the total area under the curve falls to the _left_ of NPV = 0 (the shaded area). This indicates that, when we accept this project, we accept a 9.68 percent chance that we will realize a negative NPV.

In general, do not undertake proposed projects with too large a probability that the NPV will turn out to be less than zero.

C. The _Risk-Adjusted Discount Rate_ method makes a risk adjustment to the denominator of the NPV model; that is, it adjusts the discount rate.

1. As the risk increases, the discount rate increases and PV decreases, making the project less attractive. When the risk-adjusted NPV is negative, the project is rejected.

2. The formula defining the risk-adjusted NPV is

$$\overline{NPV} = \sum_{t=1}^{n} \frac{\overline{CF}_t}{(1 + k_a)^t} - cost$$

The change from previous NPV calculations lies in the determination of k_a.

3. Determination of the risk-adjusted discount rate (k_a) is based on the risk-free interest rate and the risk premium.

   a. _Risk-free_ projects or investments (such as U.S. Government securities) have known and certain cash flows. These alternatives define the risk-free rate (i).

   b. Investments that are not risk-free require that a _risk premium_ (p) be added to reflect the degree of risk beyond the risk-free rate (i).

   c. Therefore, the risk adjusted cost of capital (k_a) is

   $$k_a = i + p$$

   d. As a project's risk increases beyond the risk-free rate, a higher k_a value is used to determine the risk-adjusted NPV.

   e. The risk-return trade-off summarizes the interaction of changes in risk and changes in expected return, as shown in the accompanying figure.

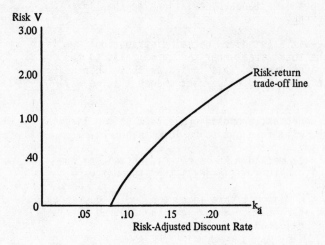

The trade-off line indicates the points at which the firm is indifferent. For example, the firm would be indifferent between a risk-free return of 8 percent and a return of 15 percent for a project with risk (V) of .90. The risk-premium adjustment for the more risky project is 15 percent - 8 percent = 7 percent. The financial officer must establish the relationship among various risk categories, coefficients of variation, and risk-adjusted discount rates in order to adjust proposed projects for varying degrees of risk.

Example: The financial officer of Parks, Inc., has developed the following estimate of investor preferences regarding risk and return.

Coefficient of Variation (V)	Risk Category	Assigned Risk-Adjusted Discount Rate (k_a), %
0	certain	8
.01-.80	lowest	10
.81-1.10	normal	12
1.11-2.10	high	16
2.10 and above	highest	20

Three projects with varying degrees of risk are being examined.

Project A: Lowest risk, expected-value annual net cash flow ($\overline{CF}_A$) of $20,000 per year for 5 years; cost = $70,000.

Project B: Normal risk, expected-value annual net cash flow ($\overline{CF}_B$) of $60,000 per year for 5 years; cost = $220,000.

Project C: Highest risk, expected-value annual net cash flow ($\overline{CF}_C$) of $100,000 per year for 5 years; cost = $250,000.

What is the risk-adjusted NPV of each project?

$$\overline{NPV}_P = \overline{CF} * PAIT \text{ (from Appendix D)} - cost$$

$$\overline{NPV}_A = (\$20,000 * 3.7908) - \$70,000 = \$5,816.00$$

$$\overline{NPV}_B = (\$60,000 * 3.6048) - \$220,000 = (\$3,712.00)$$

$$\overline{NPV}_C = (\$100,000 * 2.9906) - \$250,000 = \$49,060.00$$

Note that the following risk-adjusted discount rates were used: project A: 10 percent; project B: 12 percent; project C: 20 percent. After adjusting the $\overline{NPV}$ for this difference in risk, we can compare the projects and rank them as follows:

Ranking by risk-adjusted $\overline{NPV}$:

Project	$\overline{NPV}_P$	
C	$49,060	
		ACCEPT
A	5,816	
---------	---------	---------
B	(3,712)	
		REJECT

Therefore, after adjustment for risk, project C is preferred over project A, whereas project B is rejected. Although project C has the highest risk, it has the highest NPV after adjustment for the increased riskiness.

4. The NPV of a project found using the firm's cost of capital (unadjusted for risk) may be positive, but the same project can have a negative NPV when the risk-adjusted discount rate is used.

Example: Using project B in the previous example, assume that the firm's cost of capital is 10 percent. The unadjusted NPV is

$$\overline{NPV}_B = (\$60,000 * 3.7908) - \$220,000 = \$7,448.00$$

This indicates that the project should be accepted, because it has a positive NPV. However, as we have seen, the $\overline{NPV}$ of the project becomes negative when the risk-adjusted discount rate is used:

$$\overline{NPV}_B = (\$60,000 * 3.6048) - \$220,000 = (\$3,712.00)$$

Project B is no longer acceptable.

Note: Even a project with high expected cash flows may be unacceptable if its risk is also high.

a. The risk-oriented NPV method offers several advantages. It applies the subjective annual probability distributions to find the expected cash flows. Risk categories and associated discount rates are subjectively defined and flexible. And many financial officers find this approach easy to communicate to others.

   b. Risk-adjusted discount rates allow evaluation of the sensitivity of $\overline{NPV}$ to small changes in k_a.

IV. Fluctuations in the expected net cash flows of one project can be offset by opposite fluctuations in other projects, eliminating any significant fluctuations in the firm and reducing overall risk.

   A. Combined project risk can be less than the risk of individual projects. For example,

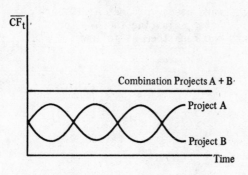

   Note that these projects have exactly opposite $\overline{CF}_t$ trends (this condition is called perfectly negative correlation). As project A's cash flows decrease, the increasing cash flows of project B offset the effect of the decline in project A. Thus the firm's cash flow position (with projects A and B) is constant. Individual project risk is reduced.

   1. Perfect positive correlation occurs when individual project flows move in the same direction. In this case, the overall risk of the firm is not reduced by combining the projects.

   2. Reduction of overall firm risk when certain projects or assets are combined is called the portfolio or diversification effect.

   B. Achieving the desired portfolio effect depends on the degree to which the combined assets are correlated, or move together. We can reduce overall risk by undertaking projects with opposing net cash flow cycles.

   1. In practice, the cash flows of projects rarely move in exactly opposite directions. Therefore, the financial manager must attempt to reduce overall risk by diversifying among projects with cash flows that do not move in perfect unison.

   2. Diversification is more likely to reduce overall risk when the net cash flows of projects fluctuate in opposite directions from one another.

STUDY PROBLEMS

7.1. What is the expected value of the annual cash flows for each of the following projects?

	Annual Cash Flow	Probability
Project C	$ 5,000	.2
	10,000	.5
	15,000	.3
Project D	60,000	.1
	70,000	.8
	80,000	.1

Solution

$\overline{CF}_C$ = ($5,000 * .2) + ($10,000 * .5) + ($15,000 * .3)

= $10,500   Answer

$\overline{CF}_D$ = ($60,000 * .1) + ($70,000 * .8) + ($80,000 * .1)

= $70,000   Answer

7.2. Calculate the standard deviation for each of the projects presented in Problem 7.1.

$$S_C = \sqrt{\sum_{t=1}^{n} (CF - \overline{CF})^2 * P_i}$$

$$S_C = \sqrt{[(\$5,000-\$10,500)^2*.2]+[(\$10,000-\$10,500)^2*.5]+[(\$15,000-\$10,500)^2*.3]}$$

= $3,500   Answer

$$S_D = \sqrt{[(\$60,000-\$70,000)^2*.1]+[(\$70,000-\$70,000)^2*.8]+[(\$80,000-\$70,000)^2*.1]}$$

= $4,472.14   Answer

7.3. The following mutually exclusive projects are available to Angels, Inc.

	Expected NPV	Standard Deviation (S)
Project X23	$100,000	$20,000
Project X19	$100,000	$35,000

Which project would you select, and why?

Solution

Both projects have the same expected NPV, $100,000; however, the risk of project X19 exceeds the risk of project X23, as measured by the standard deviation <u>and</u> by the coefficient of variation.

$$V_{X23} = \frac{\$20,000}{\$100,000} = .20 = 20\%$$

$$V_{X19} = \frac{\$35,000}{\$100,000} = .35 = 35\%$$

Project X23 would be preferred to project X19, because it has the same expected return and a lower coefficient of variation.

7.4. Richy, Inc., is considering the purchase of a $20,000 machine with a 4-year life expectancy. The following estimates apply; annual probability distribution is assumed for each of the four years:

Event	Net Cash Flow (CF_i)	Probability (P_i)
Recession	$ 6,000	.2
Mild slowdown	8,000	.4
Mild recovery	10,000	.3
Boom	12,000	.1

a. Calculate the expected net present value ($\overline{NPV}$), using a 12 percent cost of capital.

b. Calculate the standard deviation of the $\overline{NPV}$.

c. Calculate the coefficient of variation.

Solution

a. $\overline{CF}_t$ = ($6,000 * .2) + ($8,000 * .4) + ($10,000 * .3) + ($12,000 * .1)

   = $8,600

   $\overline{NPV}$ = $8,600 * (Appendix D interest factor for 4 years, 12 percent - $20,000

   = ($8,600 * 3.0374) - $20,000

   = $6,121

b. Standard deviation of annual net cash flows:

$$S_t = \sqrt{\sum_{i=1}^{n} (CF_i - \overline{CF})^2 * P_i}$$

$$S_t = \sqrt{\begin{array}{l}[(\$6,000 - \$8,600)^2 * .2] + [(\$8,000 - \$8,600)^2 * .4] + \\ [(\$10,000 - \$8,600)^2 * .3] + [(\$12,000 - \$8,600)^2 * .1]\end{array}}$$

$$S_t = \sqrt{\$1,352,000 + \$144,000 + \$588,000 + \$1,156,000}$$

$$S_t = \sqrt{\$3,240,000}$$

$$S_t = \underline{\$1,800}$$

Standard deviation of net present value:

$$S_P = \sqrt{\sum_{t}^{m} \frac{S_t^2}{(1 + k)^{2t}}}$$

$$S_P = \sqrt{\frac{\$3,240,000}{(1.12)^2} + \frac{\$3,240,000}{(1.12)^4} + \frac{\$3,240,000}{(1.12)^6} + \frac{\$3,240,000}{(1.12)^8}}$$

$$S_P = \sqrt{(\$3,240,000 * .7973) + (\$3,240,000 * .6355) + (\$3,240,000 * .5066) + (\$3,240,000 * .4039)}$$

$$S_P = \sqrt{\$2,583,252 + \$2,059,020 + \$1,641,384 + \$1,308,636}$$

$$S_P = \sqrt{\$7,592,292}$$

$$S_P = \underline{\$2,755}$$

c. $V_P = (\$2,755/\$6,121) = .45$

7.5. Cony, Inc., has developed the following set of project proposals.

Project	Expected NPV	Standard Deviation
G	$100,000	$ 60,000
H	300,000	240,000
I	500,000	200,000

If Cony is interested in minimizing the probability of realizing a negative NPV, which project should it select?

Solution

Find the number of standard deviations (Z) where a zero NPV is the expected NPV:

$$Z_G = \frac{0 - \$100,000}{\$60,000} = -1.67$$

$$Z_H = \frac{0 - \$300,000}{\$240,000} = -1.25$$

$$Z_I = \frac{0 - \$500,000}{\$200,000} = -2.5$$

Next, from the standard normal distribution table (Appendix E), find the area of the distribution to the left of Z.

The probability of Z_G (-1.67) is .0475 = 4.75 percent.
The probability of Z_H (-1.25) is .1056 = 10.56 percent.
The probability of Z_I (-2.50) is .0062 = .62 percent.

Project I would be selected, becuase it has the lowest probability of error.

7.6. In analyzing capital projects, the HIYLD Company uses the following risk categories and discount rates:

Risk Category	Adjusted Discount Rate
lowest	.10
medium	.14
high	.18
highest	.24

The following projects are under consideration.

Project B	Project D
Life = 4 years	Life = 4 years
$\overline{CF}$ = $3,000 annually	$\overline{CF}$ = $10,000 annually
Risk category: lowest	Risk category: high
Cost = $9,000	Cost = $26,391

a. What is the risk-adjusted NPV of each project?

b. Which project would you select? Why?

Solution

a. Project B:

The risk-adjusted discount rate would be .10, and the $\overline{NPV}$ is

$$\overline{NPV}_B = (\$3,000 * 3.1699) - \$9,000 = \$510$$

Project D:

The risk-adjusted discount rate would be .18, and the $\overline{NPV}$ is

$$\overline{NPV}_D = (\$10,000 * 2.6901) - \$26,391 = \$510$$

b. On the basis of the $\overline{NPV}$ calculations alone, we would be indifferent between the two projects, because the $\overline{NPV}_B$ is the same as the $\overline{NPV}_D$. This points out the fact that, even though project D is much more risky than project B, an adjustment for this additional risk (using an 18 percent rather than a 10 percent discount rate) results in a risk-adjusted $\overline{NPV}_D$ that is the same as that provided by project B.

7.7. A new company is considering expanding its activities into two new industries. The following earnings from each type of industry are expected.

Year	Industry A	Industry B
1	$ 8,000	($ 6,000)
2	($16,000)	20,000
3	20,000	(2,000)

a. What are the expected-value (mean) annual earnings for each industry?

b. Calculate the standard deviation for each industry.

c. What are the average annual earnings and standard deviation if the firm enters both industries?

d. What effect would the combination of industries have on the total firm?

Solution

a. Mean of industry A = ($8,000 - $16,000 + $20,000)/3 = $4,000
Mean of industry B = (-$6,000 + $20,000 - $2,000)/3 = $4,000

b. $$S_A = \sqrt{\frac{(\$8,000 - \$4,000)^2 + (-\$16,000 - \$4,000)^2 + (-\$20,000 - \$4,000)^2}{3}}$$

   = $14,967

   $$S_B = \sqrt{\frac{(-\$6,000 - \$4,000)^2 + (\$20,000 - \$4,000)^2 + (\$2,000 - \$4,000)^2}{3}}$$

   = $11,431

c. Both industries:

Year	Combined Industries
1	$ 2,000
2	4,000
3	18,000

Average of combined earnings = ($2,000 + $4,000 + $18,000)/3
= $8,000

Combined standard deviation:

$$S_C = \sqrt{\frac{(\$2,000 - \$8,000)^2 + (\$4,000 - \$8,000)^2 + (\$18,000 - \$8,000)^2}{3}}$$

= $7,118

d. By combining activities for both industries, the firm would reduce considerably the overall risk from either industry separately, thus indicating that earnings are negatively correlated between the industries.

7.8. Calculate the probability of acceptance error to select the better of the following two projects.

Project V	Project W
$\overline{NPV}$ = $75,000	$\overline{NPV}$ = $75,000
V = .40	V = .60

Solution

V = S/$\overline{NPV}$, so S = $\overline{NPV}$ * V. Then,

S_V = \$75,000 * .40 = \$30,000

S_W = \$75,000 * .60 = \$45,000

Therefore,

Z_V = (0 - \$75,000)/\$30,000 = -2.50, probability = .0062

Z_W = (0 - \$75,000)/\$45,000 = -1.67, probability = .0475

Select project V, because its expected net present value is the same as that of project W, and the absolute risk is much less.

REVIEW QUESTIONS

1. In forecasting, the event matrix can be used to
   a. identify the work expected to be involved in the project.
   b. identify events and assumptions.
   c. indicate the life of the project.
   d. forecast probability errors.

2. Certainty refers to
   a. a future with an infinite number of cash flows.
   b. intuitive accuracy.
   c. a future that contains only one possible net cash flow in any one year.
   d. none of these.

3. Risk differs from uncertainty in that
   a. risk contains a finite number of possibilities and uncertainty does not.
   b. risk is less certain than uncertainty.
   c. risk is easier to measure.
   d. uncertainty does not affect cash flows.

4. Probabilities indicate
   a. the number of events in the total set.
   b. the subset of events that will not occur.
   c. the assigned chances of occurrence of various events.
   d. none of these.

5. Subjective probabilities may be combined with associated annual net cash flows to determine the
   a. standard deviation.
   b. expected value.
   c. range of net cash flows.
   d. none of these.

6. The estimated net cash flow with the _____ probability is _____ likely to occur.
   a. lowest, most

b. highest, least
c. highest, most
d. lowest, least
e. both c and d

7. The width of the range of values around the expected value can be used as
    a. a measure of expected value.
    b. a measure of risk.
    c. a measure of standard deviation.
    d. none of these.

8. A wider dispersion around the expected value indicates _____ risk.
    a. less
    b. constant
    c. changing
    d. greater

9. The best measure of relative dispersion is the
    a. mean.
    b. standard deviation.
    c. coefficient of variation.
    d. none of these.

10. As a general rule, the _____ risky project has the _____ standard deviation.
    a. least, lowest
    b. least, highest
    c. most, lowest
    d. both b and c

11. The coefficient of variation indicates the
    a. standard deviation for the project.
    b. risk per dollar of expected value of cash flows among projects.
    c. degree of cash flows.
    d. none of these.

12. Projects with lower coefficients of variation are usually _____ when compared with other projects.
    a. rejected
    b. ignored
    c. preferred
    d. none of these

13. Expected NPV ($\overline{NPV}$) is an overall indication of
    a. expected dispersion.
    b. expected range.
    c. expected net dollar return from the project.
    d. none of these.

14. Which of the following approaches is(are) commonly used to incorporate risk into the capital-budgeting decision?
    a. standard deviation
    b. probability of acceptance errors
    c. risk-adjusted discount rate
    d. all of these
    e. none of these

15. Calculating the probability of acceptance error
    a. determines the probability of rejecting a good project.
    b. determines the probability that a project's realized NPV will be negative.
    c. determines the probability that a project's realized NPV will be positive.
    d. none of these.

16. When the probability of acceptance error is very large, we _____ the project.
    a. accept
    b. reject

17. The risk-adjusted discount rate method
    a. adjusts expected cash flows to certainty.
    b. adjusts expected risk measures.
    c. adjusts the discount rate.
    d. none of these.

18. When a project has a higher degree of risk than the firm wants to accept, the risk-adjusted discount rate is _____ than the overall cost of capital.
    a. higher
    b. lower
    c. the same as
    d. none of these

19. If the risk-free rate is 10 percent and investors expect a return of 18 percent, the risk premium is
    a. 18 percent.
    b. 8 percent.
    c. 10 percent.
    d. none of these.

20. The risk-return trade-off indicates that
    a. the higher the risk, the lower the expected return.
    b. the higher the risk, the higher the expected return.
    c. the lower the risk, the higher the expected return.
    d. none of these.

21. Many firms use the risk-adjusted NPV method, because
    a. it applies subjective annual probability distributions.
    b. risk categories can be subjectively defined and altered.
    c. the results are easily communicated to others.
    d. all of these.

22. When two projects are undertaken that have opposing net cash flow cycles, the _____ reduce(s) overall risk.
    a. portfolio effect
    b. expected values
    c. relative dispersion
    d. none of these

KEY DEFINITIONS

Absolute dispersion: measured as standard deviation.

Certainty: a future that contains only one possible net cash flow per year of a project.

Coefficient of Variation (V): V = standard deviation/expected value; may also be expressed as

$$\frac{S_t}{\overline{CF}_t} \quad \text{or} \quad \frac{S_P}{\overline{NPV}_P}$$

Dispersion: range of values around the expected value of the net cash flow.

Diversification: a process that can lead to the reduction of overall risk by combining assets.

Event matrix: summary of identified events that may offset net cash flows.

Expected NPV ($\overline{NPV}$): expected net present value from the project.

Expected value: weighted average, mean, or most likely value in a series.

Portfolio effect: the reduction in overall risk that often occurs due to the combining of several assets.

Probability: the likelihood of a particular outcome, expressed as a percentage of all possible outcomes.

Relative dispersion: measured as coefficient of variation.

Risk: a finite number of possible net cash flows.

Risk-free interest rate: interest rate on investments with certain cash flows.

Risk premium: additional interest added to the risk-free rate to account for additional risk in the investment.

Risk-return trade-off: a graphical illustration indicating the positive relationship between risk and expected return on investments. The trade-off shows the risk and return combinations among which the investor is indifferent.

Standard Deviation:

$$S = \sqrt{\sum_{i=1}^{n} (CF_i - \overline{CF})^2 * P_i}$$

Uncertainty: a future that contains an unknown number of possible net cash flows in any one year of a project.

CHAPTER 7

ANSWERS TO REVIEW QUESTIONS

1.	b	7.	b	13.	c	18.	a
2.	c	8.	d	14.	d	19.	b
3.	a	9.	c	15.	b	20.	b
4.	c	10.	a	16.	b	21.	d
5.	b	11.	b	17.	c	22.	a
6.	e	12.	c				

Part Three
Cost of Capital and Capital Structure

Capital is a scarce resource. For the firm to achieve its objective, this scarce resource must not only be applied efficiently through the capital budgeting process but must also be acquired at the lowest possible cost. In fact, the capital budgeting process requires an accurate estimation of the cost of capital prior to the selection of assets. Acquiring funds at the lowest overall cost depends on the financial officer's understanding of the theory of financial markets.

Part III addresses the complex issue of measuring the firm's cost of capital with the objective of selecting that set of capital resources that minimizes overall cost. Chapter 8 introduces the cost of capital concept in light of existing capital markets. Chapter 9 continues the development of capital measurements with regard to individual securities of the firm. Chapter 10 discusses the strong influence of capital structure on the firm's cost of capital. And Chapter 11 presents the financial officer's concerns with dividend policy.

At the completion of Part III, you will better understand the financial officer's complex management responsibilities in balancing the cost of individual securities, capital structure, and dividend policy. A proper balance of these elements will minimize the cost of capital while satisfying the expectations of stockholders.

Chapter Eight
An Introduction to the Cost of Capital

OVERVIEW

The second major finance function is determining how the firm should finance its long-term assets. This chapter defines capital and introduces the process of determining capital costs within the capital markets. The task of the financial manager is to evaluate the availability of capital and its cost in such a manner as to allow the firm to lower its overall cost of capital, thereby increasing shareholder wealth.

STUDY OBJECTIVES

1. To define capital and the cost of capital.

2. To identify the suppliers and demanders of funds that make up the capital market.

3. To evaluate methods of minimizing the cost of capital and develop insight into the term structure of interest rates.

CHAPTER OUTLINE

I. Defining capital and the cost of capital.

   A. Capital is the term used to represent the (1) funds supplied by external investors when they buy securities (stocks and bonds) from the firm, and (2) funds supplied internally by retained earnings.

      1. Capital can be a long-term liability of the firm, such as bonds.

      2. Capital can be a part of the equity portion of a firm, such as stocks and retained earnings.

   B. The cost of capital refers to the rate of return required by investors who purchase the securities of the firm.

II. Supply and demand factors.

    A. The cost of capital is determined by the amount of capital that investors are willing to supply and the amount of capital that corporations and others demand.

        1. When demand rises in relation to supply, the cost of capital increases.

        2. Increases in the cost of capital tend to cause the supply of capital to rise.

        3. A larger supply of capital tends to bring the supply and demand for capital to the same point (equilibrium) at a lower cost of capital.

        4. The opposite effect occurs when demand decreases in relation to supply.

        5. Financial officers attempt to time their financial needs to arise when the supply of capital is relatively high and the cost of capital is relatively low.

    B. Suppliers of capital expect to be compensated for the likelihood that the lender will default on the security. This part of the cost of capital is called the default-risk premium. But suppliers of funds also expect to be compensated for the forgone opportunity to consume in the present and also for the potential effect of inflation. This part of the cost of capital is called the default-free rate.

        1. Part of the firm's cost of capital reflects the default-free interest rate expected by suppliers of funds.

        2. Only U.S. government bonds are default-free. With all other securities, there is some degree of risk that the issuer of the security may not be able to pay the annual interest or return the principal when it is due.

        3. Investors purchasing securities other than the default-free government issues require a higher interest rate to compensate them for buying a security with the risk of default.

    C. Default-risk compensation.

        1. Default risk refers to the chance that a corporation may not be able to make interest payments or return the principal when required or meet dividend expectations.

        2. The higher the perceived degree of default risk, the higher the required rate of return expected by the supplier of funds.

        3. In extreme cases of default risk, investors may not supply funds at any rate of return.

D. Degrees of risk.

1. As the default risk <u>increases</u> from the default-free rate toward the extremes of currently defaulted securities, the demanders of funds must pay the suppliers a higher cost-of-capital rate.

2. Investors continually adjust and evaluate default-risk exposure and their matching cost-of-capital expectations.

3. The cost of capital rises as the default risk increases.

III. Defining the cost of capital and its characteristics.

A. The cost of capital (k) is the annual interest rate that occurs when the supply of funds available for investment in a particular type of security equals the demand for those funds. Symbolically,

$$k = i + \Theta$$

where k = the cost of capital, i = the default-free interest rate, and Θ = the default-risk compensation.

B. The cost of capital does not remain constant over time.

1. Investors change the default-free interest rate they demand.

2. Investors perceive the issuer's default-risk position as changing.

3. As the default risk of the issuer increases, the issuer must pay a higher cost of capital to encourage investors to supply funds (the opposite occurs when default risk decreases).

IV. <u>Capital markets</u> are the negotiating grounds where suppliers and demanders of capital meet to determine capital costs. Financial officers must identify and monitor factors and conditions in the capital markets to minimize the firm's cost of capital.

A. <u>Demanders of capital</u> include real estate mortgages, corporate securities, foreign securities, business borrowings, consumer loans, U.S. Treasury securities, and tax-exempt securities. <u>Competition</u> among demanders of capital can channel funds away from the firm, thereby increasing the firm's cost of capital. This is especially true when the U.S. government offers securities at lower risk, reducing the firm's ability to sell higher-risk securities and increasing its costs of capital. A "credit crunch" occurs when the availability of funds is highly restricted, causing many firms to stop or limit growth.

B. <u>Suppliers of funds</u> must be convinced that they should invest in the firm's securities at a relatively low cost (to the firm)--a difficult task. Suppliers include thrift institutions such as savings and loan companies (mutual savings banks), credit unions, life insurance companies, and fire and casualty insurance companies; private, noninsured pension funds; investment companies; finance companies; commercial banks; businesses and local governments; foreign investors; and individuals. Financial officers must create, evaluate, and cultivate a sustained

relationship with potential suppliers of funds to increase their availability and lower the cost of capital.

C. Forces operating within the capital markets balance supply and demand
such that the total supply equals the total demand.

1. As the demand for funds increases, individuals become the largest
suppliers, increasing the cost of capital.

2. Interest rates and the cost of capital tend to be lower when financial
institutions supply most funds.

3. Financial officers must cultivate alternative sources of funds, because periods of high capital demand lead not only to higher costs
but also to decreased availability of funds.

V. Examining the history of capital markets provides the financial officer with
an improved perspective on the cost of capital.

A. Securities in different risk classes have experienced varied and fluctu-
ating interst rates over time.

1. The cost of capital for the least risky (AAA-rated) corporate bonds
has consistently been higher than the risk-free (U.S. government
bond) rate.

2. Medium-risk (BAA-rated) bonds have consistently experienced higher
capital costs than the least risky (AAA-rated) corporate bonds.

3. A bond's cost of capital increases as the bond's risk increases.

B. Changes in the cost of capital tend to occur at about the same time for
all risk classes of securities. This simultaneous movement of most interest rates reflects the pervasive influence of general economic and
financial factors.

C. The great volatility in interest rates has been observed historically to
occur in the relatively shortest periods of time. Therefore, the timing
of security offerings can be very critical to minimize the cost of capital. The financial officer must learn to manage the impact of volatility.

D. Equity (stock) prices also exhibit cyclical volatility, so the financial
manager must also monitor this source of capital.

1. Firms prefer to sell common stock at high prices rather than low
prices, because doing so minimizes the cost of capital. Therefore,
the timing of equity offerings is extremely important.

2. Astute financial managers learn to anticipate, if possible, market
reactions to new stock issues and time their demand for equity in a
way that minimizes its cost.

VI. Insights into dealing with the dynamic cost of capital include the following
generalizations.

A. The cost of capital (k) will change.

B. The availability of funds fluctuates.

C. It may be better to demand funds when the supply is high than to delay until funds become restricted.

D. Financial officers must monitor, evaluate, and anticipate changes in supply and demand factors in the capital market.

E. The financial officer attempts to time the firm's demand for funds to arise when market conditions of high availability and low cost prevail.

VII. The term structure of interest rates plays a large part in the financial manager's objective of minimizing the cost of capital.

A. Interest rates vary; they depend not only on risk but also on the scheduled maturities (repayment dates).

    1. The investor's maturity preference affects the cost of capital.

    2. Financial officers seek to establish security offerings with maturities that minimize interest rates.

B. The term structure of interest rates is the varying pattern of interest rates among different maturities of equal-risk bonds.

    1. The yield curve (see the accompanying diagram) depicts the term structure of interest rates by graphing the relationship of interest rates and varying maturities for a security with constant risk. Using the yield curve, financial officers can identify the maturity that will minimize the cost of capital.

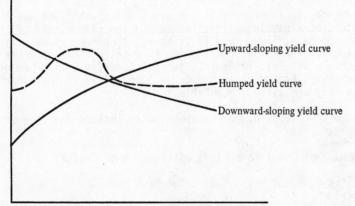

a. <u>Upward-sloping yield curves</u> indicate that long-term interest rates exceed short-term interest rates on bonds of equal risk. This relationship is typically observed during the final phases of a recession, where the first part of the curve reflects the current excess of supply over demand (lower rates) and the longer-term outlook calls for a more favorable general economy. Financial managers would interpret an upward-sloping curve as an indication of the need to evaluate marginal projects that may be accepted now in anticipation of an improved economy later.

b. <u>Downward-sloping yield curves</u> indicate that longer-term interest rates are lower than short-term interest rates. This relationship occurs when current economic activity is very high and investors anticipate an end to this activity, leading to a recession. This capital-market assessment about the future of the general economy suggests two things to the financial manager: (1) consider long-term rather than short-term financing and (2) re-evaluate projects in light of the yield curve's recession implications.

c. <u>Humped yield curves</u> indicate higher interest rates for inter- mediate-maturity bonds than for <u>either</u> short- or long-term maturities. This shape in the yield curve is usually found during the final phase of economic booms. This yield curve im- plies expectations that the current economic growth is unsus- tainable and should peak in the near future. Financial officers would be inclined to avoid intermediate-term bonds.

2. Although yield curves provide information on prospects for the economy and for interest rates, they must be interpreted carefully.

a. Shifting yield curves (from downward-sloping to upward-sloping) result in varying interest rates. The most volatile of these rates are those with short-term maturation.

b. Even when the firm observes an upward-sloping yield curve (sug- gesting the use of short-term bonds), it may be better advised to watch the maturities of the asset being purchased and the method of financing. This is because the current use of short- term bonds at lower cost to finance a long-term asset will re- quire refinancing of the funding at a later time, at unpre- dictable interest rates. In extreme cases, the firm can be hurt (even bankrupt) if the funds it requires in the future are very costly or unavailable.

VIII. Insights into the term structure of interest rates include the following generalizations.

A. Time the demand of funds to periods of low cost of capital.

B. Use maturities that offer the lowest interest rates.

C. Be aware of the risks involved in not matching long-term investments with long-term bonds.

   D. Reserve the right to replace currently high-cost sources of funds with
       lower-cost funds that might become available in the future.

STUDY PROBLEMS

8.1. Consider the characteristics of the yield curve that depicts the following
data.

Maturity (years)	Interest Rate (%)
1	9
3	10
5	11
7	12
10	13
20	16

a. What type of yield curve is this called?

b. If the firm has a project with a 10-year life, what maturity should the firm
    use for its funding?

Solution

a. Interest rates increase as maturity lengthens, so this is called an upward-
    sloping yield curve.

b. Matching maturity of assets and funding is generally the best policy, as it
    would be best to use the 10-year, 13 percent rate. It is possible to use the
    lower, short-term rates, but the risk of incurring higher interest rates when
    refinancing the short-term funding must be considered, given the long-term out-
    look of 16 percent.

8.2. As financial officer of a firm, you are evaluating the timing of a bond issue
($50 million). You are expecting long-term bond rates to decrease next year (when
the funds are needed) to 8 percent from the current rate of 10 percent.

a. What savings in interest will accrue to the firm if the financing occurs next
    year and your forecast of the decline in interest rate is correct?

b. What would be the consequence (in terms of extra interest paid) if interest
    rates on long-term bonds go up to 12 percent next year--rather than down, as
    anticipated?

Solution

a. The before-tax savings due to waiting would be .10 * $50,000,000 = $5,000,000
    the first year and (.10 - .08) * $50,000,000 = $1,000,000 per year thereafter.

b. If long-term bond rates go up to 12 percent next year, we would have to pay
    additional interest over the current 10 percent rate:
    (.12 - .10) * $50,000,000 = $1,000,000 in each year until maturity.

8.3. Treasury bonds currently pay 10 percent interest. A corporate bond is being offered that will pay 15 percent interest. What default-risk compensation is being required by the purchaser of the corporate bond?

Solution

15 percent - 10 percent = 5 percent

REVIEW QUESTIONS

1. The cost of capital is defined as
   a. the interest rate on long-term liabilities.
   b. the cost of stock.
   c. the rate of return required by investors to purchase the securities of the firm.
   d. the cost of short-term liabilities.

2. When demand rises in relation to supply
   a. the cost of capital decreases.
   b. the cost of capital remains constant.
   c. the cost of capital increases.
   d. supply does not change.
   e. none of these.

3. Only _____ are default-free.
   a. U.S. government bonds
   b. corporate bonds
   c. municipal revenue bonds
   d. common stocks

4. Default risk refers to
   a. the firm's debt-to-total-assets ratio.
   b. the chance that the firm will not be able to make its interest payments and/or return the principal.
   c. the bond issue not being sold.
   d. the business risk of the firm.

5. As the default risk _____ from the current risk-free rate, suppliers of funds require a _____ return on their investment.
   a. increases, lower
   b. increases, higher
   c. decreases, higher
   d. changes, constant

6. The financial officer of the firm must be concerned about the _____ as well as the cost of funds.
   a. availability
   b. suitability
   c. type
   d. processing

7. _____ are suppliers of funds to the capital markets.
   a. Life insurance companies
   b. Local governments

    c. Individuals
    d. All of these

8. As the demand for funds increases, _____ increasingly become the larger suppliers of funds, thereby increasing costs.
    a. life insurance companies
    b. individuals
    c. governments
    d. banks

9. Historically, the cost of capital for the least risky (AAA-rated) corporate bonds has consistently been _____ than the default-free rate.
    a. higher
    b. lower
    c. about the same
    d. less volatile

10. Financial managers must attempt to plan the timing of a stock issue carefully, because
    a. firms prefer to sell stock at the lowest price.
    b. firms cannot sell stock at more than par value.
    c. firms prefer to sell stock at higher prices rather than lower prices.
    d. stock prices do not exhibit cyclical volatility.

11. The term structure of interest rates refers to
    a. the cost of equity.
    b. the cost of debt this year.
    c. the different costs of bonds with varying risk.
    d. the varying pattern of interest rates on bonds with the same risk and varying maturities.

12. Downward-sloping yield curves suggest that
    a. interest rates will increase over time.
    b. investors anticipate that the current level of ecnomic activity will end, leading to a recessionary period.
    c. investors anticipate that the current recession will end soon, leading to a recovery period.
    d. interest rates will be stable over time.

13. The greatest volatility in interest rates occurs within _____ maturities when yield curves shift from upward to downward slopes.
    a. long-term
    b. short-term
    c. intermediate-term
    d. varying

14. By not matching asset lives with financing maturities, the firm takes on additional risk, because
    a. interest rates are changing on existing balance-sheet funds.
    b. the firm may repeatedly have to refinance short-term maturities at varying interest rates to match the lives of long-term assets.
    c. the firm may not find the funds available the next time they are needed.
    d. both b and c.

15. In obtaining funds at fixed interest rates, the financial officer should
    a. reserve the right to replace existing sources of funds with new sources at lower rates.
    b. eliminate the need to match maturities of assets and funding.
    c. insist on obtaining the funds that have the least current cost, regardless of maturity.
    d. all of these.

KEY DEFINITIONS

AAA-rated bonds: highest commercially rated bonds, indicating the lowest default risk.

BAA-rated bonds: medium-risk bonds that have a higher default risk than AAA-rated, thereby requiring a higher return for investors.

Capital: funds supplied externally by investors when they buy securities from the firm and internally from retained earnings.

Capital markets: negotiating grounds where suppliers and demanders of capital meet.

Cost of capital: the rate of return required by investors who purchase the securities of the firm.

Credit crunch: condition prevailing when the availability of funds is highly restricted, often causing many firms to stop or limit growth.

Default-free rate: rate of return that investors can earn without fear of default (loss of interest or principal). U.S. government bonds are risk-free.

Default risk: the chance that a corporation may not be able to make interest payments or return the principal to investors when required.

Downward-sloping yield curve: yield curve that indicates that long-term interest rates are lower than short-term interest rates on bonds of equal risk.

Humped yield curve: yield curve that indicates higher interest rates for intermediate-maturity bonds than for either short- or long-term maturities on bonds of equal risk.

Term structure of interest rates: interest-rate patterns over varying maturities of equal risk.

Upward-sloping yield curve: yield curve that indicates that long-term interest rates exceed short-term interest rates on bonds of equal risk.

Yield curve: graph of the relationship between interest rate and maturity for securities with equal default risk.

CHAPTER 8

ANSWERS TO REVIEW QUESTIONS

1. c	5. b	9. a	13. b
2. c	6. a	10. c	14. d
3. a	7. d	11. d	15. a
4. b	8. b	12. b	

Chapter Nine
Cost of Capital for Individual Securities

OVERVIEW

Financial managers are interested in minimizing the firm's cost of capital in order to maximize shareholder wealth. Chapter 8 provided an introduction to the concept of cost of capital, indicating that the cost reflects the risk-adjusted rate of return required by investors. This chapter extends the introduction to show how a firm estimates the cost of capital for different types of funds that it uses individually as well as collectively. The combination of various sources of funds at various individual costs leads us to define the weighted average cost of capital as the minimum acceptable rate of return of the firm.

STUDY OBJECTIVES

1. To identify the factors that determine the cost of capital for each of the firm's securities.

2. To measure the firm's components in the total capital structure.

3. To identify the individual costs of existing and new sources of capital.

4. To combine the individual costs of existing capital into an average cost of capital figure and of new sources of capital into a weighted marginal cost of capital.

5. To learn the appropriate uses of the average cost of capital for existing and new funds.

CHAPTER OUTLINE

I. Two general factors affect the cost of capital for each of the firm's securities: (1) the default-free interest rate and (2) the additional compensation required for accepting greater risk. The cost of capital for any security can be found as follows:

$$k = i + \Theta$$

where

　　k = cost of capital (as an annual percentage)
　　i = the default-free interest rate
　　Θ = risk compensation

A.　Default-free securities have zero chance of default. U.S. government
　　bonds represent the default-free rate (i), which reflects the amount
　　investors require to give up (1) the use of their money and (2) pro-
　　tection against loss of purchasing power (inflation).

　　1.　The default-free rate fluctuates as investors require a higher re-
　　　　turn for giving up the use of their money and for taking on pur-
　　　　chasing-power risk.

　　2.　While financial officers cannot control the general changes in the
　　　　default-free rate, they acknowledge the tendency of the cost of
　　　　capital to move in the same direction.

　　3.　As inflation increases, interest rates and the cost of capital for
　　　　all sources of funds increase. A large portion of a security's cost
　　　　of capital is market-determined and thus beyond the financial
　　　　officer's control.

B.　Risk compensation (Θ) makes up a large component of the cost-of-capital
　　(k) calculation. Suppliers of funds require compensation for any risks
　　unique to the firm that could reduce its ability to pay interest on
　　principal when due or dividends when expected. Business, financial,
　　and marketability risks affect the firm's risk-compensation component.

　　1.　Business risk refers to the uncertainty that the firm will pay its
　　　　scheduled bond interest and principal payments or its expected divi-
　　　　dends because of the risk inherent in its operating environment.

　　　　a.　Firms in volatile operating environments have a greater chance
　　　　　　of default due to business risks.

　　　　b.　Indicators of the degree of business risk include business cycle
　　　　　　sensitivity, quality of sales, cost and availability of materials,
　　　　　　and management depth and capability.

　　　　c.　Changes in the perceived business-risk position of the firm
　　　　　　change the cost of all sources of funds. In general, a more
　　　　　　stable operating environment reduces the firm's cost of capital,
　　　　　　and vice versa.

　　2.　Financial risk refers to the ability of the firm to meet its finan-
　　　　cial obligations (fixed charges).

　　　　a.　Financial risk increases through the excessive use of debt
　　　　　　(bonds and loans). Financial managers must monitor the pro-
　　　　　　portion of debt used in order to control perceived financial
　　　　　　risk.

b. Financial risk is also affected to a lesser degree by the security's <u>priority of claim</u> on the firm's operating profit or assets. As the claim on assets decreases in priority, financial risk increases.

c. Financial risk also increases with the <u>inept matching</u> of bond-repayment schedules and forecasted cash inflows.

d. Financial risk is the one influence on the firm's cost of capital that is totally within its control.

3. <u>Marketability risk</u> refers to the perception of the security owner regarding her or his ability to sell the instrument <u>at or near the current market price</u>. Highly marketable securities have a strong market mechanism that results in minimal marketability risk.

a. Financial officers increase marketability by selling the firm's securities to a large number of investors, creating a wide market.

b. A firm can lower marketability risk by disseminating company information widely and rapidly or by trading on the larger, nationally recognized stock exchanges.

II. Financial officers must recognize that the firm's cost of capital is affected by the default-free interest rate (including inflation), business risk (often beyond the firm's control), financial risk (totally controlled by the firm), and marketability risk (partially influenced by the firm's policies).

The financial officer can lower the firm's cost of capital by correctly anticipating changes in interest rate, using debt appropriately, and designing the offered security carefully.

III. <u>The cost of capital for debt instruments (bonds)</u> is the rate the firm must pay investors to purchase the securities offered. It is always expressed as an annual percentage. The purchase price that investors are willing to pay for the bond instrument depends on the investors' risk-adjusted cost of required rate of return, which is the firm's risk-adjusted cost of capital and which is used to determine the present value of the future interest payments and return of the principal. The discounted or present value of these benefits of purchase represents the most the investor is willing to pay.

<u>Bond example (initial sale):</u>

Annual interest payment (coupon)	$80
Maturity of bond (years)	20
Principal to be returned at maturity	$1,000
Investor-required rate of return (k)	8%

The most the investor will pay is the present value of the expected cash flows from the investment (interest and principal), which is determined as follows:

$$\text{Maximum price} = \sum_{t=1}^{20} \frac{80}{(1.08)^t} + \frac{\$1,000}{(1.08)^{20}} = \$1,000$$

Therefore, the investor requiring an 8 percent return would be willing to pay $1,000 for the firm's bond, indicating that the firm's before-tax cost of debt capital is $k_d = 8$ percent.

A. Secondary markets exist for holders of the firm's bonds. <u>Subsequent purchasers</u> of a firm's bonds have the same rights as initial purchasers. The annual interest rate and promised return of principal do not change as ownership of the bond changes.

B. Subsequent sales can occur when the sales price is lower or higher than the original price, causing the firm's cost of debt capital to be higher or lower, respectively.

<u>Bond example (subsequent sales)</u>:

Annual interest payment	$80
Maturity of bond (years)	20
Principal	$1,000
Subsequent sales price (A)	$829.73 (sold at discount)
Annual interest rate (A)	$k_d = .10$
Subsequent sale price (B)	$1,229.39 (sold at premium)
Annual interest rate (B)	$k_d = .06$

Therefore, when the price of the bond decreases to $829.73, the annual interest rate required by investors (which is the firm's cost of capital) increases to 10 percent, whereas an increase in the value of the bond to $1,229.39 reduces the interest rate required by investors to 6 percent.

Remember, a change in the bond price causes a change in the opposite direction in the firm's cost of debt capital, k_d.

C. The following formula may be used to approximate the annual interest rate or yield for a bond.

$$\hat{k}_d \cong \frac{I + \dfrac{P_n - P_o}{n}}{\dfrac{P_n + P_o}{2}}$$

$\hat{k}_d$ = approximate cost of debt capital

I = annual dollar interest (coupon) payment

P_n = principal payment at maturity

P_o = current bond price

n = remaining years in life of bond

Example:

a. Using the data given in part B, we find that the bond selling at a dis-
    count ($829.73) would have an approximate interest rate of

$$\hat{k}_d = \frac{\$80 + \dfrac{\$1,000 - \$829.73}{20}}{\dfrac{\$1,000 + \$829.73}{2}} = .0967 \text{ or } 9.67\%$$

b. Using the data for the bond selling at a premium ($1,229.39), we find that
    the interest rate would be approximately

$$\hat{k}_d = \frac{\$80 + \dfrac{\$1,000 - \$1,229.39}{20}}{\dfrac{\$1,000 + \$1,229.39}{2}} = .0615 \text{ or } 6.15\%$$

Precalculated bond-yield tables (such as Table 9.3 in the text) are also
available for financial officers to use in determining the precise pretax interest rates of various bond offerings.

D. The after-tax cost of debt represents the net effect of the costs of
    debt capital. Taxes are charged on income after expenses. Because
    interest payments are deductible expenses, income taxes are partially
    reduced by the payment of interest charges on debt. Thus the firm's
    after-tax cost of debt (k_{dt}) is always less than its before-tax cost
    (k_d).

$$k_{dt} = k_d - k_d(T)$$
$$= k_d(1 - T)$$

where

k_{dt} = after-tax cost of debt

k_d = before-tax cost of debt

T = firm's marginal tax rate

Example: A firm as acquired funding through the use of bonds that yield 10
percent. If the firm's marginal tax rate (T) is 40 percent, the after-tax cost of
this form of debt capital is

$$k_{dt} = k_d (1 - T)$$
$$= .10 (1 - .40)$$
$$= .06 \text{ or } 6\%$$

Therefore, the firm pays an annual interest rate of 10 percent before taxes, which
results in a net cost of 6 percent after taxes. Remember, the after-tax cost of
debt capital (k_{dt}) is always less than the before-tax cost of capital (k_d) due to
the tax deductibility of interest payments.

IV. <u>Preferred stock</u> is a source of capital that has characteristics of both debt and equity instruments. Investors in preferred stock are entitled to fixed, periodic dividends without a maturity date. These payments are not without risk for investors, however, because they are made after interest payments but before payment of common stock dividends. Thus preferred stock is somewhere between bonds and common stock in terms of riskiness to investors, which affects its return requirements.

A. The market price of preferred stock (P_p) represents the present value of an infinite stream of dividend payments (D_p), discounted for risk (k_p):

$$P_p = \frac{D_p}{(1 + k_p)^1} + \frac{D_p}{(1 + k_p)^2} + \cdots + \frac{D_p}{(1 + k_p)^\infty}$$

Because it is a perpetual annuity, this simplifies to

$$P_p = \frac{D_p}{k_p}$$

or

$$k_p = \frac{D_p}{P_p} \quad , \text{ the dividend yield.}$$

Therefore, the firm's cost of preferred stock represents the minimum required rate of return that investors demand for the issue, which is the dividend yield (D_p/P_p).

Example: A company issued preferred stock paying a $10 annual dividend that is currently trading at a market price of $90.00. The cost of preferred stock to the company would be

$$k_p = \frac{\$10}{\$90} = .11 = 11\%$$

Therefore, the after-tax cost of existing preferred stock would be 11 percent.

B. The market price of preferred stock varies inversely with the cost of preferred stock; that is, k_p and P_p move in opposite directions. Financial officers must monitor changes in the risk perception of investors in preferred stock, because this perception affects the price of preferred and (hence) its cost.

V. The <u>cost of common stock</u> is the rate of return investors require to purchase and hold shares.

A. The relationship between common stock's current market price and the stream of future dividends is the basis for evaluating equity costs. The current market price represents the present value of the expected dividends the investor will receive, so

$$P_0 = \sum_{t=1}^{\infty} \frac{\hat{D}_t}{(1 + k_e)^t}$$

where

D_t = expected dividend in year t

P_0 = current market price of common stock

k_e = cost of common equity capital

$\sum_{t=1}^{\infty}$ = sum of discounted future dividends into perpetuity

Given knowledge of the current market price (P_0) and expected dividends ($\hat{D}_t$) we can solve the model for the cost of common equity capital (k_e). However, this requires that we determine the future dividends expected by investors.

B. Two basic assumptions are often used to determine the expected dividends of common stock.

1. The assumption of <u>constant dividends</u> presumes that the dividend stream will remain constant for the indefinite future. The cost of common equity would be

$$k_e = \frac{D_0}{P_0} \text{ , or dividend yield}$$

where

k_e = cost of common equity capital

D_0 = current dividend per share

P_0 = current price of common stock

The cost of common stock, assuming a constant perpetual dividend, is the stock's current dividend yield (the dividend per share divided by its prevailing price per share).

<u>Example</u>: A firm with relatively stable and nongrowth characteristics is selling for $12 per share. We assume that the constant, annual dividend will be $1.80 per share. The firm's cost of common equity (k_e) is

$$k_e = \frac{1.80}{12.00} = 15\%$$

2. The assumption of <u>constant growth in dividends</u> presumes that the firm's current dividend will continually grow at a constant annual rate (g). Hence,

$$P_0 = \sum_{t=1}^{\infty} \frac{D_0(1 + g)^t}{(1 + k_e)^t}$$

If we know the current market price (P_0) and current dividend (D_0) and assume a dividend growth rate (g), we can also solve this equation for k_e:

$$k_e = \frac{D_1}{P_0} + g$$

where

k_e = cost of common equity capital

D_1 = this year's expected dividend payment or $D_0(1 + g)$

P_0 = current price of common stock

g = assumed annual growth rate in dividends

The cost of common equity capital, assuming constant dividend growth, equals the sum of the expected dividend yield (D_1/P_0) and the growth rate (g) in dividends.

Example: A firm expects to pay a $1.20 dividend this year, which is assumed to increase at a constant 8 percent annual rate in all future years. If the firm's current market price of common stock is $12.00, the cost of equity capital (k_e) is

$$k_e = \frac{\$1.20}{\$12.00} + .08 = 18 \text{ percent}$$

The required rate of return that investors demand on the firm's existing common stock is 18 percent.

C. The cost of common equity capital exceeds the cost of preferred stock and debt capital. This is a result of the position that common share-holders occupy as residual owners relative to debt and preferred securities. Common-stock dividends are more uncertain, because they are paid after interest is paid to debt capital, preferred dividends are paid, and funds are retained.

D. The cost of retained earnings (k_{re}) is the same as the cost of capital for common stock (k_e) because additions to retained earnings are simply present common-stock dividends forgone. If investors were paid the amount of the funds retained in the form of dividends, they could re-invest the dividends in the firm by purchasing additional common stock, with a required rate of return of k_e. Therefore, $k_{re} = k_e$.

VI. Debt, preferred stock, common stock, and retained earnings provide capital to the firm. A number of similarities exist in the costs of all these sources.

A. The cost of any source of capital reflects the required rate of return of the investors supplying the capital. Different costs occur because of the varying degrees of risk associated with different sources.

B. The cost of any source is the discount rate that equates the market price of the security to its promised or expected payments.

Cost of Capital for Existing Securities

Source	Expected Payment	Before-Tax Cost	After-Tax Cost
Bond	Interest, principal	$\hat{k}_d = \dfrac{I + \dfrac{P_n - P_o}{n}}{\dfrac{P_n + P_o}{2}}$	$\hat{k}_{dt} = k_d(1 - T)$
Preferred stock	Dividends	————	$k_p = \dfrac{D_o}{P_o}$
Common stock	Dividends	————	Constant dividend assumption $k_e = \dfrac{D_o}{P_o}$ Growing dividend assumption $k_e = \dfrac{D_1}{P_o} + g$
Retained earnings	————		$k_{re} = k_e$

VII. The financial officer must extend his or her examination of the individual sources of capital to determine the cost of capital that represents the total set of sources used by the firm. This total cost is determined by using the weighted average of all costs of capital, based on prevailing prices for each type of capital.

A. The weighted average cost of capital (k_a) represents the weighted cost of all capital sources, where each individual cost of capital is weighted by its relative importance in the firm's total capital.

  1. The first step in finding k_a is to determine the cost of each type of capital, using the formulas for individual cost (k_{dt}, k_p, k_e, and k_{re}).

  2. The second step in finding k_a is to find the percentage of the firm's total capital that each type of capital represents.

Example:

Capital Type	Dollar Amount	Percentage of Total
Bonds	$ 4,000,000	25%
Preferred stock	2,000,000	12.5%
Common stock	8,000,000	50%
Retained earnings	2,000,000	12.5%
Total capital	$16,000,000	100%

  3. The third step in finding k_a is to determine the weighted effect of each individual component of the capital structure by multiplying the percentage found in step 2 by the cost found in step 1.

  4. The fourth and last step in finding k_a is to add together the results of step 3.

B. The process of finding the average cost of capital is summarized by the following formula:

$$k_a = \sum_{i=1}^{n} w_i k_i$$

where

  k_a = average cost of capital

  k_i = after-tax cost of each capital source i (step 1)

  w_i = percentage of total capital that capital source i represents (step 2)

  n = number of sources used

Example: Find the average cost of capital, given our previous calculations of each component's cost and percentage of the total capital structure.

Percentage	Cost
25%	k_{dt} = 6%
12.5%	k_p = 11%
50%	k_e = 15%
12.5%	k_{re} = 15%

The average cost of capital is

$$k_a = (.25 * .06) + (.125 * .11) + (.50 * .15) + (.125 * .15)$$
$$= .0150 + .01375 + .0750 + .01875$$
$$= .1225$$
$$k_a = 12.25\%$$

    C. The weighted average cost of existing capital (k_a) is most often used in judging the average required existing rate of return. This represents the minimum required rate of return that the firm must earn on its existing securities to satisfy the expectations of the firm's investors.

        1. When a firm's realized rate of return on existing capital is <u>less than</u> the weighted average cost (k_a), dissatisfied suppliers of capital sell their securities and the market prices decline.

        2. When a firm's realized rate of return on existing capital is <u>greater than</u> the weighted average cost (k_a), the current market prices of the firm's securities increase.

        3. The firm uses the average cost of capital (k_a) to find the minimum required rate of return it must earn on <u>existing</u> capital in order to satisfy the expectations of its investors.

VIII. The <u>cost of capital for newly offered securities</u> examines the same risk factors as does existing capital (business, financial, and marketability risks) plus any costs associated with selling the new securities, which are called <u>flotation costs</u>. New issues are generally offered to raise funds to support the purchase of new assets.

    A. When the new assets being acquired through new capital will not change the risk characteristics of the firm and the marketability is the same as for existing securities, the risk premium for the new issue will be the same as the existing risk premium. Thus, for the risk premium to remain unchanged, the following conditions must be met:

        1. <u>Constant business risk.</u> No changes will occur in the operating environment as a result of the new asset being acquired.

        2. <u>Constant financial risk.</u> New capital is raised in the same proportions as existing capital, maintaining constant financial risk.

        3. <u>Constant marketability risk.</u> New securities have the same degree of marketability as existing securities.

    B. Even when the risk premium remains constant between new and existing securities, the cost may be different due to flotation costs (f). These additional expenses include commissions paid to those selling the securities, printing, advertising, registration with government agencies, and discounts required to induce investors to buy. <u>Flotation charges reduce the net receipts to the firm</u> of each security sold, increasing the security's cost to the firm.

C. The <u>cost of new capital</u> reflects the changes in risk premium and flotation charges. If no changes in risk premium occur, the price received for a new issue is the market price minus flotation cost $(p_0 - f)$. Therefore, formulas that determine individual security costs must be adjusted for flotation costs (f) as shown in the accompanying table.

Cost of Capital for Newly Offered Securities

Type	Before-Tax Cost	After-Tax Cost
Bond	$\hat{k_d} = \dfrac{I + \dfrac{P_n - (P_o - f)}{n}}{\dfrac{P_n + (P_o - f)}{2}}$	$\hat{k_{dt}} = \hat{k_d} (1 - T)$
Preferred stock	--	$k_p = \dfrac{D_p}{P_p - f}$
Common stock	--	a. Constant-dividend assumption $k_e = \dfrac{D_o}{P_o - f}$ b. Growing-dividend assumption $k_e = \dfrac{D_1}{P_o - f} + g$

The formulas for retained earnings are not adjusted, because they are an internal source of funds requiring no flotation costs.

D. The weighted cost of new capital (k_{an}), or weighted marginal cost of capital, assumes that new securities will not change the proportions currently existing in the capital structure. Therefore, the weighted cost of new capital is found by multiplying the cost of each new capital source by its proportionate weight in the total capital structure. This method is the same method used to find the weighted average cost of existing capital, with the cost of each security changed to reflect associated flotation charges, if any.

E. Calculation of the average cost of new capital can be summarized in the following formula:

$$k_{an} = \sum_{i=1}^{n} w_{in} k_{in}$$

where

k_{an} = average cost of new capital

w_{in} = proportion of each source in total capital structure

k_{in} = after-tax cost of new capital source

n = number of types of new capital

Example: Find the weighted average cost of new capital, given our previous calculation of the proportions of existing capital structure that each source represents and of new security costs.

Proportion of Total	Costs		
25%	New bonds (k_{dt})	=	6.5%
12.5%	New preferred stock (k_p)	=	11.5%
50%	New common stock (k_c)	=	15.5%
12.5%	Additional retained earnings (k_{re})	=	15%

Note that all component costs except retained earnings have increased to reflect flotation changes. The cost of retained earnings is the same as before, because flotation charges do not apply to internally generated sources of capital. Following the same steps that we followed in calculating the weighted average cost of capital for existing sources, we find that the weighted average cost of new capital is

k_{an} = (.25 * .065) + (.125 * .115) + (.50 * .155) + (.125 * .15)

   = .0163 + .0144 + .0775 + .0188

   = .1270

k_{an} = 12.7%

Note that the weighted average cost of new capital (12.7 percent) exceeds the weighted average cost of existing capital (12.26 percent) because of: (1) flotation charges that increase the net cost of external capital and (2) the greater difficulty in selling more of the same security to investors.

F. The weighted average cost of new capital (k_{an}) is used primarily in the selection of new projects. That is, the firm would use k_{an} as the minimum acceptable internal rate of return on the project being considered. If the project's internal rate of return is greater than or equal to k_{an}, the project may be accepted; otherwise, the project should be rejected. Similarly, the k_{an} figure can be used as the discount rate to determine a proposed project's net present value or profitability index.

STUDY PROBLEMS

9.1. RA, Inc., expects to pay dividends of $2.00 per share on common stock next year. The current market price of common stock is $16.00. The company's dividends have grown at a 4 percent rate over the last 8 years.

a. If the growth rate in dividends remains constant, what is the cost of common-stock capital?

b. If the growth rate in dividends remains constant and the cost of new common stock must include a flotation charge of $2.00 per share, what is the cost of new common-stock capital?

c. If the growth rate in dividends increases to 6 percent, what must happen to the prevailing stock price if the cost of existing common-stock capital (k_e) is to remain the same?

d. If the growth rate in dividends decreases to 3 percent, what must happen to the prevailing stock price if the cost of existing common stock-capital (k_e) is to remain the same?

Solution

a. Growth (g) in dividends = 4 percent

$$k_e = \frac{D_1}{P_0} + g = \frac{\$2.00}{\$16.00} + .04 = .1250 + .04 = 16.5\%$$

b. $$k_e' = \frac{D_1}{P_0 - f} + g = \frac{\$2.00}{\$16 - \$2} + .04 = \frac{2}{14} + .04 = 18.29\%$$

c. Note that the k_e formula is used and that the only unknown is P_0; k_e is derived from part a.

$$k_e = \frac{D_1}{P_0} + g$$

$$.165 = \frac{\$2.00}{P_0} + .06$$

$$.1050 = \frac{\$2}{P_0}$$

$$P_0 = \$19.05 \text{ (price increase)}$$

d. Note that the approach is the same as in part c, with growth rate <u>decreasing</u>.

$$k_e = \frac{D_1}{P_o} + g$$

$$.165 = \frac{\$2.00}{P_o} = .03$$

$$.135 = \frac{\$2}{P_o}$$

P_o = \$14.82 (price decrease)   Answer

<u>9.2.</u> AJACS, Inc., is planning to sell 15-year bonds that pay annual year-end interest of \$100 on each bond. Existing bonds that mature in 20 years pay \$80 in annual year-end interest and currently sell for \$829.73 each. At what price will AJACS be able to sell each new bond?

<u>Solution</u>

The new bonds have a face value of \$1,000 and pay an interest rate of 10 percent (100/1000). The existing bond is yielding a 10 percent return, so the new bonds must sell for \$1,000 each.

$$\$829.73 = \sum_{t=1}^{20} \frac{\$80}{(1 + k_d)^t} + \frac{\$1,000}{(1 + k_d)^{20}}$$

$$k_d = 10\%$$

<u>9.3.</u> KMARS, Inc., is interested in comparing the after-tax cost of <u>new bonds</u> to the after-tax cost of <u>new preferred stock</u>. The following information applies.

Bonds: Maturity   20 years
Face value   \$1,000 each
Expected market price   \$800 each
Flotation charge   \$20 each
Annual interest rate   9 percent

Preferred stock: Expected market price   \$54 per share
Flotation charge   \$3.49 per share
Annual dividend   \$3.44 per share

The company's marginal tax rate is 40 percent.

a. What is the after-tax cost of the new bonds?

b. What is the after-tax cost of the new preferred stock?

c. Which source of capital would you prefer? Why?

Solution

a. The approximate before-tax cost of the new bonds is

$$\hat{k}_d' = \frac{I + \dfrac{P_n - (P_0 - f)}{n}}{\dfrac{P_n + (P_0 - f)}{2}} = \frac{\$90 + \dfrac{\$1000 - (\$800 - \$20)}{20}}{\dfrac{\$1000 + (\$800 - \$20)}{2}}$$

$$\hat{k}_d' = \frac{\$101}{\$890} = .1135$$

Therefore, the approximate after-tax cost of the new bond is

$$\hat{k}_{dt}' = \hat{k}_d' * (1 - T) = .1135 * (1 - .40) = .0681 = 6.81\%$$

b. The after-tax cost of preferred stock is

$$k_p' = \frac{D_p}{P_p - f} = \frac{\$3.44}{(\$54.00 - \$3.49)} = \frac{\$3.44}{\$50.51} = .0681$$

c. We would be indifferent in terms of the after-tax cost. However, other factors such as changes in capital structure would move us to select one of the two sources. (In general, the cost of preferred stock exceeds the before-tax cost of bonds.)

9.4. The existing capital structure and current prices of MAJEL, Inc., are as follows.

Type	Amount	Present Market Price
8 percent bonds	$ 6,000,000	$935.82
$6.00 preferred stock	3,000,000	$54 per share
Common stock	12,000,000	$25 per share
Retained earnings	3,000,000	
Total capital	$24,000,000	

MAJEL is a company that has grown in dividends at a consistent annual rate of 8 percent over the last 6 years. This rate of growth is expected to continue. The next dividend is expected to be $2.00 per share. The existing bonds have 10 years to maturity, and the company's marginal tax rate is 45 percent.

a. What is the after-tax cost of the bonds?

b. What is the after-tax cost of the preferred stock?

c. What is the after-tax cost of the common stock?

d. What is the after-tax cost of the retained earnings?

e. What is MAJEL's average cost of capital?

Solution

a. After-tax cost of the bonds = k_{dt}.

$$\$935.82 = \sum_{t=1}^{10} \frac{\$80}{(1 + k_d)^t} + \frac{\$1,000}{(1 + k_d)^{10}}$$

Finding k_d by the trial-and-error method results in

$k_d = 9\%$ (before-tax cost of bonds)

Finding k_d by the approximation method results in

$$\hat{k}_d = \frac{I + \dfrac{P_n - P_0}{n}}{\dfrac{P_n + P_0}{2}}$$

$$= \frac{\$80 + \dfrac{\$1,000 - \$935.22}{10}}{\dfrac{\$1,000 + \$935.22}{2}}$$

$$= \frac{\$80 + \$6.42}{\$967.61}$$

$$= \frac{\$86.42}{\$967.61}$$

$\hat{k}_d = .0893$, or approximately .09

The after-tax cost of debt (k_{dt}) is, therefore,

$k_{dt} = k_d * (1 - T)$

$\quad = .09 * (1 - .45)$

$k_{dt} = .0495 = 4.95$ percent (after-tax cost of bonds)

b. After-tax cost of the preferred stock = k_p.

$$k_p = \frac{D}{P_0} = \frac{\$6}{\$54} = 11.11\%$$

c. After-tax cost of the common stock = k_e.

$$k_e = \frac{D_1}{P_0} + g = \frac{\$2}{\$25} + .08 = .16 = 16\%$$

d. After-tax cost of the retained earnings = k_{re}.

$$k_{re} = \frac{D_1}{P_0} + g = \frac{\$2}{\$25} + .08 = 16 = 16\%$$

e.

Type	Millions	Percentage		Cost	
Bond	$6/$24 =	.2500	*	.0495 =	.01238
Preferred stock	$3/$24 =	.1250	*	.1111 =	.01389
Common stock	$12/$24 =	.5000	*	.1600 =	.08000
Retained earnings	$3/$24 =	.1250	*	.1600 =	.02000
Total					.12627

Weighted average cost of capital (k_a) = 12.627%.

Note: Using the formula approach, we get the same result:

$$k_a = \sum_{i=1}^{n} w_i k_i = (.25 * .0495) + (.1250 * .1111) + (.5000 * .16) +$$
$$(.1250 * .16) = .12627$$

9.5. What will be the after-tax cost of debt capital if a firm sells a new 12 per-cent bond maturing in 20 years at $1,000 each, if each bond has a flotation charge of $20, and if the firm is in the 40 percent tax bracket?

Solution

By the approximation method,

$$\hat{k_d} = \frac{\$120 + \dfrac{\$1,000 - (\$1,000 - \$20)}{20}}{\dfrac{\$1,000 + \$980}{2}} = \frac{\$121}{\$990} = .1222 \text{ (before-tax cost)}$$

$$\hat{k}_{dt} = \hat{k_d} * (1 - T) = .1222 * (1 - .45) = .06722 \text{ (after-tax cost)}$$

9.6. Overway, Inc., has experienced a growth in dividends on common stock from $1.00 to $2.00 over the last 6 years. What is the firm's cost of equity capital if the current market price of common stock is $40.00?

Solution

The dividend has doubled over the last 6 years, so the growth rate is approximately 12 percent. The last dividend was $2.00 per share, so we can expect the next divi-dend to be $2.00 * (1.12)^1 = $2.24 per share.

$$k_e = \frac{D_1}{P_o} + g = \frac{\$2.24}{\$40.00} + .12 = .056 + .12 = .176 = 17.6\%$$

9.7. CCup, Inc., is investigating the purchase of a new machine that has an expected internal rate of return of 15 percent. CCup considers its optimal capital structure to be 60 percent debt, 5 percent preferred stock, and 35 percent equity. The after-tax cost of new debt will be 8 percent; of preferred stock, 10 percent; and of common stock, 18 percent.

a. What is CCup's weighted average cost of new capital?

b. Should CCup purchase the machine? Why or why not?

Solution

a. k_{an} = (.60 * .08) + (.05 * .10) + (.35 * .18) = .116 = 11.6%

b. CCup should purchase the machine. The weighted average cost of new capital is less than the expected internal rate of return of the project.

9.8. A firm has an opportunity to sell new preferred stock for $90 per share that pays a $9 annual dividend. If each share has a $5 flotation charge, what would be the cost of new preferred-stock capital to the firm?

Solution

$$k_p = \frac{D_1}{(P_o - f)} = \frac{\$9.00}{\$90 - \$5} = \frac{\$9}{\$85} = 10.59\%$$

9.9. Davis, Inc., is considering the purchase of a new machine that will provide a 10 percent internal rate of return. The machine will require Davis to obtain $10,000,000 in funds. Davis's marginal tax rate is 50 percent. The current (and optimal) capital structure is as follows:

Source	Amount
Bonds	$15,000,000
Preferred stock	5,000,000
Equity	30,000,000
Total capital	$50,000,000

New capital costs are expected to include the following characteristics:

Bonds: 20-year maturity
10 percent coupon interest rate (annual)
Market price of $1,200
Flotation charge of $100 per bond
$1,000 face value

Preferred stock: $10 dividend
$100 par value
Market price of $80
Flotation charge of $2 per share

Equity: Dividends have grown at a 6 percent annual rate
Market price of $28 per share
Flotation charge of $3 per share
Last dividend was $2 per share
No retained earnings available for this project

a. What is the firm's weighted average cost of new capital?

b. Should the company accept the project?

Solution

a. Cost of new bonds:

$$\hat{k_d} = \frac{\$100 + \dfrac{\$1,000 - (\$1,200 - \$100)}{20}}{\dfrac{\$1,000 + (\$1,100 - \$100)}{2}} = \frac{\$95}{\$1,050} = .0905 = 9.05\%$$

$$\hat{k_{dt}} = .0905 (1 - .50) = .04525 = 4.525\%$$

Cost of new preferred stock:

$$k_p = \frac{D_1}{(P_0 - f)} = \frac{\$10}{\$80 - \$2} = \frac{\$10}{\$78} = 12.82\%$$

Cost of new equity:

$$k_e = \frac{D_1}{(P_0 - f)} + g = \frac{\$2.00\ (1.06)}{\$28 - \$3} + .06$$

$$= \frac{\$2.12}{\$25} + .06$$

$$= .0848 + .06$$

$$= 14.48\%$$

$$k_{an} = [(15/50) * .04525] + [(5/50) * .1282] + [(30/50) * .1448]$$

$$= .01358 + .01282 + .08688$$

$$= .11328$$

$$k_{an} = 11.328\%$$

b. This project should not be accepted. The expected return is <u>less than</u> the average cost of new capital.

9.10. A company has a capital structure that includes 30 percent common stock and 20 percent retained earnings. The company is investigating a project that will require $7,000,000.

a. How much will be acquired through new common stock and retained earnings?

b. If retained earnings of $2,000,000 will be available to support the project, how much new common stock will be needed?

Solution

a. To maintain the capital structure within equity (stock and retained earnings), the following will be required.

    .30 * ($7,000,000) = $2,100,000 in new common stock
    .20 * ($7,000,000) = $1,400,000 in retained earnings
                         $3,500,000 total in equity

b. If $2,000,000 is available in retained earnings, $1,500,000 ($3,500,000 - $2,000,000) will be needed in new external equity (common stock) at higher cost.

REVIEW QUESTIONS

1. The cost of capital
    a. is lower for a firm in a more stable operating environment.
    b. does not depend on changes in financial risk.
    c. does not depend on the default-free rate.
    d. does not vary among companies in the same industry.
    e. both a and c

2. As inflation increases, interest rates and the cost of capital for all sources of funds
    a. decrease.
    b. increase.
    c. remain constant.
    d. are not affected.

3. The cost of capital for each source of funds includes a risk adjustment for
    a. business risk.
    b. financial risk.
    c. marketability risk.
    d. all of these.
    e. a and b only

4. The financial manager can reduce the firm's cost of capital by
    a. correctly anticipating changes in interest rate.
    b. using debt appropriately.
    c. designing the offered security carefully.
    d. all of these.
    e. a and c only.

5. The most an investor will pay for a security is
    a. the face value of the security.
    b. the present value of expected cash flows.
    c. the terminal value.
    d. none of these.

6. When a bond is sold at a discount from its face value
   a. the cost of the debt capital decreases.
   b. the cost of the debt capital remains the same.
   c. the cost of the debt capital increases.
   d. the interest charge is the same as the coupon rate.
   e. none of these.

7. The rights of subsequent purchasers of a firm's initial bond issue
   a. are changed to reflect the new interest rates.
   b. are the same as the rights of the original holders.
   c. are renegotiated.
   d. are dismissed.
   e. none of these.

8. Preferred stock is a source of capital that
   a. has tax advantages for the issuing firm.
   b. is the same as a bond issue.
   c. receives dividends prior to tax payments.
   d. has some characteristics of both debt and equity instruments.
   e. none of these.

9. The market price of preferred stock moves _____ with the firm's cost of preferred stock capital.
   a. inversely
   b. directly

10. Common stock is a source of capital that
    a. reflects the present value of expected dividends.
    b. always assumes a constant growth rate in dividends.
    c. is not used often because the cost of capital is higher.
    d. is used often because the cost of capital is lower.
    e. none of these.

11. The basic assumptions that are most often used in estimating the dividend stream of common stock are
    a. constant dividends or decreasing dividends.
    b. increasing dividends or decreasing dividends.
    c. constant dividends or constant growth in dividends.
    d. none of these.

12. When dividends are assumed to be constant for the indefinite future, the cost of common equity capital is
    a. the dividend yield.
    b. the constant-growth expectation.
    c. the current dividend amount.
    d. none of these.

13. When constant dividend growth is assumed, the cost of common equity equals
    a. the sum of the current dividend and expected growth.
    b. the sum of expected dividend yield and expected growth.
    c. the sum of the current market price and expected growth.
    d. none of these.

14. The cost of common equity capital is typically _____ the cost of pre-
    ferred stock and debt capital.
    a. less than
    b. greater than
    c. the same as

15. The cost of retained earnings is considered to be the same as the cost of
    a. debt.
    b. external preferred stock.
    c. common stock.
    d. none of these.

16. Which of the following must be considered in determining the costs of all
    sources of capital?
    a. The current commercial-paper rate
    b. The discount rate that equates the market price of the security and its
       promised or expected payments
    c. The current AAA bond rate
    d. The required rate of return of the investors supplying the capital
    e. Both b and d

17. The weighted average cost of existing capital represents
    a. the sum of the products of the proportions that individual sources repre-
       sent in the capital structure times their individual costs.
    b. the marginal cost of capital.
    c. the sum of the costs of each source.
    d. the proportion that each source used represents in the firm.

18. The weighted average cost of existing capital indicates the
    a. discount rate to use for new projects requiring new funds.
    b. the maximum return that shareholders expect.
    c. the minimum required rate of return that the firm must earn on its
       existing securities to satisfy the expectations of the firm's investors.
    d. none of these.

19. When the realized rate of return on existing capital is less than the weighted
    average cost of existing capital
    a. current market prices of the firm's securities increase.
    b. investors in the firm are satisfied.
    c. dissatisfied investors sell their securities, decreasing market prices.
    d. current market prices are not affected.
    e. none of these.

20. The weighted average cost of existing capital can differ from the weighted
    average cost of new capital because of
    a. changes in perceived risk (business, financial, and marketability risks).
    b. flotation charges.
    c. new projects with the same risk.
    d. constant capital costs.
    e. both a and b.

21. The weighted cost of new capital assumes that
    a. new funding will change the proportions currently existing.
    b. the cost of equity remains constant.
    c. the cost of debt is fixed.

    d. the use of new securities will not change the proportions currently existing in the capital structure.
    e. none of these.

22. The cost of new capital sources reflects
    a. flotation charges.
    b. changes in the capital structure.
    c. risk-premium adjustments.
    d. changes in the amount of internal funds used.
    e. both a and c.

23. The weighted average cost of new capital is used primarily in
    a. evaluating investors' expectations.
    b. analyzing past business decisions.
    c. selecting new projects.
    d. evaluating business risk.

24. If a project's internal rate of return is _____ the weighted average cost of new capital, the project may be _____.
    a. less than, accepted
    b. greater than, accepted
    c. less than, rejected
    d. greater than, rejected
    e. both b and c

25. _____ is(are) primarily responsible for the difference between the weighted average cost of existing capital and the weighted average cost of new capital.
    a. The change in capital structure
    b. Flotation charges
    c. The change in funds used
    d. Tax rates
    e. None of these

KEY DEFINITIONS

After-tax cost of debt: the before-tax cost multiplied by (1 minus the tax rate); indicates the net effect of debt-capital costs.

Business risk: uncertainty in the firm's ability to make expected payments to investors.

Constant dividends: the assumption that the common-stock dividend stream will remain constant for the indefinite future.

Constant growth in dividends: the assumption that the firm's current dividend will continually grow at a constant annual rate.

Cost of capital for debt instruments: rate the firm must pay to encourage investors to purchase bonds.

Cost of capital for new securities: the cost of capital of each new security after adjustment for changes in risk premiums required and flotation costs.

Cost of capital for retained earnings: the same as the cost of capital for common stock.

Cost of equity: the minimum acceptable rate of return that common-stock purchasers require.

Default-free securities: securities with no chance of default, such as U.S. government bonds.

Financial risk: uncertainty about the firm's ability to cover fixed charges.

Marketability risk: uncertainty about the investor's ability to sell a security easily at or near the current market price.

Preferred-stock cost of capital: minimum rate of return the firm must pay investors to buy its preferred stock.

Risk compensation (θ): adjustment in the cost of capital to reflect the risk that investors perceive in each security issued.

Secondary market: market in which sales of securities occur subsequent to initial offerings.

Weighted average cost of existing capital: the firm's weighted average cost of capital of all its sources of existing capital, with the cost of each capital source being weighted by the proportion that each type of capital represents in the total capital structure. The weighted average cost of capital is most often used in judging the average required existing rate of return of current investors.

Weighted average cost of new capital: the weighted average cost of new capital of the firm, assuming that the new securities will not change the proportions currently existing in the capital structure.

ANSWERS TO REVIEW QUESTIONS

1. a	8. d	14. b	20. e
2. b	9. a	15. c	21. d
3. d	10. a	16. e	22. e
4. d	11. c	17. a	23. c
5. b	12. a	18. c	24. e
6. c	13. b	19. c	25. b
7. b			

Chapter Ten
Capital Structure and Cost of Capital

OVERVIEW

The management of capital costs requires financial officers to balance debt and equity in the proper proportions. The judicious combination of these primary sources of funds can lead to lower total capital costs and subsequently higher profits and market prices for the firm. The interdependence of debt financing and equity financing is investigated in this chapter, as is the question of whether an optimal capital structure exists for a firm. Financial leverage (the use of debt) is examined in terms of how it affects earnings per share, the cost of equity capital, the cost of debt capital, and the search for the optimal capital structure. The impact of attaining the optimal capital structure is investigated in terms of the objective of maximizing the total market value of the firm. The traditional approach and the Modigliani and Miller argument are considered.

STUDY OBJECTIVES

1. To define financial leverage.

2. To investigate the effects of financial leverage on debt costs, equity costs, and the optimal capital structure.

3. To explore how the firm determines its optimal capital structure.

4. To examine various theories of capital structure and the impact of capital structure on the cost of capital.

5. To investigate the interactions of capital structure and overall cost of capital in maximizing the total market value of the firm.

CHAPTER OUTLINE

I. Financial leverage refers to the proportion of long-term debt used by the firm in its total capital structure. Firms without debt are said to be financially unleveraged. Firms that use debt are said to be financially leveraged to the extent of the debt used in the capital structure. The use of debt can have both positive and negative effects.

179

A. Positive financial leverage occurs when the leveraged firm's earnings per share (EPS) exceed the unleveraged or less leveraged firm's EPS, all other things being equal. This is an indication that the relative reduction in net income after taxes (NIAT) is less than the decrease in the number of common shares outstanding in the EPS calculation.

Example:

	Unleveraged Firm	Leveraged Firm
Percent debt	0	50% (8% bonds)
Percent equity	100% (10,000 shares)	50% (5,000 shares)
Total capital	$1,000,000	$1,000,000
Operating profit	$ 100,000	$ 100,000
- Interest expense	0	40,000
= NIBT	$ 100,000	$ 60,000
- Taxes	- 50,000	- 30,000
= NIAT	$ 50,000	$ 30,000
EPS = $\dfrac{\text{NIAT}}{\text{number of shares}}$	$5.00	$6.00

$$\text{Operating-profit return} = \frac{\text{operating profit}}{\text{total capital}} = \frac{\$100,000}{\$1,000,000} = 10\% \text{ for both firms}$$

The EPS of the leveraged firm is higher than the EPS of the unleveraged firm, even though the total capital and operating profits are the same. The unleveraged firm has twice as many shares outstanding as the leveraged firm, whereas the leveraged firm pays interest and the unleveraged firm does not. The positive leverage effect occurs because the reduction in NIAT between the leveraged and the un-leveraged firm ($50,000 to $30,000) is relatively less than the impact of the de-crease in the number of common shares (10,000 to 5,000). (The number of shares decreased by 50 percent, and the NIAT decreased by 40 percent.)

B. The operating-profit return on the assets financed with debt exceeds the interest cost on the debt when positive financial leverage occurs.

Example: In the previous example, the cost of debt in the leveraged firm was 8 percent and the operating-profit return was 10 percent. The 2 percent difference is available to fewer shareholders in the leveraged firm, increasing EPS. Positive financial leverage always results in higher EPS for a firm using more debt in its capital structure as long as the operating-profit return on the assets financed with debt exceeds the interest cost on the debt.

C. Negative financial leverage occurs when the operating-profit return is less than the interest cost of debt, decreasing EPS.

Example: Consider the previous example of the leveraged and unleveraged firms. If the leveraged firm had to pay 12 percent interest on its debt, its EPS would de-cline, as shown below:

Leveraged Firm

Operating profit	$ 100,000
- Interest expense (12 percent)	- 60,000
= NIBT	$ 40,000
- Taxes (50 percent)	- 20,000
= NIAT	$ 20,000

$$\text{EPS} = \frac{\$20,000}{5,000 \text{ shares}} = \$4.00$$

$$\text{Operating-profit return} = \frac{\$100,000}{\$1,000,000} = 10 \text{ percent}$$

The leverage effect is negative, because the EPS of the leveraged firm is less than that of the unleveraged firm. This occurs because the interest charge on debt (12 percent) exceeds the operating-profit return (10 percent). This effect could also be illustrated by using a change in operating profits while the interest charge on debt remains the same. Any time the operating-profit return falls below the interest charge on debt, the financial leverage is negative.

     D.   Leveraged firms are more susceptible to greater variability in EPS than identical but less leveraged or unleveraged firms. This additional risk affects all the firm's sources of capital, including equity.

    Example: Let's continue with the example in I.A, where two firms are identical in all respects except for their leverage positions. Firm A is unleveraged, and firm B has 50 percent debt in its capital structure that requires $40,000 in interest payments. The following table indicates the EPS figures for each firm at various levels of operating profit. (Assume that Firm A has 20,000 shares of common stock outstanding, Firm B has 5,000 shares outstanding, and each firm's tax rate is 50 percent.)

Operating Profit	EPS, Unleveraged Firm A	EPS, Leveraged Firm B
$300,000	$15.00	$26.00
$200,000	10.00	16.00
$100,000	5.00	6.00
$ 50,000	2.50	1.00
$ 25,000	1.25	(3.00)

Note that, as operating profit varies from $25,000 to $300,000, EPS values vary from $1.25 to $15.00 for the unleveraged firm and from ($3.00) to $26.00 for the leveraged firm. Thus the range of the unleveraged firm ($13.75) is much less than the range of the leveraged firm ($29.00), indicating a lower degree of risk associated with the unleveraged firm. The increased variability of EPS due to financial leverage is called financial risk.

    1.   Stockholders of the leveraged firm incur a greater risk of not receiving their expected dividends than stockholders of the unleveraged firm. This additional risk is called financial risk, a basic component of stockholders' required return (k_e).

    2.   Both the firm's cost of equity capital and its cost of debt capital increase as financial leverage increases, because of greater financial risk. See the accompanying graph.

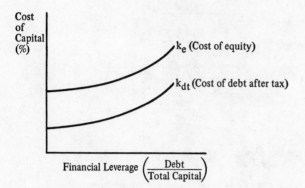

Therefore, financial leverage may have a positive or a negative impact on EPS and on the cost of all sources of capital. Although the direct cost of debt capital is the lowest of all, its total cost may be much higher because of its impact on the cost of equity capital.

E. Financial leverage affects the cost of debt capital by changing the investors' risk perceptions as additional debt is acquired relative to equity.

1. Increases in debt result in higher fixed obligations of the firm and, subsequently, in higher rate-of-return requirements of bond buyers. This occurs because the bankruptcy cushion (operating profit less interest expense) grows smaller as leverage is increased.

Example: Firm A uses no leverage. Firm B has $500,000 in 8 percent bonds. The following data apply.

Operating Profit for Both Firms	Interest Expense		Bankruptcy Cushion	
	A	B	A	B
$300,000	0	$40,000	$300,000	$260,000
200,000	0	40,000	200,000	160,000
100,000	0	40,000	100,000	60,000
50,000	0	40,000	50,000	10,000
25,000	0	40,000	25,000	(15,000)
0	0	40,000	0	(40,000)

Note that the probability that actual bankruptcy will occur is greater for firm B than for firm A. This increased probability of bankruptcy causes bond buyers to require a higher rate of return from firm B's bonds than from those of firm A.

2. As a firm issues additional debt, the claim that the more recent debt issue has on operating profit is typically of lower priority than that of more mature debt issues. Diminishing protective provisions and claim priorities increase the financial risk to investors, leading to a higher required rate of return.

3. Additional debt financing increases the complexity of <u>matching principal repayments with available cash flows</u>. Mismatching inflows and outflows can lead to greater difficulty in obtaining additional funds at a reasonable cost as the firm experiences changes in the business cycle. <u>Note</u>: In sum, the cost of both debt and equity capital increases as the proportion of debt in the capital structure increases.

II. The traditional approach to defining the optimal capital structure assumes that the firm's market value will be affected by the proper selection of debt and equity proportions. Proper balancing of these components minimizes the weighted average cost of capital and thereby maximizes the value of the firm.

A. <u>Minimizing the weighted average cost of capital</u> requires proper balancing of both the costs of various sources and the respective proportions of each capital source in the total capital structure. As the accompanying graph shows, there is a point (X) where balancing equity (k_e) and debt (k_{dt}) with their respective proportions leads to minimizing the weighted average cost of capital (k_a).

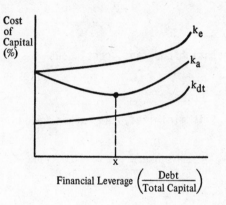

B. As long as the relative (percentage) decline in the cost of debt from the cost of equity exceeds the proportionate (percentage) change in financial leverage, the weighted average cost of capital will decline. However, k_a begins to increase when the proportionate increase in financial leverage exceeds the proportionate change in k_e and k_{dt}.

C. As the proportion of debt in the capital structure <u>increases</u>, several consequences follow.

1. There is a higher probability of variation in net profits.

2. Profits and losses are magnified.

3. The cost of debt capital increases.

4. The cost of equity capital increases.

5. The weighted average cost of capital declines to a point and then increases in a U-shaped curve.

6. Financial risk increases due to decreased coverage ratios, the imposition of greater operating restrictions on the firm, difficulties in matching repayment and cash-inflow schedules, and great variability in EPS.

D. The market value of the firm is maximized by minimizing the overall cost of capital.

1. The market value of the firm is the present value of its capital structure, or the discounted value of its equity and debt at the discount rates of k_d and k_e, respectively.

a. The market value of equity can be defined as

$$E = \frac{N}{k_e}$$

where

E = market value of equity

N = future earnings (representing constant, continuous dividends)

k_e = cost of equity capital

Thus, when the cost of equity (k_e) is minimized, the market value of equity increases.

Example: A firm has net earnings (N) of $100,000 (which are assumed to represent available dividends per year into infinity). The firm's owners have a required rate of return (k_e) of 12 percent. The market value of equity is

$$E = \frac{N}{k_e} = \frac{\$100,000}{.12} = \$833,333.33$$

If the required rate of return decreased to 8 percent, the market value of equity would increase to $1,250,000:

$$E = \frac{\$100,000}{.08} = \$1,250,000.00$$

b. The market value of debt (bonds) is defined as the sales price on new issues. Therefore, the market value of the firm is the sum of the market value of debt and the market value of equity.

Example: If the firm has $400,000 in 5 percent bonds selling at par ($1,000) and the market value of equity is $833,333.33, the market value of capital is

$400,000 + $833,333.33 = $1,233,333.33

Note that this figure ($1,233,333.33) represents what the firm's equity owners and bondholders have determined to be the value of the firm's future earnings, adjusted for risk.

        c. The <u>market value of the firm's capital</u> can be used to define the average cost of capital.

Example: Using the previous data and assuming no taxes, we find that the average cost of capital would be 9.73 percent:

$$k_a = \frac{400,000}{1,233,333.33} * .05 + \frac{833,333.33}{1,233,333.33} * .12 = 9.73\%$$

        d. An increase in the amount of debt used, without a change in the component costs (k_e, k_{dt}), would reduce the average cost of capital.

Example: Using the previous data, and still assuming no taxes, a change of capital structure to $600,000 in bonds reduces k_a to 8.89 percent:

Operating earnings	$120,000
- Interest (.05 * $600,000)	- 30,000
= Net earnings	$ 90,000
k_e	.12

$$\text{Market value of equity} = E = \frac{N}{k_e} = \frac{\$90,000}{.12} = \$750,000$$

Market value of debt is given as $600,000/$1,350,000. Therefore, the average cost of capital would be

$$k_a = \frac{\$600,000}{\$1,350,000} * .05 + \frac{\$750,000}{\$1,350,000} * .12 = 8.89\%$$

Note that, by changing the capital structure to use more debt (without allowing costs to vary), the financial management has caused the average cost of capital to decline while the value of the firm increases.

Summary of Examples

Prior to the Change in Capital Structure

Source	Cost	Market Value	Proportion	Average Cost of Capital
Bonds	5%	$400,000.00	.3243	k_a = 9.73%
Equity	12%	833,333.33	.6757	

After the Change in Capital Structure to More Debt

Source	Cost	Market Value	Proportion	Average Cost of Capital
Bonds	5%	$600,000	.4444	k_a = 8.89%
Equity	12%	750,000	.5556	

Although the operating earnings are the same in each case, the market value of the firm increases and k_a decreases as additional debt is used <u>without</u> additional costs.

      e. A point will be reached where the use of additional debt (relative to equity) will result in higher costs of both debt (k_{dt}) and equity (k_e), causing the weighted average cost of capital to increase and the value of the firm to decrease. (See the accompanying graphs.)

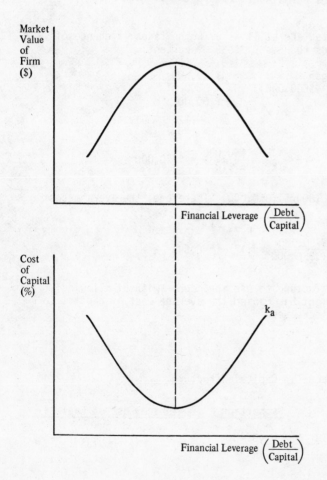

Therefore, the <u>optimal capital structure</u> (debt-to-capital ratio) maximizes the market value of the firm where the overall cost of capital is minimized.

    f.   <u>In practice</u>, it may not be possible to determine the <u>exact</u> debt-to-capital ratio that minimizes k_a. The k_a point of minimal cost is treated as a <u>range</u> of values over which the debt-to-capital ratio varies and the cost of capital is minimized. To the left of this range, the firm should sell debt; to the right of this range, it should sell equity. Movement within this range of debt-to-capital ratios should not be interpreted by investors as a change in the target leverage position.

III. <u>Opposition to the traditional approach</u> has been led by <u>Modigliani and Miller</u> <u>(M&M)</u>. The basic premise of M&M is that the financial officer <u>cannot</u> change the overall cost of capital, regardless of the amount of debt in the total capital structure.

  A. M&M make the following basic assumptions.

    1. Capital markets are perfect; there are no transaction costs, all investors have the same information, and borrowing and lending rates are the same for all investors.

    2. All investors have the same expectations.

    3. Business risk is equal among firms with similar operating environments.

    4. There are no taxes.

  B. Using these assumptions, M&M argue that investors adjust their individual holdings of stocks to reflect the degree of leverage they desire. Thus the firm's overall cost of capital will not change, regardless of the amount of leverage the firm acquires. Also assume the following:

    1. Individual investors will borrow to finance their purchases of stock if the firm does not use its own financial leverage.

    2. When a firm uses its financial leverage, individual investors do not create their own by borrowing to finance their purchases.

    3. There is an exact and identical trade-off between the firm's leverage position and that of the individual investor for all firms in the same risk class.

  C. According to the M&M proposition, two firms in the same operating risk class, with identical characteristics in every respect <u>except</u> for their debt-to-capital ratios (leverage position), must have the <u>same total</u> <u>market value</u>. If the market values differ, investors will sell shares in the overvalued (higher-market-value) firm and buy shares in the undervalued (lower-market-value) firm until a point is reached where the market values are equal.

D. Investors adjust the prices of shares to insure that total market values are equal for firms that differ only in their debt-to-capital ratios. This is achieved through <u>homemade leverage</u>. The process of creating homemade leverage is as follows:

1. Investors sell a portion of the overvalued firm.

2. Investors notice that the undervalued firm has less debt and thus less financial risk than the overvalued firm.

3. Investors then <u>borrow</u> funds in amounts that will equate the leverage positions of the firms.

4. Investors use the borrowed funds and the proceeds from the sale of the overvalued firm to purchase shares in the undervalued firm.

5. This process drives down the market price of the overvalued firm and increases the price of the undervalued firm until the return to both firms' stock is the same.

E. The process of forcing the returns of firms to equality results in a higher cost of capital for the overvalued firm (by decreasing its stock price) and a lower cost of capital for the undervalued firm (by increasing its stock price). Thus, <u>when investors use "homemade leverage," the capital structure of a firm is irrelevant</u> to determination of the cost of capital. Investors offset the firm's financial leverage with their own.

F. Several problems exist with the M&M argument, especially in their assumptions.

1. In practice, borrowing costs and the availability of funds are not the same among borrowers. Individuals cannot substitute their own homemade leverage at the <u>same</u> interest cost as the corporation. Ordinarily, the corporation would pay a lower interest cost than the individual, eliminating the tendency to use homemade leverage.

2. Institutional restrictions would make homemade leverage very difficult. Transaction costs, margin requirements, and other restrictions would make it difficult for individuals to borrow enough money to create homemade leverage.

3. The payment of <u>taxes</u> disrupts the M&M argument. Interest cost is tax-deductible, increasing the value of the firm because of the tax savings. Firms will never be identical in total market value, as M&M suggest, because of the varying tax effect of interest costs.

4. The claim of constant overall cost of capital does not hold in extreme leverage cases. M&M claim that an increase in the cost of equity capital is exactly offset by lower-cost debt capital. We know that this cannot hold in practice, because large degrees of leverage (risk) cause investors to insist on higher rates of return for debt and equity instruments.

CHAPTER 10

STUDY PROBLEMS

10.1. The Cramer Corporation is considering restructuring its capital by exchanging $2.5 million of newly issued 10 percent bonds with 20-year maturity for 50,000 shares of stock at $50 a share. The firm currently has 100,000 shares outstanding and no debt. The following financial statement (prior to restructuring capital) reflects its position.

Net operating income	$400,000
Interest expense	0
NIBT	$400,000
Taxes (50%)	200,000
NIAT	$200,000
EPS (100,000 shares)	$2.00

a. What will Cramer Corporation's EPS be after the exchange?

b. Have EPS increased or decreased? Why?

c. If net income before interest and taxes were $1,000,000, what would EPS have been (1) before the exchange and (2) after the exchange?

d. In part c, has there been positive or negative financial leverage? Why?

Solution

a. After the exchange:

Net operating income	$400,000
Interest expense	-250,000
NIBT	$150,000
Taxes	- 75,000
NIAT	$ 75,000

$$EPS = \frac{\$75,000}{50,000} \text{ shares} = \$1.50$$

b. EPS has decreased, because the interest paid on the new bonds (10 percent) exceeds the operating profit return of 8 percent (that is, $400,000 ÷ $500,000). Thus the cost of the new debt exceeds the cost savings of the exchanged equity, and negative financial leverage occurs.

c.

	Before Exchange	After Exchange
Net operating income	$1,000,000	$1,000,000
Interest expense	0	250,000
NIBT	$1,000,000	$ 750,000
Taxes	500,000	375,000
NIAT	$ 500,000	$ 375,000
EPS	$5.00	$7.50
	(100,000 shares)	(50,000 shares)

d. There has been positive leverage (EPS increased) because the interest cost of debt (10 percent) (after-tax) is less than the 5 percent operating return on capital (that is, $1,000,000 ÷ $50,000) replaced by the exchange.

189

10.2. Two firms operate in the same business environment with identical financial statements <u>except</u> for their capital structures. Firm A has a 70 percent long-term debt-to-capital ratio, and Firm B has a 20 percent long-term debt-to-capital ratio. The following data apply for each firm:

Total capital structure is $1,000,000.
All bonds outstanding charge a 6 percent interest rate (before-tax).
Common stock has a market value of $10 per share.
Tax rate is 40 percent for each firm.
Net operating income is $200,000 for each firm.

a. What are the EPS of each company?

b. What is the operating-profit return of each company?

c. What is the impact of financial leverage? Why?

d. At what point in interest costs would the leverage effect reverse?

Solution

a.

	Firm A (much leverage)	Firm B (little leverage)
Net operating income	$200,000	$200,000
Interest (6%)	- 42,000	- 12,000
NIBT	$158,000	$188,000
Taxes (40%)	- 63,200	- 75,200
NIAT	$ 94,800	$112,800

$$\text{EPS} \quad \frac{\$94,800}{\$300,000/\$10} = \$3.16 \qquad \frac{\$112,800}{\$800,000/\$10} = \$1.41$$

b. Operating-profit return $= \dfrac{\text{operating income}}{\text{total capital}}$

$$= \frac{\$200,000}{\$1,000,000} = 20\% \text{ for each}$$

c. Financial leverage is positive, because the cost of funds (6 percent) is much less than the operating-profit return (20 percent).

d. Positive leverage would occur until the interest charge exceeds the operating-profit return of 20 percent.

10.3. Consider the following data.

Firm X	Firm Y
Long-term debt-to-capital ratio = 0	Long-term debt-to-capital ratio = 80%
Total capital = $1,000,000	Total capital = $1,000,000
Shares outstanding = 20,000	Shares outstanding = 4,000
Tax rate = 35%	Tax rate = 35%
	Interest cost = 8%

a. If net operating income is $100,000, what are the EPS for each firm?

b. If net operating income is $80,000, what is the bankruptcy cushion of each firm?

c. How long could net operating income fall for each firm before bankruptcy occurred?

d. Which firm has the highest financial risk?

Solution

a.

	Firm X	Firm Y
Net operating income	$100,000	$100,000
Interest	- 0	- 64,000
NIBT	$100,000	$ 36,000
Taxes	- 35,000	- 12,600
NIAT	$ 65,000	$ 23,400
EPS	$3.25	$5.85
	(20,000 shares)	(4,000 shares)

b. Bankruptcy cushion = operating profits - interest expense. Firm X has a bankruptcy cushion of $80,000. Firm Y has a bankruptcy cushion of $16,000.

c. With no interest charges, Firm X could reduce net operating income to zero without immediate bankruptcy. With a fixed interest charge of $64,000, Firm Y must maintain a net operating income of at least $64,000 to avoid bankruptcy.

d. Firm Y has the higher financial risk, because it has the greater potential for bankruptcy.

10.4. What is the optimal capital structure (lowest average cost of capital) of the following four capital structures at prevailing market prices? Dividends are expected to grow at 9 percent per year, and 10,000 shares of preferred and 100,000 shares of common stock are outstanding; bonds are selling at $1,000 par value. (Hint: Use market value weights in this particular case.)

	Capital Structure			
	1	2	3	4
Debt	$6,000,000	$15,000,000	$25,000,000	$40,000,000
Preferred stock price	$100	$90	$80	$70
Common stock price	$8	$12	$9	$6
Retained earnings	$8,000,000	$8,000,000	$8,000,000	$8,000,000
Interest on debt	6%	8%	10%	16%
Dividend on preferred	$7	$7	$7	$7
Expected dividend on common	$1	$2	$2	$2
Tax rate	50%	50%	50%	50%

Solution

To find the average cost of capital, we must determine the respective capital costs and weights (w_i) of each type of capital. The weights (that is, the proportion that each capital source is of the total capital) for the four capital structures are as follows:

	Capital Structure #1	w_i	Capital Structure #2	w_i	Capital Structure #3	w_i	Capital Structure #4	w_i
Debt	$ 6,000,000	.38	$15,000,000	.60	$25,000,000	.72	$40,000,000	.81
Preferred stock	1,000,000	.06	900,000	.04	800,000	.02	700,000	.02
Common stock	800,000	.05	1,200,000	.05	900,000	.03	600,000	.01
Retained earnings	8,000,000	.51	8,000,000	.31	8,000,000	.23	8,000,000	.16
Total capital	$15,800,000	1.00	$25,100,000	1.00	$34,700,000	1.00	$49,300,000	1.00

The costs of the individual sources of capital for the four capital structures are as follows:

Formula	Capital Structure #1	Capital Structure #2	Capital Structure #3	Capital Structure #4
k_d	.06	.08	.10	.16
$k_p = \dfrac{D_o}{P_o}$	$7/$100 = .07	$7/$90 = .078	$7/$80 = .088	$7/$70 = .10
$k_e = \dfrac{D_1}{P_o} + g$	$\dfrac{\$1}{\$8}$ + .09 = .215	$\dfrac{\$2}{\$12}$ + .09 = .257	$\dfrac{\$2}{\$9}$ + .09 = .312	$\dfrac{\$2}{\$6}$ + .09 = .423

The k_a for the four capital structures are as follows:

#1: k_a = [.06(1 - .50) * .38] + (.07 * .06) + (.215 * .05) + (.215 * .51) = 13.6%

#2: k_a = [.08(1 - .50) * .60] + (.078 * .04) + (.257 * .05) + (.257 * .31) = 12%

#3: k_a = [.10(1 - .50) * .72] + (.088 * .02) + (.312 * .03) + (.312 * .23) = 11.9%

#4: k_a = [.16(1 - .50) * .81] + (.10 * .02) + (.423 * .01) + (.423 * .16) = 13.9%

Answer: Capital structure number 3 is the optimal capital structure.

10.5. Consider the following information.

    Debt $20,000
    Common stock 10,000 shares
    Dividends per share $2.00 (expected)
    Earnings per share $3.00
    Expected annual growth in dividends is 10%
    k_e = 20%

a. What is the expected stock price of the company?

b. If the company increased its use of debt to $60,000, decreased its use of stock to 8,000 shares, increased the expected dividend to $2.32, reduced its expected growth in dividends to 8 percent, and increased k_e to 24 percent, what would be the impact on the share price? Why?

Solution

a. To solve for P_0, use the formula

$$k_e = \frac{D_1}{P_0} + g$$

$$P_0 = \frac{D_1}{k_e - g} = \frac{\$2.00}{.20 - .10} = \frac{\$2.00}{.10} = \underline{\$20.00}$$

b. $P_0 = \dfrac{D_1}{k_e - g} = \dfrac{\$2.32}{.24 - .08} = \dfrac{\$2.32}{.16} = \underline{\$14.50}$

The new share price declines to $14.50, because the cost of equity capital increased to reflect the higher financial risk of more debt financing.

10.6. NEWS, Inc., has two alternative capital structures from which to choose, as outlined in the following table.

	Capital Structure	
	A	B
Debt 10%, 20-year maturity	$6,000,000	0
Debt 8%, 2-year maturity	0	$6,000,000
Common stock (100,000 shares)	$4,000,000	$4,000,000
Retained earnings	$4,000,000	$4,000,000
Dividends per share (expected)	$5.00	$5.00
Stock price	$40.00	$40.00
Expected dividend growth per year	8%	8%
Tax rate	40%	40%

a. What is the average cost of capital for each capital structure?

b. If the capital structure were being selected to finance a project, how would the expected life of the project affect the selection?

Solution

The weights (w_i) to find k_a for the two capital structures are as follows:

Capital Source	Capital Structure A	w_i	Capital Structure B	w_i
Debt 10%	$6,000,000	.430	0	.000
Debt 8%	0	.000	$6,000,000	.430
Common stock	4,000,000	.285	4,000,000	.285
Retained earnings	4,000,000	.285	4,000,000	.285
Total capital	$14,000,000	1.000	$14,000,000	1.000

The cost of the individual sources of capital for the two capital structures are:

	Capital Structure A	Capital Structure B
k_d	.10	.08
k_e	$\frac{\$5}{\$40} + .08 = .205$	$\frac{\$5}{\$40} + .08 = .205$
k_{re}	.205	.205

The weighted average costs of the two capital structures are as follows:

a. Capital structure A:
   $k_a = [.10(1 - .4) * .430] + (.205 * .285) + (.205 * .285) = 14.27\%$

   Capital structure B:
   $k_a = [.08(1 - .4) * .430] + (.205 * .285) + (.205 * .285) = 13.75\%$

b. If the project's life were 20 years, we would select capital structure A. Although this structure has the higher average cost, there would be a greater chance of insolvency if the 2-year maturity debt in capital structure B were used. This points out the fact that financial officers must use their projections of future capital costs as part of every decision about current capital structure. The calculation of current k_a values may not yield sufficient information.

10.7. TRIXY Corporation is interested in purchasing a new product line that will cost $5,000,000 and return 20 percent before taxes. The last balance sheet and income statement for TRIXY Corporation are as follows:

BALANCE SHEET

Current assets	$ 800,000	Current liabilities	$ 400,000
Fixed assets	10,000,000	Debt	1,400,000
Total assets	$10,800,000	Preferred stock	0
		Equity (100,000 shares)	9,000,000
		Total	$10,800,000

INCOME STATEMENT

Earnings before interest and taxes	$ 612,000
Interest	- 112,000
Earnings before taxes	$ 500,000
Taxes (50%)	- 250,000
Net income after taxes	$ 250,000
EPS	$ 2.50

Three financing alternatives are available for acquisition of the $5,000,000 project. Alternative 1 is to sell common stock at $50.00 per share. Alternative 2 is to sell bonds at par ($1,000 each), with an 8 percent interest rate and a 20-year maturity. Alternative 3 is to sell preferred stock at par ($100 each), with a 9 percent yield.

a. What are the EPS under each financing alternative?

b. Which alternative would you select? Why?

Solution

a.

	Financing Alternatives		
	1 (common)	2 (bond)	3 (preferred)
Current EBIT	$ 612,000	$ 612,000	$ 612,000
Additional EBIT (.20 * $5,000,000)	1,000,000	1,000,000	1,000,000
Total EBIT	$1,612,000	$1,612,000	$1,612,000
Interest: old	- 112,000	- 112,000	- 112,000
new	0	- 400,000	0
EBT	$1,500,000	$1,100,000	$1,500,000
Taxes (50 percent)	- 750,000	- 550,000	- 750,000
NIAT	$ 750,000	$ 550,000	$ 750,000
Preferred dividends	0	0	- 450,000
Earnings available to common	$ 750,000	$ 550,000	$ 300,000
Shares outstanding	200,000	100,000	100,000
EPS	$3.75	$5.50	$3.00

b. The bond financing scheme results in the highest EPS, but it also has the highest level of financial risk. Both common stock and preferred stock alternatives have a more dilutive effect on EPS, but the firm's financial risk is reduced. There is no clear choice. The firm must weigh the expected EPS of each alternative against the financial risk.

10.8. PR, Inc., can select either of the following capital structures.

	X	Y
Debt	$30,000	$10,000
Equity	10,000	30,000

a. What is the weighted average cost of capital under X if the after-tax cost of debt (k_{dt}) is 10 percent and the cost of equity (k_e) is 15 percent?

b. What is the weighted average cost of capital under Y if the after-tax cost of debt (k_{dt}) is 6 percent and the cost of equity (k_e) is 10 percent?

Solution

a. $k_X = (.10 * .75) + (.15 * .25) = 11.25\%$

b. $k_Y = (.06 * .25) + (.10 * .75) = 9.00\%$

REVIEW QUESTIONS

1. Financial leverage refers to
   a. the amount of current assets held.
   b. the amount of current liabilities held.
   c. the proportion of long-term debt in the firm's total capital.
   d. the total capital structure.
   e. none of these.

2. Positive financial leverage occurs when
   a. more leverage is used in the capital structure.
   b. less leverage is used in the capital structure.
   c. the leveraged firm's EPS exceeds the unleveraged firm's EPS when other characteristics of the firms are the same.
   d. none of these.

3. When the operating-profit return on the assets financed with debt exceeds the interest cost on the debt
   a. negative financial leverage occurs.
   b. positive financial leverage occurs.
   c. financial leverage is of no consequence.
   d. EPS will be decreased.
   e. none of these.

4. Leveraged firms are _____ susceptible to variability in EPS than(as) identical but unleveraged firms.
   a. more
   b. less
   c. as

5. Compared to stockholders of unleveraged firms, stockholders of leveraged firms are incurring _____ risk of not receiving their expected dividends.
   a. less
   b. greater
   c. an equal

6. The firm's cost of equity capital generally _____ as its financial leverage increases.
   a. decreases
   b. remains constant
   c. neither of these

7. The bankruptcy cushion of a firm indicates
   a. the difference between current assets and current liabilities.
   b. the excess of net after-tax profit over fixed charges.
   c. the excess of total assets over fixed charges.
   d. the difference between operating profits and interest expense.
   e. none of these.

8. Risk prevention and the cost of debt capital can change as additional financial leverage is used because of
   a. changes in the bankruptcy cushion.
   b. diminishing protective provisions and claim priorities.
   c. difficulties in matching principal repayments with cash inflows.
   d. all of these.
   e. none of these.

9. The traditional approach to management of capital structure assumes that
   a. no taxes exist.
   b. perfect capital markets exist.
   c. the firm's market value is affected by the firm's capital structure.
   d. the cost of capital cannot be controlled.

10. When the weighted average cost of capital is minimized
    a. the market value of the firm is maximized.
    b. the market value of the firm is minimized.
    c. the market value of the equity is minimized.
    d. none of these.

11. As the proportion of debt in the capital structure increases
    a. the cost of debt capital increases.
    b. the cost of equity decreases.
    c. the cost of equity increases.
    d. financial risk decreases.
    e. both a and c.

12. When the debt-to-capital ratio of the firm moves above its optimal point
    a. debt costs increase.
    b. only equity costs increase.
    c. both debt costs and equity costs increase.
    d. financial risk is reduced.

13. In practice, a _____ of various debt-to-capital ratios results in only insignificant changes in investor perception and in the average cost of capital.
    a. group
    b. range
    c. point estimate
    d. none of these

14. The Modigliani and Miller (M&M) approach to capital structure suggests that
    a. managing debt proportions is one way to minimize the cost of capital.
    b. investors have divergent views on the future.
    c. taxes are 50 percent.
    d. the financial officer cannot manipulate the overall cost of capital through changes in capital structure.
    e. none of these.

15. "Homemade leverage" refers to
    a. a corporation borrowing from other corporations.
    b. investors borrowing funds to purchase shares of undervalued firms, thereby creating equivalent leverage positions.
    c. eliminating taxes.
    d. creating additional debt in each firm purchased.

16. M&M argues that the use of _____ by rational investors makes the capital structure of a firm irrelevant.
    a. tax savings
    b. growth stocks
    c. homemade leverage
    d. perfect information
    e. none of these

17. The M&M proposition assumes that
    a. capital markets are perfect (without taxes).
    b. business risk is equal among like firms.
    c. all investors have the same expectations.
    d. all of these.
    e. none of these.

18. One of the major problems with the M&M argument is that
    a. capital structures are constant over time.
    b. the cost of capital is constant over time.
    c. institutional restrictions make the use of homemade leverage very difficult (or impossible).
    d. all of these.
    e. none of these.

19. M&M claim that
    a. an increase in the cost of equity capital is exactly offset by lower-cost debt capital.
    b. an increase in the cost of equity capital is not affected by the use of lower-cost debt.
    c. taxes are important considerations in capital structure.
    d. all of these.
    e. none of these.

20. The more accepted, traditional approach to the theory of capital structure differs from the M&M approach in recognizing that
    a. minimizing the cost of capital maximizes the value of the firm.
    b. adjusting the capital structure affects the overall cost of capital.
    c. taxes are important factors in decisions affecting capital structure and the cost of capital.
    d. all of these
    e. none of these.

KEY DEFINITIONS

<u>Bankruptcy cushion</u>: operating profits less interest expense.

<u>Financial leverage</u>: the proportion of long-term debt used by the firm in its total capital.

<u>Financial risk</u>: the risk that shareholders will not receive their expected dividends or interest payments.

<u>Homemade leverage</u>: the position that, according to the M&M premise, investors create for themselves as they operate in perfect markets, without taxes or transaction costs, to borrow funds to invest. In this view, the leverage position of the firm is irrelevant.

<u>Market value of equity (E)</u>: net earnings divided by the cost of equity capital. This figure represents investors' valuation of the firm's future earnings adjusted for risk. A special case of the dividend valuation model that assumes that all future earnings are paid as dividends and are constant.

<u>Market value of the firm</u>: the market value of debt plus the market value of equity (B + E); the present value of the firm's capital.

<u>Modigliani and Miller (M&M)</u>: an approach to capital structure that assumes that investors use homemade leverage in place of the firm's use of leverage. It maintains that the firm's capital structure cannot affect its cost of capital and market value. Thus the financial officer cannot change the overall cost of capital by financial leverage.

<u>Negative financial leverage</u>: condition prevailing when the EPS of the leveraged firm are less than the EPS of the unleveraged firm (operating-profits return is less than the cost of debt).

<u>Operating profit return</u>: net operating income divided by total capital.

<u>Optimal capital structure</u>: that ratio of long-term debt to total capital that minimizes the overall cost of capital and maximizes the market value of the firm.

<u>Positive financial leverage</u>: condition prevailing when the EPS of the leveraged firm exceed the EPS of the unleveraged firm (operating-profit return exceeds cost of debt).

<u>Unleveraged firm</u>: a firm without long-term debt.

ANSWERS TO REVIEW QUESTIONS

1. c	6. c	11. e	16. c
2. c	7. d	12. c	17. d
3. b	8. d	13. b	18. c
4. a	9. c	14. d	19. a
5. b	10. a	15. b	20. d

Chapter Eleven
Dividend Policy

OVERVIEW

   Managing the dividend policy of a firm is an exercise in compromise. This chapter examines the conflicting viewpoints of shareholders, who expect dividends, and the corporation, which attempts to minimize its cost of capital and reinvest earnings. Investor expectations can also shift from periods of high expectation to periods in which shareholders expect the firm to retain earnings to meet growth objectives. Factors affecting the dividend policy of the firm (cash dividends or stock dividends) are examined from the viewpoint of both investor and corporation.

STUDY OBJECTIVES

1. To define the mechanics of dividend payments.

2. To summarize the common dividend policies used by the corporation.

3. To outline factors that are considered in setting dividend policies.

4. To determine the relationship between dividends and share prices.

5. To evaluate the impact of stock dividends and that of cash dividends on share prices and ownership position.

CHAPTER OUTLINE

   I. The financial officer is usually responsible for implementing the firm's dividend policy. Several steps are involved in making dividend payments.

      A. The board of directors meets to determine the dividend payment, if any. If dividends are to be paid, a <u>declaration</u> statement is issued specifying the dollar amount of the dividend, the date it was declared, the date it will be paid, and who is entitled to receive it. The declaration statement indicates the date on which the registrar examines the stockholder records to determine which shareholders receive the dividend.

B. The transfer of ownership is a common practice. To facilitate the administrative process, the stock sells <u>ex-dividend</u> four business days prior to the date of record. For example, if the date of record is December 12, 1980 (a Friday), the ex-dividend date is December 8, 1980.

II. Corporations today commonly adhere to one of several basic policies.

A. Many financial analysts believe that investors favor <u>stable dividends</u> that are always greater than or equal to the dividend paid in the previous period. Investors view this dividend stream as more certain, which boosts the price they are willing to pay for the stock and reduces the firm's cost of equity capital.

   1. Many regulated institutions that purchase large quantities of stocks are restricted to purchasing those with a record of continuous and stable dividends.

   2. Most analysts believe that investors view changes in dividends as a source of information about the firm's profitability. Stable dividends bolster the image of the company as stable. Increasing dividends indicate permanent upswings in earnings, whereas a decrease indicates an unfavorable change in the earnings outlook.

B. Other analysts suggest the use of a stable <u>payout ratio</u>. This policy maintains the same percentage of net profit after taxes each year, but dividends per share fluctuate and may decrease the investor's valuation of the firm. Combining the policy that favors a stable payout ratio with the policy that favors stable dividends can lead to a <u>target-dividend</u> policy that maintains a cushion for periods of decreased earnings.

C. The <u>policy of extra dividends</u> refers to the declaration of dividends at the end of the year (in addition to the regular dividend) in recognition of extraordinary earnings performance. This creates a "bonus" perception among investors and mitigates the problem of increasing the <u>regular</u> dividend in good years and reducing it in other accounting periods.

D. A small number of firms use a <u>residual-dividend policy</u> that pays out whatever remains after the firm's capital needs are satisfied. This can lead to a volatile dividend payout and subsequent investor dissatisfaction.

III. Many other factors are important in the decision about dividend policy.

A. <u>Ability to borrow</u> can affect dividend policy. A more liberal dividend policy may be adopted by firms with easy access to capital.

B. <u>Liquidity</u> conditions affect dividend policy. When excess liquidity exists, the firm may consider a more liberal payout policy.

C. The board of directors may retain large portions of earnings to avoid selling more voting stock to the public, diluting their control.

D. <u>Taxes</u> can affect dividend policy.

   1. Federal taxing authorities can impose tax penalties on firms that have excessively retained earnings to avoid paying personal taxes on dividends.

2. Firms typically attract investor groups with homogeneous tax positions. Groups in high tax brackets want the firm to retain earnings to eventually lead to higher stock prices and lower capital-gains taxes. Groups in lower tax brackets are interested in receiving dividends and paying taxes on unearned revenue rather than incurring the uncertainty associated with achieving capital gains.

E. Low payout ratios are desired by the firm when a large number of acceptable projects are available. Retaining earnings to invest in projects is more convenient and less costly than acquiring new equity. This approach also keeps the debt-to-equity ratio of the capital structure in line, increasing the base on which the firm can borrow additional funds in the future.

F. Existing loan restrictions may limit the firm's ability to pay dividends, increasing the reinvestment of earnings. Reinvesting earnings decreases the leverage position of the firm, creating a larger cushion for existing lenders. Restrictions can apply to the declaration of new dividends, increased dividends, or dollar amount of retained earnings required before the firm can declare a dividend.

G. Several states regulate the payment of dividends when such payments will impair the firm's capital position (capital = common stock + additional paid-in capital).

1. The firm is limited to making dividend payments out of its retained earnings (not more than existing retained earnings).

2. The state may prohibit a firm from borrowing funds to pay dividends.

3. If the firm is currently insolvent, it cannot pay dividends until creditor claims have been satisfied.

H. When the early repayment of debt is more desirable than the declaration of a dividend, funds may be retained to pay off the debt.

I. During periods of rapid inflation, some firms look to retained earnings as a means of making up the difference between depreciation-generated funds and the funds required to replace old assets. Thus their dividend policy would be conservative.

J. A firm may choose to retain earnings rather than declare dividends in order to repurchase shares from existing stockholders.

1. EPS should increase after repurchase, because net earnings remain the same while the numeber of shares outstanding decreases. (This could lead to an increase in market prices.)

2. Share repurchase offers several advantages.

a. The selling stockholder pays a tax on capital gains rather than the higher regular income tax on dividends.

b. The firm can use repurchased shares for acquisition, exercise of stock options, or future resale without the need for a new issue.

     c. Repurchased shares are removed from the possible control of un-
friendly hands.

     d. Exchanges of repurchased shares for debt can increase financial
leverage.

   3. Share repurchase also has several <u>disadvantages</u>.

     a. Existing shareholders may prefer dividends to repurchase.

     b. The reduced number of shares outstanding may decrease trading
activity, reducing marketability.

     c. Share repurchase may decrease growth prospects by shifting the
reinvestment of funds or acquisitions to repurchase.

     d. Control of the firm shifts to fewer individuals.

     e. Repurchases usually occur at prices higher than the current market
price, which is expensive and can result in legal problems.

IV. <u>Dividend policy affects</u> investors' expectations of growth and risk, thereby
affecting the firm's <u>share price</u>.

  A. <u>Stable dividends tend to result in increased share prices</u>. This approach
avoids the reduction of dividends and the negative impact it has on share
price.

  B. <u>Increasing dividends creates the perception of prosperity</u>. Shareholders
may acquire stock to participate in the expected earnings growth, placing
upward pressure on the stock price. Increasing the dividend yield also
helps the stock compete with investment alternatives during varying market conditions.

  C. When investors favor growth over current dividends, higher stock prices
should follow the reinvestment of retained earnings in the asset base of
the firm. Thus investor expectations of growth in earnings increase.

  D. Reinvesting retained earnings instead of paying dividends is expected to
place upward pressure on stock prices. Downward pressure also occurs due
to the increased uncertainty of realizing the expected dividends and the
risk that growth (and capital gains) will not occur.

  E. <u>Investors have not exhibited a clear preference for dividends or retained
earnings</u>. Dividends are often preferred when interest rates are rising,
stock prices declining, and earnings prospects uncertain. However, investors prefer earnings to be retained and reinvested when the firm has
superior investment opportunities. The ability of the corporate board
of directors to accurately match corporate goals, dividend policy, and
investor preferences can lead to favorable pressure on stock prices.

  F. Automatic dividend reinvestment can potentially satisfy investors who
demand dividends <u>and</u> investors who want growth. Under this method,
<u>dividends are automatically reinvested in newly issued shares</u> of the
firm, without commission. The firm reinvests earnings in projects for

growth, while the stockholder increases his or her ownership shares and subsequent dividends and capital gains.

V. Stock dividends represent returns to shareholders in the form of additional shares instead of cash. Financial officers investigate the impact of stock dividends on the accounting books, the stock price, and other factors before choosing what dividend policy to follow.

A. Both stock dividends and cash dividends must be paid out of retained earnings. However, stock dividends are charged to retained earnings at the current market price of the stock. The mechanics of declaring stock dividends are as follows:

1. Increase the common-stock account by the number of additional shares times the stock's par value.

2. Add to the paid-in capital account the difference between the market value of the stock dividend and the par-value adjustment.

3. Reduce the retained-earnings account by the total market value of the stock dividend. The net effect on the dollar amount of a stockholder's equity has been absolutely zero.

B. When a stock dividend is paid, previously reported EPS figures must be adjusted to provide a reasonable comparison, as follows:

$$\text{Adjusted EPS} = \frac{E_0}{1 + D_s}$$

where

E_0 = the original earnings per share

D_s = the stock dividend rate

Example: A firm pays a 20 percent stock dividend (to 600,000 shares). The original EPS were $2.20 (when 500,000 shares were outstanding).

$$\text{Adjusted EPS} = \frac{2.20}{1 + .20} = \$1.83$$

The $1.83 EPS figure can be reasonably compared to subsequent EPS announcements, because it reflects the current number of shares outstanding. Future EPS figures will not be adjusted.

C. Stock dividends result in adjustments to stock prices. The ex-dividend price is adjusted as follows:

$$\text{Adjusted share price} = \frac{M}{1 + D_s}$$

where

M = the ex-dividend market price

D_s = the stock dividend rate

Example: If the ex-dividend price of the stock is $42.00, a 20 percent stock dividend would result in an adjusted share price of

$$\text{Adjusted share price} = \frac{\$42.00}{1 + .20} = \$35.00$$

Note that a shareholder's total value does not change. The new ownership position is 1.20 shares for each one held, so the value of a shareholder's investment, ex-dividend, is

($35.00 * 1.20) = $42.00

which is the original ownership position. Proportional ownership in the firm does not change when a stock dividend is paid.

    D. Stock dividends offer some advantages to stockholders.

        1. They are not taxed when received.

        2. They are taxed at the capital-gains rate when sold.

        3. Increased ownership can occur when the dividend is sold by some of the present stockholders.

        4. Marketability of the stock can be improved.

        5. The total cash payment to dividends is increased for the firm that currently pays dividends.

    E. Issuing stock dividends can also be advantageous to the firm.

        1. It preserves cash and yet provides something to shareholders.

        2. It communicates the concern of the board of directors with shareholder interests.

STUDY PROBLEMS

11.1. Wilomax, Inc., has declared the payment of a quarterly dividend on common stock, payable March 15, 19X1 to stockholders of record at the close of business on March 1, 19X1. How long can current shareholders sell their stock and still receive the dividend declared?

Solution

Shareholders can sell any time on or after the ex-dividend date of March 11 (assuming that no holidays or weekends occur between March 11 and March 15) and still receive the dividend.

11.2. Mono, Inc., had earnings of $3.25 per share this year prior to declaring a 20 percent stock dividend.

a. What will the EPS be after the dividend?

b. If the firm reported an EPS figure of $2.50 two years ago, what is the EPS figure after adjusting for the latest stock dividend?

Solution

a. $\dfrac{\$3.25}{1 + .20}$ = $2.71 per share

b. $\dfrac{\$2.50}{1 + .20}$ = $2.08 per share

11.3. Colortrain, Inc., is evaluating its dividend policy. It is currently paying a $.20 quarterly dividend. Last year's earnings per share were $3.20, and the current market price of the stock is $14.00 per share. Using the present payout ratio, the board of directors anticipates a 10 percent rate of growth in dividends per share. If the payout ratio is increased 6 percentage points, the growth rate in dividends per share is expected to decrease to 9 percent. Similar firms, with the same payout ratio as Colortrain, have a dividend yield of 7 percent. Firms with a payout ratio 6 percentage points higher have a dividend yield of 9 percent. (Assume that the capital structure does not change.)

a. What is the present payout ratio?

b. What is the cost of common-stock capital with the present payout ratio?

c. The payout ratio is increased 6 percentage points.

   1. What is the cost of common equity?

   2. What is the stock price likely to be in relation to other companies <u>after</u> the increased stock dividend?

   3. What is the cost of common equity, based on your answer to part 2?

Solution

a. Payout = $\dfrac{\$.20 \ast 4}{\$3.20}$ = 25%

b. Cost of equity = $k_e = \dfrac{D_1}{P_o} + g = \dfrac{\$.80}{\$14.00} + .10 = 15.71\%$

c. New dividend = (.25 + .06) * $3.20 = $.99

   1. $k_e = \dfrac{\$.99}{\$14.00} + .09 = 16.07\%$

   2. $.07 = \dfrac{\$.99}{P_o}$

      $P_o = \$14.143$

   3. $k_e = \dfrac{\$.99}{\$14.143} + .09 = 16\%$

<u>11.4.</u> POLYWAY, Inc., has 14 million shares of common stock outstanding.

a. How many shares will POLYWAY have after declaring a 12.5 percent stock dividend?

b. If the EPS figure before the dividend is $4.22, what will it be after the 12.5 percent stock dividend is declared?

<u>Solution</u>

a. 14 + (14 * .125) = 15.75 million shares

b. $\dfrac{\$4.22}{1 + .125} = \dfrac{\$4.22}{1.125} = \$3.75$

<u>11.5.</u> POLYWAY stock sells for $20.00 per share. What will the share price be on the ex-dividend date after the 12.5 percent stock dividend?

<u>Solution</u>

Adjusted stock price = $\dfrac{\$20.00}{1 + .125} = \$17.78$

<u>11.6.</u> You own 5,000 shares of Zero, Inc. Zero had 100,000 shares outstanding prior to declaring a 20 percent stock dividend.

a. How many shares do you own after the dividend?

b. What percentage of the firm do you own before the dividend? after the dividend?

<u>Solution</u>

a. Total after dividend = 5,000 * (1 + .20) = 6,000

b. Ownership before dividend = $\dfrac{5,000}{100,000}$ = 5%

   Ownership after dividend = $\dfrac{6,000}{120,000}$ = 5%

   Thus a stock dividend does not alter an investor's percentage share of the firm's outstanding stock.

<u>11.7.</u> Horngrin, Inc., had earnings per share and stock dividends as shown in the following table.

Year	Reported EPS	Stock Dividend
19X0	$3.00	10%
19X9	2.80	5%
19X8	2.40	5%
19X7	2.20	10%

What would be the adjusted earnings per share each year?

Solution

19X0 $\frac{\$3.00}{1.10}$ = $2.73   19X8 $\frac{\$2.60}{1.05}$ = $2.48

19X9 $\frac{\$2.73}{1.05}$ = $2.60   19X7 $\frac{\$2.48}{1.10}$ = $2.25

11.8 Consider the following information.

Year	Cash Dividends per Share	Stock Dividend
19X0	$1.50	5%
19X9	1.50	5%
19X8	1.50	5%
19X7	1.50	5%

a. What is the adjusted cash dividend per share for each year?

b. If you owned and held 1,000 shares of the stock since 19X7, what total dollar amount of cash dividends did you receive?

Solution

a. 19X0 = $\frac{\$1.50}{1.05}$ = $1.43   19X8 = $\frac{\$1.36}{1.05}$ = $1.30

   19X9 = $\frac{\$1.43}{1.05}$ = $1.36   19X7 = $\frac{\$1.30}{1.05}$ = $1.23

b. Per-share return = $1.00 * $(1.05)^4$ = $1.00 * 1.21551 = $1.21551

   For 1,000 shares = 1,000 * 1.21551 = $1,215.51

REVIEW QUESTIONS

1. The declaration date of a dividend announcement is
   a. the day the dividend will be paid.
   b. the day the records are searched to determine ownership.
   c. the day the declaration statement is announced.
   d. none of these.

2. The ex-dividend date is
   a. the day after which the stock sells without the benefit of a declared dividend.
   b. the day the share owners are declared.
   c. four business days prior to the date of record.
   d. both a and c.

3. Investors are said to view a _____ dividend policy as more certain, thereby _____ the price they are willing to pay for the shares.
   a. stable, decreasing
   b. stable, increasing
   c. growth, decreasing
   d. both a and c

4. Many regulated institutions that purchase stocks are restricted to the purchase of
   a. low-priced stocks.
   b. stocks that pay no dividends.
   c. stocks that have a history of paying continuous, stable dividends.
   d. large quantities of low P/E stocks.

5. The _____ approach will retain the same percentage of net profit after
taxes each year, but dividends per share will vary.
   a. constant-dollar-dividends
   b. continuous-growth
   c. residual-dividend
   d. stable-payout-ratio

6. The _____ pays out whatever remains after capital requirements are satisfied, but it can lead to volatile dividends and investor dissatisfaction.
   a. residual-dividend policy
   b. stable-dividend policy
   c. continuous-growth dividend policy
   d. none of these

7. Which of the following factors is (are) considered in managing the firm's
dividend policy?
   a. liquidity
   b. ability of the firm to borrow
   c. control dilution
   d. taxes
   e. all of these

8. Firms typically attract investor groups that have _____ tax positions.
   a. homogeneous
   b. heterogeneous
   c. low
   d. none of these

9. Which of the following factors may limit the amount of dividends paid?
   a. the number of shareholders
   b. existing loan restrictions
   c. the number of acceptable projects available
   d. legal (state) regulations
   e. b, c, and d

10. During periods of rapid inflation, some firms concentrate on _____ as a
means of maintaining the value of productive/depreciable assets.
    a. dividend income
    b. the use of retained earnings
    c. new equity
    d. all of these

11. When a firm repurchases shares from existing shareholders
    a. EPS should decrease.
    b. EPS should increase.
    c. the value of the firm increases.
    d. none of these.

12. Repurchasing shares has the advantage of
    a. obtaining shares to use in acquisitions.
    b. decreasing the tax liability of the firm.
    c. decreasing exposure to external, undesirable control.
    d. both a and c.
    e. both b and c.

13. The disadvantages of share repurchase include
    a. possible decreased trading activity in the stock.
    b. the shift of control to larger numbers of investors.
    c. increased growth prospects through reinvestment of earnings.
    d. all of these.

14. Stable dividends tend to result in _____ share prices.
    a. decreased
    b. increased
    c. stable

15. Increasing the dividend yield helps the stock
    a. compete with investment alternatives during varying market conditions.
    b. by facilitating the repurchase of more shares.
    c. by decreasing investor trading.
    d. none of these.

16. Investors have exhibited a clear preference for _____ over _____.
    a. dividends, retained earnings
    b. retained earnings, dividends
    c. cash dividends, repurchase of shares
    d. none of these

17. _____ has the potential of satisfying investors who demand dividends and investors who require growth.
    a. Stock repurchase
    b. Automatic dividend reinvestment
    c. Declaring stock dividends
    d. None of these

18. Both stock dividends and cash dividends must be paid out of
    a. cash.
    b. paid-in capital.
    c. retained earnings.
    d. none of these.

19. The net effect of a stock dividend on the dollar amount of a stockholder's equity is
    a. an increase in ownership.
    b. a decrease in treasury stock.
    c. absolutely zero.
    d. the same as the percentage of the dividend payment.

20. Stock dividends have the advantage of
    a. being nontaxable when received.
    b. improving marketability of the stock.
    c. increasing cash payment to dividends.
    d. all of these.

KEY DEFINITIONS

Adjusted EPS: the EPS that reflects the effect of a stock dividend, $E_0/(1 + D_s)$.

Adjusted share price: the stock price that reflects the effect of a stock dividend $M/(1 + D_s)$.

Automatic dividend reinvestment: the automatic reinvestment of dividends in newly issued shares of the firm.

Date of record: the day the registrar establishes ownership of the shares on which the dividends will be paid.

Declaration statement: account of the details of a dividend payment to be made in the future.

Ex-dividend date: four days prior to the date of record, after which new stock-holders are no longer eligible for the most recently declared dividend.

Payout ratio: ratio of dividends per share to earnings per share.

Payout-ratio dividend policy: the policy of retaining the same percentage of net profit after taxes by using a stable payout ratio.

Policy of extra dividends: the policy of paying a "bonus" dividend at the end of the year in recognition of extraordinary earnings performance.

Repurchase of shares: the firm's use of retained earnings to buy shares back from existing stockholders, thereby artificially increasing EPS.

Residual-dividend policy: the policy of paying out whatever remains after the firm's capital needs are satisfied.

Stable-dividends policy: the policy of always paying the same dollar dividend, regardless of earnings.

Stock dividends: returns to shareholders in the form of additional shares rather than cash.

ANSWERS TO REVIEW QUESTIONS

1. c	6. a	11. b	16. d
2. d	7. e	12. d	17. b
3. b	8. a	13. a	18. c
4. c	9. e	14. b	19. c
5. d	10. b	15. a	20. d

Part Four
Working Capital Management

In all firms, regardless of size, a significant amount of the financial officer's attention is devoted to managing the firm's working capital investment. In
addition to examining the objectives of working capital management, Chapter 12
investigates methods available to the firm for improving its cash management and
discusses various types of marketable securities in which idle cash balances can
be invested. Chapter 13 covers the basic principles of inventory and accounts
receivable management.

Chapter Twelve
Cash and Marketable Securities

OVERVIEW

A firm's working capital investment in current assets provides the firm with the liquidity it needs to conduct its normal business activities. However, this working-capital investment is not without related costs. Therefore, the objective of working-capital management is to balance the firm's need for liquidity against these costs. One important aspect of working-capital management involves determining optimal cash balances and acting to minimize these balances. Financial managers must also be aware of appropriate investments in which temporarily idle cash balances can be invested to enhance the firm's profitability without jeopardizing its liquidity.

STUDY OBJECTIVES

1. To examine both the uses of working capital and the objectives of working-capital management.

2. To investigate techniques available to the firm for improving its cash management.

3. To probe the various types of marketable securities in which the firm can invest its idle cash balances.

CHAPTER OUTLINE

 I. Working capital and its uses

   A. Working capital is the firm's investment in current assets such as cash, marketable securities, accounts receivable, and inventory. Net working capital is the firm's current assets minus its current liabilities.

   B. The primary motive for the firm's working-capital investment is to provide the firm with sufficient liquidity both to meet current obligations that come due and to conduct the firm's routine business.

1. The firm maintains cash balances consisting primarily of checking accounts at commercial banks to:

   a. Satisfy minimum cash balance requirements that lenders may impose on the firm.

   b. Make timely payments to its suppliers, employees, and lenders.

   c. Take advantage of profitable business opportunities (such as trade discounts from suppliers) that are available to the firm.

   d. Accommodate either seasonal or unexpected changes in the firm's operating cash flows.

2. Although the investment in cash helps satisfy the firm's liquidity requirements, it does little to enhance profitability. Marketable securities are both liquid and profitable, however, so the firm should always try to keep its idle cash balances invested in these "near money" instruments.

3. Unless all sales are on a cash basis, the firm must maintain some investment in accounts receivable. Although such an investment increases the firm's financing and administrative costs, effective management of accounts receivable can both control these costs and provide the firm with a relatively stable source of liquid assets. Furthermore, the increased investment in accounts receivable that results from a liberal credit policy to customers may produce greater profitability to the firm due to larger sales volume.

4. An investment in inventory is necessary to competitively satisfy sales demands for the firm's products. Inventory control procedures (discussed in Chapter 13) can be implemented to balance inventory expenses against the potential sales opportunities that result from the firm's inventory investment.

II. The objective of working-capital management

A. Arriving at the appropriate level of a firm's investment in working capital involves a trade-off between liquidity and profitability. Although a greater working-capital investment improves the firm's liquidity, the increased costs may weaken profits. Thus the objective of working-capital management is to minimize the costs associated with the firm's working-capital investment without jeopardizing the firm's liquidity or disrupting its operations, sales, and profit potential.

B. The costs related to the firm's working-capital investment can be classified as:

1. Investment costs incurred through the financing of working capital.

2. Operating costs (such as administrative, accounting, and maintenance) necessary to effectively manage and control the firm's working-capital investment.

3. <u>Shortfall costs</u> associated with maintaining too small a working-capital investment. Examples of these costs include lost sales, forgone discounts from suppliers, and penalties imposed by lenders for insufficient cash balances.

III. Cash balance analysis

A. To determine the firm's appropriate level of cash balances, it is necessary to prepare <u>cash budgets</u> so that future cash inflows and outflows can be synchronized. The preparation of cash budgets is discussed in Chapter 4.

B. The objective of cash balance analysis is to determine the optimal level of the firm's cash balances such that the firm maintains its necessary liquidity while minimizing the total costs (the sum of investment, operating, and shortfall costs) related to its investment in cash.

IV. Techniques for lessening cash needs

A. The firm's financial management can minimize idle cash balances by accelerating cash collections and slowing cash disbursements.

B. Accelerating collections

1. Billing promptly and accurately.

2. Offering discounts to customers who pay their bills quickly.

3. Supplying customers with self-addressed envelopes in which to pay their bills.

4. Using either a lock-box system with regional banks or regional collection offices. These devices can vastly reduce both mailing and check-processing time, but their benefits must be weighed against their higher costs of operation.

5. Using electronic funds-transfer devices to make the proceeds from a sale immediately available to the firm.

C. Slowing disbursements

1. Delaying payments to suppliers.

2. Using the check-clearing float.

3. Issuing less frequent payrolls.

4. Using zero-balance checking accounts to eliminate the accumulation of idle cash balances.

V. Marketable securities

A. When the firm has temporary excess cash balances, they should be invested in marketable securities that are <u>liquid</u>, <u>low-risk</u>, and <u>price-stable</u>.

B. <u>Liquidity</u> of a financial asset has two dimensions: (1) the time required to convert the asset into cash and (2) the possibility of a financial loss upon the asset's conversion into cash. Most liquid assets have strong secondary markets with enough buyers and sellers so that no single asset trade adversely affects the asset's market price.

C. An asset's <u>default risk</u> relates to the likelihood that the holder will be paid in full the asset's promised principal and interest. There is a direct relationship between an asset's expected return (or yield) and its level of risk. That is, lower-risk assets have lower yields than higher-risk assets.

D. Assets with long maturities are generally subject to volatile price changes. Therefore, firm's excess cash balances should be restricted to assets with maturities not in excess of one year.

E. <u>Money market instruments</u> are financial assets that usually are actively traded in secondary markets, possess little default risk, and have maturities less than one year. The firm's temporary excess cash balances should be invested in money market instruments, because they are liquid, low-risk, and price-stable. The major money market instruments include United States Treasury bills (T bills), tax anticipation bills (TAB), short-term federal agency obligations, banker's acceptances, commercial paper, repurchase agreements, negotiable certificates of deposit, Euro-dollar deposits, federal funds, money market funds, foreign treasury bills, local-agency tax-exempt notes, and business savings accounts. Features of these money market instruments are summarized in Table 12.1. Most money market instruments are sold on a <u>discount basis</u>, which means that the buyer pays less than par value for the instrument. The difference between the purchase price P_0 and the par value P_N represents the investor's dollar return. The investor's annual interest rate (yield) on a money market instrument can be calculated as follows:

$$\text{Yield} = (360/N)[(P_N - P_0)/P_0]$$

where N is the number of days to maturity.

Table 12.1   Money Market Instruments

Instrument	Denominations	Maturities	Special Features
U.S. Treasury Bills Obligations of the United States Treasury.	$10,000 to $1,000,000	91 to 365 days	Excellent secondary markets. No default risk. Interest is exempt from state income taxes.
Tax Anticipation Bills Obligations of states, municipalities, or political subdivisions.	$1,000 to $1,000,000	91 to 365 days	Good secondary markets. Default risk varies with issuer but is generally quite low. Interest is exempt from federal income taxes.
Federal Agency Issues Issued by federally sponsored or endorsed agencies and corporations such as the Government National Mortgage Association (GNMA), Federal National Mortgage Association (FNMA), Veteran's Administration (VA), Housing and Urban Development (HUD), and the Federal Home Loan Bank (FHLB).	$1,000 to $100,000	Varies up to 365 days. Longer maturities available.	Good secondary markets. Low default risk. Interest on most issues is exempt from state income taxes.
Bankers' Acceptances Time draft with future payment guaranteed by a commercial bank.	$25,000 to $1,000,000	Usually 91 to 182 days	Good secondary markets for acceptances issued by the larger banks. Default risk varies with issuing bank but is generally low.
Commercial Paper Short-term, unsecured promissory notes issued by large corporations.	$1,000 to $5,000,000	Varies with issue up to 270 days	Poor secondary market since each issue is uniquely designed to the needs of the borrowing and lending parties. Default risk varies with issuer but is normally low, since only the more creditworthy firms borrow in the commercial paper market.

Table 12.1   Money Market Instruments (cont.)

Instrument	Denominations	Maturities	Special Features
Repurchase Agreements An agreement between a borrower and a lender whereby the borrower sells the lender a financial asset with a promise to repurchase the asset at a negotiated future date for a higher predetermined price.	$500,000	Usually 1 to 30 days	Poor secondary market since each issue is self-liquidating within a few days; however, repurchase agreements are very liquid because of their short maturities. Low default risk since lender has the underlying securities to be repurchased.
Negotiable Certificates of Deposit Large time deposits at commercial banks.	$100,000	30 to 180 days	Fair secondary market. Default risk varies with issuing bank, however the principal is insured up to $100,000 if the issuing bank is federally insured by the Federal Deposit Insurance Corporation (FDIC).
Eurodollar Deposits Time deposits or certificates of deposit in foreign banks denominated in U.S. dollars.	$500,000 to $5,000,000	Overnight to 360 days	Poor secondary market. Default risk varies with issuing foreign bank, and no portion of the principal is FDIC-insured.
Federal Funds Overnight loans to commercial banks.	$1,000,000	Overnight	No secondary market but very liquid, since federal funds have short maturities. Low default risk, but it depends on the borrowing bank.

Table 12.1   Money Market Instruments (cont.)

Instrument	Denominations	Maturities	Special Features
Money Market Funds Mutual funds that invest in a portfolio of money market instruments.	$1,000 to $10,000	No fixed maturity	No secondary market but highly liquid, since shares can be sold back to the fund at any time. Very little default risk.
Foreign Treasury Bills Issues of foreign governments denominated in foreign currency.	Similar to U.S. Treasury bills	Similar to U.S. Treasury bills	Excellent foreign secondary markets. Little default risk; however the investor is subject to the risk that the foreign currency in which the treasury bill is denominated will devalue against the dollar.
Business Savings Accounts Savings and time deposits of partnerships or corporations in commercial banks.	Up to $150,000	Subject to negotiation	No secondary market since these accounts must be held to maturity. Little default risk. Federally insured up to $100,000 if the bank is FDIC-insured.
Local-Agency Tax-Exempt Notes Obligations of local agencies.	$1,000 to $1,000,000	Various, depending on date taxes are due	Exempt from federal income tax. Highly liquid. Well-developed secondary market.

STUDY PROBLEMS

<u>12.1.</u> The Ace Company has the following balance sheet as of 12/31/79:

```
Cash . . . . . . . . . . . . . . . . . . . . . . . . . .   $ 15,000
Marketable securities  . . . . . . . . . . . . . . . . .     12,000
Accounts receivable  . . . . . . . . . . . . . . . . . .     28,000
Inventory  . . . . . . . . . . . . . . . . . . . . . . .     38,000
Net fixed assets . . . . . . . . . . . . . . . . . . . .    226,000
        Total assets . . . . . . . . . . . . . . . . . .   $319,000

Accounts payable . . . . . . . . . . . . . . . . . . . .   $ 18,000
Wages payable  . . . . . . . . . . . . . . . . . . . . .      6,000
Taxes payable  . . . . . . . . . . . . . . . . . . . . .     15,000
Notes payable  . . . . . . . . . . . . . . . . . . . . .     30,000
Long-term debt . . . . . . . . . . . . . . . . . . . . .     60,000
Capitalized leases . . . . . . . . . . . . . . . . . . .     65,000
Common-equity net worth  . . . . . . . . . . . . . . . .    125,000
        Total liabilities and net worth  . . . . . . . .   $319,000
```

a. What is Ace's working-capital investment?

b. Determine Ace's net working-capital position.

<u>Solution</u>

a. Working capital is the firm's current assets. Therefore, for the Ace Company,

> Working capital = cash + marketable securities + accounts receivable
> + inventory = <u>$93,000</u>

b. Net working capital is current assets minus current liabilities. Ace's current liabilities are the sum of accounts, wages, taxes, and notes payable. Since Ace's current assets are $93,000 and its current liabilities are $69,000, Ace's net working capital = $93,000 - $69,000 = <u>$24,000</u>.

<u>12.2.</u> Bannock Lumber Company is attempting to determine its optimal level of cash balances. Four alternative cash balances (A, B, C, and D) are being considered. They have the following characteristics:

Cash Balance Alternatives

	A	B	C	D
Cash Balance	$10,000	$20,000	$30,000	$40,000
Expected Shortfall Costs	$ 4,800	$ 2,700	$ 1,000	$ -0-
Operating Costs	$ 8,000	$ 8,000	$ 8,000	$ 8,000

Bannock's cost of capital is 14 percent. Determine its optimal cash balance.

Solution

Alternative	Investment Costs	Operating Costs	Shortfall Costs	Total
A	$1,400	$8,000	$4,800	$14,200
B	$2,800	$8,000	$2,700	$13,500
C	$4,200	$8,000	$1,000	$13,200
D	$5,600	$8,000	0	$13,600

Alternative C is the cash balance that has the minimum total costs ($13,200). Bannock Lumber should maintain a cash balance of $30,000.

12.3. The bank with which Scott Hardware does business has an agreement with the store's owner that, if Scott maintains a minimum balance of $15,000 in its checking account, the store receives both free checking services and a 1 percent reduction in its borrowing rate on any loans with the bank. On average, Scott Hardware issues 50 checks per month and maintains an $80,000 loan balance at the bank. The bank's regular fee for processing checks is $.25 per check plus a service charge of $5 per month. The owner has maintained $15,000 in the store's checking account for years, but he recently noticed that one-year Treasury bills are yielding 11 percent.

a. Should Scott Hardware continue its current practice or maintain a zero checking account balance and invest the $15,000 currently in the account in one-year Treasury bills?

b. What rate of return would one-year Treasury bills have to yield in order for it to be profitable for Scott Hardware to maintain a zero checking account balance?

Solution

a. The annual return on a $15,000 investment in T bills yielding 11 percent a year would be .11 * $15,000 = $1,650. However, if Scott were to invest its present minimum checking account balance in T bills, the store would have the following additional banking expenses:

> Loan interest expense = .01 * $80,000 = $800
> Checking service charges = (50 * $.25 * 12) + ($5 * 12) = $210

Therefore, total increased annual banking expenses would be $800 + $210 = $1,010. Since investment income exceeds the additional bank expenses by $640, Scott Hardware should maintain a zero checking account balance and invest the $15,000 minimum balance in one-year T bills.

b. The rate X on one-year T bills would have to be large enough for investment income on the $15,000 invested in T bills to at least equal the $1,010 additional annual banking costs that Scott Hardware expects to pay the bank. Therefore,

> $15,000X = $1,010
> X = .06733
> = 6.733%

12.4. Holland Instruments has annual sales of $32,850,000 that occur uniformly throughout the year (365 days). Although the company has regional offices throughout the country, it currently has all its customers remit payment checks to its

Houston corporate headquarters. The company receives an average of 200 checks per day in Houston. Holland's main bank has suggested that the company establish five regional lock-box systems with the bank's affiliates in San Francisco, Denver, Chicago, New York, and Atlanta. With the exception of customers in Texas and Louisiana, Holland's customers will then be instructed to mail their payments to a Post Office box in one of these cities rather than to Houston. The affiliate banks will collect the checks daily from the Post Office, credit Holland's checking account at each regional bank by the amount of daily collections, and forward all paperwork to Holland's Houston office. Finally, the affiliate banks will wire-transfer to Holland's checking account at its Houston bank the daily balance in each checking account, so that Holland maintains a zero end-of-day checking account balance with each of the five regional affiliate banks. Each regional bank will perform these tasks 260 working days per year. The Houston bank estimates that lock-box systems will speed up Holland's cash collections by 4 days. However, each check cleared will cost the company $.50, and wire transfers are $8.00 per transfer. Holland's cost of capital is 15 percent. Should the lock-box system recommended by the bank be used?

Solution

Annual added costs incurred with the lock-box system include:

Check-clearing fees = 200 checks/day * 365 days/yr * $.50/check
= $36,500
Wire-transfer costs = 5 transfers/day * 260 days/yr * $8.00/transfer
= $10,400

Hence the total increased annual cost is $36,500 + $10,400 = $46,900. Annual savings that result from Holland's reducing its investment in accounts receivable by 4 days of daily sales can be determined as follows:

Annual savings = 4 days * $32,850,000/365 days * .15 = $54,000

Conclusion: Holland should use the lock-box system, because annual savings ($54,000) exceed annual added costs ($46,000).

12.5. Determine the annual yield on the following money market instruments:

a. A 75-day T bill selling for $9,850 with a $10,000 par value.

b. A 30-day banker's acceptance selling for $24,800 with a $25,000 par value.

c. A 3-day repurchase agreement selling for $99,940 with a $100,000 par value.

d. A 220-day T bill selling for $9,300 with a $10,000 par value.

Solution

Y = yield = $[(P_N - P_0)/P_0] * [360/N]$, where P_N = par value, P_0 = current price, and N = days to maturity.

a. Y = ($10,000 - $9,850)/($9,850 * 360/75) = .0731 = 7.31%

b. Y = ($25,000 - $24,800)/($24,800 * 360/30) = .0968 = 9.68%

c. $Y = (\$100,000 - \$99,940)/(\$99,940 * 360/3) = 0.720 = 7.20\%$

d. $Y = (\$10,000 - \$9,300)/(\$9,300 * 360/220) = .1232 = 12.32\%$

REVIEW QUESTIONS

1. Net working capital is the firm's
    a. current assets.
    b. current liabilities.
    c. current assets minus current liabilities.
    d. total assets minus total liabilities.
    e. cash balances.

2. A firm maintains its working-capital investment primarily to
    a. enhance its profitability.
    b. provide it with sufficient liquidity to conduct its business.
    c. insure its ability to pay cash dividends to stockholders.
    d. reduce its reliance on debt financing.
    e. take advantage of high-yielding marketable securities.

3. Firms with excessive working-capital investments are likely to be
    a. both profitable and liquid.
    b. profitable but illiquid.
    c. both unprofitable and illiquid.
    d. liquid but unprofitable.
    e. growth-oriented.

4. Which of the following is not a motive for the firm's investment in cash?
    a. to meet required cash balances imposed by lenders
    b. to make timely payments to suppliers, employees, and lenders
    c. to take advantage of unexpected and profitable business opportunities
    d. to accommodate seasonal or unexpected cash flows
    e. to maximize the firm's earnings

5. Which of the following are shortfall costs resulting from the firm's policy of working-capital management?
    a. administrative costs incurred to manage accounts receivable
    b. financing costs related to the firm's investment in inventory
    c. lost sales resulting from insufficient inventory
    d. bank service charges on the firm's checking account
    e. expenses related to managing the firm's portfolio of marketable securities

6. One of the most important aspects of cash balance analysis is
    a. sales forecasting.
    b. preparing cash budgets.
    c. preparing pro forma income statements
    d. capital budgeting.
    e. determining the firm's dividend policy.

7. The firm can minimize idle cash balances by
    a. accelerating cash collections.
    b. acquiring more profitable product lines.
    c. slowing cash disbursements.
    d. both a and b.
    e. both a and c.

8. All of the following are methods for accelerating cash collections <u>except</u>
   a. accurate billings to customers.
   b. giving discounts to customers who pay their bills promptly.
   c. the use of electronic funds-transfer devices.
   d. less frequent payrolls.
   e. the use of a lock-box system.

9. The firm's idle cash balances should always be invested in marketable securities that
   a. have little default risk.
   b. are liquid.
   c. possess long maturities.
   d. both a and b.
   e. both b and c.

10. The two basic aspects of a financial asset's liquidity are
    a. speed of conversion into cash and possibility of financial loss.
    b. speed of conversion into cash and profit potential.
    c. profit potential and possibility of financial loss.
    d. default risk and maturity.
    e. profit potential and default risk.

11. Money market instruments:
    a. always have high yields
    b. include common stock and municipal bonds
    c. have maturities in excess of one year
    d. usually have no secondary markets
    e. are normally sold on a discount basis

12. A $100 par-valued money market instrument selling for $97.50 with a 180-day maturity has an annual yield of approximately
    a. 5.00 percent.
    b. 5.13 percent.
    c. 1.28 percent.
    d. 2.56 percent.
    e. 8.45 percent.

KEY DEFINITIONS

Cash budget: a projection of both cash inflows and cash outflows during a specific time period. Cash budgets are important in forecasting both the firm's future cash balances and its short-term borrowing needs.

Default risk: the uncertainty about whether a borrower will be able to pay either a loan's interest or its principal.

Discount basis: a term applied to the method by which most short-term marketable securities are sold. A security sold on a discount basis is bought by an investor for less than its par (or face) value. However, the investor is repaid the par value at the security's maturity. Thus the difference between the security's par value and its purchase price reflects the investor's profit.

Investment costs: the firm's financing costs that result from its investment in working capital.

<u>Liquidity</u>: a property of a financial asset determined by (1) the time required to convert the asset into cash and (2) the possibility of a financial loss upon the asset's conversion into cash. The most liquid of all financial assets are coin, currency, and checking accounts.

<u>Money market instrument</u>: a marketable security that has both good liquidity and a maturity that is less than one year. Treasury bills, commercial paper, negotiable certificates of deposit, and banker's acceptances are popular examples of money market instruments in which firms can invest their idle cash balances.

<u>Negotiable certificates of deposit</u>: large-time deposits ($100,000 minimum) at commercial banks that are liquid (via the secondary markets) and have maturities between 30 days and 180 days.

<u>Net working capital</u>: a firm's current assets minus its current liabilities.

<u>Operating costs</u>: in reference to a firm's working capital, the administrative, accounting, and maintenance costs involved in management of the firm's working-capital investment.

<u>Shortfall costs</u>: lost sales, forgone discounts from supplies, and penalties imposed by lenders that are incurred because a firm maintained an insufficient working-capital investment.

<u>Treasury bills</u>: short-term (maturities less than one year) marketable securities issued by the U.S. Treasury that have both good liquidity and no default risk (popularly referred to as T bills).

<u>Working capital</u>: a firm's investment in current assets such as cash, marketable securities, accounts receivable, and inventory.

ANSWERS TO REVIEW QUESTIONS

1. c	4. e	7. d	10. a
2. b	5. c	8. d	11. e
3. d	6. b	9. d	12. b

Chapter Thirteen
Inventory and Accounts Receivable Management

OVERVIEW

Since inventory and accounts receivable make up the largest investment in current assets for most firms, financial managers must be familiar with factors that affect their optimal levels. For either asset, the optimal level of investment is the one at which total costs are minimized. With inventory management, these total costs include ordering, carrying, and shortfall costs. The total costs related to accounts receivable management include operating, investment, and shortfall costs. With accounts receivable management, additional matters must be considered, such as (1) credit terms, (2) credit standards, (3) techniques to quantify credit risks, (4) sources of credit information, (5) monitoring of accounts receivable, and (6) alternative methods of financing accounts receivable.

STUDY OBJECTIVES

1. To become aware of methods by which the firm can determine its <u>optimal investment</u> in both inventory and accounts receivable.

2. To introduce techniques that financial officers can use to analyze the <u>risks</u> involved in extending credit to their firm's customers.

CHAPTER OUTLINE

I. Inventory management

   A. The objective of inventory management is to determine optimal inventory levels such that the firm's total inventory costs are minimized. These costs include ordering, carrying, and shortfall costs.

      1. <u>Ordering costs</u> are incurred each time the firm places an order. Included in ordering costs are the expenses related to preparing order requisitions and to receiving and inspecting newly ordered goods. Ordering costs increase with smaller, more frequently placed orders.

228

2. Carrying costs are associated with the warehousing and the financing of inventory. Unlike ordering costs, carrying costs increase with larger, less frequently placed orders.

3. Shortfall (stockout) costs result when the firm loses sales because it maintains an insufficient level of inventory. The firm can maintain safety stock to reduce its shortfall costs, but higher levels of safety stock increase the firm's inventory carrying costs.

B. At the firm's optimal level of inventory, its total inventory costs are minimized. This ideal inventory level can be achieved in a stepwise manner. Step 1 is to determine the economic order quantity (EOQ) at which both ordering and carrying costs are minimized. The following equation can be used to determine the EOQ:

$$EOQ = \sqrt{2PS/C}$$

where P = ordering costs per order, S = annual sales in units, and C = carrying costs per unit of inventory.

Step 2 is to determine the optimal level of safety stock necessary to minimize shortfall costs without incurring large additional carrying costs. Step 3 is to find the firm's optimal initial level of inventory by adding the EOQ (from Step 1) to the minimum-cost level of safety stock (from Step 2). If sales occur throughout the year in a uniform manner, the optimal average level of inventory is half the EOQ plus the minimum-cost level of safety stock.

Example: The Apex Company has annual sales S of 300,000 units and ordering costs P of $600 per order. The costs C of carrying inventory are $2 per unit. Further, the company estimates that, at various levels of safety stock, its shortfall costs are as follows:

Safety Stock	Shortfall Costs
15,000 units	$ 0
8,000 units	$17,000
1,000 units	$40,000

Determine both the optimal initial level and the average level of Apex's inventory.

Solution: The objective is to determine the level of inventory that has minimum total costs. The stepwise method can be used to solve this problem.

Step 1

$$EOQ = \sqrt{2 * 600 * 300,000/2} = \underline{13,416 \text{ units}}$$

229

Step 2

Safety Stock Level	Carrying Costs @ $2/unit	Shortfall Costs	Shortfall plus Carrying Costs
15,000 units	$30,000	$ 0	$30,000
8,000 units	$16,000	$17,000	$33,000
1,000 units	$ 2,000	$40,000	$42,000

The safety stock level that minimizes combined carrying and shortfall costs is 15,000 units.

Step 3

The minimum-cost initial level of inventory is 28,416 units, which equals 13,416 units (EOQ) plus 15,000 units (the optimal level of safety stock). The optimal average level of Apex's inventory is 21,708 units (half the EOQ plus the safety stock level).

II. Accounts receivable management

    A. The objective of accounts receivable management is to determine the firm's ideal accounts receivable investment--the investment that minimizes total costs. The costs associated with the firm's investment in accounts receivable include operating, investment, and shortfall costs.

        1. Operating costs are administrative and collection costs, delinquency costs, and default costs.

            a. The expenses that result from both maintaining and staffing a credit department are reflected in administrative and collection costs.

            b. When the firm's customers are untimely in paying their bills, expenses such as collection agency fees and legal fees result in delinquency costs. Furthermore, the lost profit opportunities on any funds invested in delinquent accounts receivable increase these delinquency costs.

            c. When a delinquent account becomes uncollectible, the entire account balance must be written off as a default cost.

        2. Investment costs result from the expenses associated with financing the firm's investment in accounts receivable.

        3. Shortfall costs are incurred when the firm loses collectible credit sales due to its stringent credit policy.

        4. As the firm liberalizes its credit policy, its investment in accounts receivable increases and its shortfall costs are reduced. However, a larger investment in accounts receivable also increases the firm's operating and investment costs. The firm's financial management should try to achieve the optimal level of accounts receivable such that the trade-off among these various costs results in maximum profitability for the firm.

B. A firm can offer its customers credit subject to numerous terms (conditions). The firm's financial management must be aware of these various credit terms, because their impact on the firm's investment in accounts receivable affects the firm's profitability.

   1. Cash before delivery (CBD) requires payment prior to the shipment of merchandise to customers. CBD can be used if the firm is wary of a customer's credit record.

   2. Cash on delivery (COD) requires customers to pay the bill upon delivery of the merchandise. Although COD terms insure prompt payment, the firm is responsible for transportation costs should the customer refuse to accept delivery.

   3. Sight draft - bill of lading (SD-BL) terms assure that the firm will be paid before the customer takes possession of the merchandise. With SD-BL terms of credit, a commercial bank designated by the firm assists the firm in the collection process.

   4. Cash/no discount credit terms require payment after the customer has taken possession of merchandise. Payment is to be made within a predetermined time period, and the customer receives no discount for early payment.

   5. Discount terms allow the customer a discount from the purchase price if payment is made before the entire credit period has expired. If the customer fails to take the discount, full payment is due by the end of the extended credit period. For example, if the discount terms were 3/15 net 60, the customer would receive a 3 percent discount if she or he paid the bill prior to the fifteenth day after the billing date. The full balance would be due by the sixtieth day should the customer decide not to accept the discount terms.

   6. Seasonal billing can be made available to customers whose sales are seasonal. Although the firm does not receive payment until after the seasonal period, its inventory carrying costs are reduced due to the earlier shipment of finished goods.

   7. Free on board (FOB) implies that the firm is responsible for all expenses (insurance, inspection, transportation, and so on) up to a designated shipping point. Thereafter, the customer bears these expenses.

   8. Cost, insurance and freight (CIF) means that the price quoted the customer includes the cost of merchandise, insurance, and freight charges to a specific destination.

C. The firm's billing frequency affects the shortfall, investment, and operating costs that are related to its accounts receivable. For example, less frequent billing reduces both shortfall and operating (administrative) costs. Higher investment costs will result from the firm's larger investment in accounts receivable. Consequently, billing frequency is one factor to consider in determining the firm's optimal investment in accounts receivable.

D. The firm's financial management must establish <u>credit standards</u> in order to assess the creditworthiness of its customers. If these standards are too stringent, the firm may lose sales from creditworthy customers. But if the credit standards are too loose, the firm's default costs may increase as uncollectible accounts receivable build up. In determining credit standards, financial managers should be aware of traditional credit standards, methods to quantify credit risk, sources of credit information, and techniques that can be used to monitor accounts receivable.

1. <u>Traditional standards</u> are referred to as the <u>five Cs</u> of credit. They are capital, character, conditions, capacity, and collateral.

   a. <u>Capital</u> measures the customer's financial strength.

   b. <u>Character</u> refers to the customer's credit reputation.

   c. <u>Conditions</u> reflect current economic circumstances that may affect the customer's present ability to pay bills.

   d. <u>Capacity</u> relates to the customer's liquidity (both the quality of the customer's current assets and the nature of his or her current liabilities).

   e. <u>Collateral</u> consists of assets of the customer that could be pledged to the firm in the event that the customer defaults on payment of bills.

2. It is possible to quantify the credit risk a given customer represents. For example, certain financial ratios tend to be good indicators of a customer's ability to pay his or her bills. Historic averages of these key ratios can be calculated for two groups of customers: a low-credit-risk group and a high-credit-risk group. These same key ratios can then be determined for a customer (either current or potential) and compared with the historic averages of both the low- and the high-credit-risk groups. A cumulative credit rating score can then be awarded the customer, depending on how each of his or her key ratios compares with the corresponding key ratio of the two groups. In this manner, the firm's financial management can assess the credit risk that each of its customers represents.

3. Sources of credit information on the firm's customers can be obtained from Dun and Bradstreet, customers' financial statements, bank references, and either national or local credit bureaus.

4. After having established credit standards, it is important for financial officers to continually monitor the firm's accounts receivable.

   a. Individual customer accounts should be monitored to bring to light any changes that may occur in a customer's creditworthiness.

   b. Collectively, the firm's accounts receivable should be monitored to judge the effectiveness of the firm's accounts receivable policy. In this manner, policy changes can be implemented in accordance with changes in either general economic conditions or individual customers' creditworthiness.

      c. Within each credit risk class of the firm's customers, the ratio of the percentage of actual defaults to the percentage of expected defaults should also be monitored to determine whether policy changes are needed. For example, a ratio in excess of 1 may suggest that the firm either has been too liberal in its credit policy to customers in that credit risk class or has inappropriately classified customers in that credit risk class. In either event, this finding suggests that changes in the firm's accounts receivable policy may be needed.

      d. Monitoring the age (the number of days outstanding) of the firm's accounts receivable can help financial officers determine the effectiveness of the firm's credit screening policy and its credit collection practices.

E. Alternative methods of financing the firm's accounts receivable include factoring, credit insurance, and captive finance companies.

    1. <u>Factoring</u> is the sale of a firm's accounts receivable to a factor (a firm that buys other firms' accounts receivable). The factor can perform all the normal tasks (credit analysis, billing, collection) of the firm's credit department. The factor's fee is determined by both the number of these tasks performed by the factor and the credit risk associated with the accounts receivable. Factors sometimes buy accounts receivable on a <u>without-recourse</u> basis, whereby the factor assumes all default risk. Naturally, the factor's fee increases when the factoring arrangement is without recourse. Factoring benefits the firm in several ways. The firm reduces (or eliminates) the cost of maintaining a credit department, and it has no default risk if without-recourse factoring is used. The firm can reduce its investment costs in accounts receivable, because payments are received more quickly from the factor than from the firm's collection of the accounts. However, these benefits must be weighed against an additional cost: the factor's fee.

    2. With credit insurance, an insurance company insures the firm against unusually large defaults. The firm benefits by reducing its default costs. In determining whether to purchase credit insurance for their firm, financial officers must weigh these reduced default costs against the expense of credit insurance.

    3. A <u>captive finance company</u> is a wholly owned subsidiary of the firm established to finance the firm's accounts receivable.

STUDY PROBLEMS

<u>13.1.</u> The Roggers Slacks Company has annual sales S of 40,000 units that occur in a uniform manner throughout the year. Inventory ordering costs P are $1,000 per order, and inventory carrying costs are $4 per unit. The financial officers at Roggers have prepared the following table, which gives their best estimates of shortfall costs that result from lost sales at various levels of inventory safety stock.

Safety Stock	Shortfall Costs
5000 units	$ 0
4000 units	$ 3,300
3000 units	$ 6,800
2000 units	$10,500
1000 units	$15,000

Determine the following:

a. Roggers's EOQ.

b. The optimal safety stock level.

c. The company's optimal initial inventory level and average inventory level.

d. The optimal number of orders that Roggers must place each year to replace its inventory.

Solution

a. EOQ = $\sqrt{2PS/C}$ = $\sqrt{2 * 1,000 * 40,000/4}$ = 4,472 units

b.
Safety Stock Level	Shortfall Costs	Carry Costs @$4/unit	Shortfall plus Carrying Costs
5000 units	$ 0	$20,000	$20,000
4000 units	$ 3,300	$16,000	$19,300
3000 units	$ 6,800	$12,000	$18,800
2000 units	$10,500	$ 8,000	$18,500 (minimum costs)
1000 units	$15,000	$ 4,000	$19,000

The minimum-cost (optimal) level of safety stock is 2,000 units.

c. The optimal initial inventory level is 6,472 units (EOQ plus the optimal safety stock level). The optimal average inventory level is 4,236 units (half of EOQ plus the optimal safety stock level).

d. The optimal number n of inventory orders per year can be determined as follows:

   n = S/EOQ = 40,000/4472 = 8.94 orders/year

Assuming a 365-day year, Roggers should reorder inventory about every 41 days (365/8.94).

13.2. Reflexo Ski Poles is considering tightening its credit policy. Presently, Reflexo has annual sales of $3 million. However, the company's financial officer is concerned about the high investment and default costs associated with Reflexo's accounts receivable. The proposed change in credit policy would reduce annual sales to $2.8 million, but it would also reduce the average collection period (based on a 360-day year) from the current 45 days to an estimated 30 days. Reflexo's cost of capital on funds invested in the company's assets is 12 percent. Regardless of credit policy, the company's gross profit margin is 30 percent of sales. The following table summarizes accounts receivable operating-expense characteristics both currently and after the proposed change in credit policy.

Expense Item	Current Policy	Proposed Policy
Administrative and collection costs	$30,000 plus .5% of sales	$45,000 plus .75% of sales
Delinquency costs	1% of sales	.5% of sales
Default costs	3% of sales	2% of sales

In the ski pole business, all sales are credit sales. Should Reflexo change its credit policy on the basis of this information?

Solution

The better credit policy is the one that minimizes total costs, so Reflexo must analyze its operating, investment, and shortfall costs to reach a decision.

Step 1 Operating Costs Analysis

Expense Item	Current Policy	Proposed Policy
A. Administrative and collection costs	$30,000 + (.005 * $3,000,000) equals $45,000	$45,000 + (.0075 * $2,800,000) equals $66,000
B. Delinquency costs	.01 * $3,000,000 equals $30,000	.005 * $2,800,000 equals $14,000
C. Default costs	.03 * $3,000,000 equals $90,000	.02 * $2,800,000 equals $56,000
D. Total operating costs (A + B + C)	$165,000	$136,000

Step 2 Investment Costs Analysis

For either alternative,

IC = investment costs = cost of capital * daily sales * average collection period * 1 - profit margin

For current policy,

IC = .12 * ($3,000,000/360) * 45 * .7 = $31,500

For proposed policy,

IC = .12 * ($2,800,000/360) * 30 * .7 = $19,600

Step 3 Shortfall Costs Analysis

With either alternative, Reflexo's gross profit is 30 percent of annual sales. Currently this profit is .3 * $3,000,000 = $900,000. With the proposed change in credit policy, this profit is expected to be .3 * $2,800,000 = $840,000. Therefore, shortfall costs resulting from a change in credit policy are $60,000 ($900,000 - $840,000).

Step 4   Total Costs Analysis

Total costs for either alternative equal the sum of operating, investment, and shortfall costs. With current policy,

   Total costs = $165,000 + $31,500 + zero shortfall costs = $196,500

With the proposed policy,

   Total costs = $136,000 + $19,600 + $60,000 = $215,600

Since the total costs associated with the proposed changes in credit policy are higher (by $19,100), Reflexo should retain its present credit policy. That is, the firm should reject the proposed change.

13.3.   Regal Can Company offers its customers credit terms of 1/15 net 60. Annual sales (all credit) are $300,000, on which 50 percent are discounted by customers paying on the fifteenth day after the billing date. The remaining customers pay on the sixtieth day after the billing date. Regal finances its accounts receivable investment at 12 percent, and its gross profit margin is 20 percent. The company is contemplating a change in its credit terms to 2/10 net 30. Although this change is not expected to affect the level of sales, management feels the change will prompt 70 percent of its sales to be discounted on the tenth day after billing. However, only 75 percent of the nondiscounted sales are expected to pay on the thirtieth day after billing, with the balance of nondiscounted sales paid on the sixtieth day after billing.

a.   Calculate the average collection period for both alternatives, assuming a 360-day year.

b.   Determine Regal's investment in accounts receivable both currently and with the proposed change in credit terms.

c.   What impact would the change have on Regal's investment costs?

d.   Assuming that all other credit costs are the same for the two alternatives, determine whether the company should change its credit terms.

Solution

a.   With 1/15 net 60,

   Average collection period = (.5 * 15 days) + (.5 * 60 days) = 37.5 days

   With 2/10 net 30,

   Average collection period = (.7 * 10 days) + .3 * [(.75 * 30 days)
                                    + (.25 * 60 days)] = 18.25 days

b.   With either alternative, daily sales are the same.

   Daily sales = $300,000/360 = $833.33/day

The investment in accounts receivable is the product of daily sales times the average collection period times (1 - gross profit margin). Therefore, for the current policy (1/15 net 60),

Investment in accounts receivable = $833.33/day * 37.5 days * .8
= $25,000.

For the new policy (2/10 net 30),

Investment in accounts receivable = $833.33/day * 18.25 days * .8
= $12,167

c. With each alternative,

Investment costs = cost of financing * accounts receivable

With 1/15 net 60,

Investment costs = .12 * $25,000 = $3,000

With 2/10 net 30,

Investment costs = .12 * $12,167 = $1,460

d. The credit costs of each alternative are the sum of investment costs and the sales discount, where

Sales discount = annual sales * % of sales discounted * discount percentage

For the current 1/15 net 60 policy

Credit costs = $3,000 + $300,000 * .5 * .01 = $3,000 + $1,500 = $4,500

For the contemplated 2/10 net 30 policy,

Credit costs = $1,460 + $300,000 * .7 * .02 = $1,460 + $4,200 = $5,660

Since the objective is to minimize total costs, the proposed policy (2/10 net 30) should not be adopted by Regal Can. Its total costs exceed the total costs of the present policy by $1,160 ($5,660 - $4,500).

13.4. The credit department at the Bebo Corporation uses the following credit scoring model to classify its customers according to credit risk:

Z = credit score = .26 (current ratio) + .61 (quick ratio)
+ .08 (receivable turnover) + .32 (inventory turnover) - .30
(debt/equity ratio) + .06 (return on assets)

The amount of credit that Bebo will extend to a customer depends on the customer's credit score Z, obtained from this model and listed in the following table:

Credit Score Z	Maximum Credit as Percent of Purchase
0-2.80	no credit
2.81-3.50	20%
3.51-4.00	50%
4.01-4.50	80%
above 4.50	100%

Two new customers (Burswick and Alpha Wire) have placed large orders ($100,000 by Burswick and $60,000 by Alpha Wire) with Bebo. How much credit would Bebo extend to each customer if they had the following financial characteristics?

Ratio	Burswick	Alpha Wire
Current	1.7	2.1
Quick	1.3	1.6
Receivable Turnover	10.2	10.1
Inventory Turnover	4.8	5.3
Debt/Equity Ratio	.8	2.4
Return on Assets	15.9	13.8

Solution

Credit score for Burswick:

$$Z = (.26 * 1.7) + (.61 * 1.3) + (.08 * 10.2) + (.32 * 4.8) - (.30 * .80) + (.06 * 15.9) = \underline{4.30}$$

Credit score for Alpha Wire:

$$Z = (.26 * 2.1) + (.61 * 1.6) + (.08 * 10.1) + (.32 * 5.3) - (.30 * 2.4) + (.06 * 13.8) = \underline{4.13}$$

Since the credit score for each company is greater than 4.01 but less than 4.5, Bebo would allow a maximum of 80 percent of the purchase to be credit sales for either customer. Therefore, the maximum credit allowed by Bebo for Burswick and Alpha Wire would be $\underline{\$80,000}$ and $\underline{\$48,000}$, respectively.

13.5. Kristi Shambers, Inc. (KSI) is negotiating with a factor to handle its accounts receivable. Since the factor would handle all customer billings and collections, KSI could eliminate its credit department, thereby saving $35,000 in operating costs. Before costs related to accounts receivable are taken into account, KSI has a 25 percent gross profit margin. Annual sales (all credit) are $900,000, and the average collection period is 45 days (based on a 360-day year). The default rate is 1.5 percent of sales, and KSI's cost of capital is 14 percent. The factor's service charge (fee) is 8 percent of sales if the arrangement is without recourse. With 20 percent recourse, the factor's service charge drops to 6 percent of sales. Regardless of recourse, the factor will advance KSI 100 percent of its credit sales when presented to the factor.

a. Determine KSI's current total credit costs.
b. Calculate KSI's total credit costs, using the factor both with and without recourse.
c. Should KSI use the factor? If so, with or without recourse?

Solution

a. Operating costs = $35,000
   Investment costs = daily sales * average collection period
                   (1 - gross profit margin)
                   cost of capital
           = $900,000/360 * 45 * .75 * .14
           = $\underline{\$11,813}$

Default costs = .015 * $900,000 = $13,500
Current total credit costs = $35,000 + $11,813 + $13,500 = $60,313

b. Factor credit costs without recourse = .08 * $900,000 = $72,000
Factor credit costs with 20% recourse = service charge + 20% of default costs
= .06 * $90,000 + .2 * $13,500 = $57,700

c. KSI's credit costs with the various alternatives are:

$60,313 (current without factor)
$72,000 (factor without recourse)
$57,700 (factor with 20% recourse)

Since KSI's objective is to minimize total credit costs, the factor should be used on a 20 percent recourse basis.

REVIEW QUESTIONS

1. The objective of inventory management is to minimize the sum of
   a. shortfall and ordering costs.
   b. default, shortfall, and ordering costs.
   c. carrying, shortfall, and ordering costs.
   d. delinquency, investment, and shortfall costs.
   e. ordering and carrying costs.

2. The objective of accounts receivable management is to determine the firm's optimal investment in accounts receivable--in other words, the investment that
   a. maximizes sales.
   b. minimizes delinquency and shortfall costs.
   c. is determined by the firm's EOQ.
   d. minimizes operating, investment, and shortfall costs.
   e. minimizes collections, delinquency, and default costs.

3. A firm has annual sales of 400,000 units and inventory ordering costs are $2,000/order. Inventory carrying costs are $8/unit, and the firm maintains a safety stock of 10,000 units. The EOQ is approximately
   a. 10,000 units.
   b. 14,142 units.
   c. 15,657 units.
   d. 22,236 units.
   e. 40,000 units.

4. For the company described in Question 3, the optimal number of days between inventory orders (assuming a 360-day year) is approximately
   a. 9 days.
   b. 11 days.
   c. 13 days.
   d. 15 days.
   e. 23 days.

5. For the company described in Question 3, the average optimal level of inventory is
   a. 10,000 units.
   b. 14,142 units.

    c. 14,444 units.
    d. 17,071 units.
    e. 22,236 units.

6. If a firm were very wary of a new customer's creditworthiness, appropriate credit terms for that customer would be
    a. COD
    b. SD-BL
    c. 2/10 net 15
    d. 3/15 net 60
    e. CBD

7. ABC Corporation ships an order from Boston to one of its customers in Seattle. Terms of the sale are FOB Boston. The order is destroyed due to the carrier's mishandling in Chicago. An insurance claim for the destroyed shipment would be filed by
    a. the customer in Seattle.
    b. the carrier responsible for the damage in Chicago.
    c. ABC Corporation.
    d. both the Seattle customer and ABC Corporation.
    e. both the ABC Corporation and the carrier.

8. Which of the following is not one of the traditional five Cs of credit?
    a. conditions
    b. collateral
    c. character
    d. coverage
    e. capacity

9. After having established a credit policy, it is important for the firm's management to continually monitor
    a. aging of the firm's accounts receivable.
    b. individual customer accounts.
    c. default percentages with each risk class of the firm's accounts.
    d. both a and c.
    e. combined a, b, and c.

10. Alternative methods to finance accounts receivable include the use of
    a. credit insurance, commercial banks, and commercial paper.
    b. lease finance and factors.
    c. factors and commercial banks.
    d. captive and sales finance companies.
    e. factors and captive finance companies.

11. A factor's fee increases when
    a. the factoring arrangement includes recourse.
    b. the factoring arrangement is without recourse.
    c. the factor assumes all the firm's credit-related tasks.
    d. both a and c.
    e. both b and c.

12. Capital Supply offers its customers 2/10 net 30 credit terms. Its records show that 30 percent of sales are discounted on the last available day of the discount, 50 percent of sales are paid on the last day before they become

delinquent, and 20 percent of sales are 20 days delinquent. The average collection period for Capital Supply is approximately
a.   2 days.
b. 10 days.
c. 22 days.
d. 28 days.
e. 30 days.

KEY DEFINITIONS

Age of accounts receivable: a schedule of accounts receivable classified according to the number of days they have been outstanding. Credit managers should monitor changes in this aging schedule.

Captive finance company: a firm's wholly owned subsidiary organized to finance the firm's accounts receivable.

COD: credit terms that require "cash on delivery." The selling firm receives payment quickly but incurs the risk of transportation costs should the merchandise not be accepted by the customer.

Dun & Bradstreet: a nationally known company that sells credit reports useful to firms in determining their customers' creditworthiness.

EOQ: the economic order quantity; that is, the optimal inventory ordering quantity that minimizes the sum of ordering and carrying costs.

Factor: a company that specializes in both buying and managing the accounts receivable of another firm.

FOB: credit terms that mean "free on board." The selling firm is responsible for all shipping, inspection, and insurance costs to a particular destination. Beyond this destination, the customer is responsible for these costs.

Investment costs: in accounts receivable management, the firm's costs involved with financing its investment in accounts receivable. Similar to the carrying costs associated with inventory management.

Operating costs: the sum of administration and collection, delinquency, and default costs involved in the management of a firm's accounts receivable.

Recourse: a term used in factoring whereby the firm shares with the factor a portion (or all) of the default risk involved in the firm's accounts receivable. If factoring is without recourse, the factor is solely responsible for bearing this risk.

Safety stock: the optimal level of inventory a firm holds that minimizes the sum of shortfall and carrying costs related to the inventory investment.

Shortfall costs: in accounts receivable management, a firm's implicit costs of lost sales from desirable customers due to either too low a minimum inventory investment (safety stock) or too stringent a credit policy.

CHAPTER 13

ANSWERS TO REVIEW QUESTIONS

1. c	4. c	7. a	10. e
2. d	5. d	8. d	11. e
3. b	6. e	9. e	12. d

Part Five
Short and Intermediate-Term Sources of Funds

The following two chapters focus on issues related to the firm's short-term and intermediate-term financing. Sources, types, and effective costs of the many forms of short-term financing available to the firm are probed in Chapter 14, whereas Chapter 15 addresses the characteristics and the traditional suppliers of the firm's intermediate-term financing. Additionally, Chapter 15 examines the many facets of lease financing, from the classification of leases to methods for evaluating lease-purchase alternatives.

Chapter Fourteen
Sources and Forms of Short-Term Financing

OVERVIEW

For most firms, the major sources of short-term credit are suppliers and banks. Other sources include Eurodollar loans, business finance company loans, and commercial paper. Short-term financing can take various forms. Suppliers provide trade credit, whereas bank loans can be unsecured loans, loans secured by either the firm's accounts receivable or its inventory, single-purpose loans, simple-interest loans, discount loans, installment loans, lines of credit, or revolving credit agreements.

Financial managers are concerned about both the sources and the forms of short-term financing, because these factors affect not only the availability but also the effective (true) costs of the firm's short-term funds.

STUDY OBJECTIVES

1. To become familiar with the sources and the forms of short-term financing.

2. To learn how a financial manager calculates the effective costs of the various sources and forms of short-term credit available to the firm.

CHAPTER OUTLINE

I. Trade credit and accrued current liabilities

   A. Trade credit results when suppliers extend short-term credit to the firm. The basic forms of trade credit include open accounts, consignments, and trade acceptances.

      1. An open account is a prearranged extension of the short-term credit a supplier extends to the firm.

         a. Terms include the credit period and any discount available to the firm if payment is made prior to the end of the discount period. For example, if terms were 1/10 net 30, the credit period would be 30 days after the invoice date, and the firm would be given a 1 percent discount from the invoice amount for payment made prior to the tenth day past the invoice date.

b. The cost of using an open account depends on the terms. When no discount is offered, open-account credit is free during the credit period. When a discount is available, open-account credit is free during the discount period, but there is a cost to the firm if it forgoes the discount. The annual percentage cost of forgoing the discount and paying at the end of the credit period can be approximated with the following equation:

$$\text{Annual \% cost} = \frac{\text{discount \%}}{100\% - \text{discount \%}} * \frac{360 \text{ days}}{\text{credit} - \text{discount} \atop \text{period} \quad \text{period}}$$

The firm should compare this cost with the costs of alternative sources of short-term credit when making its short-term financing decision. In the event that the discount is forgone, payment should be delayed until the end of the payment period to minimize the cost of not using the discount.

Example: If short-term bank loans are available at 16 percent and open-account credit terms are 1/10 net 30, should the firm take advantage of the discount?

Solution: The annual percentage cost of forgoing the 1 percent discount and using the funds for the 20 available days past the discount period is 18 percent:

$$\text{Annual \% cost} = \frac{1}{100 - 1} * \frac{360}{30 - 10} = .18 = \underline{18\%}$$

Therefore, the firm should take advantage of the discount and use the less expensive bank credit.

2. With a consignment, the firm allows the vendor to sell its goods in the firm's stores in return for a percentage of the sales. Since ownership of the consigned goods remains with the vendor, the vendor (rather than the firm) is responsible for financing the goods until they are sold.

3. Trade acceptances are time drafts (checks payable at a future date) issued to a supplier by the firm for payment of goods. From the date of their issuance until their payment date (usually 30 to 90 days hence), trade acceptances provide short-term financing to the firm. A trade acceptance on which the firm's bank guarantees payment is known as a banker's acceptance. Banker's acceptances are often used by firms involved in international trade.

B. Accrued current liabilities are interest-free sources of short-term financing that result when the firm delays its payment of accrued expenses such as wages, taxes, and interest.

II. Borrowing against accounts receivable and inventory

   A. Financial institutions (notably banks) will provide a firm with short-term credit secured by the firm's accounts receivable.

      1. The security agreement is the document that sets forth the terms and conditions of the loan.

      2. The percentage of the collateral value of the firm's accounts receivable that the financial institution will lend the firm depends on the quality of the accounts receivable pledged against the loan.

      3. Loans secured by accounts receivable are often made on a recourse basis to protect the lender in the event that the accounts receivable should be uncollectible in case of default by the borrower.

   B. The firm can also obtain short-term financing from lending institutions with loans secured by the firm's inventory.

      1. The loan's security agreement sets forth the conditions of the lien (a legal document that entitles the lender to possession of an asset pledged against a loan in the event of default) as well as the borrower's responsibility to document the inventory and assure its safekeeping during the period of the loan.

      2. In addition to the loan's interest rate, the cost of an inventory loan is affected by expenses incurred by the firm to comply with the loan's security agreement. Consequently, the firm's financial management should take these expenses into account when negotiating the terms of an inventory loan.

      3. Inventory-secured loans can be obtained under various arrangements, including terminal warehousing, field warehousing, trust receipts, floating collateral liens, and chattel mortgages.

         a. With terminal warehousing, the firm places merchandise in a public warehouse and obtains a terminal warehouse receipt. The lender then advances the firm funds against the warehoused merchandise upon presentation of the terminal warehouse receipt. Henceforth, the lender's authorization is usually required for the firm to remove merchandise from the warehouse.

         b. Field warehousing is similar to terminal warehousing, except that the merchandise is warehoused on the firm's premises rather than in a public warehouse. Under this arrangement, the firm leases a portion of its premises to a public warehouser for storage of the field warehoused goods. The warehouser controls access to these premises, usually with fences and security personnel. The warehouser then issues the firm a field warehouse receipt for merchandise placed on these controlled premises. When it is impractical to remove inventoried goods from the firm's premises prior to their ultimate sale, field warehousing may be preferred to terminal warehousing. However, the costs involved in field warehousing can make this type of inventory loan quite expensive.

      c. With a <u>trust receipt</u> arrangement, the lender retains title to the specific inventory items but they remain in the firm's possession. Proceeds from the sale of these specific goods are used to repay the loan, at which time the lender relinquishes title to these goods to either the firm or the buyer. This type of short-term financing is often referred to as <u>floor planning</u>, and it is popular with automobile dealers.

      d. A <u>floating collateral lien</u> requires the pledge of either a given quantity or a fixed inventory value of the firm's general inventory. From the firm's viewpoint, this type of inventory financing arrangement is less restrictive than other types. However, the lender may require additional liens on specific assets to reduce the risk.

      e. A <u>chattel mortgage</u> allows the firm to retain both possession of and title to specific inventory pledged against a loan. The lender must consent to the firm's sale of any inventory covered by the chattel mortgage, which reduces the flexibility of this method of financing.

III. Short-term bank loans

  A. Commercial banks are a major supplier of short-term credit to business firms. Therefore, selecting a bank (or banks) is an important task of the firm's financial management. Among the factors that influence the selection of a bank are the bank's <u>checking account services</u>, <u>international banking capabilities</u>, <u>bookkeeping and accounting services</u> that may be helpful to the firm, <u>flexibility</u> in tailoring loans to meet the firm's needs, <u>size</u> to accommodate large loan requests, <u>loyalty</u> to its customers during periods of tight credit, <u>lending rates</u>, <u>compensating balance</u> requirements, <u>management talent</u>, <u>location</u>, <u>financial conditions</u> that may affect the bank's ability to reliably meet loan demands, and participation in the <u>FDIC</u> (Federal Deposit Insurance Corporation) program.

  B. When approaching a bank for a loan, the firm's financial managers should be prepared to provide the bank with the following information:

    1. The loan's purpose and the amount of borrowed funds desired.

    2. Pro forma financial statements indicating the firm's ability to service the loan.

    3. Recent financial statements and past records of the firm's short-term borrowings.

    4. A profile of the firm's financial management.

    5. A list of collateral or endorsement guarantees that the firm is willing to offer as security on the loan.

    6. A review of the firm's past relations with the bank if the firm has been a regular customer of the bank.

C. Interest rates on bank loans are calculated in many ways. Therefore, in order to determine the effective (true) cost of borrowed funds, it is important to be aware of interest rate terminology, the compensating balance requirement, and various methods used to calculate effective interest rates.

   1. The prime rate is the nominal interest rate that a bank charges its best and most creditworthy customers. Other customers pay interest rates above the prime rate depending on the credit risk they represent. Many banks use a floating prime rate that varies in accordance with other short-term interest rates. Interest rates on loans with maturities in excess of one year can be quoted on a prime plus basis, whereby the loan's interest varies directly with the prevailing prime rate plus a few additional percentage points. The magnitude of the premium above the prevailing prime rate is determined by the borrower's credit risk.

   2. The effective interest rate on a loan is the true percentage interest cost paid by the borrower for the use of new funds made available by the loan. Thus the effective rate takes into account the loan's nominal interest rate and other factors (such as compensating balances, loan service fees, and expenses the borrower incurs in complying with the loan agreement) that affect the total cost of the loan.

   3. When the borrower has the use of total loan funds over the entire loan period and repays both the principal and the interest in a lump sum payment at the end of the period, the loan's nominal and effective interest rates are the same. The effective interest rate on loans of this nature is called simple interest, and such loans are referred to as simple-interest loans.

   4. A compensating balance requirement is a loan condition that requires the borrower to maintain a percentage of the loan in either a checking account or a time deposit at the lending bank. Thus compensating balance requirements increase a loan's effective interest rate. If the dollar amount (either absolute or average, depending on the loan agreement) in the borrower's compensating balance falls below the required level during the life of the loan, the borrower is subject to predetermined penalty charges assessed by the bank.

   Example: Suppose a one-year $900,000 loan has a 12 percent nominal interest rate but requires a $100,000 compensating balance in a time deposit that pays 6 percent per year. What is the effective rate on this loan?

   Solution: The total interest expense on the loan is $108,000 (.12 * $900,000). However, the $100,000 compensating balance in the time deposit will generate $6,000 (.06 * $100,000) in interest income, so the net interest expense related to the loan is $102,000. Since the loan has made $800,000 in net funds available to the borrower, the loan's effective rate is

   $$\frac{\$102,000}{\$800,000} = .1275 = 12.75\%$$

5. With a discount loan, the bank deducts the loan's interest expense from the principal when the loan proceeds are advanced to the borrower. Thus the net usable funds that the loan makes available to the borrower are reduced by the amount of this prepaid interest. At the end of the period of the loan, the borrower repays the loan's full principal. The effective interest rate on a discount loan always exceeds the loan's nominal rate.

Example: Determine the effective annual rate on a 180-day $100,000 discount loan that has a 14 percent nominal rate. Assume a 360-day year.

Solution: Total interest expense for 180 days on this loan is $7,000 (.14 * (180/360) * $100,000). Because this $7,000 is discounted from the loan's principal, the net loan proceeds available to the borrower are $93,000. Thus the loan's effective annual rate is calculated as follows:

$$\text{Effective annual rate} = \frac{\$7,000}{\$93,000} * \frac{360 \text{ days}}{180 \text{ days}} = .1505 = 15.05\%$$

6. An installment loan requires the borrower to make equal payments at regular intervals (monthly, quarterly, or annually) over the life of the loan. After the final payment, the loan's principal balance is reduced to zero. The effective annual interest rate on an installment loan can be approximated by using the equation

$$\text{Effective annual rate} = \frac{2 * K * I}{P * (N + 1)}$$

where K is the number of payment periods per year (12=monthly, 4=quarterly, and so on); I is total interest expense on the loan; P is the loan's original principal; and N is the number of total payments on the loan.

Example: A firm borrows $2,000 for 9 months on an installment loan. The monthly payments (end-of-month) are $240 each, and total interest on the loan is $160. Find the loan's effective interest rate.

Solution: Since payments are monthly, K = 12. Therefore,

$$\text{Effective annual rate} = \frac{2 * 12 * \$160}{\$2,000 * 10} = .192 = 19.2\%$$

D. In addition to the loan's nominal interest rate, other general terms of a bank loan, which are negotiable, include the loan's maturity, size, collateral, repayment terms according to the type of loan (simple, discount, or installment), compensating balance requirements, and covenants (the borrower's obligations under the loan contract).

E. A business firm can arrange several types of short-term loans with a bank.

1. A single loan is negotiated for both a specific amount and a fixed maturity.

2. A <u>line of credit</u> is a continuous borrowing relationship with a bank over a specific period of time. The bank agrees to lend the firm a maximum amount over that period of time (commonly one year), and the firm can call for advances (known as "take-downs") against the line of credit at its discretion. Interest rates on funds borrowed with take-downs are negotiated when the line of credit is established. Also negotiated are compensating balances, loan collateral (if any), and repayment obligations. The firm is usually required to repay ("<u>clean up</u>") all outstanding take-down balances for a set period of time (normally 30 days) during each year.

3. In a <u>revolving credit agreement</u>, the bank is legally obligated by the credit contract to lend the firm up to a maximum amount negotiated with the firm. Terms of a revolving credit agreement (compensating balances, collateral, clean-up period, and so on) are similar to those applied with a line of credit, except that the firm pays a <u>commitment fee</u> on any funds not borrowed (taken down) during the commitment period.

4. <u>Eurodollars</u> are dollar-denominated time deposits in banks located in foreign countries. With the assistance of a domestic bank that has either foreign branches or correspondents, a firm can borrow these Eurodollar deposits. Eurodollar loans usually have maturities of less than one year and interest rates that correspond closely to short-term interest rates in the United States.

IV. Commercial paper

A. Commercial paper issues are unsecured promissory notes issued by large firms with good credit ratings. Maturities on commercial paper vary from a few days up to 270 days (the average maturity is from 3 to 6 months). Interest rates on commercial paper are normally less than the prime rate, and they vary with the issuer's credit rating. Most issues of commercial paper are in excess of $10 million, so issuers of commercial paper tend to be the large and nationally prominent firms. Repayment on a commercial paper issue is at maturity, but issues are often refinanced (rolled over) with a new issue. Issuers of commercial paper usually have a back-up line of credit with a bank to assure investors of repayment at maturity.

B. Commercial paper is classified according to the method of issue.

1. With a <u>dealer-placed</u> issue, the issuer sells (for a fee) the entire issue to an investment banking group that resells the issue at a higher price to the public.

2. The issuer can by-pass the dealer (and his fee), with a <u>direct placement</u> of the issue to the public. With direct-placed commercial paper, however, the issuer assumes the risk that the entire issue will not be placed.

3. <u>Finance company paper</u> is issued by a finance company rather than by a nonfinancial firm. Since these issues are usually quite large, they are sold at lower prices (higher yields) than their nonfinancial counterparts.

V. Firms can also borrow short-term funds from a business <u>finance company</u> that specializes in making high-risk loans that banks may reject. Due to this higher risk, interest rates on business finance company loans tend to be higher than lending rates at banks.

STUDY PROBLEMS

14.1. Determine the effective annual rate (annual percentage cost) of forgoing the trade discount and using trade credit for short-term financing through the end of the credit period if credit terms were:

a. 2/10 net 30.   b. 2/10 net 45.   c. 1/15 net 60

Solution

a. Effective annual rate = (2/98) * (360/20) = .3673 = <u>36.73%</u>

b. Effective annual rate = (2/98) * (360/35) = .2099 = <u>20.99%</u>

c. Effective annual rate = (1/99) * (360/45) = .0808 = <u>8.08%</u>

14.2. Suppose that a firm pledges $450,000 of inventory against a 300-day inventory-secured loan of $380,000. The nominal rate on the loan is 12 percent per year, but the loan's security agreement requires the firm to spend an additional $9,000 to field warehouse the inventory. Calculate the loan's effective annual rate, assuming a 360-day year.

Solution

The total cost of obtaining this loan has two components: interest charges and field warehousing expenses ($9,000). Interest on the 300-day loan is calculated as follows:

Interest = $380,000 * .12 * 300/360 = $38,000

Total loan costs equal $47,000 ($38,000 + $9,000). Therefore,

Effective annual rate = ($47,000/$380,000) * (360/300) = .148 = <u>14.8%</u>

14.3. Find the effective annual rate on a $40,000 discount loan that has a 180-day maturity. The loan's nominal annual interest rate is 10 percent.

Solution

The discount (prepaid interest) amount = .10 * $40,000 * (180/360) = $2,000. Since the discount is deducted from the loan's principal, only $38,000 is available to the borrower. Therefore,

$$\text{Effective annual rate} = \frac{\$2,000}{\$38,000} * \frac{360}{180} = .1053 = 10.53\%$$

14.4. A company borrows $200,000 for 8 months with an installment loan from a bank. Repayment on the loan is to be 8 equal payments (R) of $27,000 each at the end of each month. Determine the loan's effective annual rate.

Solution

Total interest I equals the total amount of loan payments minus the loan's principal. Hence, for this loan,

$$I = (8 * \$27,000) - \$200,000 = \$16,000$$

Since payments on this loan are monthly, K (in the effective annual rate equation for a business installment loan) equals 12. Therefore,

$$\text{Effective annual rate} = \frac{2 * 12 * \$16,000}{\$200,000 * 9} = .2133 = \underline{21.33\%}$$

14.5. Tanner Supply negotiated a one-year revolving credit agreement with its bank for a credit line of $600,000. The nominal annual rate on any take-downs was 12 percent. To obtain this loan, Tanner had to pay a commitment fee of $9,000 at the beginning of the loan period and to maintain a ¢60,000 compensating balance in its checking account at the bank. Tanner normally carries a $20,000 checking account balance at the bank to accommodate its normal business transactions. If Tanner had $500,000 borrowed for the entire year, what was Tanner's effective annual interest on the funds made available by the revolving credit agreement?

Solution

From the $500,000 initial borrowing, Tanner had to pay $9,000 to the bank for the commitment fee and to deposit an additional $40,000 in its checking account to satisfy the loan's compensating balance requirement. Thus net proceeds from the loan to Tanner were $451,000 ($500,000 - $40,000 - $9,000). Total costs of the borrowed funds were the $9,000 commitment fee plus one year's interest on the $500,000 take-down. Because interest amounted to $60,000 (.12 * $500,000), total costs were $69,000. Therefore,

$$\text{Effective annual rate} = \frac{\text{total costs}}{\text{net funds}} = \frac{\$69,000}{\$451,000} = .153 = \underline{15.3\%}$$

REVIEW QUESTIONS

1. The annual cost of forgoing the trade discount with 1/10 net 20 credit terms is
   a. 1 percent.
   b. 10 percent.
   c. 18 percent.
   d. 20 percent.
   e. 36 percent.

2. Which of the following financing instruments are commonly used to finance international business transactions?
   a. trust receipts
   b. chattel mortgages
   c. banker's acceptances
   d. floating collateral liens
   e. trade acceptances

3. Floor planning is a financing arrangement using
   a. trust receipts.
   b. chattel mortgages.
   c. open-account trade credit.
   d. field warehouse receipts.
   e. consignments.

4. The effective annual rate on a $45,000 discount loan with a 120-day maturity and total prepaid interest of $3,000 is
   a. 6.67 percent.
   b. 7.14 percent.
   c. 14.29 percent.
   d. 20.00 percent.
   e. 21.43 percent.

5. A firm borrows $400,000 for 270 days with a simple-interest loan. What is the loan's effective annual rate if the nominal interest rate on the loan is 12 percent?
   a. 9.00 percent
   b. 9.89 percent
   c. 10.24 percent
   d. 12.00 percent
   e. 16.00 percent

6. A business's installment loan for $80,000 requires equal end-of-month payments of $7,200 each for the next 12 months. The loan's effective interest rate is approximately:
   a. 8.00 percent.
   b. 8.70 percent.
   c. 9.00 percent.
   d. 12.43 percent.
   e. 14.77 percent.

7. Which of the following forms of short-term credit are not available to most local business firms?
   a. revolving credit agreements
   b. commercial paper
   c. discount loans
   d. bank installment loans
   e. line-of-credit agreements

8. Determine the effective annual rate on a $200,000 loan for 10 months that has an 8.5 percent nominal interest rate and requires a 20 percent compensating balance in the firm's checking account.
   a. 10.20 percent
   b. 10.63 percent
   c. 12.60 percent
   d. 12.75 percent
   e. 14.27 percent

9. In the situation described in Question 8, recalculate the $200,000 loan's effective annual rate if the borrowing firm normally maintained $25,000 in its checking account at the lending bank.
   a. 8.50 percent
   b. 8.88 percent

    c. 9.19 percent
    d. 10.94 percent
    e. 12.15 percent

10. A bank will lend a firm $1,000,000 for 6 months if the firm agrees to maintain a 15 percent compensating balance in a time deposit at the bank. This time deposit pays 5.25 percent per year. The loan's principal and $60,000 interest come due at the end of the loan period. What is the effective annual rate on this loan?
    a. 6.13 percent
    b. 7.06 percent
    c. 12.54 percent
    d. 13.19 percent
    e. 15.04 percent

11. In order to obtain a $3,000,000 bank loan secured by its inventory, a firm must place its loan-related inventory in a warehouse under a terminal warehousing agreement. The firm must bear the warehousing expense of $42,000. The loan is for one year and has a 10 percent nominal annual rate. If the loan were set up as a discount loan, the loan's effective annual rate would be:
    a. 10.42 percent.
    b. 11.11 percent.
    c. 11.40 percent.
    d. 12.67 percent.
    e. 13.34 percent.

12. On a $2,000,000 revolving credit agreement for one year with a firm, the bank charges a nominal annual rate of 14 percent on any take-downs, plus a .5 percent per month commitment fee on any funds not borrowed. The loan agreement also stipulates that 10 percent of any funds borrowed must be maintained in a noninterest time-deposit account at the bank. If the firm had an average loan balance of $1,700,000 over the year on the revolving credit loan, what was the firm's effective annual rate on its loan?
    a. 14.96 percent
    b. 16.73 percent
    c. 17.44 percent
    d. 18.10 percent
    e. 20.36 percent

KEY DEFINITIONS

Banker's acceptances: checks payable at a future date and guaranteed (accepted) for payment at that future date by the bank on which they are drawn. They are a popular means of short-term financing available to firms engaged in international trade.

Commercial paper: unsecured, short-term promissory notes issued by large, nationally known firms with good credit ratings.

Compensating balance: either checking or time-deposit account balances that a bank requires a borrower to maintain as a condition for a loan. Compensating balances increase a loan's effective rate, because they reduce the funds that the loan makes available to the borrower.

<u>Consignment</u>: an arrangement that allows a vendor to sell its goods in a firm's store. The firm receives a percentage of the sales revenue from the consigned goods without having to pay finance charges on the consigned goods (that is, financing is the vendor's responsibility).

<u>Discount loan</u>: a loan for which the interest is prepaid and deducted from the loan proceeds before they are disbursed to the borrower. At the loan's maturity, the borrower repays the loan's full principal. The effective rate on a discount loan always exceeds its nominal rate.

<u>Eurodollars</u>: dollar-denominated time deposits in foreign banks that can be lent to domestic firms in the form of short-term Eurodollar loans.

<u>Floating collateral lien</u>: a lien that gives the lender the right to possession of either a fixed quantity or a fixed inventory value of a borrower's general inventory in the event of a loan default.

<u>Floor planning</u>: a method of short-term financing popular with automobile dealers that allows a dealer possession of automobiles financed by a bank that holds the titles. The bank passes the title to either the dealer or the purchaser when the automobile is sold and the proceeds of the sale fully pay the loan balance.

<u>Lien</u>: a legal instrument that gives the lender the right to possession of a specific asset in the event that the borrower defaults.

<u>Line of credit</u>: a continuing borrowing agreement with a bank that allows a firm to borrow up to a maximum amount (<u>line</u>) over a specific period of time (usually one year). Generally, all advances (<u>take-downs</u>) against the line of credit must be repaid each year for a set number of days (often one month) known as the <u>clean-up period</u>.

<u>Revolving credit agreement</u>: a line-of-credit agreement wherein the bank is legally obligated by the loan contract to make available loan funds to the borrower up to the maximum amount of the line over the loan period. In return for this guarantee, the bank charges the borrower a commitment fee on funds not borrowed during the commitment period.

<u>Trade credit</u>: short-term financing made available to a firm by its suppliers subject to prenegotiated terms and conditions.

ANSWERS TO REVIEW QUESTIONS

1. e	4. e	7. b	10. d
2. c	5. d	8. b	11. d
3. a	6. e	9. c	12. b

Chapter Fifteen
Sources and Forms of Intermediate-Term Financing

OVERVIEW

Intermediate-term financing in the form of either loans or leases provides the firm with financing over a span from one to ten years. The most common types of loans for intermediate-term financing include term loans, equipment financing loans, and conditional sales contracts. Institutional suppliers of these loans are commercial banks, life insurance companies, pension funds, business finance companies, equipment manufacturers, the Small Business Administration, and small business investment companies. Among the negotiable terms of such loans are the loan's repayment (amortization) schedule, interest rate, and covenants. Leases are an alternative to intermediate-term financing loans. The means of accounting for a lease depends on whether the lease is classified as a capital or an operating lease. Within this classification system are many types of leases (leveraged, sale-lease-back, net). In addition to understanding the various types of leases, financial managers should be aware of the advantages and disadvantages of leasing and should know how to evaluate lease-purchase alternatives.

STUDY OBJECTIVES

1. To become acquainted with the types and the sources of intermediate-term financing.

2. To understand the classification system for leases and the various types of leases that a firm's financial management encounters.

3. To learn how to evaluate lease-purchase alternatives.

CHAPTER OUTLINE

  I. Types of intermediate-term financing

     A. Term loans from either commercial banks or other financial institutions can be obtained with maturities between one and ten years. The negotiable features of a term loan include the loan's repayment schedule, interest rate, and covenants.

1. The repayment terms of most term loans require the borrower to repay (amortize) at a stated interest rate the loan's principal (amount borrowed) in periodic (monthly, quarterly, or annual) installments over the duration of the loan. The installments are usually uniform such that their present value, when discounted at the loan's interest rate, equals the original principal. In the event that the present value of these installments is less than the loan's original principal, a balloon payment at the end of the loan's duration will be large enough to fully amortize the principal. The loan's amortization schedule depicts both principal and interest components of each installment.

Example: Assume that a firm borrows $80,000 ($A_0$) for 3 years (n) at 10 percent (i) with a term loan. The loan is to be repaid with equal end-of-year installments such that the loan's principal is fully amortized at the end of the third year. Determine the size of each annual installment (R), and construct an amortization schedule for this loan.

Solution: The present value of the installments (R) discounted at 10 percent (i) for 3 years (n) equals the loan's principal (A_0). So, from Chapter 5,

$$A_0 = R * PAIT \text{ (where i = 10\%, n = 3)}$$

Substituting both A_0 = $80,000 and PAIT (from Appendix D) = 2.4864 into this equation yields $80,000 = R * (2.4868). Therefore, R = $32,169/year.

Amortization Schedule (to the nearest dollar)

(1) Year	(2) Beginning-of-Year Principal	(3) Installment (R)	(4) Interest [.10 * (2)]	(5) Principal [(3) - (4)]	(6) End-of-Year Principal [(2) - (5)]
1	$80,000	$32,169	$8,000	$24,169	$55,831
2	55,831	32,169	5,583	26,586	29,245
3	29,245	32,169	2,924	29,245	0
	Totals		$16,507	$80,000	

2. The interest rate charged on a term loan varies with the credit risk of the borrower. However, because the lender is committing funds for longer than a year, the interest rate is normally higher than the prime rate in effect when the loan is negotiated. The interest rate can be fixed over the loan's duration, or it can be a floating rate that changes with conditions in the credit market during the life of the loan. With a floating rate, any alterations in the loan's interest rate change the size of the installment payments and the loan's amortization schedule.

3. The loan's covenants are security provisions intended both to protect the lender and to help assure that the borrower is financially able to repay the loan's principal and interest. These covenants place restrictions on the borrowing firm--restrictions that can

materially affect the choices available to financial management in its future decisions. Therefore, the borrowing firm's financial officers should carefully negotiate the loan's covenants with the lender. Covenants associated with a term loan address such matters as:

a. Loan collateral and its maintenance.

b. Working-capital requirements placed on the borrower.

c. Dividend restrictions with which the borrower must comply.

d. Mandatory life insurance on the firm's key management, which would fully repay the loan's principal in the event of the death of an insured officer.

e. Lender approval prior to major changes in assets (or collateralization) by the borrowing firm.

f. Accelerated repayment, which may require the immediate repayment of the loan's principal in the event that the borrower either defaults on any loan or violates any covenant of the term loan.

g. Early-repayment penalties that may be imposed on the borrower for repaying the loan's principal prior to maturity.

h. Restrictions on the borrowing firm's use of the loan proceeds and on future salary increases for the firm's executives.

B. Equipment financing loans are used to finance specific equipment purchases, with the purchased equipment serving as collateral. In order to provide the lender with a margin of safety, the loan-to-value ratio associated with equipment financing loans is less than 1. That is, the lender lends less than the full market value of the pledged equipment. Interest rates on this type of loan vary with both the credit risk of the borrower and the marketability of the collateral. Although they are usually less restrictive than term loans, equipment financing loans are subject to covenants.

C. Equipment manufacturers can provide the firm with intermediate-term financing in the form of conditional sales contracts. The equipment sold to the firm serves as collateral, and the manufacturer holds title to the equipment until the loan's principal is repaid. Interest rates vary with the marketability of the equipment being financed, the borrower's creditworthiness, and the competitive market in which the manufacturer operates. Unlike other forms of intermediate-term financing, conditional sale contracts usually contain few restrictive covenants.

II. For a list of suppliers of intermediate-term financing, refer to Table 15.1.

Table 15.1   Suppliers of Intermediate-Term Financing

Lender	Term Loans	Equipment Financing Loans	Conditional Sales Contracts
Commercial Banks	Yes	Yes	-
Life Insurance Co.	Yes[1]	Occasionally	-
Pension Funds	Yes	Occasionally	-
Business Finance Co.[2]	Yes	Yes	-
Small Business Administration (SBA)[3]	Yes	-	-
Equipment Manufacturers	-	-	Yes
Small Business Investment Co. (SBIC)[4]	Yes	-	-

[1]Life insurance companies prefer longer maturities than other suppliers of term loans. Term loans from life insurance companies are often secured by real estate, and they may have stiff early-repayment penalties.

[2]Interest rates on intermediate-term financing from business finance companies are usually higher than rates on similar loans from other lenders. This is because business finance companies often provide financing to firms that represent high credit risks.

[3]The SBA is a federal agency that was established to help small businesses get financing. The SBA lends directly to small firms that meet certain criteria, and it also guarantees loans made to small businesses by private lending institutions (usually commercial banks).

[4]SBICs are federally chartered private lenders designated to provide venture (high-risk) capital to small businesses. SBIC loans usually give the lending SBIC the option to obtain an equity interest in the borrowing firm at some future date.

III. Leases

    A. A lease is a unique form of intermediate-term financing common in equipment financing and real estate financing. The asset's owner (lessor) allows the asset's user (lessee) to have the economic use of the asset in accordance with the basic provisions of the lease agreement. Consequently, financing of leased assets is provided by the lessor.

    B. Leases are generally classified as either capital or operating leases. Both the accounting for and the tax treatment of a lease depends on its classification. Within this classification system, several types of leases can be negotiated. They include the sale-leaseback, leveraged leases, and net leases.

        1. For a lease to be classified as a capital lease, any one of the following four criteria must be met:

      a. <u>Ownership</u> of the leased asset is transferred to the lessee at the termination of the lease.

      b. The lease has a <u>bargain purchase option</u> that allows the lessee to purchase the asset at the end of the lease at a price that is below the asset's market value at that time.

      c. The <u>lease's duration</u> is greater than 75 percent of the leased asset's economic life.

      d. The <u>present value of the minimum lease payments</u> exceeds 90 percent of the leased asset's market value when the lease went into effect. The discount rate used in this calculation is the lessee's borrowing rate that prevailed at the commencement of the lease.

2. All leases not classified as capital leases are <u>operating leases</u>.

3. When a firm sells an asset and then leases (as the lessee) the asset from the new owner (who becomes the lessor), the arrangement is known as a <u>sale-leaseback</u>. A sale-leaseback can be either a capital lease or an operating lease.

4. In a <u>leveraged lease</u>, three parties are involved: the lessee, the lessor, and a creditor who provides partial financing (leverage) to the lessor for the initial purchase of the leased asset. If a leveraged lease does not meet at least one of the criteria of a capital lease, it is classified as an operating lease.

5. A <u>net lease</u> (which can be either a capital lease or an operating lease) indicates the extent to which the lessee is required to assume certain expenses (property taxes, insurance, and maintenance) associated with the leased asset. The degree of the "net" reflects how many of these expenses are the lessee's responsibility. For example, with a double-net lease (also known as a net-net lease), the lessee assumes any two of these expenses and the lessor assumes the third.

C. The <u>basic lease provisions</u> are important to both the lessee and the lessor during negotiation of a lease. They determine the legal responsibilities and rights of both parties during the lease's life. Included in these provisions are:

1. The lease's <u>term</u> (duration).

2. The amount and frequency of <u>lease payments</u>.

3. The <u>degree of the "net"</u> in the lease; that is, which party bears what expenses associated with the leased asset.

4. The <u>covenants</u> (security provisions) of the lease contract, which specify what actions of either party to the lease constitute a default on the lease and the legal remedies of either party in the event of a default.

5. Escalation clauses that specify how increases in lease payments (if any) during the term of the lease are to be determined.

6. Option clauses, which determine such matters as the right of either party to the lease to renew the lease contract and the terms that apply if the lessee has an option to purchase the leased asset from the lessor at the lease's termination.

7. Insurance that the lessee may be required to carry for the benefit of the lessor in the event that the lessee defaults on the lease.

D. Any item can be leased, but those items most commonly leased include transportation equipment (airplanes, trucks, railroad cars), real estate (office buildings, shopping centers, farm land, stores), mineral rights, and computers.

E. The financial institutions that regularly engage in lease financing as lessors include subsidiaries of commercial banks, pension funds, specialized leasing companies, and insurance companies. The SBA occasionally guarantees the lease if the lessee is a small business.

F. Before deciding to lease assets, the lessee firm's financial management should consider both the advantages and the disadvantages associated with leasing.

Advantages

1. Leases afford flexibility to the firm in that they provide piecemeal financing. Furthermore, a lease's covenants (particularly those that pertain to the firm's dividend and working-capital policies) are usually less restrictive than similar covenants associated with other forms of intermediate-term financing.

2. The firm can shift the risk of the leased asset's possible obsolescence to the lessor. If the asset becomes obsolete during the lease's term, however, the firm is still obliged to honor the lease.

3. Leases can offer tax advantages. For example, if the alternative to leasing were equity financing of the leased asset, the firm would only receive a depreciation deduction for tax purposes. With leasing, however, the firm could possibly deduct the entire lease payment from its taxable income, thereby reducing its taxes because the lease payment usually exceeds the asset's depreciation deduction. In the case of older assets that are almost fully depreciated, the firm could sell the asset and simultaneously enter into a sale-leaseback on the asset with the new owner. The firm would gain a substantial tax advantage if the lease payments significantly exceeded the remaining depreciation charges on the old asset.

4. Leases can sometimes be used to circumvent loan restrictions imposed on the firm by its previous lenders to prevent the firm from using additional debt financing. However, because many lenders view leases as another form of debt, the ability of the lessee firm to avoid these restrictions may be limited.

5. If the firm is a poor credit risk, many lenders may not be interested in lending the firm new funds to purchase additional assets. But a lessor may be willing to lease assets to such a firm, because the lessor retains title to the leased assets.

6. Operating leases may have a favorable balance sheet effect for the lessee firm. Such leases are required to be reported only as a note to the firm's financial statements rather than as a liability on the firm's balance sheet.

7. Leases allow the firm some advantages in a bankruptcy. Since title to the leased asset is held by the lessor, the asset cannot be taken by the firm's other creditors. Furthermore, the lessor's legal claims against the firm may be limited to three (or fewer) annual lease payments in the event that the lessee breaks the lease, thereby giving the lessee firm more flexibility during a reorganization subsequent to a bankruptcy.

Disadvantages

1. Leases are often more expensive than debt funds provided by other sources of intermediate-term financing.

2. The firm loses both the depreciation and the investment credit tax deductions associated with assets leased under operating leases, because the deductions accrue to the lessor. (In certain cases, however, the tax advantage of the lease payments may outweigh these lost tax deductions.) Any residual value of the leased assets also accrues to the lessor rather than to the lessee.

3. Most leases are noncancelable. Therefore, even if the firm abandons the lease, it is still financially obligated to make the remaining lease payments. Thus leases usually represent fixed financial commitments of the firm that reduce the firm's future borrowing capacity.

G. Accounting treatment of leases

1. If a lease meets any of the four requirements of a capital lease, the minimum lease payments during the lease's term are capitalized (appear as a present value) on the lessee firm's balance sheet at the firm's borrowing rate that prevails when the lease commences. The asset entry to the balance sheet is made to Leased Property Under Capital Leases, and the liability entry is made to Capital Lease Obligations. The lease payments amortize this liability during the lease's term in a manner similar to the amortization of the principal of a term loan by periodic payments. Thus the imputed principal component of each lease payment reduces the firm's liability associated with the lease, whereas the imputed interest component is recorded on the firm's income statement as an interest expense. The leased asset is then depreciated as if it were owned by the lessee firm. Capital leases and their minimum lease payments in future years are also disclosed in the footnotes to the firm's financial statements.

2. The lease payments of an operating lease are simply expensed on the firm's income statement. They are not capitalized on the balance

sheet. Nevertheless, the firm must disclose in the footnotes to its financial statement the minimum future lease payments associated with its operating leases.

H. The lease-versus-purchase decision

  1. The first step in the lease-purchase decision is to determine the firm's annual <u>after-tax cash outflows</u> associated with each alternative. With the lease alternative, the relevant cash outflows include the lease payments less any tax deductions that would occur with leasing. With the purchase alternative, the yearly cash outflows to be considered include:

     a. Annual loan payments if the asset's purchase is debt financed, otherwise the firm's equity investment in the asset

     b. <u>Plus</u> maintenance expenses associated with the asset's ownership that would be included in the lease payments if the asset were leased

     c. <u>Less</u> the after-tax salvage value (if any) that the firm would receive when the asset was either sold or taken out of service

     d. <u>Less</u> all tax deductions related to interest, depreciation, and maintenance expenses

  2. The second step involves calculating the <u>present value</u> of the annual cash outflows related to each alternative. The discount rate to apply to each annual cash outflow is chosen in accordance with the riskiness of the outflow.

  3. The final step is to select the alternative with the cash outflow that has the minimum <u>present value</u>.

STUDY PROBLEMS

15.1. Construct a loan amortization schedule for a 4-year $25,000 term loan with a 12 percent interest rate. Equal end-of-year installments (R) are to be made on the loan.

<u>Solution</u>

    $25,000 = R * PAIT (where i = 12%, n = 4)
            = R * 3.037 (from Appendix D)

Therefore,

    R (the annual installment) = <u>$8,230.86</u>

Loan Amortization Schedule

(1) Year	(2) Beginning-of-Year Principal	(3) Installment	(4) Interest [.12 * (2)]	(5) Principal [(3) - (4)]	(6) End-of-Year Principal [(2) - (5)]
1	$25,000.00	$8,230.86	$3,000.00	$5,230.86	$19,769.14
2	19,769.14	8,230.86	2,372.30	5,858.56	13,910.58
3	13,910.58	8,230.86	1,669.27	6,561.59	7,348.99
4	7,348.99	8,230.86	881.87	7,348.99	0
	Totals		$7,923.44	$25,000.00	

15.2. Gavin Broadcasting leases its transmitter equipment with a 10-year lease that requires end-of-year payments of $65,000 each. The economic life of the equipment is 15 years, and its original cost (if purchased) would have been $500,000. When Gavin originally negotiated the lease, its borrowing rate was 7 percent. At the end of the lease's term, Gavin has the option of purchasing the equipment at its fair market value at that time. Is this lease an operating lease?

Solution

Gavin's lease is an operating lease only if none of the four requirements of a capital lease are satisfied. Therefore, we must consider each of these four requirements.

1. Ownership is not transferred to Gavin at end of the lease's term, so the first requirement is not met.

2. Gavin has an option to buy the equipment at the termination of the lease, but at fair market value, so the second requirement is not fulfilled.

3. Nor is the third requirement satisfied. The lease's duration is 67 percent of the equipment's economic life rather than the required 75 percent.

4. The present value of the minimum lease payments, discounted at Gavin's borrowing rate (7 percent) in effect at the lease's inception, is $456,533 [$65,000 * 7.0234 (from Appendix D with i = 7 percent and n = 10)]. The ratio of this present value to the equipment's original market value is 91.3 percent ($456,533/$500,000). This ratio exceeds the maximum 90 percent value, so the fourth requirement of a capital lease is met.

Gavin's equipment lease is a capital lease rather than an operating lease.

15.3. Suppose that the Gavin lease described in Problem 15.2 is just entering its third year.

a. Currently, what is recorded for this lease on Gavin's balance sheet under the liability account entitled Capital Lease Obligations?

b. Determine the imputed interest component of the third year's lease payment.

Solution

Partial Amortization Schedule of Gavin's Lease (to the nearest dollar)

(1) Year	(2) Beginning-of-Year Capital Lease Obligation	(3) Lease Payment	(4) Imputed Interest [.07 * (2)]	(5) Imputed Principal [(2) - (4)]	(6) End-of-Year Capital Lease Obligation [(2) - (5)]
1	$456,533	$65,000	$31,957	$33,043	$423,490
2	423,490	65,000	29,644	35,356	388,134
3	388,134	65,000	27,169	37,831	350,303

a. At the end of the second year (that is, at the beginning of the third year), $388,134 appears on Gavin's balance sheet as a liability under the account Capital Lease Obligations.

b. The imputed interest associated with the third year's lease payment is $27,169.

15.4. Suppose that a machine could be either purchased for $15,000 or leased for 3 years with an operating lease. The lease payments would be $6,600/year to be paid at the end of years 1, 2, and 3. The lease payments would be tax deductible. If the machine were purchased, annual depreciation charges would be $3,000/year, and the machine's purchase would be financed with a 3-year term loan at 9 percent requiring equal end-of-year payments of $5,926 each. The annual lease payments include a maintenance contract on the machine over the lease's term. The firm estimates that, without the maintenance contract, the annual maintenance expense related to the machine would be $600/year. The after-tax salvage of the machine at end of the third year is estimated to be $6,000 if the purchase alternative is chosen. The firm is in a 50 percent tax bracket, and all cash flows are to be discounted at the firm's cost of capital (11 percent). Should the firm purchase or lease this machine?

Solution

Step 1 - Determining cash outflows

Lease Alternative Cash Outflows

(1) Year	(2) Lease Payment	(3) Tax Deduction [.5 * (2)]	(4) After-Tax Cash Outflow [(1) - (3)]
1	$6,600	$3,300	$3,300
2	6,600	3,300	3,300
3	6,600	3,300	3,300

Loan Amortization Schedule (to the nearest dollar)

(1) Year	(2) Beginning-of-Year Principal	(3) Loan Installment	(4) Interest [.09 * (2)]	(5) Principal [(3) - (4)]	(6) End-of-Year Principal [(2) - (5)]
1	$15,000	$5,926	$1,350	$4,576	$10,424
2	10,424	5,926	938	4,988	5,436
3	5,436	5,926	490	5,436	0

Purchase Alternative Cash Outflows

(1) Year	(2) Loan Installment	(3) Interest Expense	(4) Depre- ciation	(5) Mainte- nance	(6) Total Tax Deduct. [.5*[(3)+(4)+(5)]]	(7) After-Tax Outflow [(2)+(5)-(6)]
1	$5,926	$1,350	$3,000	$600	$2,475	$4,051
2	5,926	938	3,000	600	2,269	4,257
3	5,926	490	3,000	600	2,045	-1,519*

*Note: The third year's after-tax cash outflow (R_3) must be adjusted to include the asset's after-tax salvage value ($6,000 inflow). Therefore, R_3 = $5,926 + $600 - $2,045 - $6,000 = $1,519 (a net inflow).

Step 2 - Calculating present values of outflows

PV of lease = $3,300 * PAIT (where i = 11%, n = 3)
= $3,300 * 2.4437 (from Appendix D)
= $8,064

PV of purchase = $4,051/(1.11) + $4,257/(1.11)^2 - $1,519/(1.11)^3
= $5,994

Step 3 - Selecting the minimum-present-value alternative

The asset should be purchased. The present value ($5,994) of the purchase alternative's outflows is less than the present value ($8,064) of the lease alternative's outflows.

REVIEW QUESTIONS

1. A firm is planning to borrow $100,000 for 4 years at 14 percent with a bank term loan. The loan's principal will be amortized with four equal end-of-year installments. The magnitude of each installment (to the nearest dollar) will be
   a. $9,467.
   b. $20,321.
   c. $25,000.
   d. $34,320.
   e. $37,653.

2. For the loan described in Question 1, what would be the loan's approximate principal balance after the third year's installment?
   a. $0
   b. $4,215
   c. $19,219
   d. $25,000
   e. $30,105

3. For the loan described in Question 1, the total interest paid on the loan over its life would be approximately
   a. $28,314.
   b. $37,282.
   c. $46,791.
   d. $56,000.
   e. $100,000.

4. Which of the following are not sources of business term loans?
   a. commercial banks
   b. non-life insurance companies
   c. pension funds
   d. business finance companies
   e. SBIC

5. SBICs typically
   a. are state chartered.
   b. provide high-risk (venture) capital to small businesses.
   c. have options to obtain an equity interest in their clients.
   d. both a and b.
   e. both b and c.

6. All leases that are not capital leases are classified as
   a. net leases
   b. gross leases
   c. operating leases
   d. leverage leases
   e. sale-leaseback leases

7. A tractor is to be leased for 5 years with noncancelable lease payments of $6,000 due at the end of each of the next 5 years. The tractor's economic life is 8 years, and its market value at the beginning of the lease is $33,070. At the end of the lease, the lessee has an option to buy the tractor at its fair market value. The lessee currently could borrow money to buy the tractor at 14 percent per year. This lease will
   a. be disclosed only in the footnotes to lessee's financial statements.

b. be classified as an operating lease.
c. appear on the lessee's balance sheet as a liability under Operating Leases.
d. appear on the lessee's balance sheet as a liability under Capital Leases.
e. both a and b.

8. Which of the following are usually considered <u>disadvantages</u> of leasing from the lessee's viewpoint?
   a. Leases seldom offer any tax advantages.
   b. Leasing is an expensive way to obtain intermediate-term financing.
   c. Lease covenants are more restrictive than those associated with term loans.
   d. Leases offer few advantages in a bankruptcy.
   e. Both a and d.

9. M. K. Dike & Company has a 6-year capital lease on a computer. The lease requires minimum annual end-of-year payments of $5,000/year. Dike's borrowing rate when the lease was signed was 9 percent, and the computer's market value at the commencement of the lease was $20,000. This lease originally appeared on Dike's financial statements as
   a. a balance sheet liability under Capital Lease Obligations in the amount of $20,000.
   b. a balance sheet liability under Capital Lease Obligations in the amount of $30,000.
   c. a balance sheet liability under Capital Lease Obligations in the amount of $22,430.
   d. a balance sheet asset under Leased Property Under Capital Leases in the amount of $20,000.
   e. both a and d.

10. For the Dike computer lease described in Question 9, approximately how much of the second year's lease payment was imputed principal for reducing Dike's Capital Lease Obligations?
    a. $900
    b. $1,750
    c. $2,980
    d. $3,250
    e. $5,000

11. Duvall Pump can buy a new press for $50,000 and finance the purchase with a 3-year term loan at 8 percent that requires end-of-year installments of $19,402 each. Maintenance expenses are expected to be $800/year, and annual depreciation expenses will be $10,000/year. Duvall plans to use the press for only 3 years, after which time Duvall estimates that the press could be sold for its book value ($20,000). Alternatively, Duvall could lease the press for 3 years with an operating lease that requires end-of-year lease payments. The lease payments would be fully tax deductible. Duvall is in a 50 percent tax bracket, and the company discounts all after-tax cash associated with either leased or purchased assets at 10 percent. The present value of the purchase alternative's after-tax cash outflows is approximately
    a. $18,282.
    b. $22,721.
    c. $25,312.
    d. $33,308.
    e. $50,000.

12. Determine the approximate magnitude of each lease payment in Question 11 such that Duvall would be indifferent between the lease and the purchase alternatives.
    a. $7,351
    b. $9,926
    c. $13,200
    d. $14,703
    e. $19,402

KEY DEFINITIONS

Amortization schedule: a detailed table of installment loan payments that shows the principal and the interest components of each installment and the principal balance remaining on the loan after each installment.

Balloon payment: in an installment loan, the final payment necessary to fully repay the loan's principal in the event that the regular installments on the loan do not completely amortize (repay) that principal.

Capital lease: a lease that meets any one of four criteria that tend to make the lease resemble purchase of the asset by the lessee. The present value of the minimum lease payments must appear on the lessee's balance sheet as a liability.

Conditional sales contract: a method of intermediate-term financing often provided by equipment manufacturers, whereby title to the equipment is held by the manufacturer that sold the equipment as collateral on the loan.

Covenants: security provisions on a loan that are intended to protect the lender by placing restrictions on the borrower during the duration of the loan.

Equipment financing loan: a loan that is secured by specific equipment and is similar to a conditional sales contract except that the lender is a commercial bank, pension fund, life insurance company, or business finance company rather than the equipment manufacturer.

Lessee: the party to a lease that obtains the economic benefits of the leased property during the lease's term.

Lessor: the party to a lease that both owns the leased property and conveys to the lessee the right to use that property during the lease's term.

Leveraged lease: a lease that involves three parties: the property's owner (lessor), the lessee, and a creditor that provides financing to the lessor so that the lessor can acquire the property.

Operating lease: any lease that does not meet one of the four criteria for a capital lease. Although the present value of the minimum lease payments need not appear on the lessee's balance sheet as a liability, the lessee must disclose those minimum lease payments in the footnotes to its financial statements.

Sale-leaseback: a lease arrangement in which a first party sells property to a second party and the first party (now the lessee) leases the property back from the property's new owner (now the lessor).

<u>Term loan</u>: intermediate-term loan with a maturity of up to ten years that is available from commercial banks and other institutional lenders. The negotiable features of a term loan include the loan's amortization (repayment) terms, interest rate, and covenants (security provisions).

ANSWERS TO REVIEW QUESTIONS

1.	d	4.	b	7.	e	10.	d
2.	e	5.	e	8.	b	11.	a
3.	b	6.	c	9.	c	12.	d

Part Six
Long-Term Sources of Funds

Chapters 16 through 19 investigate the types and characteristics of financial instruments the firm can use to meet long-term financing requirements. Chapter 16 provides an overview of financial markets in which long-term funds are obtained and the methods a firm can employ to issue its long-term securities. The specific aspects of debt financing (bonds) and equity financing (both common and preferred stocks) are examined in Chapters 17 and 18, respectively. In Chapter 19 attention is on long-term instruments (convertible securities and warrants) that sometimes offer the firm greater flexibility in its long-term financing plans than would be available with either straight debt or equity financing.

Chapter Sixteen
Marketing Long-Term Securities

OVERVIEW

Although most firms do not issue long-term securities on a regular basis, financial managers should be familiar with the marketing process by which long-term financing is obtained. When planning a new issue, many firms engage the services of investment bankers to provide them with professional advice on such matters as market conditions that may affect the issue's timing and different methods that can be used to market the issue. Among these various methods are negotiated under-writings, competitive bid underwriting, commission (best efforts) sales, direct sales, and private placements. If the offering is made to the public, the issue must comply with the registration requirements of the Securities and Exchange Commission and of the various states in which the new securities are to be sold. Since security markets are highly regulated, financial managers must also be aware of federal and state laws affecting the issuing of new securities and the trading of existing securities.

STUDY OBJECTIVES

1. To become familiar with the services and the functions of <u>investment bankers</u>.

2. To understand the various <u>methods</u> available to the firm for issuing new long-term securities.

3. To develop an understanding of <u>security markets</u> and their <u>regulatory environment</u>.

CHAPTER OUTLINE

I. Investment banking

   A. An <u>investment banker</u> is a company that (for a fee) helps firms sell their long-term securities (common stock, preferred stock, and bonds) to investors. Thus investment bankers bring buyers (investors) and sellers (firms issuing long-term securities) together. Investment banking firms also serve as <u>underwriters</u> by purchasing newly issued securities from firms and then reselling these securities to investors. In this underwriting

275

role, the investment banker bears the risk that the resale price of the securities will be lower than the price it paid the issuing firm for the securities. Due to their familiarity with both individual and institutional investors, many stock brokerage houses are also investment bankers.

B. Numerous issuing costs (collectively known as <u>flotation costs</u>) are incurred by a firm that attempts to sell a new issue of long-term securities.

    1. Flotation costs include:

        a. The investment banker's selling or underwriting commissions.

        b. Filing fees related to registering the issue with the Securities and Exchange Commission (SEC).

        c. Legal and accounting expenses.

        d. Costs associated with printing the issue's prospectus.

        e. The transfer agents' fees.

    2. An issue's flotation costs vary with:

        a. The <u>type of security</u> (for example, more expense is usually associated with stock issues than with bond issues).

        b. The <u>risk</u> of the security.

        c. <u>Market conditions</u> prevailing when the securities are issued.

        d. The <u>size</u> of the issue (per-security flotation costs tend to vary inversely with issue size).

        e. The issuing firm's <u>public image</u> (less-known firms usually have higher flotation costs than nationally prominent firms).

C. Functions of an investment banker.

    1. <u>Underwriting</u> and <u>distributing</u> newly issued securities are the main functions of investment bankers.

    2. Investment bankers also <u>advise</u> their clients on financial market conditions and the favorable timing of a new issue. In addition, investment bankers sometimes serve on their clients' boards of directors. Through this director's role, an investment banker can provide the firm with general advice about such matters as management of the firm's pension plans or possible merger offers. As a director, however, an investment banker must be careful to avoid possible <u>conflicts of interest</u>.

    3. By using the <u>prestige</u> associated with a reputable investment banker, many firms that lack national recognition among investors find it easier to sell new issues of their long-term securities.

    4. <u>Other services</u> offered by investment bankers include assisting their clients with private placements of long-term securities, lease

financing, mergers, real estate financing, international financing, commercial paper placements, and stock repurchases.

II. Methods of selling the firm's long-term securities

A. A <u>public offering</u> occurs when the firm sells its new securities to the general community of investors. Investment bankers are used if the public offering is on the basis of <u>negotiated underwriting</u>, <u>competitive bid underwriting</u>, or <u>commission (best efforts)</u>. Alternatively, the firm can make a public offering without the services of investment bankers through a <u>direct sale</u>.

1. A <u>negotiated underwriting</u> is a sequential process.

Step 1 - Initiate discussions

Once the firm decides to use long-term financing, the firm's financial management is directed to initiate discussions with an investment banker. However, these discussions can be initiated by either the investment banker or a third party (known as a <u>finder</u>), to which the firm pays a fee if the discussions result in an underwriting agreement.

Step 2 - Pre-underwriting conferences

After an investment banker is selected, but prior to the underwriting, the investment banker and the firm hold conferences to discuss the issue's <u>size</u>, <u>market conditions</u> that may affect the issue's timing, the <u>approximate price</u> that the investment banker is willing to pay the firm for its new securities, and the investment banker's <u>underwriting fee</u>. These conferences also establish the issue's <u>upset price</u>--that is, the minimum market price (or the maximum yield in the case of bonds) which, if it is reached prior to the sale, gives the firm the option to cancel the issue.

Step 3 - Syndication

Following a formal agreement between the firm and its investment banker, the investment banker establishes an <u>underwriting syndicate</u> with other investment banking firms that will assist in underwriting the firm's new securities. The firm's investment banker usually serves as the syndicate's general manager and negotiates with the syndicate's other underwriters such matters as each underwriter's responsibilities, liabilities, compensation, and proportion of the issue to be sold. The syndicate's underwriters then sign an agreement with the firm.

Step 4 - Registration

Subsequent to the formation of the syndicate, the firm must register the proposed new issue with the Securities and Exchange Commission (SEC) at least 20 days prior to the issue's public offering. Separate registrations may be required by state authorities of the various states in which the securities are to be sold. The SEC registration is accompanied by a preliminary prospectus (known as a <u>red herring</u>), which includes a brief history of the firm, the firm's recent financial statements (certified by its accountants), an explanation of the proposed use of funds raised by the new issue, a profile of the firm's management, both the characteristics and the amount of securities to be sold, the recent price ranges for the firm's existing securities, pending litigation (if any) involving the firm, the names of the issue's underwriters and the underwriting agreement, and a list of the firm's assets. In the minimum 20-day waiting period, during which the SEC confirms the validity of the firm's registration materials, the red herring can be distributed to potential investors only to advertise the new issue. Following SEC approval, a final prospectus (which includes the issue's offering price) must be distributed to all investors who purchase the new issue. The intent of the registration process is to insure that the issuing firm accurately discloses enough information for the investing public to make informed decisions about the new issue.

Step 5 - Selling group

During the registration process, the underwriting syndicate forms a selling group made up of security firms and brokerage houses that will actually sell the new securities to the public. The underwriting syndicate acts as a wholesaler of the issue, then, whereas members of the selling group serve as retailers to the public. Members of the underwriting syndicate can also be included in the selling group. Participants in the selling group receive a commission for their services from the underwriting syndicate in accordance with a formal agreement. This agreement specifies the allotment of the issue to be sold by each member of the selling group, the party that bears the responsibility in the event that a member of the selling group fails to sell its allotment, the minimum price (usually the initial offering price) at which the securities can be sold to the public, the conditions that must be satisfied for a commission to be paid to a member of the selling group, and the selling group's duration.

Step 6 - Setting the offering price

Following SEC approval of the registration process, a due diligence meeting is held between the issuing firm and its underwriters to set the offering price and prepare the final prospectus. This last-minute meeting derives its name from the fact that the meeting's participants are expected to diligently insure that all relevant information is disclosed in the final prospectus.

Step 7 - Sale

After the final prospectus is printed, the selling group begins selling the issue to the public. During the selling period, the underwriters try to stabilize the market so that the market price of the new securities will not fall below the initial offering price. (The underwriters' intent to stabilize the market price during the selling period must be disclosed in the SEC registration statement.) It is hoped that the issue will be sold quickly. If the issue is slow to sell, the offering price may have to be abandoned in favor of a lower market price, which could result in a financial loss to the issue's underwriters. Alternatively, the issue may be oversubscribed with more potential buyers than available securities. In this case, the underwriting syndicate may have the option to issue the securities necessary to handle the oversubscription.

Step 8 - Termination

Following the sale, the underwriting syndicate is terminated and all remaining securities in the underwriters' inventories are sold at current market prices.

2. A competitive underwriting is similar to a negotiated underwriting in most respects, except that competing underwriting syndicates bid against each other for the initial purchase of the firm's new securities. The issuing firm solicits bids and awards the issue to the syndicate offering the highest price for the securities. Many publicly regulated companies (for example, railroads and electric utilities) are required by their respective regulatory agencies to have competitive bidding to insure the highest possible price for the company's securities. Since it is difficult for a firm that employs competitive underwritings to establish a permanent relationship with an investment banker, the issuing firm usually retains an external financial advisor (often an investment banker) to provide advice on market conditions, timing of issues, and legal requirements.

3. When new securities are sold on a commission (best efforts) basis, the investment banker serves only as a selling agent (paid by commissions) rather than as an underwriter. Because an underwriter is not employed, the issuing firm has no assurance that the entire issue will be sold. Sometimes the offering is conditional on a specified portion of the issue being sold. Under these conditions, an escrow account is normally established both to receive any proceeds from the sale and to hold any purchased securities until the conditions of the sale are met. When these requirements have been satisfied, the funds in the account are released to the issuing firm and the new securities held in escrow are issued to the investors. Otherwise, the offering is cancelled and the contents of the account are returned to the respective parties. The commission (best efforts) method is usually best suited for high-risk firms that offer securities that investment bankers do not want to underwrite.

4. A firm can use a direct sale of its new securities to the public to by-pass investment bankers during the selling process. This reduces the firm's flotation costs in that both selling and underwriting fees are eliminated, but the firm must still bear the expense of registering the issue. Small issues are often sold directly to the public, because their size makes it impractical to use investment bankers as either sellers or underwriters.

B. As an alternative to a public offering, the firm may offer its new securities via a private placement to a few investors rather than to the general public. In a private placement, both the issue's terms and its price are negotiated directly with the investors. However, the issuing firm may use the advisory services of an investment banker during these negotiations. Institutional investors frequently involved in private placements include life insurance companies and pension funds. Private placements do not have to be registered, because the public is not involved.

1. The advantages of a private placement include:

      a. Flexibility to tailor the issue's size to the financial needs of the issuer (many issues are too small to justify the flotation costs of a public offering).

      b. Speed, because the issue is not delayed in the registration process.

      c. Lower flotation costs due to the elimination of sales commissions, underwriters' fees, and registration expenses.

  2. The disadvantages of a private placement include:

      a. More restrictive covenants (provisions) imposed on the issuing firm to protect the investors.

      b. A possible commitment by the issuing firm to bear future registration expenses should the investors decide to resell the issue to the public later.

      c. Either lower issuing prices (in the case of stock issues) or higher interest rates (in the case of long-term debt issues).

III. Organization and regulation of security markets

  A. All issues of new securities via either public offerings or private placements occur in primary markets. Thus the economic function of primary markets is to bring together the buyers (investors) and sellers (issuers) of new securities.

  B. Securities that are resold among investors after their issuance are traded in secondary markets. The economic function of secondary markets is to enhance the liquidity of securities issued in the primary markets.

    1. Organized exchanges provide a physical location where security dealers meet for the purpose of trading securities in the secondary market. Examples of domestic exchanges include the New York Stock Exchange (NYSE), the American Stock Exchange (AMEX), and the Midwest Stock Exchange. For a firm's securities to be traded on a particular exchange, the firm must meet certain listing requirements established by the exchange. These requirements usually pertain to such matters as the firm's size, the number of securities that the firm has outstanding, minimum financial performance standards, and the diversity and number of the firm's security holders. Due to these listing requirements, securities of the more established firms tend to be traded on the organized exchanges. Thus a certain amount of prestige is associated with having securities listed on an exchange. This prestige sometimes enhances the liquidity of the firm's securities in the secondary market, thereby making it easier for the firm to issue new long-term securities in the primary market.

    2. Unlisted securities in the secondary market are traded over the counter (OTC). Rather than being physically located in one trading area, OTC dealers are dispersed throughout the country. These dealers are connected by telephones and by the computerized telecommunications network of the National Association of Securities Dealers' Automatic Quotation (NASDAQ). In addition to unlisted stocks, most corporate bonds are traded OTC.

C. <u>Government regulations</u> apply to most corporate securities either issued to the public in the primary market or publicly traded in the secondary markets.

1. The <u>Securities Act of 1933</u> (amended in 1934) empowered the Securities and Exchange Commission (SEC) to monitor compliance with federal laws pertaining to the issuance of corporate securities to the public. The SEC can stop a firm's public offering if the law is violated and can bring criminal or civil charges against a firm or its officers. The intent of SEC regulations is to insure that a firm publicly offering securities <u>fully discloses</u> to potential investors both sufficient and accurate information so that investors can make informed decisions about purchasing the securities. In a public offering, the following SEC requirements must be satisfied.

   a. SEC <u>registration</u> of the issue (including a preliminary prospectus) at least 20 days prior to the issue's sale to the public is required. During this period, the SEC can delay the issue indefinitely until information in the registration material complies with the SEC's disclosure criteria.

   b. After the SEC approves the sale, a <u>final prospectus</u> must be supplied to each purchaser (investor) of the new issue.

   c. <u>Exemptions</u> to these SEC regulations include securities issued by firms regulated by another federal agency, by financial institutions regulated by either federal or state banking authorities, by firms involved in a reorganization under the authority of bankruptcy courts, by nonprofit organizations, for less than $450,000 in any 12-month period, and with maturities less than 270 days.

2. In addition to complying with federal laws, a firm publicly offering securities must obey any applicable state laws (popularly referred to as <u>blue sky laws</u>). These laws may require a separate registration statement to be filed with the states' regulatory authorities.

3. Under the <u>Securities Exchange Act of 1934</u>, the SEC was granted the authority to monitor the secondary market for publicly traded corporate securities. This authority includes the regulation of insider trading, public disclosure, and certain trading activities.

   a. <u>Insiders</u> include the firm's directors, the firm's key officers, and any investor who has a beneficial interest in more than 10 percent of the firm's stock. Insiders must submit monthly reports of their security holdings in the firm to the SEC and must return to the firm any profits they make from the sale of the firm's stock that they held for less than 6 months. They are forbidden from <u>short selling</u> the firm's stock (selling borrowed stock in the expectation of profiting from a future decline in the stock's market value.

   b. The firm's financial management is legally obligated to make certain that any information that might materially affect the firm's stock price is publicly disseminated in an expedient manner. Thus management should be cautious about making public statements on the firm's prospects for future earnings. In addition, the firm must file periodic (annual, quarterly, or monthly) financial statements with the SEC.

c. Certain trading practices, such as wash sales and pools, which are designed to defraud both the investment community and the public, are illegal.

1. A wash sale occurs when two or more investors buy and sell a firm's stock to each other in order to create the false impression of vast investor interest in the stock. Misled investors may then pay unwarrantably high prices for the stock, resulting in sizable profits for the investors involved in the scheme.

2. In a pool, a group of investors or insiders clandestinely acquires large holdings in a firm's stock and then attempts to inflate the stock's price with fraudulent information about the stock or with wash sales. If they are successful in manipulating the stock's price, the members of the group sell their stock and reap large profits.

REVIEW QUESTIONS

1. Per-security flotation costs tend to be higher for
   a. bond issues.
   b. low-risk securities.
   c. small issues.
   d. privately placed issues.
   e. stocks listed on the NYSE.

2. An investment banker that underwrites an issue
   a. assumes the risk of selling the issue to the public.
   b. is usually a subsidiary of a life insurance company.
   c. is precluded from being a member of the selling group.
   d. both a and b.
   e. both b and c.

3. Which one of the following services do investment bankers not perform for their clients?
   a. providing advice on financial market conditions
   b. offering advisory services in private placements
   c. helping in commercial paper placements
   d. assisting in arranging international financing
   e. conducting audits of their clients' financial statements

4. Which of the following methods used to issue new securities is dissimilar to the rest?
   a. negotiated underwriting
   b. commission (best efforts) offering
   c. direct sale
   d. private placement
   e. competitive bid underwriting

5. ABQ Company plans to issue 200,000 shares of common stock with a negotiated underwriting. During the pre-underwriting conference with its investment banker, ABQ establishes an upset price of $14/share and an investment banker's total fee of $2/share. All other flotation costs will be $100,000. The mini-mum net proceeds from the issue to ABQ are
   a. $2,300,000
   b. $2,400,000
   c. $2,500,000
   d. $2,700,000
   e. $2,800,000

6. In a commission (best efforts) offering
   a. the investment banker serves as an underwriter.
   b. investment bankers are not used.
   c. the firm is assured of selling the entire issue.
   d. the offering may be conditional on a specified portion of the issue being sold.
   e. registration with the SEC is not required.

7. Which of the following financial institutions are frequent investors in securi-ties issued via a private placement?
   a. pension funds
   b. commercial banks
   c. casualty insurance companies
   d. mutual funds
   e. investment bankers

8. A company issuing new common stock with a direct sale
   a. is taking part in a secondary market transaction.
   b. must register the issue with the SEC.
   c. uses an investment banker to underwrite the issue.
   d. will do so in the OTC market.
   e. sells the issue directly to either pension funds or commercial banks.

9. Which of the following pertain to the secondary markets?
   a. AMEX
   b. Securities Act of 1933
   c. Securities Exchange Act of 1934
   d. Both a and b
   e. Both a and c

10. Blue sky laws
   a. refer to the SEC's power under the Securities Act of 1933.
   b. exempt new issues of commercial bank stocks from SEC registration.
   c. pertain to state laws governing public offerings.
   d. are federal regulations that address public offerings of nonprofit organi-zations.
   e. control the activities of the NASDAQ.

11. Which one of the following sets of secondary market activities is illegal?
   a. noninsider short sells and pools
   b. both insider and noninsider short sells
   c. wash sales and insider ownership of stock
   d. wash sales and insider short sales
   e. pools and insider ownership of stock

12. A red herring
   a. may be distributed to potential investors to advertise an issue during the issue's registration process.
   b. must be distributed to all investors who purchase securities of a new issue.
   c. is a final prospectus.
   d. must contain the issuing price of securities to be issued.
   e. is required by blue sky laws.

KEY DEFINITIONS

Blue sky laws: state laws that govern public offerings of securities within the various states.

Flotation costs: the firm's various costs associated with issuing new securities.

Insider: any of a firm's key officers and directors or any investor who has a beneficial interest in more than 10 percent of the firm's stock. Insider trading of a firm's stock is permitted, provided that it is done in accordance with SEC regulations.

Investment banker: a company that specializes in both the distribution (selling) and underwriting of new security issues to the public.

Pool: an illegal practice whereby a group of investors acquires a large block of a firm's securities (usually stock) in the secondary market and then fraudulently attempts to manipulate the market price of the securities for the group's benefit.

Private placement: a firm's nonpublic offering of new securities to a few investors (often life insurance companies and pension funds). Private placements are exempt from SEC registration, because the public is not involved.

Public offering: the sale of new securities by a firm to the general community of investors via a negotiated underwriting, a competitive bid underwriting, a commission (best efforts) offering, or a direct sale.

Red herring: a preliminary prospectus that may be distributed to potential investors during a new issue's SEC registration process in order to advertise the issue.

Securities and Exchange Commission (SEC): the federal agency that regulates both the primary and the secondary markets for publicly traded corporate securities.

Short sale: the sale of borrowed stock in anticipation of a future decline in the stock's market price.

Underwriting: the process whereby an investment banker (for a fee) buys an entire issue of new securities from the issuing firm. Thus the investment banker (rather than the firm) bears the risks of reselling the issue to the public. The fee (usually a discount from the issue's offering price) is intended to compensate the investment banker for taking this risk.

Wash sale: an illegal, secondary market transaction involving two or more investors who trade (buy and sell) a firm's stock among themselves in an attempt to fraudulently inflate the stock's market price in order to make a profit.

CHAPTER 16

ANSWERS TO REVIEW QUESTIONS

1. c	4. d	7. a	10. c
2. a	5. a	8. b	11. d
3. e	6. d	9. e	12. a

Chapter Seventeen
Long-Term Debt

OVERVIEW

Once a firm has decided to use long-term sources of debt capital, it is important that the firm's financial officers be familiar with terminology, types of bonds, methods of repayment, and restrictive provisions associated with long-term debt financing. Understanding these topics will help the firm's management to design long-term debt offerings in such a way that they will be attractive to potential investors but not place unnecessary financial burdens on the firm. Before issuing bonds, the firm's financial officers should review both the advantages and the disadvantages of long-term debt financing. It is also helpful for financial managers to know how to assess the advisability of bond refunding. Market conditions may change after bonds have been issued, and the firm may have an opportunity to retire the old bond issue and replace it with new bonds that have terms more favorable to the firm.

STUDY OBJECTIVES

1. To get acquainted with the terminology typically used by investors and financial officers in dealing with long-term debt.

2. To be able to distinguish between the various types of long-term bonds.

3. To appreciate the restrictions often associated with long-term financing that may affect the firm's future operating and financial decisions.

4. To learn how to evaluate the advisability of bond refunding.

CHAPTER OUTLINE

I. Types and features of long-term debt (bonds)

   A. Bonds are long-term debt instruments that promise repayment to the bondholder (investor) of the bond's principal (the amount borrowed, referred to as the bond's face or par value) over a specified time period (maturity) at a specific annual interest rate. Most corporate bonds have $1,000 par values and maturities that range from 20 to 30 years. The

286

indenture is the legal agreement between the investor and the firm issuing the bond. It specifies such details as the bond's maturity, annual interest rate, denomination (the dollar size of the bond's par value), restrictions (covenants), repayment schedule, and collateral. The bond's trustee is the party (usually the trust department of a commercial bank) that serves in behalf of the bondholders to make sure that the issuing firm fulfills its obligations in accordance with the bond's indenture.

B. The annual interest rate paid on a bond's par value is known as the coupon rate. The current yield (CY) is the bond's annual dollar interest payments divided by the bond's current market price. An investor's annual rate of return on the bond if the bond were bought today and held to maturity is referred to as the bond's yield to maturity (YTM). For a bond that matures in the nth year, the exact YTM is found by determining the discount rate that equates the present value of both the bond's annual interest payments (I) and the bond's par value (P_n) to the bond's current market price (P_0). The following equation allows us to determine the bond's YTM if we know I, P_0, and P_n:

$$P_0 = \sum_{t=1}^{n} I/(1 + YTM)^t + P_n/(1 + YTM)^n$$

For approximation purposes, the formula for a bond's YTM is

$$YTM = \frac{I + (P_n - P_0)/n}{(P_n + P_0)/2}$$

Example: Suppose that a bond ($1,000 par) matures in 25 years and has a 6 percent coupon rate (that is, the annual interest on the bond is $60). Determine the bond's CY and its appropriate YTM if the bond's market price is $850.

Solution: CY = $60/$850 = .0706 = 7.06%

$$YTM = \frac{\$60 + (\$1,000 - \$850)/25}{(\$1,000 + \$850)/2} = .0714 = 7.14\%$$

Note: The bond's exact YTM is 7.33 percent.

C. A bond is trading at par whenever its market value and its par value are equal. These conditions occur when the bond's coupon rate equals its YTM. When the coupon rate is less than the bond's YTM, the bond's market value is lower than its par value and it trades at a discount from its par value. When the coupon rate is greater than the YTM, the bond trades at a premium, because its market value exceeds its par value. The dollar amount of either the discount or the premium associated with a bond is determined by both the bond's duration to maturity and the difference between the bond's YTM and coupon rate. In our example, the bond's discount is $150.

D. Types of bonds.

1. Ownership of a bearer bond is evinced by the investor's physical possession of the bond. Annual interest is paid when the investor presents to the firm a dated coupon that has been clipped from the bond. Upon maturity of a bearer bond, the bond's par value is paid to the investor, who surrenders the bond to the firm. A registered bond, on the other hand, is registered in the bondholder's name on the firm's official records. These official ownership records are referred to as the bond's registry. Both annual interest payments and the par value (at maturity) are mailed directly to the investor of record in the bond's registry.

2. A mortgage bond is secured (via a lien) by specific assets of the firm. In the event of a default on mortgage bonds, bondholders can take possession of the mortgaged assets in an attempt to satisfy their claims against the firm. However, the bondholders have no guarantee that the liquidated value of these mortgaged assets will fully repay the bonds' principal and unpaid interest. Numerous types of mortgage bonds exist.

    a. Holders of first-mortgage bonds (or senior-mortgage bonds) have a priority claim to the bonds' mortgaged assets over the claims of any other bondholders whose bonds (known as junior mortgages) are secured by the same assets. Second-mortgage bonds are junior mortgages that are subordinated to first-mortgage bonds. Because second mortgages provide less security than first mortgages, they must offer higher interest rates to attract investors.

    b. Closed-end mortgage bonds prohibit the firm from issuing future mortgage bonds that have an equal claim priority to the original bonds' pledged assets. Open-end mortgage bonds don't have this restriction; however, the provisions of such mortgages may require that subsequently acquired assets that have the same general nature as the mortgaged assets also be included in the bonds' collateral. Limited open-end mortgage bonds permit the firm to issue only a predetermined amount of future mortgages with the same claim priority to the bonds' mortgaged assets.

    c. Rather than being secured by specific assets, general (or blanket) mortgage bonds are secured by all or most of the firm's assets.

3. Other types of secured bonds include equipment trust certificates and collateral trust bonds.

    a. Equipment trust certificates are usually collateralized by transportation equipment of railroads and other transportation companies. Defaults on equipment trust certificates are few. Their collateral is easily repossessed and is crucial to the operations of the firm issuing them.

    b. Collateral trust bonds are secured by the issuing firm's financial assets (stocks and bonds of other firms or of the issuing firm's subsidiaries). These pledged securities are held in a trust account to protect the investors, even though the firm that pledged these assets continues to have a voting right (in the case of pledged common stock) and to receive any income (either dividends or interest) from the pledged securities.

4. Debentures are unsecured, long-term bonds backed only by the borrowing firm's creditworthiness. If a default occurs, debenture holders become general creditors of the firm.

   a. A debenture can be subordinated to either other bonds or bank loans (that is, it can have a lower claim priority). The degree of subordination of a debenture depends on the conditions specified in the bond's indenture. For example, senior subordinated debentures have a higher-priority claim than junior subordinated debentures.

   b. Debentures are sometimes convertible into a specific number of shares of the borrowing firm's common stock. (Convertible debentures are discussed in Chapter 19.)

   c. Income bonds and receiver's certificates are special types of debentures.

      i. The interest on income bonds is payable only if it is earned; that is, the issuing firm is not obliged to pay the bond's annual interest unless sufficient earnings are available. Most income bonds have an accumulation feature requiring the firm to pay all interest that is in arrears as soon as the firm's earnings improve. Income bonds are typically issued by firms that are being reorganized in bankruptcy and are too financially weak to withstand the burden of fixed-interest obligations.

      ii. Receiver's certificates are issued by the bankruptcy court when it takes over the firm's operation in receivership (see Chapter 21). In order to entice potential investors, receiver's certificates normally have a priority claim over all the firm's existing debt.

5. Even though most bonds have fixed annual interest rates, certain types of bonds are exceptions to this general rule.

   a. The interest rate on index bonds fluctuates with the rate of inflation. (Index bonds are uncommon in the United States.)

   b. Within predetermined limits, the interest rate associated with a floating-rate note adjusts (with a slight lag) to changes in market interest rates. Holders of these bonds often have the option of converting their bonds into either a fixed number of shares of the issuing firm's common stock or a fixed-interest-rate subordinated debenture.

6. The interest and principal on certain types of bonds are sometimes either guaranteed or assumed by a third party.

a. Guaranteed bonds are usually unsecured, but their interest and principal are guaranteed by either the issuing firm's parent company or a more creditable corporation.

b. Assumed bonds are bonds for which a firm other than the firm that originally issued the bonds has assumed the responsibility of making the interest and principal payments. Such bonds are frequently issued in a merger, when the acquiring firm assumes the debt obligations of the acquired firm.

c. Joint bonds are bonds issued by a firm that was created as a joint venture of two or more firms. Both parent firms guarantee the debt of the issuing firm.

d. Industrial revenue bonds are issued by a governmental authority for the purpose of purchasing land, buildings, or equipment that will be leased to a business firm. In a sense, the firm's associated lease payments to the governmental authority guarantee the bonds, because these payments are negotiated large enough to satisfy the bonds' interest and principal obligations over the bond's duration. Being exempt from federal income taxes, the interest on industrial revenue bonds is less than the fully taxable interest that would be paid if the firm issued the bonds in its own name.

7. A unit offering is a combination of several types of the firm's securities (usually bonds and common stock) in one investment package. The issuing firm can sometimes market the components of a unit offering more easily (and at terms more favorable to the firm) than would be possible if the securities making up the unit were sold individually.

E. Repayment terms

1. Sinking funds provide for the periodic repayment of a bond issue's principal during the issue's life. Annual sinking-fund payments can be made into an interest-paying escrow account such that, at the bonds' maturity, sufficient funds will have accumulated in the account to retire the entire issue of bonds. Alternatively, the firm may have the option to repurchase a fixed amount of the issue's outstanding debt annually in the open market at prevailing market prices. The firm benefits with this alternative if the bonds' market price is below their par value.

2. Serial bonds require the firm to redeem at par value a certain percentage of the bond issue each year. The bonds to be redeemed each year are randomly selected according to the serial numbers appearing on the bonds.

3. Some bond issues (notably those associated with state and local governments) have staggered maturities such that various segments of the issue mature at different times.

4. If a bond has a call provision, the firm has the option of retiring the bond prior to its maturity. This option gives the firm's financial management considerable flexibility in the event that interest

rates fall after the bond is issued. Under these conditions, the firm can retire the original bond issue and replace it with a new issue of bonds that have a lower interest rate. Since the call option benefits the firm rather than the firm's bondholders, the call price is usually at a premium above the bond's par value to compensate the bondholder for surrendering a bond that pays a higher interest rate than a replacement bond would pay. This premium can be constant during the bond's duration, or it can be reduced uniformly each year until it is zero at the bond's maturity. If the bond has a deferred call provision, the firm is prohibited from calling the bond for a certain number of years (usually five to ten years) after the bond is issued. Investors in bonds that have a call provision are interested in the bond's yield to first call (YTFC) as well as in the bond's yield to maturity (YTM) and its current yield (CY). A bond's exact YTFC and its approximate YTFC can be found by substituting the bond's call price for the bond's par value (P_n) and the number of years to first call for the bond's maturity (n) in the appropriate YTM formula.

5. A balloon repayment provision allows the firm to retire either all or a portion of a bond issue at the issue's maturity.

F. Bonds are rated according to their quality (investors' risk) by rating agencies such as Moody's or Standard & Poor's. Lower ratings (which imply higher risks) tend to raise the firm's cost of debt. A bond's rating worsens as its claim priority declines. For example, mortgage bonds usually have a lower rating than debentures issued by the same firm.

II. Advantages and disadvantages of long-term debt

A. Advantages to the firm.

1. Since bonds offer investors greater protection than stock, the interest rate on the firm's long-term debt is typically lower than the dividend rate on the firm's stock. Furthermore, the firm's interest expense is tax deductible for bonds. Its stock dividend payments don't receive this tax benefit. Consequently, bonds provide the firm with a relatively inexpensive source of long-term financing that may result in a lower after-tax cost of capital for the firm.

2. Bonds typically have lower flotation costs than other sources of long-term financing.

3. The use of bonds results in less dilution of both the firm's per-share earnings and the current stockholders' control of the firm.

4. Long-term debt is less risky than short-term debt, because it has a longer maturity. Therefore, financing with bonds offers the firm greater liquidity than short-term financing.

5. The firm's earnings per share may be increased by the positive effects of financial leverage resulting from the firm's use of long-term debt financing.

B. <u>Disadvantages</u> to the firm.

   1. Since interest and sinking-fund payments are fixed financial obliga-
      tions of the firm, both the firm's <u>financial risk</u> and its <u>risk of in-
      solvency</u> are increased with the use of long-term financing. These
      higher risks tend to raise the firm's costs of long-term financing
      and its cost of capital.

   2. The restrictive covenants specified in bond indentures can result in
      <u>less flexibility</u> in the firm's future dividend policy, working-capital
      management, and financing decisions.

III. When considering the use of long-term debt as a source of funds, the firm's
     financial management should bear in mind the following factors:

   A. The impact of long-term debt on the firm's <u>cost of capital</u>.

   B. The possible positive effects on the firm's earnings per share resulting
      from increased <u>financial leverage</u>.

   C. The <u>earnings stability</u> necessary to service the firm's new debt.

   D. Any restrictions on management's <u>flexibility</u> imposed by the debt's
      covenants.

   E. Current stockholders' <u>control</u> of the firm.

   F. Improved <u>liquidity</u> that could result from less reliance on short-term
      financing.

   G. <u>Market receptiveness</u> to new issues of either the firm's long-term debt or
      its stock.

   H. Current <u>market conditions</u> and prevailing <u>interest rates</u>, which affect the
      timeliness of long-term debt financing.

IV. If the firm's existing bonds are callable, the firm can retire them and re-
    issue new bonds at a lower interest rate whenever market interest rates fall
    below the interest rate on the old bonds. This <u>bond refunding</u> can be evalu-
    ated in a stepwise manner.

   A. <u>Step 1</u> is to determine the total <u>investment outlay</u> necessary both to re-
      tire the old bonds and to issue new bonds. The cash flows associated
      with this investment include:

      1. The <u>call premium</u> less its tax savings. (The call premium is fully
         tax deductible, and the related tax savings are immediately available
         to the firm.)

      2. The <u>flotation costs</u> of the new issue. (Although these flotation
         costs are tax deductible, they must be amortized over the life of
         the new issue.)

      3. The <u>after-tax overlapping interest expense</u> from the old bonds that
         results from the fact that both the new and the old issues are simul-
         taneously outstanding while the old bonds are being retired.

      4. The <u>tax savings</u> that immediately occur from the unamortized portion of the old bonds' issuing expense.

  B. <u>Step 2</u> is to calculate the future <u>cash flow savings</u> that result from the refunding decision. Included in the future savings are:

      1. The difference between the <u>annual after-tax interest expense</u> of the new bonds and that of the higher-interest-rate old bonds.

      2. The difference between the <u>annual tax savings</u> associated with the amortization of each issue's flotation costs.

  C. <u>Step 3</u> is to find the <u>net present value</u> of the refunding decision by sub-tracting the investment outlay (determined in step 1) from the present value of the future cash savings (calculated in step 2) discounted at the firm's average cost of capital. If this net present value is greater than zero, the firm should refund the old bonds.

STUDY PROBLEMS

<u>17.1.</u> The Welster Corporation has $20,000,000 of bonds outstanding, which carry a 13 percent coupon rate. The par value of each bond is $1,000 and the bonds mature in 25 years. The bond's flotation costs when they were issued 5 years ago were $240,000. The bonds are callable, but their call premium is $130 per bond. If the old bonds were refunded, $20,000,000 of new 25-year bonds could be issued for $300,000 (flotation costs) with an 11 percent coupon rate. Like the old bonds, the new bonds would have a par value of $1,000 per bond. Welster is in a 40 percent tax bracket and has a 12 percent average cost of capital. Should the old 13 per-cent bonds be refunded if the overlapping interest period on the existing bonds would be one month?

<u>Solution</u>

  <u>Step 1</u> - Investment outlay

  a. Bonds to be called = $20,000,000/$1,000 = 20,000 bonds
     Call premium = 20,000 bonds * $130/bond = $2,600,000
     Call premium tax savings - $2,600,000 * .4 = $1,040,000
     Net after-tax call premium cash outflow = $2,600,000 - $1,040,000
                                    = $1,560,000

  b. Flotation costs of new issue = $300,000

  c. Overlapping after-tax interest expense of the old bonds
     = (1/12 * .13 * $20,000,000) * (1.0 - .4)
     = $130,000

  d. Tax savings from the unamortized portion of the old bonds' flotation costs
     = 25/30 * $240,000 * .4
     = $80,000

<u>Total cash investment</u> = a + b + c - d
                    = $1,560,000 + $300,000 + $130,000 - $80,000
                    = $1,910,000

Step 2 - Future cash flow savings

a. Annual after-tax interest expense savings
    = (.13 - .11) * $20,000,000 * (1.0 - .4)
    = $240,000

b. Annual tax savings associated with the unamortized portion of each issue's flotation costs
    = [(1/25 * $300,000) - (1/30 * $240,000)] * (.4)
    = (12,000 - 8,000) * (.4)
    = $1,600

Total future annual cash savings = a + b
    = $240,000 + $1,600 = $241,600

Step 3 - Net present value of refunding decision

Present value PV of future annual cash savings
= $241,600 * PAIT (where i = 12%, n = 25)
= $241,600 * 7.8431 (from Appendix A.4) = $1,894,893

Net present value of refunding = PV - investment outlay
    = $1,894,893 - $1,910,000
    = -$15,107

Conclusion: Do not refund the old bonds. The present value of the future annual cash savings does not exceed the investment outlay required to refund. That is, the net present value of the refunding decision is negative (-$15,107).

17.2. A $1,000 par value bond that matures in 10 years has a 12 percent coupon rate. The bond's market price is $1,100. Determine the bond's current yield (CY) and yield to maturity (YTM).

Solution

CY = (.12 * $1,000)/$1,100 = $120/$1,100 = .1091 = 10.91%

$$\text{YTM (approx.)} = \frac{\$120 + (\$1,000 - \$1,100)/10}{(\$1,000 + \$1,100)/2} = .1048 = 10.48\%$$

17.3. Suppose the bond described in Problem 17.2 could be called in 3 years at a call price of $1,200. Calculate both the bond's approximate yield to first call (YTFC) and its call premium.

Solution

$$\text{YTFC (approx.)} = \frac{\$120 + (\$1,200 - \$1,100)/3}{(\$1,200 + \$1,100)/2} = .1333 = 13.33\%$$

Call premium   = $200 [$1,200 - $1,000 (par value)]

17.4. Idaho Bell has an issue of senior subordinated debentures ($1,000 par) out-
standing that mature in 12 years with an 8½ percent coupon rate. The debentures'
sinking fund requires the company to either deposit $700,000 annually in the sinking
fund's escrow account or annually repurchase $900,000 of the issue's par value in
the open market. Currently, the debentures are trading at a $166.67 discount from
their $1,000 par value. Idaho Bell is in a 46 percent tax bracket.

a. What is the market price of each debenture?

b. Determine the approximate YTM for the debentures.

c. How many bonds could be retired with a repurchase option?

d. If Idaho Bell wanted to minimize its sinking-fund cash outflow, which
    alternative should it select?

e. Calculate the savings in annual after-tax interest expense available to
    the company if the repurchase option is chosen.

Solution

a. Market price = par value - discount = $1,000 - $166.67
                 = $833.33/debenture

b. YTM = $\dfrac{\$85 + (\$1,000 - \$833.33)/12}{(\$1,000 + \$833.33)/2}$ = .1079 = 10.79%

c. Debentures retired = $900,000/$1,000 par value = 900 debentures

d. Escrow account cash outflow = $700,000

    Repurchase cash outflow = 900 debentures * $833.33/debenture
                            = $749,997

    To minimize its sinking-fund cash outflow, Idaho Bell should select the
    escrow account option. Its cash outflow is $49,997 less than cash out-
    flow of the repurchase option.

e. Annual interest per debenture = (.085) * ($1,000) = $85. Therefore,
    savings in annual after-tax interest expense associated with the repur-
    chase option are

        $85/debenture * 900 debentures * (1 - .46) = $41,310

REVIEW QUESTIONS

1. Restrictions (covenants) associated with a bond are specified in the bond's
    a. sinking fund.
    b. debenture.
    c. call provision.
    d. indenture.
    e. escrow.

2. FMA Corporation debentures ($1,000 par) have a 9 percent coupon rate and a re-
maining maturity of 11 years. The debentures' current market value is $1,050
per debenture. Which one of the following sets of yields corresponds to the
debentures' current yield (CY) and their approximate yield to maturity (YTM),
respectively?
   a. 8.34 percent, 9.00 percent
   b. 8.57 percent, 8.34 percent
   c. 8.57 percent, 9.00 percent
   d. 9.00 percent, 8.57 percent
   e. 9.47 percent, 11.21 percent

3. If the FMA debentures in Question 2 were first callable in 4 more years at a
call price of $1,090, the debentures' approximate yield to first call (YTFC)
would be
   a. 8.34 percent.
   b. 8.57 percent.
   c. 9.35 percent.
   d. 9.47 percent.
   e. 11.21 percent.

4. A bond will sell at a discount whenever
   a. the yield to maturity exceeds the coupon rate.
   b. the yield to maturity exceeds the current yield.
   c. the coupon rate exceeds the yield to maturity.
   d. the coupon rate exceeds the current yield.
   e. the current yield equals the coupon rate.

5. Which of the following bonds have the highest claim priority?
   a. senior subordinated debentures
   b. closed-end mortgages
   c. open-end mortgages
   d. debentures
   e. income bonds

6. Bonds secured by the issuing firm's financial assets are called
   a. unit offerings.
   b. floating-rate notes.
   c. limited open-end mortgages.
   d. collateral trust bonds.
   e. junior mortgages.

7. Which of the following bonds are exempt from federal income taxes?
   a. assumed bonds
   b. callable bonds
   c. joint bonds
   d. industrial revenue bonds
   e. bearer bonds

8. Which of the following is not a possible advantage that using long-term debt
financing may offer the firm?
   a. inexpensive source of capital on an after-tax basis
   b. less dilution of the firm's earnings per share
   c. positive effects of financial leverage on earnings per share
   d. lower flotation costs than stock
   e. favorable impact on the firm's financial risk

9. When considering the possible use of long-term debt financing, the firm's financial management should consider all the following factors except
    a. the impact of debt financing on the firm's business risk
    b. additional restrictions imposed by debt covenants
    c. current market conditions
    d. the stability of the firm's earnings
    e. the firm's cost of capital

10. Suppose a firm could satisfy a bond issue's sinking-fund requirement with the repurchase of $300,000 of the bonds' par value in the open market. The par value is $1,000 per bond, and the bonds are trading at a $75 discount. What cash outflow must the firm have to comply with the sinking-fund requirement?
    a. $75,000
    b. $277,500
    c. $292,500
    d. $300,000
    e. $322,500

11. Bengal Airlines has $14,000,000 of 10½ percent debentures outstanding that mature in 15 years. Each debenture has a $1,000 par value and is currently callable for a call premium of $90 per debenture. The debentures were issued 10 years ago and their flotation costs were $175,000. Bengal is considering refunding the entire old issue, because new 15-year debentures ($1,000 par value) could be issued with an 8 percent coupon rate. The flotation costs of the new issue would be $225,000. Bengal is in a 45 percent tax bracket. Bengal estimates that the firm would have overlapping interest on the old issue for about one month. What total cash investment would be required to refund the old debentures?
    a. $67,375
    b. $225,000
    c. $693,000
    d. $938,125
    e. $1,032,625

12. In Question 11, assume that Bengal's cost of capital is 9 percent. Determine the approximate present value of the annual after-tax savings that would result if the old debentures were refunded.
    a. $808,500
    b. $1,214,800
    c. $1,580,700
    d. $2,327,200
    e. $2,941,500

KEY DEFINITIONS

Bond refunding: the process of retiring (or calling) an existing issue of bonds and replacing them with bonds that have a lower coupon (interest) rate.

Call provision: the firm's option to retire a bond issue prior to its maturity. The firm may exercise this option when current interest rates fall below the callable bonds' interest rate. When bonds are called, the firm is usually required to pay bondholders a call premium in addition to the bonds' par value. Some bonds have no call provision.

Coupon rate: the annual interest rate paid on a bond's par value.

Current yield (CY): the ratio of a bond's annual interest payments to its current market price.

Debenture: an unsecured, long-term bond backed only by the issuing firm's credit-ability.

Denomination: the dollar amount of a bond's principal or par value.

Indenture: the legal agreement between the firm issuing a bond and the bondholder specifying the bond's restrictions (covenants) placed on the firm, collateral, re-payment provisions, maturity, annual interest rate, and denomination.

Par value (face value): the amount borrowed (or principal) associated with a long-term bond. The par value of most corporate bonds is $1,000.

Registry: the firm's official books for a bond issue, which indicate the bonds' registered owners.

Sinking fund: a prepayment provision of some bonds requiring the firm to gradually repay the bonds' principal at regular intervals prior to the bonds' maturity. Sinking funds may be established as escrow accounts, or they may allow the firm to repurchase a fixed quantity of outstanding bonds annually at prevailing market prices.

Yield to first call (YTFC): the annual rate of return an investor would receive if a bond were bought today and sold back to the issuing firm for the bond's call price at the first available call date.

Yield to maturity (YTM): the annual rate of return an investor would receive if a bond were bought today and held to maturity.

ANSWERS TO REVIEW QUESTIONS

1. d	4. a	7. d	10. b
2. b	5. b	8. e	11. d
3. c	6. d	9. a	12. c

Chapter Eighteen
Preferred and Common Stock

OVERVIEW

The firm's two sources of long-term equity financing are preferred stock and common stock. Both types of stock make up the firm's equity base, and they are somewhat similar. For example, both are subordinated to the firm's debt in their priority claims to either the firm's assets or its earnings. However, financial managers should be aware of the numerous distinctions between preferred and common stock. Before deciding which source of equity financing is more appropriate for the firm, they must consider the advantages and the disadvantages of each source. In the case of common stock, a rights offering may be a suitable alternative method. of issuing new stock. Therefore, financial officers must understand the unique characteristics of rights offerings. And, after a firm's common stock has been issued, management may be confronted with decisions involving stock splits, reverse splits, and stock repurchases.

STUDY OBJECTIVES

1. To appreciate the similarities and the differences between preferred and common stock.

2. To gain a fundamental grasp of the issues involved in a rights offering.

3. To become familiar with methods (such as stock splits, reverse splits, and stock repurchases) available to the firm for altering the market price of its common stock.

CHAPTER OUTLINE

 I. Preferred stock

   A. Preferred stock is part of the firm's equity base. Its priority claim to the firm's earnings and to its assets falls between the priority claim of the firm's debt and that of its common stock. In other words, preferred stock has a priority claim above common stock but below debt.

B. <u>Characteristics</u> of preferred stock.

1. <u>Par value</u> represents the liquidation claim per share of preferred stock. The most common par value associated with preferred stock is $100 per share.

2. Preferred stock normally has no fixed maturity. However, preferred stock often has a <u>redemption</u> feature that allows the firm to retire the stock after a specified period of time has elapsed since the stock was issued. If stock is redeemed, the firm must usually pay investors a premium over the stock's par value. If the preferred stock is <u>convertible</u>, the stockholder has the option of converting the preferred stock into a fixed number of shares of the firm's common stock.

3. Most preferred stocks have <u>protective provisions</u> (covenants). Although not so restrictive as debt covenants, a preferred stock's protective provisions commonly include restrictions on the firm's:

a. Future issuance of securities that have higher claim priority than the firm's existing preferred stock.

b. Common stock dividends.

c. Minimum working-capital levels.

4. <u>Dividends</u> on preferred stock are stated as an annual percentage of the par value, and they are usually paid quarterly. Unlike the interest on bonds, preferred stock dividends may be omitted. If the preferred stock has a <u>cumulative</u> feature, however, all preferred stock dividends in arrears must be paid before any subsequent dividends can be paid on the firm's common stock. Some preferred stocks are <u>participating</u>. That is, if the firm's after-tax earnings exceed a certain level, preferred stockholders may receive a special dividend in addition to the regular preferred stock dividend.

5. Although preferred stockholders seldom have the right to vote for the firm's board of directors, most preferred stocks allow substantial voting power in the event that dividends are omitted for a specific number of quarters.

C. <u>Advantages</u> of preferred stock.

1. <u>Dividend omission</u> on the firm's preferred stock does not constitute a default, as would be the case if the firm missed an interest payment on its debt.

2. Preferred stock affords the firm greater <u>financing flexibility</u> than bonds. Because preferred stock has no fixed maturity, the firm has no financial obligation to retire a preferred stock issue. Or, if the preferred stock has a redemption feature, the firm can retire the stock and seek refinancing at more favorable terms should the proper market conditions exist in the future.

3. Financing with preferred stock normally results in <u>less dilution</u> of the firm's earnings per share than financing with common stock.

4. The firm's current common stockholders retain their <u>control</u> of the firm when preferred stock is issued, because preferred stock is ordinarily nonvoting.

5. Preferred stock is a good bargaining tool in <u>acquisition negotiations</u> when the selling firm's stockholders are interested in income rather than capital appreciation.

6. If <u>market conditions</u> are such that investors are unreceptive to a new issue of the firm's common stock, preferred stock may be the only source of equity financing available to the firm.

D. <u>Disadvantages</u> of preferred stock.

1. Preferred stock is an <u>expensive</u> source of long-term funds, because preferred stock dividends are not deductible from a firm's income for tax purposes.

2. Since the firm has a more binding dividend commitment with preferred stock than with common stock, <u>growth firms</u> wishing to retain their earnings for promising expansion opportunities may prefer to use common stock for their equity financing.

E. Buyers of preferred stock have typically been corporate investors (such as <u>life insurance companies</u>) interested in stable dividend income.

1. For corporate investors, preferred stock dividends are <u>85 percent tax exempt</u>. This tax exemption results in a high after-tax dividend yield to corporate investors owning preferred stock.

2. Nevertheless, many investors are wary of preferred stock for several reasons.

   a. Preferred stock prices are more <u>interest-rate sensitive</u> than bond prices.

   b. Preferred stocks are not actively traded in the secondary markets, so they often have poor <u>marketability</u>.

   c. Dividends on preferred stock are <u>nonobligatory</u>. Thus investors are usually attracted to preferred stock issued by only the more creditworthy firms.

II. Common stock

A. <u>Common stock</u> is similar to preferred stock in that both are a part of the firm's equity base, but common stock is subordinate to preferred stock in its priority claims to the firm's earnings and its assets. Dividends can be paid on common stock (at the board of directors' discretion) only after all the firm's other financial claims (from both debt and preferred stock) have been satisfied. However, when these other claims have been fulfilled, all the firm's residual profits accrue to the common stockholders. Thus, even though the firm's common stockholders are exposed to the greatest risks, they enjoy the potential for the largest dividend returns on their investment.

B. Characteristics of common stock.

1. A common stock's par value is an arbitrarily fixed value that usually has little significance other than for accounting purposes. For example, if a firm sold 100 shares of new common stock with a $1 per share par value for $20 per share, the following accounting entries would be made on the firm's balance sheet.

    Common stock ($1 par value) . . . . $ 100
      (100 shares @ $1/share)
    Additional paid-in capital $1,900
      (100 shares @ $19/share)
    Total common stock and additional
      paid-in capital $2,000

2. Book value per share of common stock is the difference between the book value of the firm's assets and both the firm's liabilities and preferred stock divided by the number of shares of common stock that are outstanding. Liquidation value reflects the residual per-share worth of a firm's common stock in the event that the firm's assets were sold at prevailing market prices, with the proceeds from the sale being used first to pay both the firm's creditors and preferred stockholders the amounts due them. Thus book value is based on the historical prices of the firm's assets, whereas liquidation value reflects the assets' market value if the firm were liquidated. The book value usually exceeds the liquidation value, because the firm's assets may have to be sold at discount prices during liquidation. Neither value has a significant effect on a common stock's market value. Market value is influenced more by the level and the riskiness of the firm's future after-tax earnings that accrue to common stock.

3. Common stock has no maturity.

4. The sale of new common stock usually results in an immediate dilution in the firm's earnings per share. However, if the proceeds from the sale are prudently invested, the effects of this dilution are temporary.

5. The common stockholders collectively control the firm. In this capacity they perform several important duties, which include:

    a. Electing the board of directors.

    b. Selecting the firm's independent auditors, who periodically examine the firm's books and report their findings to the stockholders.

    c. Amending the firm's by-laws and charter.

    d. Authorizing the maximum number of shares of both preferred and common stock that can be issued.

    e. Approving mergers.

In addition to these duties, the firm's common stockholders have the right to _transfer_ their ownership in the firm to another party and to _inspect_ (within reason) the firm's books.

6. Of all the firm's securities, common stock tends to exhibit the largest _price fluctuations_ in the market. Much of this price volatility is due to the uncertainty associated with a common stock's future dividend stream.

7. The _authorized shares_ of a firm's common stock represent the maximum number of shares that the firm can issue in accordance with its charter. This number cannot be changed without the common stockholders' approval. The _issued shares_ are the number of authorized shares that have been sold. _Treasury stock_ is common stock that has been issued and later reacquired by the firm but not retired from the firm's books. Treasury stock is often held by the firm for such purposes as mergers and employee stock option plans. The firm's _outstanding shares_ of common stock are its issued shares less its treasury stock. Per-share earnings are calculated using the firm's outstanding shares.

8. Occasionally, a firm's common stock is _classified_ according to both its voting rights and its dividend claims. For example, class A common stock may have full voting rights, whereas class B common stock may have limited voting rights but a preferential claim to the firm's dividends. Most organized stock exchanges prohibit the trading of classified stocks that have no voting rights. _Restricted common stock_ contains provisions that limit the rights of ownership. Restricted stock frequently provides the right of first refusal, which requires that the firm's current stockholders be given the first opportunity to buy any shares of common stock being sold. This provision is designed to keep control of the firm with the current stockholders. _Letter stock_ is common stock that has not been registered with the Securities and Exchange Commission and hence cannot be publicly traded. As a result, letter stock is relatively illiquid.

9. Unless classified in terms of _voting rights_, common stock entitles its holders to vote in the election of the firm's board of directors and in all other voting matters brought to the common stockholders. Stockholders can vote for directors (and other matters) at the firm's annual meeting either in person or by proxy votes. A _proxy_ is a temporary assignment of a common stockholder's vote to an appointed trustee who has been instructed how to vote. The proxy can be revoked should the stockholder later decide to vote in person. Proxy voting is regulated by the Securities and Exchange Commission, but collecting and processing proxy votes are the firm's responsibility.

C. The method used to elect the firm's directors is specified in the firm's charter. The _direct majority_ method limits stockholders to casting one vote per share of common stock for each director being elected. The _cumulative_ process also allows each stockholder one vote per share per director being elected, but these votes can be accumulated and then cast for any number of directors. With cumulative voting, minority stockholders have an opportunity to elect at least one director. The number N of shares required to elect a desired number D of directors can be determined with the following formula:

$$N = \frac{D * S}{T + 1} + 1$$

where T equals the number of directors to be elected and S equals the number of shares of common stock that are outstanding. Regardless of the voting method used, firms sometimes schedule staggered elections to prevent dissident stockholders from electing a majority of directors to the board.

D. The main advantage of common stock financing is freedom from the restrictions and fixed financial obligations that are associated with debt financing and preferred stock financing. The disadvantages of using common stock as a long-term source of funds include:

a. Its high cost of capital and its expensive flotation costs.

b. Its dilution effects on both the firm's earnings per share and the present stockholders' control of the firm.

c. The loss of the favorable influence that financial leverage may exert on the firm's earnings.

III. Subscription rights

A. Subscription rights (also referred to as pre-emptive rights) give the firm's present common stockholders the first option to purchase new shares of common stock issued by the firm. When a firm has a rights offering, rights are distributed to stockholders on the basis of one right for each share of outstanding common stock. During the rights offering, a specific number of rights allows each stockholder to purchase one new share of common stock at a stated price (known as the subscription price), which is set below the stock's current market price. If stockholders exercise their rights, their percent ownership in the firm will not be diluted.

B. After a rights offering has been publicized by the firm on the announcement date, all stockholders who are registered on the firm's books on the record date will be entitled to their rights. Due to bookkeeping time lags, an investor must purchase the stock before the fourth business day (called the ex-rights date) prior to the record date in order to receive any rights. The rights offering terminates on the expiration date. After the announcement date but before the ex-rights date, the stock is referred to as trading rights-on. After the ex-rights date, the stock trades ex-rights.

C. The number N of rights required to purchase one new share of common stock can be calculated using the following equation:

$$N = \frac{\text{existing number of shares outstanding} * S}{\text{dollar amount of new common stock issue}}$$

where S equals the offering's subscription price. When the stock is trading rights-on, the theoretical rights-on value R_0 of a right is determined by

$$R_0 = (M_0 - S)/(N + 1)$$

where M_0 equals the rights-on market value per share of common stock. Since the subscription price S is set less than the stock's rights-on market price M_0, rights are valuable to their owners. Investors who purchase the stock after the ex-rights date lose their privileges to receive rights. Therefore, the stock's market price M_x on the ex-rights date should decline from its rights-on market price M_0 by the theoretical value of a right. That is,

$$M_x = M_0 - R_0$$

After the ex-rights date, the theoretical ex-right value R_x of a right can be determined from the following relationship:

$$R_x = (M_x - S)/(N)$$

If all market conditions remain constant during the rights offering, the theoretical value of a right will be the same both before and after the ex-rights date. However, because rights are traded as separate securities after the ex-rights date, supply and demand forces in the market affect a right's market price. On the expiration date, rights become worthless.

Example   L & N Controls currently has 2,000,000 shares of common stock outstanding, which have a market price of $25/share. L & N is planning a rights offering with a $15/share subscription price in order to raise $10,000,000. Assuming stable market conditions during the offering, determine:

a. The number N of rights required to purchase one new share of L & N common stock.

b. The theoretical rights-on value R_0 of a right.

c. The price M_x of L & N common stock on the ex-rights date.

d. The theoretical ex-rights value R_x of a right.

Solution

a. $N = \dfrac{2{,}000{,}000 \text{ shares} * \$15/\text{share}}{\$10{,}000{,}000} = \underline{3 \text{ rights}}$

b. $R_0 = (\$25 - \$15)/(3 + 1) = \underline{\$2.50/\text{right}}$

c. $M_x = \$25 - \$2.50 = \underline{\$22.50/\text{share}}$

d. $R_x = (\$22.50 - \$15)/3 = \underline{\$2.50/\text{right}}$

   D. Stockholders who receive rights have three options. They can exercise their rights, sell their rights to other investors, or let their rights expire. If stockholders with rights select either of the first two options, they normally will not suffer a financial loss due to the rights offering. If they choose the third option, however, they may incur a financial loss equal to the value of the rights that they allowed to expire. When a stockholder has an odd (insufficient) number of rights to purchase a share of new stock, the stockholder can either <u>sell</u> the odd rights or <u>buy</u> enough rights to combine with the odd rights in order to have the number of rights required to purchase a share of new stock.

E. A firm often employs an investment banker to assist with a rights offering. If a <u>standby agreement</u> is arranged, the investment banker will (for an underwriting fee) guarantee the firm that all the new shares being offered will be bought, even if the investment banker is the ultimate buyer. Alternatively, the firm can have a rights offering without the services of an investment banker. In these cases, the subscription price is normally set significantly below the market price of the firm's stock to insure that the offering will be successful.

F. <u>Advantages</u> of a rights offering.

   1. Current stockholders are given an opportunity to retain their <u>percent ownership</u> in the firm.

   2. Investment bankers' <u>underwriting fees</u> are typically lower for a rights offering than for a public offering.

   3. A rights offering may strengthen <u>stockholder loyalty</u> to the firm.

   4. An <u>alternative method</u> to sell new common stock is made available to the firm.

G. <u>Disadvantages</u> of a rights offering.

   1. The subscription price of a rights offering is usually lower than the price the firm could receive for its common stock with either a public offering or a private placement. As a consequence, a rights offering may result in greater <u>dilution</u> of the firm's earnings than another marketing technique.

   2. Rights offerings are often <u>cumbersome</u> to the firm due to the amount of paperwork involved. As a result, the firm's total <u>issuing expenses</u> may be higher with a rights offering than with other methods that could be used to issue new common stock.

IV. Stock splits and revenue splits

A. A <u>stock split</u> is a proportionate increase in the number of the firm's shares of common stock. A split is accomplished via distribution of additional shares to the firm's stockholders of record on the date of the split.

   1. The <u>effects</u> of a stock split are:

      a. A proportionate <u>decrease</u> in the price of the firm's common stock on the date of the split.

      b. A proportionate <u>decrease</u> in each share of common stock's par value.

      c. A proportionate <u>increase</u> in the number of shares of common stock.

     A stock split has <u>no effect</u> on the dollar amount of total stockholders' equity recorded on the firm's balance sheet.

  2. There are several <u>reasons</u> for stock splits.

      a. The lower stock price after a split may attract <u>new investors</u> to the firm's stock, resulting in improved <u>marketability</u> of the shares.

      b. The increased number of shares that result from a stock split may qualify the firm for <u>listing</u> on an organized stock exchange.

B. A <u>reverse split</u> is the opposite of a stock split; that is, it is a proportionate decrease in the number of the firm's shares of common stock. A firm will sometimes have a reverse split to raise the market price of its common stock into a more respectable <u>trading range</u>. Since fewer shares of common stock are outstanding, a reverse split may even allow the firm to offer its investors a meaningful <u>per-share dividend</u>.

V. Stock repurchase

A. A firm can repurchase its shares of common stock in the secondary markets either through stockbrokers or with a tender offer. A <u>tender offer</u> is a formal solicitation by the firm to purchase the firm's common stock from existing stockholders. In announcing the tender offer to stockholders, the firm discloses the offer's tender price, minimum obligation, expiration date, and rights that are reserved for the firm. The <u>minimum obligation</u> is the minimum number of shares that the firm is obligated to repurchase in the tender offer. Included in the offer's <u>reserved rights</u> are the firm's options to:

  1. Buy either fewer or more shares than the offer's minimum obligation.

  2. Extend the offer's expiration date.

  3. Return all tendered shares if the minimum obligation is not met.

  4. Alter the tender's terms. (Term alterations do not affect shares tendered under the previous terms.)

B. There are several <u>reasons</u> for repurchase.

  1. During a period of generally depressed stock prices, the firm may consider its common stock a <u>good investment</u>.

  2. The firm may repurchase the shares of stockholders who own 25 or fewer shares to reduce the firm's <u>administrative expenses</u>.

  3. A repurchase may frustrate the attempts of another corporation that is seeking a <u>controlling interest</u> in the firm.

4. The firm's <u>financial leverage</u> is increased as a result of a repurchase.

5. <u>Per-share earnings</u> of the firm are enhanced, because a repurchase reduces the number of shares of common stock that are outstanding.

6. A repurchase allows the firm to acquire <u>treasury stock</u>, which can later be used for either merger negotiations or employee stock option plans.

STUDY PROBLEMS

18.1. A corporate investor owns 10 subordinated debentures and 100 shares of preferred stock. Each debenture ($1,000 par value) has a 12 percent coupon rate, and each share of preferred stock ($100 par value) has a 10 percent annual dividend rate. The corporate investor is in a 45 percent tax bracket. Both investments were originally purchased at their respective par values. Determine the corporate investor's annual after-tax yield associated with each investment.

Solution

Subordinated debentures:

Annual after-tax income = $10,000 * .12 * (1 - .45) = $660

Annual after-tax yield = $660/$10,000 = .066 = <u>6.60%</u>

Preferred stock:

Annual before-tax income = $10,000 * .10 = $1,000

Dividend-income tax exemption = .85 * $1,000 = $850

Taxes on nonexempt dividend income = .45 * ($1,000 - $850) = $67.50

Annual after-tax dividend income = $1,000 - $67.50 = $932.50

Annual after-tax yield = $932.50/$10,000 = .09325 = <u>9.325%</u>

18.2. Fischer Properties, Inc. has 5,000,000 shares of common stock authorized, but only 3,000,000 shares are outstanding. Fischer's after-tax net income is $7,200,000. Fischer plans to acquire 400,000 shares of treasury stock via a tender offer. The tender price will be $22/share, and the repurchase will be financed with a bank loan at 11 percent annual interest. Fischer is in a 45 percent tax bracket. Determine the impact of the proposed stock repurchase on Fisher's earnings per share (EPS).

Solution

Current EPS = $7,200,000/3,000,000 shares = <u>$2.40/share</u>

Amount borrowed to finance repurchase = 400,000 shares * $22/share
= <u>$8,800,000</u>

After-tax cost of borrowed funds = $8,800,000 * .11 * (1 - .45)
$$= \$532,400$$

After-tax net income following the repurchase = $7,200,000 - $532,400
$$= \$6,667,600$$

Shares outstanding after the repurchase = 3,000,000 shares - 400,000 shares
$$= \underline{2,600,000 \text{ shares}}$$

EPS after repurchase = $6,667,600/2,600,000 shares = $\underline{\$2.56/\text{share}}$

Thus Fischer's planned stock repurchase will improve the firm's EPS from $2.40/share to $2.56/share.

18.3. Picabo National Bank has twelve directors on its board and 800,000 shares of common stock outstanding. Picabo has staggered elections for its directors, electing four directors each year. The bank uses the cumulative method of voting. How many shares of common stock would a group of the bank's stockholders need to insure that the group could elect at least three directors at each election?

Solution

Number of shares required to elect at least three directors $= \dfrac{3 * 800,000}{4 + 1} + 1 = \underline{480,001 \text{ shares}}$

18.4. Federal Telephone plans to sell $24,000,000 of new common stock with a rights offering. The offering's subscription price is $15/share. Currently, Federal has 14,400,000 shares of common stock outstanding. The record day is Monday, October 15.

a. Determine both the day and the date that Federal's stock will trade ex-rights.

b. How many new shares of stock does Federal plan to issue with the rights offering?

c. What number N of rights will be required to purchase one new share of stock?

d. Assume that the market price M_0 of Federal's common stock was $20/share prior to the ex-rights date. Calculate the rights-on value R_0 of a right.

e. Determine both the theoretical value R_x of a right and the stock's market price M_x on the ex-rights date, assuming that no other events affect the market price of Federal's common stock.

Solution

a. The ex-rights date is <u>four</u> business days before the record date (Monday, October 15). Since Saturday and Sunday are not considered business days, the ex-rights day is <u>Tuesday, October 9</u>.

b. Number of new shares issued = dollar amount of new stock divided by subscription price. Therefore,

New shares = $24,000,000/($15/share) = <u>1,600,000 shares</u>

c. $N = \dfrac{14,400,000 \text{ shares} * \$15/\text{share}}{\$24,000,000}$ = <u>9 rights</u>

d. R_0 = ($20 - $15)/(9 + 1) = <u>$.50/right</u>

e. M_X = $20 - $.50 = <u>$19.50/share</u>

R_X = ($19.50 - $15.00)/9 = <u>$.50/right</u>

18.5. Debco Homes announced an 8-for-5 stock split. Prior to the split, the company had 3,000,000 shares of $2 par value common stock outstanding, and each share had a market price of $24/share. Determine the following after the split:

a. The number of shares outstanding.

b. The par value and the market value of each share of common stock.

<u>Solution</u>

a. Shares outstanding after the split = 8/5 * 3,000,000 shares
    = <u>4,800,000 shares</u>

b. Par value per share after the split = 5/8 * $2/share = <u>$1.25/share</u>

    Market price per share after the split = 5/8 * $24/share = $15/share

REVIEW QUESTIONS

1. Stock that has not been registered with the Securities and Exchange Commission is referred to as
    a. restricted stock.
    b. authorized stock.
    c. issued stock.
    d. private stock.
    e. letter stock.

2. Most preferred stocks have
    a. protective provisions.
    b. maturities less than 30 years.
    c. $1/share par values.
    d. cumulative voting rights.
    e. both b and d.

3. Preferred stock
    a. is often ideal for growth-oriented companies.
    b. is a less expensive source of capital than long-term bonds.
    c. is frequently convertible into subordinated debentures.

    d. usually results in greater dilution of the firm's earnings per share than common stock.

    e. may be useful to the firm in acquisition negotiations.

4. Old Stagg Insurance Company owns 700 shares of Leadore 8½ percent preferred stock ($100 par value), which it bought at $87/share. If Old Stagg is in a 35 percent corporate tax bracket, the after-tax dividend yield on the Leadore investment is approximately

    a. 2.98 percent.

    b. 5.53 percent.

    c. 8.05 percent.

    d. 9.26 percent.

    e. 11.49 percent.

5. If Old Stagg (see Question 4) wants to replace its Leadore preferred stock with an investment in mortgage bonds ($1,000 par value), what approximate coupon rate must the bonds have in order to offer Old Stagg the same after-tax current yield as the after-tax dividend yield of the Leadore preferred stock? Assume that the mortgage bonds could be bought for their par value.

    a. 8.50 percent

    b. 9.6 percent

    c. 10.91 percent

    d. 13.08 percent

    e. 14.24 percent

6. A common stock's book value

    a. must equal its par value.

    b. usually exceeds its liquidation value.

    c. is regulated by the Securities and Exchange Commission.

    d. ultimately determines the maximum value of the stock's market value.

    e. cannot be changed under any circumstances.

7. Common stockholders do not have the explicit right to

    a. select the firm's investment banker.

    b. amend the firm's charter and by-laws.

    c. elect the board of directors.

    d. examine the firm's books.

    e. approve mergers.

8. Jutland Industries has 9,000,000 shares of common stock authorized, of which 7,500,000 shares have been issued. The company has 700,000 shares of treasury stock. Determine Jutland's earnings per share if its after-tax net income was $18,000,000.

    a. $2.00/share

    b. $2.40/share

    c. $2.65/share

    d. $9.47/share

    e. $25.71/share

9. If a company had a rights offering with a record date on Wednesday, July 23, and an expiration date on Friday, August 29, the ex-rights date would be

    a. Wednesday, July 16.

    b. Thursday, July 17.

    c. Friday, July 18.

    d. Monday, August 25.

    e. Tuesday, August 26.

10. Jones Labs has 2,500,000 shares of common stock outstanding, each share with a $1 par value. The market price of the stock is $48/share and Jones's earnings per share (EPS) are $7.25. Jones has just announced a 3-for-5 reverse split. Which of the following sets of information about Jones's common stock after the reverse split is correct?
    a. EPS = $4.35/share and market price = $80.00/share.
    b. Par value = $1.67/share and EPS = $4.35/share.
    c. Market price = $28.80/share and par value = $.60/share.
    d. EPS = $12.08/share and shares outstanding = 1,500,000 shares.
    e. Par value = $.60/share and shares outstanding = 900,000 shares.

11. Coulter Mills plans to have a rights offering to raise $8,000,000. Currently, Coulter has 2,560,000 shares of common stock outstanding, which have a market price of $18.75/share. The offering's subscription price will be $12.50/share. Calculate the number of rights required to buy a new share of Coulter common stock.
    a. 3.25 rights
    b. 4.00 rights
    c. 4.50 rights
    d. 5.00 rights
    e. 5.75 rights

12. Dr. Stratton owned 500 shares of Coulter's common stock. However, during the rights offering discussed in Question 11, Dr. Stratton took an extended vacation. While on vacation, Dr. Stratton paid little attention to either the Coulter investment or the rights offering. In fact, the doctor let her rights expire. Assuming that no factors other than those associated with the rights offering had an impact on the market price of Coulter's common stock during the rights offering, determine Dr. Stratton's probable reaction upon first scanning Coulter's stock price in the <u>Wall Street Journal</u>.
    a. comfort in finding no change in the value of her stock.
    b. a $575 smile
    c. idle speculation about what to do with her $78.25 profit
    d. red-faced anger to the tune of $625
    e. a stormy tantrum over her $3,125 loss

KEY DEFINITIONS

<u>Book value per share</u>: for each share of common stock outstanding, the difference between the book value of the firm's assets and the sum of its liabilities and preferred stock.

<u>Classified stock</u>: a type of common stock that has different voting rights or dividend claims from other types of the firm's common stock.

<u>Cumulative voting</u>: a method of voting for a firm's board of directors that allows stockholders to accumulate their votes and cast them for any number of directors.

<u>Direct-majority voting</u>: a method of voting for a firm's board of directors in which no more than one vote per share of voting common stock outstanding can be cast for any director.

<u>Ex-rights date</u>: four business days prior to the record date of a rights offering. Either on or after the ex-rights date, an investor who purchases the firm's common stock will not receive the subscription rights associated with the stock.

Letter stock: common stock that has not been registered with the Securities and Exchange Commission. Letter stock is relatively illiquid, because it cannot be publicly traded in the secondary markets.

Proxy: a revokable assignment of a common stockholder's vote to an appointed third party who must cast the vote in a prescribed manner.

Reverse split: a reduction in the number of a firm's outstanding shares of common stock that causes a proportionate increase in each share's par value, earnings, and market price.

Stock split: an increase in the number of a firm's outstanding shares of common stock that causes a proportionate decrease in each share's par value, earnings, and market price.

Subscription rights: options given the firm's common stockholders to purchase additional shares of common stock at a specified price during a rights offering.

Tender offer: a formal solicitation by the firm to purchase a fixed number of shares of common stock from the firm's existing stockholders at a stated per-share price.

Treasury stock: a firm's issued common stock that has been repurchased by the firm. Shares of treasury stock owned by the firm are not used in calculating the firm's per-share statistics.

ANSWERS TO REVIEW QUESTIONS

1.	e	4.	d	7.	a	10.	d
2.	a	5.	e	8.	c	11.	b
3.	e	6.	b	9.	b	12.	d

Chapter Nineteen
Convertible Securities and Warrants

OVERVIEW

Convertible securities are either bonds or preferred stocks that their holders can exchange for shares of the firm's common stock. The firm may be able to use convertible securities to obtain inexpensive long-term financing that has relatively few restrictive covenants. Further, convertible securities often represent a way for the firm to defer its equity financing until the securities' conversion options are exercised. Such deferred equity financing usually results in less dilution of the firm's earnings per share than would have occurred had common stock been issued originally. Warrants are options to purchase common stock during a limited time at a specific price. When warrants are exercised, the firm is provided with new common stock financing, thereby increasing its equity base. When warrants are attached to new bonds, the firm may be able to entice potential investors who would otherwise have little interest in the firm's bond issue. Both convertible securities and warrants can play important roles in the firm's long-term financing plans. But, before using either, financial managers must be familiar with their special characteristics.

STUDY OBJECTIVES

1. To develop a working knowledge of the <u>characteristics</u> associated with convertible securities and warrants.

2. To examine the <u>advantages</u> and the <u>disadvantages</u> that result from the use of either convertible securities or warrants.

CHAPTER OUTLINE

I. Convertible securities

    A. <u>Convertible securities</u> are bonds and preferred stocks that, at the option of the holders of these securities, may be exchanged for a predetermined number of shares of the issuing firm's common stock during a specific period of time. (Convertible bonds and convertible preferred stocks have similar characteristics, and only convertible bonds will be discussed here.)

B. Characteristics of convertible bonds.

1. The bond's <u>conversion ratio</u> is the number of common stock shares that may be exchanged for the convertible bond.

2. The <u>conversion price</u> reflects the issuing price of each share of common stock as recorded on the firm's books upon conversion of the bond. To determine the conversion price, the bond's par value (usually $1,000) is divided by the conversion ratio. For example, if a convertible bond ($1,000 par value) has a conversion ratio of 40 (that is, each bond is convertible into 40 shares of common stock), the conversion price per share of common stock issued when the bond is converted would be $25/share ($1,000/40 shares). During a convertible bond's duration, the conversion ratio can either remain fixed or decrease at predetermined intervals. Thus the conversion price could increase during the bond's life if the conversion ratio were reduced.

3. The period during which the holder of a convertible bond has the conversion option is referred to as the <u>conversion period</u>. The conversion period is often, but not always, the same as the bond's duration. For example, a <u>deferred conversion period</u> prohibits conversion of the bond for a specific number of years after the bond has been issued, and a <u>limited conversion period</u> prohibits conversion of the bond for a specific number of years prior to the bond's maturity.

C. Convertible bond values.

1. The <u>conversion value</u> (CV) is the bond's worth if it were converted into shares of common stock.

$$CV = N * P$$

where N is the bond's conversion ratio and P is the per-share market price of the firm's common stock.

2. The <u>bond value</u> is a convertible bond's worth if it were appraised as a long-term debt security without a conversion option. This value indicates the present value of both the bond's future annual interest payments (I) and its principal (P_n). The discount rate (i) used in the present-value calculation represents the convertible bond's yield to maturity (the bond investors' required annual rate of return) if the bond were traded as a straight debt security. Thus,

$$\text{Bond value} = \sum_{t=1}^{n} I/(1 + i)^t + P_n/(1 + i)^n$$

where n is the convertible bond's remaining maturity. Alternatively, because the convertible bond's annual interest payments (I) are usually uniform, we can also use the tables in Appendices A.2 and A.4 to determine this present value.

Bond value = I * PAIT (from Appendix A.4) + P_n * PIT (from Appendix A.2)

3. A convertible bond's <u>market value</u> is the price at which the bond trades in the secondary markets. <u>Arbitrageurs</u> (investors who seek profit opportunities by simultaneously buying and selling equivalent securities that have different market prices) keep a convertible bond's market price from falling below either its conversion value or its bond value. Consequently, the higher of these two values establishes a <u>price floor</u> for a convertible bond's market value.

4. The difference between a convertible bond's market value and its price floor is referred to as the <u>conversion premium</u>. A convertible bond will trade at a premium over its price floor, because it offers investors a fixed-income long-term bond with the potential for capital appreciation should the firm's common stock increase in value. Furthermore, investors are exposed to less risk with convertible bonds than with an equivalent investment in the firm's common stock, because the market value of a convertible bond cannot fall below its bond value regardless of the market price of the firm's common stock.

   Whenever a convertible bond's conversion value is significantly below its bond value, the bond's conversion premium will be near zero. That is, the convertible bond's market value will be only slightly higher than its bond value. Usually, the conversion premium then increases as the difference between conversion value and the bond value decreases. As the bond's conversion value begins to exceed its bond value, the conversion premium starts to get smaller. Most convertible bonds are callable, as the bond's market price and its conversion value tend to converge when the conversion value is beyond the bond's call price. Therefore, the bond's conversion premium is very small when the bond has a high conversion value. Apart from the relationship between the bond value and the conversion value associated with a convertible bond, the bond's conversion premium tends to decrease as the per-share dividends on the firm's common stock increase.

Example: Burnet Natural Gas has convertible debentures outstanding that mature in 15 years. Each debenture ($1,000 par value) has a 9 percent coupon rate and a conversion ratio N of 25. Debentures in the same risk class as Burnet's convertible debentures are priced to have a 12 percent yield to maturity. Burnet common stock pays a $4/share dividend and has a market price P of $45/share. The convertible debentures are currently callable for $1,090 per debenture, and their market value is $1,130 each.

a. Determine the debentures' conversion price, conversion value, bond value, and price floor.

b. Calculate the conversion premium and provide an explanation for its magnitude.

   <u>Solution</u>:

a. Conversion price = debentures' par value/conversion ratio N
                    = $1,000/25 shares = <u>$40/share</u>

   Conversion value = N * P = 25 shares * $45/share
                    = <u>$1,125/debenture</u>

$$\text{Bond value} = \sum_{t=1}^{15} \$90/(1.12)^t + 1{,}000/(1.12)^{15}$$

= $90 * PAIT (i = 12%, n = 15) + $1,000 * PIT (i = 12%, n = 15)

= $90 * 6.8109 (from Appendix A.4) + $1,000 * .1827 (from Appendix A.2)

= $795.68/debenture

The price floor is either a convertible bond's conversion value or its bond value, whichever is greater. Therefore, for Burnet's convertible debentures, price floor = conversion value = $1,125/debenture.

b. Conversion premium = market value - floor price
                       = $1,130 - $1,125 = $5/debenture

There are two reasons why the conversion premium ($5) is so small. First, the debentures' conversion value ($1,125) exceeds their call price ($1,090). In the event that the convertible debentures were called (which is likely when a convertible bond's conversion value is greater than its call price), debenture holders would exercise their conversion option to receive 25 shares of common stock (worth $1,125) rather than take the $1,090 call price. Thus, because investors are apt to view each debenture as a unit of 25 shares of Burnet common stock rather than as a bond, they are less apt to pay a high premium for the bond features associated with each debenture. In addition, an investment in 25 shares of Burnet common stock would generate $100 (25 * $4) in dividend income, whereas an investment in a Burnet convertible bond would produce only $90 of interest income. Income-oriented investors may be more inclined to buy Burnet's common stock, thereby reducing the market demand for the convertible debentures.

D. Advantages of convertible bonds.

1. If convertible bonds are callable, the firm can call the bonds and hope to create a forced conversion of the bonds into common stock. Most forced conversions are successful if the bonds' conversion value exceeds their call price by 20 percent or more. Since the conversion of a convertible bond issue into common stock both reduces the firm's debt and increases its equity base, the firm is in a much better position to seek new long-term debt financing after a forced conversion.

2. Convertible bonds can represent delayed equity financing. A firm may want to issue new common stock, but depressed market conditions for new equity issues could temporarily rule out this possibility. However, the firm may be able to obtain its financing with convertible bonds and, later, when the market price of the firm's common stock improves, attempt a forced conversion. If successful, the forced conversion would provide the firm with the equity capital that it originally wanted. Further, delayed equity financing of this nature often results in less dilution of the firm's earnings per share, because the bond's conversion price is normally higher than the prevailing market price of the firm's common stock when the convertible bonds were issued.

3. Convertible bonds can be used as a <u>sweetener</u> to entice potential investors who would otherwise not be interested in a new issue of the firm's common stock or straight bonds.

4. The firm may be able to negotiate both a <u>lower coupon rate</u> and <u>less restrictive covenants</u> for its new bonds if the bonds have a conversion feature.

5. Interest payments associated with convertible bonds are tax deductible, so convertible bonds have a lower after-tax <u>cost of capital</u> than common stock.

E. <u>Disadvantages</u> of convertible bonds.

1. When a convertible bond is exchanged for common stock, the firm's earnings per share are reduced. This is due to the <u>dilution effects</u> resulting from the increased number of common stock shares and to loss of the favorable influence from <u>financial leverage</u> that may have been associated with debt financing.

2. The convertible bond issue could <u>overhang</u>; that is, the firm's common stock price may not increase enough to allow the firm to have a successful forced conversion. In this event, the firm is caught in an awkward position with very little financing flexibility. The firm may not be able to issue new debt with the existing convertible bonds outstanding. Likewise, the firm may find that investors are unreceptive to a new common stock issue if the firm has convertible bonds that could later be converted into common stock, resulting in dilution of the firm's future per-share earnings. The possibility of an overhang always exists with convertible bonds. A firm that does not expect its common stock to appreciate enough in the future to prevent an overhang is ill-advised to use convertible bonds as a source of long-term financing.

II. Warrants

A. A <u>warrant</u> is an option to purchase a specific number of shares of common stock at a predetermined price (known as the <u>exercise price</u>) prior to an <u>expiration date</u>.

B. <u>Characteristics</u> of warrants.

1. A warrant normally has a fixed exercise price during its life. However, some warrants either allow the firm to lower the exercise price or have an exercise price that increases at predetermined future dates.

2. The number of shares of common stock that each warrant holder is entitled to purchase is specified in the warrant. Most warrants permit one share per warrant, although some warrants permit either several shares per warrant or only a fractional share per warrant.

3. Warrants pay no dividends.

4. Warrants usually expire in a fixed number of years after they are issued, but they are occasionally issued without an expiration date.

5. In the event of either a stock split or a stock dividend, a warrant's antidilution provision requires the number of shares that can be purchased with a warrant to be proportionately increased and the exercise price to be proportionately reduced.

C. Warrant values.

1. A warrant's theoretical value (V) can be determined as follows:

    V = (P - E) * N

    where P = the common stock's market price, E = the warrant's exercise price, and N = the number of shares that each warrant entitles its holder to purchase.

2. A warrant's market value is ultimately determined by supply and demand in the market. However, a warrant's market value will never fall below the larger of its theoretical value and zero (should the warrant's theoretical value be negative). After its expiration date, a warrant becomes worthless.

3. The difference between the warrant's market value and its theoretical value is the warrant's premium.

    a. Warrants offer their investors more leverage (that is, the opportunity to make a large profit on a small investment) than would be available with an equivalent investment in the common stock associated with the warrants. This leverage opportunity enhances a warrant's premium. However, the effect of the warrant's leverage is diminished as its theoretical value increases, causing the premium to decrease.

    b. As a warrant nears its expiration date, its premium decreases.

    c. Warrant premiums tend to be higher when the associated common stock is volatile.

    d. Large cash dividends on a warrant's affiliated common stock have a negative impact on the warrant's premium. Since warrants pay no dividends, investors who purchase warrants must forgo dividends that they would have received had they invested in the firm's common stock. These lost dividends become an opportunity cost associated with warrants. A high cash dividend on the firm's common stock increases this opportunity cost, causing investors to be less inclined to invest in the firm's warrants. With less investor interest in the firm's warrants, their premium will be lower.

D. Advantages and disadvantages of warrants.

1. Due to the leverage opportunities that warrants offer investors, a firm sometimes attaches warrants to its bonds to stimulate investor interest in a new debt issue. And the use of warrants to lure potential investors may allow the firm to offer its new debt under more favorable terms.

2. When warrants are exercised, the firm is supplied with <u>new funds</u> and its <u>equity base</u> is expanded.

3. Warrants may be useful to the firm in <u>merger negotiations</u>.

4. However, warrants must be treated as though they had been exercised when the firm reports its earnings. Consequently, warrants <u>dilute</u> the firm's reported earnings per share.

STUDY PROBLEMS

<u>19.1.</u> A Tricor Industries convertible debenture ($1,000 par value) has an 8 percent coupon rate and matures in 7 years. The debenture's conversion price is $25/share. Tricor's common stock has a market value of $21.50/share. Straight debt with a 7-year maturity that is in the same risk class as the Tricor convertible debenture is priced in the market to have a 10 percent yield to maturity.

a. Determine the convertible debenture's conversion ratio, conversion value, bond value, and price floor.

b. Assuming that the Tricor convertible debenture had a 6 percent conversion premium, calculate its market value.

<u>Solution</u>

a. Conversion ratio = par value/conversion price
                    = $1,000/$25 = <u>40 shares/debenture</u>

   Conversion value = $21.50/share * 40 shares/debenture
                    = <u>$860/debenture</u>

   Bond value = $80 * 4.8684 (Appendix A.4: i = 10%, n = 7) + $1,000 * .5132
              (Appendix A.2: i = 10%, n = 7)
            = <u>$902.67/debenture</u>

   Price floor = higher of conversion value and bond value
               = <u>$902.67/debenture</u>

b. Market value = (1 + conversion premium) * price floor
               = 1.06 * $902.67
               = <u>$956.83/debenture</u>

<u>19.2.</u> An investor owns a Glasco convertible bond ($1,000 par value) that has both a conversion ratio of 36 and a one-year maturity. Glasco's common stock sells for $27/share, and its value is expected to increase by 13 percent over the next year. The convertible bond's market value is $1,020.

a. Determine the convertible bond's coupon rate if the investor expects an 11 percent return on his or her Glasco investment over the next year.

b. Recalculate the coupon rate if the bond's conversion ratio was 32 and the investor's one-year expectation remained 11 percent.

Solution

a. The bond value in one year will equal the bond's par value ($1,000), because the bond will come due. However, conversion value in one year = 36 * $27 * 1.13 = $1,098.36. Therefore, the investor will either exercise the bond's conversion option or sell the bond in one year, rather than take the $1,000 par value when the bond is retired. Consequently,

$$.11 = \frac{(\text{coupon rate} * \$1,000) + (\$1,098.36 - \$1,020)}{\$1,020}$$

Solving this equation for the coupon rate yields

Coupon rate = .0338 = 3.38%

b. If the conversion ratio were 32,

Conversion value in one year = 32 * $27 * 1.13 = $976.32

In this case, the investor would take the bond's $1,000 par value in one year, because that value is greater than the bond's conversion value ($976.32). To provide the investor with an 11 percent return during the year, the bond's coupon rate would have to exceed 3.38 percent.

$$.11 = \frac{(\text{coupon rate} * \$1,000) + (\$1,000 - \$1,020)}{\$1,020}$$

Coupon rate = .1322 = 13.22%

19.3. Avery Scientific has $30,000,000 of 5 percent convertible bonds ($1,000 par value) outstanding that have a conversion ratio of 30. The bond value of each convertible bond is $800, but Avery's common stock sells for $42/share. The conversion premium of each bond is only 1 percent. In an attempt to force conversion, Avery has announced its plans to call the convertible bonds in one month for $1,040/bond. The firm's after-tax earnings presently are $26,000,000, and 5,800,000 shares of common stock are outstanding.

a. What is each convertible bond's market value?

b. Is a successful forced conversion likely? Explain.

c. If the bonds were converted, what would be Avery's earnings per share (EPS) both after and before the conversion, assuming that Avery is in a 45 percent tax bracket?

Solution

a. Conversion value = 30 * $42 = $1,260/bond

Bond value = $800 (given)

Price floor = larger of conversion value and bond value = $1,260

Market value = (1 + conversion premium) * price floor
              = 1.01 * $1,260 = $1,272.60

321

b. With the conversion value 21.15 percent [($1,260 - $1,040)/$1,040 = .2115] above the call price, it would be foolish for investors not to exercise their bonds' conversion option. Conversion of the issue is relatively certain.

c. New shares of common stock issued upon conversion = ($30,000,000/$1,000) * 30
    = 900,000 shares

    Total outstanding shares after conversion = 5,800,000 + 900,000
    + 6,700,000 shares

    Increase in after-tax net income due to a reduction in interest expense
    = .05 * $30,000,000 * (1 - .45)
    = $825,000

    After-tax net income following the conversion = $26,000,000 + $825,000
    = $26,825,000

    EPS after the conversion = $26,825,000/6,700,000 shares
    = $4.00/share

    EPS before conversion = $26,000,000/5,800,000 shares
    = $4.48/share

    Due to both the loss of financial leverage and the effects of dilution, Avery's EPS would decline after the conversion.

19.4. Texas Gas has 200,000 warrants outstanding that expire in 3 years. Each warrant allows its holder to purchase 2 shares of Texas Gas common stock for $20/share. The firm has 6,250,000 shares of common stock outstanding. Each share has a market value of $18 and pays a $1.50 dividend. The warrants are traded on the New York Stock Exchange for $2 each. The firm's after-tax earnings are $20,870,000.

a. Find the theoretical value V of each warrant.

b. Determine the premium associated with each warrant.

c. Does the premium seem justifiable from an investor's viewpoint?

d. What are the firm's stated earnings per share (EPS)?

Solution

a. V = ($18 - $20) * 2 = -$4.00/warrant

b. Premium = market value - theoretical value V
    = $2.00 - (-$4.00) = $6.00

c. The warrants have 3 years before they expire, so investing in Texas Gas warrants offers investors a significant amount of leverage should the firm's stock price increase during the warrants' life. Therefore, the $6.00 premium seems reasonable. For example, an investor could buy either 100 shares of Texas Gas common stock or 50 warrants. Suppose that, in one year, the common stock had increased 20 percent in value to $21.60/share and the premium on each warrant had declined to $1/warrant. Examine the annual return (neglecting taxes and brokers' fees) available to the investor on each investment.

	100 Shares of Stock	50 Warrants
Initial investment	100 * $18 = $1,800	50 * $2 = $100
Dividend income	100 * $1.50 = $150	none
Value of investment after one year . . .	100 * $21.60 = $2,160	50 * [($21.60 - $20) * 2] + $50 (premium = 50 * $1) = $210
Return on investment . .	$\frac{(\$2,160 + \$150 - \$1,800)}{\$1,800}$	$\frac{\$210 - \$100}{\$100}$ = 1.10
	= .2833 = 28.33%	= 110%

Note that, due to the leverage associated with the warrant investment, the investor is potentially able to obtain a much higher return on his or her investment than is available to an investor in the firm's common stock.

d. If exercised, the warrants would result in 400,000 shares of new common stock (400,000 shares = 200,000 warrants * 2 shares/warrant). Thus the potential exists for the firm's earnings to be diluted by 400,000 additional shares. Current accounting standards require that the firm's stated earnings per share reflect this possible dilution, so

    Stated EPS = $20,870,000/(6,250,000 shares + 400,000 shares)
              = $3.14/share

REVIEW QUESTIONS

1. What is the conversion ratio of a share of convertible preferred stock ($100 par value) that has a conversion price of $12/share?
   a. 8.33 shares
   b. 12 shares
   c. 100 shares
   d. $24/share
   e. $100/share

2. An ADEX convertible bond ($1,000 par value) has a 6 percent coupon rate and 14 years to maturity. The conversion ratio of each bond is 50. Straight debt with a 14-year maturity that is in the same risk class as the ADEX convertible bonds has a 10 percent yield to maturity (YTM). Which of the following sets of information about an ADEX convertible bond is correct?
   a. Conversion price = $20/share and bond value = $637.
   b. Conversion price = $20/share and bond value = $705.
   c. Conversion price = $50/share and bond value = $1,000.
   d. Conversion price = $50/share and YTM = 10 percent.
   e. YTM = 6 percent and bond value = $825.

3. If ADEX common stock sells for $19/share, the conversion value of an ADEX convertible bond (described in Question 2) is
   a. $380.
   b. $637.

    c. $825.
    d. $950.
    e. $1,000.

4. Assuming that ADEX convertible bonds referred to in Questions 2 and 3 sell for a 7 percent conversion premium, determine each bond's market value.
    a. $681.50
    b. $754.30
    c. $883.50
    d. $1,016.50
    e. $1,070.00

5. A convertible bond's price floor cannot fall below
    a. either its call price or its par value.
    b. either its conversion value or its call price.
    c. either its conversion value or its bond value.
    d. either its par value or its bond value.
    e. either its par value or its conversion value.

6. A Doge-Winn warrant entitles its holder to purchase 3 shares of Doge-Winn common stock for $18.75/share. The common stock currently has a market value of $23.50/share. Each warrant's theoretical value is
    a. $1.58.
    b. $3.75.
    c. $4.75.
    d. $9.82.
    e. $14.25.

7. The Doge-Winn warrants described in Question 6 have an antidilution provision. If Doge-Winn has a 5-for-4 stock split, each warrant's exercise price would become
    a. $15.00/share.
    b. $18.80/share.
    c. $23.44/share.
    d. $25.50/share.
    e. $29.38/share.

8. A convertible bond issue that overhangs often
    a. reduces the firm's after-tax cost of capital.
    b. can be used as a sweetener to entice new investors.
    c. results from a forced conversion.
    d. enhances the firm's earnings per share.
    e. reduces the firm's future financing flexibility.

9. A warrant's premium tends to increase
    a. should its theoretical value increase significantly.
    b. if its associated common stock is volatile.
    c. as the leverage opportunity of the warrant is reduced.
    d. when the firm pays higher dividends on its common stock.
    e. when the warrant's exercise price is increased.

10. Talex has 6,000,000 shares of common stock authorized, but only 4,000,000 shares have been issued. The company owns 400,000 shares of treasury stock and has 100,000 warrants outstanding. Each warrant allows its holder to purchase one share of Talex common stock at $12/share. Talex's after-tax earnings are $8,000,000. The firm's stated earnings per share are approximately

    a. $1.25/share
    b. $1.45/share.
    c. $2.05/share.
    d. $2.16/share.
    e. $2.71/share.

11. After a warrant's expiration date, the warrant's value
    a. approaches its exercise price.
    b. equals the par value of the associated common stock.
    c. is reduced to $1.
    d. exceeds its conversion price.
    e. is zero.

12. A Markel convertible bond ($1,000 par value) has a 4 percent coupon rate and matures in one year. The bond's market value is $1,065, and Markel common stock trades for $46/share. However, the price of the common stock is expected to increase by 8 percent during the next year. If an investor bought a Markel convertible bond today and held it for one year, what approximate conversion ratio would be necessary to give the investor a 12 percent return on her or his investment?
    a. 8.6 shares
    b. 18.0 shares
    c. 23.2 shares
    d. 25.6 shares
    e. 42.4 shares

KEY DEFINITIONS

Antidilution provision: in the event of either a stock split or a stock dividend, a provision in a warrant that requires (1) the number of shares that can be purchased with a warrant to be proportionately increased and (2) the warrant's exercise price to be proportionately reduced.

Arbitraguers: investors who seek profit opportunities by simultaneously buying and selling equivalent securities that have different prices.

Bond value: a convertible bond's value if it were appraised as a bond without a conversion feature.

Conversion premium: the excess of a convertible bond's market price over its price floor.

Conversion price: the issuing price per share of common stock that is recorded on the firm's books upon the conversion of a convertible security into common stock.

Conversion ratio: the number of shares of common stock into which a convertible bond can (at its holder's option) be converted.

Conversion value: a convertible bond's value if it were converted into common stock.

Convertible security: either a bond or a share of preferred stock that grants its holder the option to exchange the security for a predetermined number of shares of the firm's common stock during a specific time period.

Exercise price: the per-share price at which a warrant entitles its holder to purchase the firm's common stock.

Overhang: the situation that exists when a convertible bond issue that would probably not be converted into common stock if the firm attempted to force a conversion of the issue by calling the bonds.

Price floor: the minimum market price of a convertible bond, established by the higher of the bond's conversion value and its bond value.

Warrant: an option to purchase a specific number of shares of the firm's common stock at a predetermined price prior to an expiration date.

ANSWERS TO REVIEW QUESTIONS

1. a	4. d	7. a	10. d
2. b	5. c	8. e	11. e
3. d	6. e	9. b	12. c

Part Seven
Special Situations in Financial Management

The final three chapters address special topics in finance that challenge financial managers to coordinate their full range of skills in the areas of ratio analysis, capital budgeting, risk analysis, working capital management, and long-term financing. Chapter 20 examines various issues involved in merger decisions, and Chapter 21 probes both the reasons that firms fail and methods available to the ailing firm (and its creditors) in attempting to alleviate the firm's financial distress. Chapter 22 investigates the added scope of the financial manager's tasks when a firm engages in international operations.

Chapter Twenty
Mergers

OVERVIEW

Mergers are exciting and challenging, because they require financial managers to integrate all the functional areas of corporate finance. With a merger, a firm can enhance its shareholders' wealth (the firm's stock price) by either altering its risk profile or increasing its earnings. Financial managers should be familiar with all of the numerous types of mergers. Each type often presents a unique set of factors to be considered. For example, some types of mergers significantly modify the legal status of the firm, whereas other types change the firm's financial characteristics as a result of their various economic effects on the firm. In accounting for a merger, we use either the pooling-of-interests method or the purchase method, depending on the conditions associated with the merger. Seldom will both methods have the same postmerger effects on the firm's income statement and balance sheet.

STUDY OBJECTIVES

1. To understand the principal <u>types</u> of mergers in terms of their legal and economic impact on the firm.

2. To investigate the various <u>motives</u> for a merger.

3. To learn about the different <u>accounting implications</u> associated with a merger.

CHAPTER OUTLINE

I. Types of mergers

A. Mergers based on <u>legal status</u>.

1. A <u>statutory merger</u> occurs when the acquiring firm obtains all the assets, liabilities, and legal responsibilities of the acquired firm. Either a simple majority or a two-thirds majority approval (depending on the firms' charters and bylaws) by the common stockholders of each firm is required to authorize the merger. The stockholders of the

329

acquired firm are compensated with either cash or the acquiring firm's securities. After a statutory merger, the acquired firm ceases to exist as a legal entity.

2. In a consolidation, two firms merge to form a new firm. After the consolidation, each firm loses its status as a legal entity. As in a statutory merger, approval by the stockholders of each firm is usually required to effect a consolidation.

3. With a sale of assets, one firm purchases a portion of another firm's assets but both firms continue to exist as legal entities after the sale. If a significant amount of the selling firm's assets are involved in the sale, approval by the selling firm's stockholders and bondholders may be required.

4. A holding company is a firm that owns controlling interests in the common stock of other firms. All firms involved in a holding company's organization retain their legal identities.

Note: Except in situations that require explicit legal distinctions, the terms merger, consolidation, and sale (or acquisition) of assets will be used interchangeably.

B. Mergers based on economic impact.

1. When two firms that have very similar lines of business (often in the same geographic markets) merge, the merger is referred to as a horizontal merger. For example, a merger between two local retail clothing chains would be considered a horizontal merger.

2. A vertical merger results from the merging of two firms that are involved at different levels of a product's production chain. The merging of a manufacturing firm with one of its suppliers is an example of a vertical merger.

3. A conglomerate merger occurs between two firms that have either non-competing products or noncompeting markets. Conglomerate mergers are classified into one of three categories.

   a. A product extension involves two firms that are in functionally related lines of business (for example, newspapers and textbooks) but create products that do not compete directly against each other.

   b. The merging of two firms that have identical lines of business in different geographic markets is a market extension.

   c. A pure conglomerate merger joins firms that exhibit apparent similarities in either their products or their geographic markets.

II. Motives for mergers

A. The underlying motive for any merger is to maximize shareholders' wealth (the firm's stock price) by either enhancing earnings (and dividends) or reducing risks.

B. Earnings.

1. A merger may reduce the acquiring firm's costs through <u>economies of scale</u> in the production phase or the marketing phase of the firm's business. These reduced costs result in greater future income for the firm's stockholders. This positive effect on the firm's earnings is called <u>synergism</u>.

2. A profitable firm can often gain future <u>tax savings</u> by acquiring an unprofitable firm that has accumulated tax-loss carryforwards that may be unusable without a merger.

3. The acquiring firm may need the acquired firm's <u>managerial talents</u>, particularly those of middle management.

4. If the acquired firm has little debt in its capital structure, a merger could expand the acquiring firm's <u>equity base</u>, thereby increasing its future <u>debt capacity</u>.

5. A merger is often a quicker and more profitable avenue into either <u>new products</u> or <u>new markets</u> than would be available to the acquiring firm through internal expansion.

6. Historically, firms have used mergers to <u>eliminate competition</u> by acquiring their competitors. In the past few decades, however, state and federal antitrust laws have established strict guidelines to prevent mergers that could result in reduced competition. The Department of Justice and the Federal Trade Commission have the primary responsibility to enforce such laws that have been federally enacted.

7. Under certain conditions, a merger may produce short-term <u>growth in earnings per share</u> for the acquiring firm that could appear quite impressive to investors. However, both investors and financial managers should be more concerned with the long-term effects of a merger on the firm's per share earnings than with the short-term effects.

Example: Suppose that Carey Iron acquired Rupert Mines in a merger. Prior to the merger, both firms had the financial characteristics shown in the accompanying table.

	Carey	Rupert
After-tax earnings	$600,000	$300,000
Shares of common stock	200,000 shares	300,000 shares
Earnings per share	$3/share	$1/share
Price to earnings ratio	10X	5X
Common stock per share price	$30/share	$5/share

Carey paid $7/share for Rupert's common stock. Determine Carey's earnings per share (EPS_X) subsequent to the merger if:

a. No economies of scale were available from the merger. That is, no synergistic earnings would result after the merger.

b. New synergistic earnings would be $20,000.

In both cases, assume that Carey could issue new common stock at $30/share to Rupert's stockholders in exchange for their common stock.

Solution: The number N of new shares of Carey common stock that must be issued at $30/share to finance the acquisition of Rupert's 300,000 shares of common stock at a price of $7/share can be determined in the following manner:

N = 300,000 shares * ($7/$30) = <u>70,000 new shares</u>

Therefore, Carey would have 270,000 shares (200,000 original and 70,000 new) of common stock outstanding after the merger.

a. Without synergistic earnings:

Carey's EPS_x = combined earnings of Carey and Rupert/270,000 shares
= ($600,000 + $300,000)/270,000 shares
= <u>$3.33/share</u>

b. With synergistic earnings ($20,000):

Carey's EPS_x = ($600,000 + $300,000 + $20,000)/270,000 shares
= <u>$3.41/share</u>

Example: In the previous Carey-Rupert merger, determine Carey's postmerger earnings per share (EPS_x) if Rupert's common stock was valued at $12/share for the merger and no synergistic earnings resulted from the merger. Assume that Carey's stock was worth $30/share to Rupert's stockholders in the merger negotiations.

Solution:

New shares issued by Carey = 300,000 shares * ($12/$30)

= 120,000 new shares

Therefore,

EPS_x = ($600,000 + $300,000)/(200,000 shares + 120,000 shares)

= <u>$2.81/share</u>

Note that if Rupert's common stock were valued at $12/share for purposes of the merger, the merger would result in a dilution of Carey's earnings per share from $3.00/share prior to the merger to $2.81/share after the merger. In fact, with Carey's common stock at $30/share, the maximum price at which Rupert's common stock could be valued, if the merger were to leave Carey's postmerger earnings per share unchanged at $3/share, would be <u>$10.67/share</u>.

C. Risk reduction

1. A merger sometimes gives a firm the opportunity to reduce its overall risk exposure. Having less risk, the firm may be able to lower its after-tax cost of capital, thereby increasing the value of its stock as a consequence of a merger.

2. Types of risks affected by a merger

   a. The firm's business risk will decline if a merger leads to less volatility in the firm's operating profits. In this regard, a merger can often stabilize the firm's sales, expand the firm's base of customers, or diversify the firm's projects.

   b. A firm may be able to reduce its financial risk by acquiring another firm that has very little debt in its capital structure. A merger of this nature expands the acquiring firm's asset base without resulting in a corresponding increase in the firm's financial commitments to creditors. Thereafter, the acquiring firm would be in a better position to service its existing debt.

3. When a merger is financed by the issuance of new common stock, there is an increase in the number of the acquiring firm's stockholders and shares of common stock outstanding. These increases tend to reduce the marketability risk associated with the acquiring firm's common stock. Having less marketability risk (or greater liquidity in the secondary markets), the firm's stock enjoys an increase in market value.

III. Accounting treatment of mergers

A. Whether the pooling-of-interests method or the purchase method is used to account for a merger depends on the circumstances of the merger. The effects of the two methods on the balance sheet and the income statement of the merged firm can be significantly different.

B. Requirements of the pooling-of-interests method.

1. The firms to be merged are independent and have been autonomous for at least two years prior to the merger.

2. The merger is effected either in a single transaction or within one year, in accordance with a prenegotiated plan.

3. The acquiring firm issues only common stock to exchange for at least 90 percent of the acquired firm's voting common stock. Further, the common stock issued for the exchange must be identical to the issuing firm's voting common stock that was outstanding prior to the merger.

4. After the merger, the acquired firm's stockholders have a proportionate ownership position in the acquiring (or combined) firm.

5. The accounting basis for the acquired firm's assets remains unchanged after the merger.

6. The acquiring firm cannot dispose of a significant portion of the acquired firm's assets during the first two years after the merger.

C. Pooling-of-interests method.

1. With a pooling of interests, the Assets (based on historical costs), Liabilities, and Total Shareholders' Equity accounts of the firms involved in the merger are simply added together to determine the postmerger balance sheet of the acquiring firm (also referred to as the merged firm). However, the postmerger number of common stock shares of the merged firm depends on the amount of common stock issued by the acquiring (merged) firm that was exchanged for the acquired firm's stock.

2. The income statement of the merged firm is derived by combining the income statements of the merging firms. The merged firm's earnings per share are calculated using its postmerger number of shares of common stock.

D. Purchase method.

1. The purchase method assumes that both the assets and the liabilities of the acquired firm are purchased by the acquiring firm. If the per-share price paid by the acquiring firm for the acquired firm's common stock equals the acquired firm's book value per share, accounting treatment of the merger in the purchase method is similar to the accounting procedures used in the pooling-of-interests method. If any other price is paid, however, the assets of the acquired firm must be adjusted either upward or downward. In the event that the acquiring firm pays more than the book value for each of the acquired firm's shares of common stock, the adjustment equals the per-share difference between these values multiplied by the number of the acquired firm's shares. This upward adjustment appears on the merged firm's balance sheet as an intangible asset called goodwill. If a downward adjustment of the acquired firm's assets is necessary, due to the acquired firm's per-share selling price being less than its per-share book value, the adjustment is made to specific asset accounts (such as Inventory and Fixed Assets) of the acquired firm during the consolidation of the firms' balance sheets. With this downward adjustment of the acquired firm's specific assets, the merged firm will show no goodwill on its postmerger balance sheet as a result of the merger.

2. The merged firm's earnings per share are determined by dividing the merging firms' combined after-tax net incomes (plus any synergistic earnings created by the merger) by the postmerger shares of the merged firm. However, if goodwill was created in the merger, it must be amortized as a non-tax-deductible expense in determining the merged firm's after-tax net income. Thus goodwill reduces the merged firm's postmerger earnings per share. For this reason, most firms prefer to use the pooling-of-interests method when the necessary conditions can be met. Alternatively, if the acquired firm's assets were adjusted downward during the merger, the amount of the downward adjustment cannot be amortized as a credit against expenses on the merged firm's income statement.

E. Example problem.

Prior to the acquisition of XYZ by ABC, the two firms had the following financial characteristics:

	ABC	XYZ
Total assets	$1,000	$350
Total liabilities	$ 250	$ 75
Common stock ($1 par value)	$ 200	$ 50
Additional paid-in capital	$ 400	$125
Retained earnings	$ 150	$100
Shareholders' equity	$ 750	$275
Total liabilities and shareholders' equity	$1,000	$350
After-tax net income	$ 800	$150
Shares outstanding	200 shares	50 shares
Earnings per share	$4.00/share	$3.00/share

ABC financed the merger by issuing new common stock at $25/share. The total price paid for XYZ was $500 (that is, ABC paid $10/share for XYZ's common stock). Therefore, ABC had to issue 20 new shares of its common stock to finance the merger. The following postmerger financial statements of ABC indicate the accounting differences between the pooling-of-interests and purchase methods.

	ABC's Postmerger Financial Statements	
	Pooling of Interests Method	Purchase Method
Premerger combined assets	$1,350	$1,350
Goodwill	$ 0	$ 225
Postmerger total assets	$1,350	$1,575
Total liabilities	$ 325	$ 325
Common stock (220 shares @ $1 par)	$ 220	$ 220
Additional paid-in capital	$ 555	$ 880
Retained earnings	$ 250	$ 150
Shareholders' equity	$1,025	$1,250
Total liabilities and shareholders' equity	$1,350	$1,575
Premerger after-tax net income	$ 950	$ 950
Less goodwill expense	$ 0	($ 25)
Postmerger after-tax net income	$ 950	$ 925
Shares outstanding	220 shares	220 shares
Postmerger earnings per share	$4.32/share	$4.20/share

Comments on the pooling-of-interests method:

1. The assets and the liabilities of the merging firm are simply combined.

2. Goodwill is not created.

3. Retained earnings of the merging firms are summed. But the merged firm's postmerger Additional Paid-In Capital account serves as a balancing account to make the Shareholder's Equity account of the merged firm equal to the sum of the Shareholders' Equity accounts of the merging firms.

Comments on the <u>purchase method</u>:

1. The book value of XYZ's common shareholder equity was $275, yet ABC paid $500 (50 shares * $10/share) to XYZ's stockholders. The difference ($225) is goodwill on the balance sheet of the acquiring firm (ABC).

2. The $25 goodwill expense assumes that goodwill resulting from the merger is amortized over 9 years. This expense is non-tax-deductible, and it reduces ABC's postmerger earnings from $4.32/share to $4.20/share.

3. The acquiring firm's postmerger Additional Paid-In Surplus account was calculated in the following manner:

    $880 = ABC's premerger amount + <u>new</u> additional paid-in surplus
    = $400 + (20 shares * $24/share)
    + $400 + $480 = <u>$880</u>

IV. When management of the firm to be acquired (referred to as the <u>target firm</u>) is opposed to a proposed merger, the acquiring firm may attempt to obtain a controlling interest in the target firm by means of a <u>tender offer</u>. The tender offer may be successful if the target firm's stockholders are unhappy with the firm's current management or if the tender price is attractive enough. The target firm's management can attempt to thwart a tender offer by going to court, by issuing new common stock to acquire a third firm, or by seeking a more friendly acquisition by another firm.

STUDY PROBLEMS

<u>20.1.</u> Eagle Motors acquired Winkler Auto Parts in a merger with an exchange of common stock. Prior to the merger, the following premerger conditions existed.

	Eagle	Winkler
After-tax earnings	$3,680,000	$6,200,000
Shares of common stock	1,200,000 shares	4,000,000 shares
Earnings per share (EPS)	$3.07/share	$1.55/share
Price-to-earnings ratio	5.9X	7.0X
Market price of common stock	$21.18/share	$10.85/share

It is anticipated that, due to economies of scale, approximately $300,000 in synergistic after-tax earnings will result from the merger. Assuming that Eagle paid $12/share for Winkler's common stock, (a) how many new shares (N) of Eagle common stock would have to be issued at $21/share, and (b) what would be Eagle's postmerger earnings per share (EPS_x)?

Solution

a. N = 4,000,000 shares * ($12/$21)
    = 2,285,714 new shares to be issued by Eagle

Therefore, after the merger, Eagle would have 3,485,714 shares (1,200,000 original shares plus 2,285,714 new shares) of common stock outstanding.

b. To determine Eagle's postmerger earnings per share (EPS_x):

EPS_x = ($3,680,000 + $6,200,000 + $300,000)/3,485,714 shares
     = $2.92/share

Although the Eagle-Winkler merger (under the above conditions) would result in a slight dilution of Eagle's earnings per share (from $3.07/share to $2.92/share), the merger may still be in the best interests of Eagle's stockholders if the long-run benefits of the merger overshadow this short-run dilution.

20.2. In the Eagle-Winkler merger discussed in Problem 20.1, find Eagle's post-merger earnings had Eagle financed the merger by issuing debt at 11 percent and paying the Winkler stockholders in cash rather than in Eagle common stock. Assume that the purchase price for Winkler's stock remained $12/share. Eagle is in a 45 percent tax bracket, and the book value of Winkler's common stock was $5/share prior to the merger. Further, Eagle amortizes goodwill resulting from mergers over 10 years. Before answering this question, consider which accounting method was applicable to the merger under these conditions.

Solution

The purchase method must be used for the Eagle-Winkler merger, because Eagle paid Winkler's stockholders in cash. Thus the merger created $7 of goodwill for each share of Winkler common stock purchased. Total goodwill was $28 million (4 million shares of Winkler common stock * $7/share). The following information is also known:

Amount borrowed = 4,000,000 * $12 = $48,000,000

After-tax interest expense = $48,000,000 * .11 * (1 - .45)
                          = $2,904,000

Amortization of goodwill = $28,000,000/10 years
                        = $2,800,000/year

Postmerger after-tax net income
   before interest and amortization = $3,680,000 + $6,200,000 + $300,000
                                   = $10,180,000

Postmerger after-tax net income
   after interest and amortization = $10,180,000 - $2,904,000 - $2,800,000
                                   = $4,476,000

(Note that the $2,800,000 amortization of goodwill is non-tax-deductible.) Eagle didn't issue new stock for the merger, so its number of shares of common stock after the merger remained 1,200,000 shares. Consequently,

Postmerger EPS = $4,476,000/1,200,000 shares
             = $3.73/share

Although Eagle could substantially improve its postmerger earnings with debt financing rather than with an exchange of stock, $48,000,000 in new debt increased the firm's financial risk. As a result of this added risk, Eagle's cost of capital could have increased and its price-to-earnings ratio could have dropped after the merger.

20.3. Prior to a proposed merger in which Smith Steel would acquire Phoenix Pipe, the firm's balance sheets are as follows:

	Smith	Phoenix
Current assets	$24,000	$ 8,000
Fixed assets	$65,000	$20,000
Total assets	$89,000	$28,000
Current liabilities	$ 6,000	$ 2,000
Long-term debt	$18,000	$ 6,000
Total liabilities	$24,000	$ 8,000
Common stock ($1 par value)	$10,000	$ 2,000
Additional paid-in capital	$25,000	$ 7,000
Retained earnings	$30,000	$11,000
Shareholders' equity	$65,000	$20,000
Total liabilities and shareholders' equity	$89,000	$28,000

Smith is considering two alternative means of completing the merger.

a. An exchange of two shares of its common stock for every five shares of Phoenix's common stock. This alternative would allow Smith to use the pooling-of-interests method.

b. A cash purchase of Phoenix's common stock at $18/share. To finance this purchase, Smith could issue new common stock at $45/share. With this alternative, Smith must use the purchase method.

Construct Smith's balance sheet after the proposed merger for both alternatives.

Solution

	Smith's Postmerger Balance Sheet	
	Pooling	Purchase
Current assets	$ 32,000	$ 32,000
Fixed assets	$ 85,000	$ 85,000
Goodwill	$ 0	$ 16,000 (Note 3)
Total assets	$117,000	$133,000
Current liabilities	$ 8,000	$ 8,000
Long-term debt	$ 24,000	$ 24,000
Total liabilities	$ 32,000	$ 32,000
Common stock ($1 par value)	$ 10,800 (Note 1)	$ 10,800 (Note 4)
Additional paid-in capital	$ 33,200 (Note 2)	$ 60,200 (Note 4)
Retained earnings	$ 41,000	$ 30,000
Shareholders' equity	$ 85,000	$101,000
Total liabilities and shareholders' equity	$117,000	$133,000

Notes:

1. Smith and Phoenix currently have 10,000 shares and 2,000 shares of common stock, respectively. If Smith's stock were exchanged on a 2-for-5 basis for the Phoenix stock,

   New Smith shares = 2,000 shares * (2/5)
   $\qquad\qquad\qquad$ = 800 shares

   Therefore, after the merger,

   Smith's common stock at par value = 10,800 shares * $1/share
   $\qquad\qquad\qquad\qquad\qquad\qquad\qquad$ = $10,800

2. Smith's postmerger additional paid-in capital = $85,000 - $10,800 - $41,000
   $\qquad\qquad\qquad\qquad\qquad\qquad\qquad\qquad\qquad\qquad\qquad$ = $33,200

3. Phoenix's premerger book value = $20,000/2,000 shares = $10/share. Therefore,

   Goodwill = 2,000 Phoenix shares * ($18 - $10) = $16,000

4. To finance the merger associated with the second alternative,

   New Smith shares = 2,000 * ($18/$45) = 800 shares

   As a consequence of 800 shares being issued at $45/share, Smith's postmerger common stock and additional paid-in capital accounts would be

   Common stock (10,800 shares @ $1/share par value) $10,800
   Additional paid-in surplus (25,000 + [800 * ($45 - $1)]) $60,200

REVIEW QUESTIONS

1. A merger in which both firms lose their original identities as legal entities is classified as a
   a. vertical merger.
   b. merger into a holding company.
   c. statutory merger.
   d. product extension merger.
   e. consolidation.

2. If a perfume manufacturer in the northeast acquired a western electrical appliance retailer, the resulting merger would be considered a
   a. statutory merger.
   b. pure conglomerate merger.
   c. product extension merger.
   d. market extension merger.
   e. vertical merger.

3. The merging of a firm that brews beer and one that produces soft drinks would be a
   a. product extension.
   b. market extension.
   c. vertical merger.
   d. horizontal merger.
   e. consolidation.

4. Synergism in a merger results from
   a. financial leverage.
   b. goodwill.
   c. reduction of business risk.
   d. economies of scale.
   e. the acquiring firm's expanded equity base after the merger.

5. Before Wasaff Concrete acquired Thomas Yarn, the after-tax incomes of the two firms were $75,000 and $31,000, respectively. Wasaff had 25,000 shares of common stock, and Thomas had 14,000 shares of common stock. To finance the merger, Wasaff issued new common stock (valued at $15/share) to Thomas's stockholders. Ignoring possible economies of scale, determine Wasaff's post-merger earnings per share had Thomas's common stock been valued at $10/share in the merger negotiations.
   a. $2.75/share
   b. $3.09/share
   c. $3.17/share
   d. $3.40/share
   e. $3.72/share

6. For the Wasaff-Thomas merger described in Question 5, calculate Wasaff's post-merger earnings per share had Wasaff paid $12/share for Thomas's common stock and had its additional after-tax income (as a result of the merger's synergism) been $8,000. Wasaff's common stock was valued at $15/share.
   a. $2.93/share
   b. $3.00/share
   c. $3.15/share
   d. $3.27/share
   e. $3.48/share

7. A merger that reduces the volatility of the acquiring firm's operating profits tends also to lower the acquiring firm's
   a. business risk.
   b. financial risk.
   c. marketability risk.
   d. price-to-earnings ratio.
   e. earnings per share.

8. The primary objective of a merger should be to improve the firm's
   a. earnings per share.
   b. growth in earnings.
   c. risk profile.
   d. stock price.
   e. competitive position.

Use the following information to answer Questions 9-12.

	Premerger Financial Data	
	Air-Temp, Inc.	Horner Stoves
Total assets	$4,200,000	$1,480,000
Total liabilities	$1,000,000	$ 450,000
Common stock shares outstanding	150,000 shares	70,000 shares
Par value	$1/share	$1/share
Additional paid-in capital	$1,050,000	$360,000
Retained earnings	$2,000,000	$600,000
Shareholders' equity	$3,200,000	$1,030,000
After-tax earnings	$3.75/share	$2.90/share
Market price of stock	$28.00/share	$17.50/share

9. Suppose Air-Temp acquired Horner with an exchange of common stock based on current market stock prices. If the pooling-of-interests method was used for the merger, how many shares of common stock would Air-Temp have outstanding after the merger?
   a. 168,200 shares
   b. 181,275 shares
   c. 193,750 shares
   d. 204,133 shares
   e. 220,000 shares

10. Assuming a merger under the conditions mentioned in Question 9, determine Air-Temp's postmerger Additional Paid-In Capital account.
    a. $390,750
    b. $1,410,000
    c. $1,436,250
    d. $4,730,000
    e. $5,425,000

11. Had Air-Temp paid Horner's stockholders $17.50/share for their common stock in cash rather than with an exchange of Air-Temp's common stock
    a. $195,000 of goodwill would have been created in the merger.
    b. the merger would have resulted in no goodwill.
    c. Horner's assets would have been adjusted downward by $735,000 during the merger.
    d. the pooling-of-interests method could have been used to account for the merger.
    e. both b and c.

12. Air-Temp expects no synergistic earnings to result from its acquisition of Horner. Suppose that the acquisition discussed in Question 11 was financed with Air-Temp issuing the necessary amount of debt at 13 percent, and determine Air-Temp's postmerger earnings per share. Assume that goodwill, if any, is amortized over 10 years and that Air-Temp is in a 40 percent tax bracket.
    a. $2.95/share
    b. $3.75/share
    c. $4.02/share
    d. $4.34/share
    e. $4.69/share

KEY DEFINITIONS

Consolidation: a merger in which two firms are combined to form a new firm. The firms involved in a consolidation lose their separate corporate identities after the merger.

Holding company: a company that owns a controlling interest in the common stock of other firms.

Horizontal merger: a merger involving firms that have very similar lines of business. In a horizontal merger, the merging firms usually have the same geographic markets also.

Market extension: a merger that results from the merging of firms that have the same line of business in different geographic markets.

Pooling of interests: an accounting method for a merger that simply combines the Assets, Liabilities, and Total Shareholders' Equity accounts of the merging firms when the merged firm's balance sheet is constructed. No goodwill is created when the pooling-of-interests method is used.

Product extension: a merger between firms that have functionally related (but not identical) lines of business.

Purchase method: an accounting treatment of a merger that does not meet the conditions required for the pooling-of-interests method. The purchase method assumes that the shareholders' equity of the acquired firm was purchased by the acquiring firm. If the price paid by the acquiring firm exceeds the book value of the acquired firm's shareholders' equity, goodwill is created on the acquiring (merged) firm's balance sheet.

Pure conglomerate: a merger of firms that have neither competing lines of business nor the same product markets.

Sale of assets: although not technically classified as a merger, a situation in which one firm purchases a portion of the selling firm's assets. After the sale, both firms retain their legal identities as separate corporations.

Statutory merger: a merger that results when the acquiring firm obtains all the assets, liabilities and legal obligations of the acquired firm. Subsequent to the merger, the acquired firm ceases to exist as a legal entity.

Synergism: the favorable influence on a firm's postmerger earnings that is made possible by cost savings due to economies of scale in a merger.

Vertical merger: a merger between firms at different levels of a product's production chain.

ANSWERS TO REVIEW QUESTIONS

1.	e	4.	d	7.	a	10.	c
2.	b	5.	b	8.	d	11.	a
3.	a	6.	c	9.	c	12.	d

Chapter Twenty-One
Failure and Reorganization

OVERVIEW

A firm can experience various degrees of financial distress, such as poor profitability, liquidity problems, or the inability to meet its existing debt obligations. Financial distress is seldom a welcome condition for any firm. However, financial managers can develop contingency plans to help cope with the firm's financial problems if they are aware of what causes these problems and sensitive to the early warning signals associated with oncoming financial distress. Should the financial condition of the firm deteriorate to a point that threatens the firm's existence, the firm can attempt to negotiate with its creditors an extension, a composition, or a recapitalization. Creditors usually prefer these voluntary agreements to a formal bankruptcy, because bankruptcy proceedings are often prolonged and expensive. But, if a voluntary agreement cannot be arranged, the only remaining alternative may be a bankruptcy proceeding. A petition for bankruptcy can be submitted to the bankruptcy court either by the firm or by its unsecured creditors (under certain conditions). In a bankruptcy proceeding, the bankruptcy court usually tries to devise a reorganization plan for the financially distressed firm that is both fair and equitable to the firm's creditors. If such a plan is unworkable or unlikely to provide a lasting remedy for the firm's financial problems, the court will supervise the firm's liquidation.

STUDY OBJECTIVES

1. To recognize the degrees, causes, and symptoms of financial distress that a firm can experience.

2. To become aware of the voluntary agreements and the formal bankruptcy procedures that are available to a firm and its creditors for relieving the firm's financial distress.

CHAPTER OUTLINE

I. Degrees of financial distress

A. A firm that is not earning profits or is obtaining an insufficient return on its investment is often considered a financial failure. According to these criteria, a firm that is currently very profitable could have been a financial failure at some time in its past. Poor profitability is a mild degree of financial distress. It does not necessarily imply that the firm is about to go out of business.

B. Insolvency occurs when the firm is having a liquidity problem. The firm is technically insolvent if it does not have sufficient cash (or access to cash) to satisfy its present financial commitments. A technical insolvency doesn't usually pose a serious threat to the firm's existence unless it continues for a long time. However, the firm is legally insolvent whenever the sum of its debts (total liabilities) exceeds the current value of its assets. Legal insolvency suggests that the firm is in considerable financial distress.

C. Bankruptcy is a legal declaration of a firm's insolvency by the bankruptcy court. A bankruptcy petition can be filed with the court by the firm or by its creditors. If filed by the firm, the petition requests that the court (1) protect the firm from its creditors while it tries to improve its financial condition, (2) assume the management responsibilities of the firm, or (3) liquidate the firm.

D. Liquidation of the firm represents the most severe degree of financial distress. In a liquidation, the firm's assets are either sold for the benefit of the firm's creditors or given to them.

II. Causes of a firm's financial distress include insufficient working capital, poorly timed cash flows, declining sales, mismanagement, production problems, excessive debt obligations, overbearing loan restrictions, and external factors (such as government regulations, labor problems, natural disasters, inflation, and recessions).

III. Both the trends over time and the deviations from industry (or peer group) norms of certain financial ratios can act as early warning signals that a firm is in financial trouble. Among the symptoms of a financially ailing firm are:

A. A lower ratio of net cash flow to total debt.

B. A rapidly declining market price of the firm's stock.

C. A deterioration in the ratio of working capital to total assets.

D. A diminishing ratio of sales to total assets.

E. A decline in the ratio of retained earnings to total assets.

F. A waning ratio of earnings before interest and taxes to total assets.

G. A falling ratio of the market value of the firm's equity to the book value of its debt.

IV. Financial managers should continually monitor the early warning signals that may help alert them to a decline in the firm's financial condition. When indications of possible financial distress arise, well-executed contingency plans can often prevent severe financial difficulties. Contingency plans help the firm's management determine the following:

1. Cash reserves and lending sources available to the firm.

2. Methods to reduce either cash expenditures or operating expenses quickly.

3. Assets that could be liquidated to raise cash.

4. The approximate time that would be required for the firm to accumulate the liquid funds it needs.

V. Voluntary agreements

A. In the event that a firm's financial condition has deteriorated so much that it can no longer fulfill its financial commitments, the firm and its creditors may be able to negotiate a voluntary agreement. Extensions, compositions, and recapitalizations are the major types of voluntary agreements that can be arranged.

B. The first phase of a voluntary agreement is the formation of a creditors' committee consisting of several larger creditors, a few smaller creditors, and an independent credit bureau. All the firm's creditors must agree with the committee's proposed plan before the plan can be adopted. The committee is responsible for both implementing and overseeing the adopted plan. The degree of managerial control that is assigned to the committee depends on the severity of the firm's financial problems. In some cases, the committee may even have the authority to replace the firm's existing management.

1. Advantages of a creditors' committee.

a. Details of the agreement can be kept confidential.

b. Legal costs are minimized.

c. The firm's existing management is sometimes able to retain a part of its control over the firm.

2. Disadvantages of a creditors' committee.

a. The committee lacks the legal authority to refuse payment on questionable claims presented by creditors.

b. Unanimous approval by the firm's creditors is often difficult to obtain for the committee's proposed plan.

C. Types of voluntary agreements.

1. In an extension, the firm's creditors consent to grant the firm more time to resolve its financial difficulties. Usually, an extension allows the firm to lengthen the maturity of its debt that is either past due or coming due in the near future. An extension is typically arranged by the firm's bank. In this capacity, the bank also serves as the chief negotiator for the firm's creditors. In order to protect their financial interests, the firm's creditors usually take an active role in the firm's managerial duties during an extension.

2. If creditors feel that the firm has little chance of ever being able to make full payment on its financial obligations, they can agree to a <u>composition</u>. With a composition, creditors reduce their original claims against the firm to a level which (in their opinion) the firm will be able to pay. Compositions are sometimes preferred to other types of voluntary agreements. They can be completed more promptly, and they leave the firm with a more manageable financial structure.

3. In a <u>recapitalization</u>, the firm's capital structure is changed and the terms of its existing debt are usually altered. Creditors may receive shares of the firm's preferred or its common stock in exchange for their debt holdings in the firm. Such exchanges require the existing stockholders' approval (via amendments to the firm's charter) if the recapitalization necessitates either an increase in the number of authorized shares of common stock or the issuance of new preferred stock. In addition to this change in the firm's capital structure, the maturity of the firm's remaining debt is often lengthened. (In this respect, a recapitalization is similar to an extension.)

VI. Bankruptcy

A. When a voluntary agreement cannot be arranged between the firm and its creditors, the firm may be forced into either a <u>reorganization</u> or a <u>liquidation</u>, in accordance with Chapters 11 and 7, respectively, of the Federal Bankruptcy Act of 1978. However, voluntary agreements are usually preferred to formal bankruptcy proceedings, which are lengthy and expensive.

B. If the bankruptcy court believes that the firm has a reasonable chance of repaying its debts and operating profitably in the future, it can supervise a <u>reorganization</u> of the firm. During the reorganization, the firm is protected from its creditors until it has had enough time to solve its financial problems. A reorganization is a stepwise process.

Step 1 - A formal <u>petition</u> of bankruptcy is submitted to the court either <u>voluntarily</u> by the firm or <u>involuntarily</u> by its unsecured creditors. Three or more unsecured creditors with combined claims of more than $5,000 may file an involuntary petition. If the firm has fewer than 12 unsecured creditors, any unsecured creditor can file the petition with the court.

Step 2 - When a voluntary bankruptcy petition is submitted by the firm, the court automatically issues an <u>order of relief</u>, which protects the firm from further action by its creditors during the balance of the bankruptcy proceedings. Should creditors submit the bankruptcy petition, the court issues an order of relief only if it judges that the petition offers sufficient grounds to merit continued proceedings. Once the order of relief has been issued, both the firm and its creditors are subject to the court's jurisdiction.

Step 3 - Next the court appoints a <u>creditors' committee</u> made up of the firm's unsecured creditors. The creditors' committee serves an advisory function. The court may also appoint other advisory committees to represent other groups (stockholders, secured creditors, etc.) that have an interest in the firm.

Step 4 - The court then decides whether to allow the firm's existing management to continue operating the firm or to appoint a trustee to manage the firm's affairs during the proceedings. The court may seek the opinion of an examiner before making this decision.

Step 5 - The firm has 120 days after the bankruptcy petition is submitted to file a reorganization plan with the court. If the firm fails to file a plan, or if the court does not accept the firm's plan within 180 days following the submission of the bankruptcy petition, the court will receive reorganization plans filed by the firm's creditors. A proposed reorganization plan normally addresses such issues as included and excluded claims covered by the plan, the treatment of claims according to the plan, the method of implementing the plan, and amendments to the firm's charter that are required before the plan can be put into effect.

Before a plan is adopted by the court, hearings are held to discuss possible modifications to the plan that may have been recommended by any interested party (including the Securities and Exchange Commission, when necessary). With its decision, the court hopes to adopt a plan that is fair, equitable, and likely to allow the firm to continue operating successfully with a more tolerable level of debt obligations. Reorganization plans often combine some of the features of extensions, compositions, and recapitalizations.

Step 6 - The three possible outcomes of an attempted reorganization are a dismissal, a conversion, and a discharge.

   a. The court can order a dismissal of the bankruptcy petition. In this event, an order of relief is not issued and the proceedings go no further.

   b. If the reorganization plan proves to be unworkable, the court can order a conversion of its reorganization efforts into liquidation of the firm.

   c. If the reorganization is successful, the court can discharge the firm from bankruptcy.

C. When a reorganization attempt is unsuccessful, the court may order the firm's liquidation. The steps involved in a liquidation are similar to those in a reorganization, but the end results are quite different.

Step 1 - Either the firm (voluntarily) or its creditors (involuntarily) can commence a liquidation proceeding by submitting a formal petition to the court.

Step 2 - If an <u>order of relief</u> is issued by the court, the court appoints an <u>interim trustee</u> to operate the firm and preserve its assets until a permanent trustee is appointed.

Step 3 - A <u>permanent trustee</u> is elected by the firm's creditors, and <u>creditors' committees</u> representing the various types of the firm's creditors are established.

Step 4 - The permanent trustee <u>sells the firm's assets</u>, using the proceeds from the sale <u>to pay creditors</u> in the following order.

    a. <u>Secured creditors</u>, from the proceeds generated by the sale of assets on which specific liens are held. (If the proceeds from this sale don't fully repay secured creditors, they become unsecured creditors for the difference.)

    b. The <u>bankruptcy court's expenses</u>, such as accounting, legal, and administrative fees.

    c. A limited amount of the firm's <u>wages, salaries, and commissions</u> that were payable prior to the bankruptcy.

    d. Court-allowed claims for unpaid contributions to the firm's <u>employee pension plans</u>.

    e. <u>Deposits</u> (up to $800) made by individuals for the purchase of the firm's products.

    f. Federal, state, and local <u>taxes</u> that are payable by the firm.

    g. <u>Unsecured claims</u> (trade credit, commercial paper, debentures) of the firm.

    h. <u>Subordinated</u> unsecured claims (for example, both senior and junior subordinated debentures).

    i. <u>Preferred stockholders</u>.

    j. <u>Common stockholders</u>.

STUDY PROBLEMS

<u>21.1.</u> Pawar Sleek Shops, a regional beauty parlor chain, is currently negotiating a 180-day loan with its bank for $300,000. The following information was obtained from Pawar's financial statements for the past two years.

	1980	1981	Industry
Working capital	$ 400,000	$ 440,000	$ 500,000
Total debt at book value	$ 650,000	$ 970,000	$ 700,000
Total assets	$1,700,000	$2,100,000	$2,000,000
Retained earnings	$ 400,000	$ 480,000	$ 700,000
Sales	$2,600,000	$2,700,000	$3,000,000
Earnings before interest and taxes (EBIT)	$ 270,000	$ 250,000	$ 360,000
Net cash flow	$ 190,000	$ 175,000	$ 235,000
Shares of common stock outstanding	50,000 shares	50,000 shares	60,000 shares
Market price of common stock . .	$20.50/share	$13.50/share	$22.50/share

This table also indicates industry averages for beauty parlor chains of the same size as Pawar. The chief financial officer at Pawar has told the bank that the company needs the loan to temporarily reduce its reliance on trade credit. Should the bank grant Pawar the loan?

Solution

Before making a decision on the Pawar loan application, the bank's loan officer calculated the following ratios.

Ratio			
Sales/total assets	1.53X	1.29X	1.50X
EBIT/total assets	15.9%	11.9%	18.0%
Net cash flow/total debt	29.2%	18.0%	33.6%
Working capital/total assets	23.5%	21.0%	25.0%
Retained earnings/total assets	23.5%	22.9%	35.0%
Total equity (market value)/ total debt	1.58X	.70X	1.93X (see note)
Stock price	$20.50/share	$13.50/share	$22.50/share

Note: Total market value of equity = shares of common stock outstanding * market price/share.

A review of these ratios (and their two-year trend) reveals several alarming aspects of Pawar's financial condition.

1. Both Pawar's asset turnover (sales/total assets) and its operating profitability (EBIT/total assets) ratios are low compared to industry norms. Further, both of these ratios have had poor trends over the last two years.

2. Pawar's ratio of net cash flow to total debt deteriorated significantly in 1981. The company's weak operating profitability and low asset turnover no doubt explain some of this weakening in cash flow, but Pawar also increased its debt to $970,000 during 1981. Thus it is highly questionable whether Pawar has sufficient debt capacity to repay a $300,000 loan in such a short time as six months.

3. The company's working-capital and returned-earnings ratios are unimpressive. The low ratio of returned earnings to total assets further suggests that Pawar's equity base is very weak compared to the industry norm.

4. Stock prices reflect investor expectations about future earnings and risks. And clearly, investors in the stock market are not too excited about Pawar's prospects for the future.

On the basis of these observations, the bank would probably refuse the loan application. Pawar is beginning to show many of the early warning signals of a firm that may be in financial distress.

21.2. Blotz Brewery has earnings before interest and taxes (EBIT) of $455,000 and the following debt obligations.

Debt	Amount	Maturity	Annual Principal Repayment
Bank loan (10%)	$ 250,000	1 year	$250,000
First-mortgage bonds (11%)	$1,200,000	15 years	$ 80,000
Subordinated debentures (12%)	$ 400,000	8 years	$ 50,000

Blotz is in a 40 percent tax bracket and has 120,000 shares of common stock outstanding. The firm's noncash expenses (such as depreciation) are $200,000. In an attempt to lighten its financial burden, Blotz has voluntarily submitted a plan to its creditors that combines certain attributes of both an extension and a recapitalization. The following details are the essential aspects of the plan.

Bank loan . . . . Extend the maturity to two years, reduce annual principal repayments to $125,000/year, and increase the loan's annual interest rate to 12 percent.

Morgage bonds . . . . No change in terms.

Subordinated debentures . . . . Exchange each debenture ($1,000 par value) for an income bond ($1,000 par value) that has: (1) a 14 percent coupon rate, (2) a 20-year maturity, (3) a $20/year principal repayment, and (4) 10 warrants attached. Each warrant expires in five years and allows its holder to purchase one share of Blotz's common stock at the stock's current market price.

Assuming that Blotz's creditors approve the plan:

a. Calculate Blotz's stated earnings per share (EPS) both before and after the plan is adopted.

b. Will the plan improve Blotz's debt service capabilities?

c. Does the plan seem reasonable to both Blotz's creditors and its stockholders?

Solution

Blotz's Income and Cash Flow Calculations

	Before Plan	After Plan
EBIT	$455,000	$455,000
Interest expense (Note 1)	($205,000)	($218,000)
Taxable income	$250,000	$237,000
Taxes (40%)	($100,000)	($ 94,800)
After-tax income	$150,000	$142,200
Noncash expenses	$200,000	$200,000
After-tax cash flow (Note 2)	$350,000	$342,200
Principal repayment (Note 3)	($380,000)	($225,000)
Cash flow after debt service	($ 30,000)	$117,200
Diluted shares (Note 4)	120,000 shares	124,000 shares
Stated EPS	$1.25/share	$1.15/share

Notes

1. Interest expense (before) = (.10 * $250,000) + (.11 * $1,200,000)
   + (.12 * $400,000) = $205,000
   Interest expense (after) = (.12 * $250,000) + (.11 * $1,200,000)
   + (.14 * $400,000) = $218,000

2. After-tax cash flow = after-tax income + noncash expenses

3. Principal repayment (before) = $250,000 + $80,000 + $50,000 = $380,000
   Principal repayment (after) = $125,000 + $80,000 + $20,000 = $225,000

4. The possible dilution that could occur due to the warrants being exercised must
   be reflected in Blotz's stated EPS. If the warrants were exercised,

   New shares = 400 bonds * 10 warrants/bond * 1 share/warrant = 4,000 shares

   Consequently, common stock shares that reflect possible dilution from the
   warrants equal 124,000 shares (120,000 original shares plus 4,000 possible new
   shares).

a. After the plan is adopted, Blotz's stated EPS will decline from $1.25/share to
   $1.15/share.

b. The plan will significantly improve Blotz's debt service capabilities. Although
   interest expense will be higher after the plan is implemented, the firm's annual
   principal repayments will be reduced from $380,000 to $225,000. Perhaps the
   best indicator of this improvement is Blotz's cash flow after debt service. If
   the plan were not implemented, the firm would have a $30,000 deficit; that is,
   Blotz could not service its existing debt. With the plan, however, Blotz will
   have a $117,200 surplus after all its debt obligations have been fulfilled.

c. Realizing that, without the plan, Blotz would be unable (by $30,000) to service
   all its debt, the firm's creditors would probably prefer this voluntary plan to
   formal bankruptcy. Perhaps the firm's debenture holders may be circumspect

about their new income bonds. However, the priority claims of Blotz's debenture holders will not be materially diminished with the income bonds, even though a missed interest payment on the new bonds would not constitute a default. Furthermore, the warrants may be of some value to the former debenture holders if Blotz can regain its financial strength after the plan is put into effect. From the stockholders' point of view, both the increased interest expense and the mild dilution effects of the warrants will have very little impact on the firm's EPS. Like Blotz's creditors, the firm's stockholders would have little to gain from a bankruptcy. Also, if the plan is accepted by Blotz's creditors, the firm may be able to pay a cash dividend on its common stock. Without the plan, dividend payment would be impossible.

21.3. Matson Fence Company has been in bankruptcy for some time while the court has been trying to reorganize the company. No suitable reorganization plan could be arranged, however, so the court ordered a conversion of the reorganization attempt to a liquidation. When the bankruptcy petition was filed with the court, Matson had the following liabilities and net worth on its balance sheet.

Account	Balance
Trade credit	$ 7,000,000
Wages payable	$ 1,300,000
Taxes payable	$ 100,000
Bank loan	$ 4,600,000
First-mortgage bonds	$25,000,000
Subordinated debentures	$ 6,000,000
Common equity	$20,000,000
Total liabilities and net worth	$64,000,000

The bank loan is secured by Matson's inventory. A lien on all the firm's fixed assets secures the first-mortgage bonds, and the debentures (which are unsecured) are subordinated to both Matson's bank loan and its first-mortgage bonds. The following table indicates the book value of Matson's assets and the actual proceeds obtained by the court when the assets were sold.

Asset	Book Value	Liquidation Proceeds
Cash and marketable securities	$ 1,100,000	$ 1,000,000
Accounts receivable	$10,100,000	$ 8,100,000
Inventory	$16,000,000	$ 8,800,000
Fixed assets	$36,800,000	$20,100,000
Totals	$64,000,000	$38,000,000

Determine the distribution of proceeds to each group that had a financial claim against Matson if court costs were $1,200,000 and the court ruled that only $1,100,000 of the firm's wages payable would be allowed. (The court discharged the remaining $200,000 of Matson's wages payable.)

Solution

The initial distribution of proceeds would be as follows:

```
First-mortgage bonds . . . . . . . . . . .   $20,100,000 (from fixed assets)
Bank loan . . . . . . . . . . . . . . . .    $ 4,600,000 (from inventory)
Court costs . . . . . . . . . . . . . . .    $ 1,200,000
Court-allowed wages payable . . . . . . .    $ 1,100,000
Taxes payable . . . . . . . . . . . . . .    $   100,000
Total initial distribution . . . . . . .     $27,100,000
```

After the initial distribution, the $10,900,000 ($38,000,000 - $27,100,000) in re-
maining funds would be allocated to the firm's unsecured debt claims on a proportional basis. Sufficient funds were available from the sale of Matson's inventory
to completely repay the bank loan. However, because the proceeds from the sale of
Matson's fixed assets would not fully repay the claims of first-mortgage bondholders,
their remaining unsecured claim = $25,000,000 - $20,100,000 = $4,900,000. Both the
unsecured claims after the initial distribution of proceeds and the proportional
distribution (adjusted for subordination) of the remaining $10,900,000 to these un-
secured claims are shown in the following table.

Unsecured Claim	Amount	Proportion	Proportioned Distribution	Subordination Adjustment	Adjusted Distribution
Trade credit	$ 7,000,000	.3911	$ 4,262,990	0	$ 4,262,990
Mortgage bonds	$ 4,900,000	.2737	$ 2,983,330	$1,916,670	$ 4,900,000
Debentures	$ 6,000,000	.3352	$ 3,653,680	($1,916,670)	$ 1,737,010
Totals	$17,900,000	1.0000	$10,900,000	$ 0	$10,900,000

Unsecured claims amounted to $17,900,000 and only $10,900,000 was available to
service these claims, so neither the trade credit nor the subordinated debenture
claims would be completely fulfilled. However, the mortgage bond would be paid in
full after the subordination adjustment from the debentures' proportional distribution. In any event, Matson's stockholders would receive nothing. The following
table indicates the proportion of each claim that would ultimately be paid after
Matson's liquidation.

Account	Original Claim	Initial Distribution	Unsecured Distribution	Total Distribution	Percent of Claim Paid
Trade credit	$ 7,000,000	$ 0	$ 4,262,990	$ 4,262,990	60.9%
Wages payable	$ 1,300,000	$ 1,100,000	$ 0	$ 1,100,000	84.6%
Taxes payable	$ 100,000	$ 100,000	$ 0	$ 100,000	100.0%
Bank loan	$ 4,600,000	$ 4,600,000	$ 0	$ 4,600,000	100.0%
Mortgage bonds	$25,000,000	$20,100,000	$ 4,900,000	$25,000,000	100.0%
Subordinated debentures	$ 6,000,000	$ 0	$ 1,737,010	$ 1,737,010	29.0%
Common equity	$20,000,000	$ 0	$ 0	$ 0	None
Totals	$64,000,000	$25,900,000	$10,900,000	$36,800,000	57.5%

REVIEW QUESTIONS

1. When a firm's liabilities exceed the current value of its assets, the firm is
   a. technically insolvent.
   b. bankrupt.
   c. in reorganization.
   d. in a composition.
   e. legally insolvent.

2. Bankruptcy is
   a. the same as insolvency.
   b. a legal term.
   c. an automatic consequence whenever a firm becomes technically insolvent.
   d. always initiated by the firm's creditors.
   e. declared by the firm if a reorganization is unsuccessful.

3. Creditors may agree to reduce their original financial claims against the firm to a level that the firm may be able to repay. Such an arrangement is called
   a. a reorganization.
   b. a bankruptcy.
   c. an extension.
   d. a composition.
   e. a recapitalization.

4. The causes of a firm's financial distress often include
   a. a rapid decline in the market value of the firm's common stock.
   b. declining sales.
   c. poor timing of the firm's cash flows.
   d. both a and b.
   e. both b and c.

5. In a liquidation
   a. both preferred and common stockholders receive at least the par value of their stock.
   b. a creditors' committee must approve the liquidation plan.
   c. taxes payable and court costs are paid.
   d. trade credit has a priority claim over subordinated debentures.
   e. all wages payable are usually dismissed by the bankruptcy court.

6. How many days after a bankruptcy petition has been entered into the bankruptcy court does the firm have to file a reorganization plan?
   a. 30 days
   b. 60 days
   c. 90 days
   d. 120 days
   e. 180 days

7. After the bankruptcy court has issued an order of relief
   a. the firm's creditors cannot take further action against the firm.
   b. a liquidation of the firm occurs.
   c. the firm is technically insolvent.
   d. the creditors' committee is disbanded.
   e. the firm's management cannot be replaced for 180 days.

8. A formal bankruptcy petition can be involuntarily filed
   a. if a majority of the creditors' committee vote to do so.
   b. when the bankruptcy court orders the petition.
   c. by an unsecured creditor if the firm has 12 or fewer unsecured creditors.
   d. by preferred stockholders if the firm misses 4 consecutive preferred stock dividends.
   e. by 3 or more secured creditors that have more than $50,000 in combined claims against the firm.

9. In a reorganization supervised by the bankruptcy court, the reorganization plan should address all the following issues except
   a. the composition of the creditors' committee that will supervise the plan.
   b. amendments to the firm's charter that may be necessary.
   c. the plan's treatment of creditors' claims.
   d. which claims will be affected by the plan.
   e. implementation of the plan.

Use the following information to answer Questions 10-12.

Vermont Glass Works was in a court-supervised liquidation. Prior to the liquidation, the firm had the following balance sheet.

(Thousands of Dollars)

Cash and marketable securities	$ 680	Trade credit	$ 4,350
Accounts receivable	9,220	Wages payable	1,850
Inventory	14,300	Taxes payable	2,800
Plant structures	16,000	Pension plans payable	200
Equipment	8,400	Notes payable	8,600
Land	2,600	First-mortgage bonds	11,000
Total assets	$51,200	Second-mortgage bonds	2,000
		Equipment trust bonds	6,400
		Subordinated debentures	5,000
		Common equity	9,000
		Total liabilities and net worth	$51,200

The following table indicates the proceeds actually obtained by the court when Vermont's assets were sold.

(Thousands of Dollars)

Cash and marketable securities	$ 670
Accounts receivable	8,500
Inventory	10,530
Plant structures	4,000
Equipment	5,600
Land	2,900
Total liquidation value	$32,200

The court ruled that all of Vermont's wages and pension plans payable must be fully paid. Court costs during the entire bankruptcy proceeding were $250,000. Vermont's notes payable were secured by a lien on the firm's inventory. Both the first- and second-mortgage bonds had liens on Vermont's plant structures and its land, but the second-mortgage bonds had a lower-priority claim to these assets than the first-mortgage bonds. The debentures were subordinated to the second-mortgage bonds, and the equipment trust bonds were secured by Vermont's equipment assets.

10. What approximate percentage of the equipment trust bonds' original claim
    ($6,400,000) was paid in the liquidation?
    a. none
    b. 37 percent
    c. 77 percent
    d. 92 percent
    e. 100 percent

11. How much was the total liquidation payment to subordinated debenture holders?
    a. none
    b. $584,800
    c. $1,261,400
    d. $1,846,200
    e. $3,640,600

12. Which one of the following statements is true of the distribution of proceeds
    obtained from Vermont's liquidation?
    a. The first-mortgage bonds were paid in full.
    b. The second-mortgage bonds were paid $725,000.
    c. The common stockholders received nothing.
    d. Vermont's trade creditors were paid $2,780,200.
    e. Subordinate debentures were paid $3,077,000.

KEY DEFINITIONS

Bankruptcy: a legal declaration of a firm's insolvency by the bankruptcy court.
A bankruptcy petition can be submitted to the court either voluntarily by the firm
or involuntarily by its unsecured creditors (under certain conditions).

Composition: a type of voluntary agreement between the firm and its creditors in
which creditors reduce their original claims against the firm.

Conversion: an order by the bankruptcy court to liquidate the firm, issued when a
successful reorganization of the firm seems unlikely.

Creditors' committee: a committee made up of a cross section of the firm's creditors.
The creditors' committee is responsible for overseeing any voluntary agreement negotiated with the firm. Or, in a bankruptcy proceeding, the creditors' committee
serves the bankruptcy court in an advisory capacity.

Extension: a voluntary agreement between the firm and its creditors whereby creditors
agree to lengthen the maturity of the firm's existing financial obligations. The
purpose of an extension is to grant the firm temporary relief from its debt burdens
until it can regain its financial strength.

Financial failure: a term applied to a firm that has been unprofitable. Although
unprofitability does not necessarily result in the firm's financial collapse, it is
often an early warning signal of financial distress to come.

Legal insolvency: a condition that exists when a firm's total liabilities exceed
the current value of its assets.

Order of relief: an order issued by the bankruptcy court to protect the firm from
further action of its creditors during the ensuing bankruptcy proceedings.

Recapitalization: a voluntary change in the firm's capital structure negotiated between the firm and its creditors. In a recapitalization, creditors agree either to modify the terms of the firm's existing debt or to exchange their present debt holdings for new securities (such as common stock, preferred stock, or income bonds) that may reduce the firm's current financial burden.

Reorganization: a plan supervised by the bankruptcy court to allow the firm to successfully fulfill its financial obligations to the firm's creditors in a fair and equitable manner. A reorganization plan often combines several features of extensions, compositions, and recapitalizations.

Technical insolvency: a condition of poor liquidity in which a firm has insufficient cash (or access to cash) to meet its financial obligations that are due. Technical insolvency sometimes indicates financial distress that could become serious if the firm fails to act to solve its liquidity problems.

Voluntary agreements: arrangements (such as extensions, compositions, and recapitalizations) negotiated between a firm and its creditors to assist the firm in reducing its financial burdens. Creditors often prefer voluntary agreements to formal bankruptcy proceedings, which are usually expensive (in court costs) and time-consuming.

ANSWERS TO REVIEW QUESTIONS

1. e	4. e	7. a	10. d
2. b	5. c	8. c	11. b
3. d	6. d	9. a	12. c

Chapter Twenty-Two
Multinational Financial Management

OVERVIEW

During the past few decades, many firms (foreign as well as domestic) have expanded the scope of their operations into the international arena. With this proliferation of multinational firms has come a need for financial managers to be aware of special considerations related to their firms' international activities. Financial managers of multinational firms must understand international credit instruments, ways to minimize foreign exchange risk, international cash (and working-capital) management, capital budgeting in an international context, sources of international funds, and the accounting implications of foreign ventures. In addition, they must understand the basic balance-of-payments mechanisms, because fluctuations in the exchange rates of a country's currency are vastly affected by the country's balance of payments.

STUDY OBJECTIVES

1. To understand the various types of international credit instruments.

2. To examine both foreign exchange risk (and ways to reduce this risk) and the relationship between a country's balance of payments and its exchange rates for foreign currencies.

3. To investigate working-capital management, capital budgeting, and accounting in an international context.

4. To probe the various international sources of capital available to a multinational firm.

CHAPTER OUTLINE

I. International credit instruments

A. A bill of exchange is a draft (check) made payable to an exporter by an importer. A sight draft is a bill of exchange that can be cashed or deposited immediately by the exporter. Time drafts cannot be either cashed or deposited by the exporter until a specified payment date.

B. A <u>banker's acceptance</u> is a time draft on which a bank guarantees payment. Since a banker's acceptance is guaranteed, it can be sold prior to the payment date by its holder (originally the exporter who received the banker's acceptance from the importer) at a discount from its face value. The amount of the discount (which is the purchaser's investment profit) varies directly with prevailing interest rates.

C. When exported goods are shipped to the importer, the exporter receives from the transporting company a <u>bill of lading</u>, which serves as the exporter's official shipping receipt. A bill of lading specifies the exporter, the transportation company, the party to which the goods are to be shipped, and shipping terms. If shipping terms are FOB (free on board), the title to the goods and all shipping costs are passed to the importer at the point of export. Alternatively, with CIF (cost, insurance, and freight) shipping terms, the exporter both retains title to the goods and pays all shipping costs until the importer has received the goods.

D. To reduce the exporter's credit risk associated with selling goods to an importer, the importer's bank may issue the exporter a <u>letter of credit</u>. The letter of credit assures the exporter that the importer has a line of credit at the issuing bank that can be drawn against for payments to the exporter. Naturally, an exporter prefers to have an irrevocable letter of credit. But, even if it is revocable at the issuing bank's option, a letter of credit indicates to the exporter that the importer's creditworthiness has been prescreened by the importer's bank.

II. <u>Export-import assistance</u> is available from several sources (both governmental and private) that facilitate international trade.

A. The Department of Commerce, through its <u>Bureau of International Commerce</u>, provides information to domestic (U.S.) exporters concerning such matters as foreign <u>trade missions</u>; potential <u>foreign markets</u> for U.S. exports; foreign <u>tariffs</u>, <u>duties</u>, and <u>import restrictions</u>; foreign <u>trade shows</u>; and <u>credit ratings</u> on potential importers.

B. <u>Foreign branches</u> of U.S. banks also assist domestic exporters by providing information on <u>business conditions</u> in foreign countries and by arranging <u>letters of credit</u> for prospective foreign importers.

C. The <u>Foreign Credit Insurance Association</u> (FCIA) insures domestic exporters against payment default by foreign importers up to 90 percent of the value of the exported goods. FCIA insurance terms (and premiums) vary with the stability (both economic and political) of the importer's country, the security offered by the importer (such as letters of credit), and restrictions on currency conversions imposed by the importer's country. However, FCIA does <u>not</u> insure the exporter against losses that result from foreign exchange rate fluctuations.

III. Foreign exchange risk and markets

A. <u>Foreign exchange</u> is a term applied to the currencies of other countries. A country's <u>exchange rate</u> with a foreign currency is the number of units of domestic currency required to buy one unit of the foreign money. From the U.S. viewpoint, the dollar's exchange rate with a foreign currency is the dollar price of one unit of the other currency. From the other country's viewpoint, its exchange rate for U.S. dollars is the number of units of its currency required to purchase one U.S. dollar. Consequently, the exchange rates for any two countries are simply reciprocals of each other. For example, if the U.S. exchange rate for British pounds were $2.40/pound (£), the British exchange rate for U.S. dollars would be approximately £.42/dollar, the reciprocal of $2.40/£.

B. Exchange rates vary from time to time (usually daily) as a result of supply and demand forces in foreign exchange markets. A currency is said to suffer devaluation when more of it is necessary to purchase a unit of foreign currency. On the other hand, revaluation is said to occur when it takes fewer units of the domestic currency to purchase a unit of foreign currency. For example, if the dollar price of the German mark (DM) increases from $.55/DM to $.57/DM, the dollar has incurred a devaluation. But if the dollar price of the DM declines from $.55/DM to $.53/DM, the dollar has been revalued; that is, it has increased in value. Similarly, if country A's currency devalues against country B's currency, then B's currency correspondingly revalues against A's currency.

For example, if the U.S. dollar devalues against the German mark (DM) from $.55/DM to $.57/DM, the mark experiences a revaluation against the dollar from DM 1.8182/$ to DM 1.744/$. The accompanying table illustrates the impact of various U.S. exchange rates for German marks on the dollar import price of a German camera that is exported to a U.S. importer for 300 marks. Note that as the dollar devalues from $.55/DM to $.61/DM, the dollar price of the German camera increases accordingly, even though the camera's export price remains unchanged at 300 marks.

U.S. Exchange Rate	German Exchange Rate	U.S. Import Price per Camera (DM 300)
$.55/DM	DM 1.8182/$	$165.00
$.57/DM	DM 1.7544/$	$171.00
$.59/DM	DM 1.6949/$	$177.00
$.61/DM	DM 1.6393/$	$183.00

C. Foreign exchange risk is the uncertainty associated with changes in exchange rates. This risk can significantly affect both a multinational firm's profits and the value of its assets and liabilities that are denominated in foreign exchange. However, a multinational firm can reduce its vulnerability to foreign exchange risk by either negotiating domestic currency contracts for its international sales whenever competitive circumstances allow or matching the foreign-denominated assets and liabilities of its international subsidiaries.

Example: Suppose an American firm produces cars in the United States and sells them in Mexico. Each car costs $4,200 to produce and is sold to Mexican distributors for 50,000 Mexican pesos. What is the dollar profit for each car sold in Mexico if the exchange rate between dollars and pesos is: a. $.10/peso; b. $.07/peso?

Solution

a. At $.10/peso,

Dollar profit/car = (50,000 pesos/car * $.10/peso) - $4,200/car
= $800 (profit)

b. At $.07/peso,

Dollar profit/car = (50,000 pesos/car * $.07/peso) - $4,200/car
= -$700 (loss)

This example illustrates the impact of foreign exchange risk on the American car manufacturer's profits. All of this risk could have been eliminated had the American firm denominated its Mexican car sales in dollars rather than in pesos.

Example: Robinson Boats has a wholly owned German subsidiary that has the following balance sheet (DM denotes German marks).

Total assets . . . . DM 8,000,000
Total liabilities . . . . DM 2,000,000
Net worth . . . . DM 6,000,000

Determine the dollar value of Robinson's investment in its German subsidiary (the subsidiary's net worth) if the exchange rate is: a. $1.50/DM; b. $2.00/DM.

Solution

Account	Value in Dollars at $1.50/DM	Value in Dollars at $2.00/DM
Total assets	$12,000,000	$16,000,000
Total liabilities	$ 3,000,000	$ 4,000,000
Net worth (that is, Robinson's investment) . .	$ 9,000,000	$12,000,000

Since the mark-denominated assets and liabilities of the German subsidiary are mismatched (not the same in marks), Robinson's dollar-denominated investment in the subsidiary is subject to fluctuations in the exchange rate between dollars and marks.

D. Foreign exchange can be bought or sold in foreign exchange markets. Immediate transactions in foreign exchange occur in the spot market, whereas foreign exchange transactions that are to occur at a later date occur in the forward (or future) market. In the forward market, buyers and sellers of foreign exchange agree to a specific date and a specific price for the foreign exchange transaction. Financial managers can use the forward market to eliminate much of the risk related to fluctuations in exchange rates. Daily quotes on both spot and forward contracts of the more popularly traded foreign exchanges in the United States (such as German marks, Swiss francs, French francs, British pounds, Japanese yen, and Canadian dollars) can be found in the Wall Street Journal or supplied by foreign exchange dealers in major U.S. cities.

Example: A U.S. heavy truck manufacturer has received an order from a French firm to buy five trucks. The price negotiated for each truck is 9,500 French francs (FF), but payment is not due for 90 days. Currently, the spot rate for French francs is $.25/FF, but the U.S. firm could sell a forward contract of French francs for delivery in 90 days for $.247/FF. The U.S. firm's financial management estimates that, over the next 90 days, the French franc could devalue against the dollar by as much as 3 percent. Given these expectations, should the U.S. firm sell a 90-day forward contract of French francs to be received from the sale of the trucks?

Solution: The present spot rate of U.S. dollars in French francs is FF 4.0/$ (the reciprocal of $.25/FF). If the French franc devalues by 3 percent against the dollar during the next 90 days, the dollar's spot rate in 90 days will be FF 4.12/$ (1.03 * FF 4.0/$). Thus, assuming a 3 percent devaluation of the French franc, each French franc received by the U.S. firm will be worth $.243 (the reciprocal of FF 4.12/$) in 90 days. The current 90-day forward rate ($.247/FF) exceeds the expected spot rate ($.243/FF) in 90 days, so the U.S. firm should sell a 90-day forward contract of FF 47,500 (5 trucks * FF 9,500/truck). Let us compare the total dollar revenues resulting from selling the trucks under these conditions. Without a forward contract,

Anticipated dollar revenue = FF 47,500 * $.243/FF = $11,543

With a forward contract,

Anticipated dollar revenue = FF 47,500 * $.247/FF = $11,733

IV. Balance of payments

   A. A country's balance of payments measures the net flow of foreign exchange into or out of the country. An increase in imports of goods, services, or financial instruments reduces a country's supply of foreign exchange, because foreigners must be paid in foreign currencies for their exports. Thus increased imports result in an outflow of foreign currencies, which decreases the importing country's foreign exchange supply. On the other hand, whenever a country increases its exports, it experiences an inflow of foreign exchange, because foreigners must purchase domestic currency from the exporting country with foreign currencies in order to pay the exporting country's exporters. In this manner, exports tend to increase a country's supply of foreign exchange.

   B. If a country's inflows and outflows of foreign exchange are equal, the country has an equilibrium in its balance of payments. Such an equilibrium occurs only when the values of the country's imports and its exports are the same. However, should a country's foreign exchange inflows (resulting from exports) exceed its outflows of foreign exchange (resulting from imports), the country has a surplus in its balance of payments. Likewise, a deficit in a country's balance of payments occurs when an excess of imports over exports causes a net outflow of foreign exchange from the deficit country.

   C. Categories of foreign exchange flows that make up a country's balance of payments include:

      1. Purchases (imports) and sales (exports) of either goods or services (including travel).

      2. Net unilateral transfers, such as foreign aid and military assistance.

3. Net <u>direct investments</u> in long-term financial securities (such as stocks, bonds, and mortgages), real estate, or international subsidiaries.

4. Net <u>portfolio investments</u> in short-term financial instruments (for example, government securities, commercial paper, and negotiable certificates of deposit).

D. <u>Causes</u> of balance of payments surpluses or deficits.

1. Relative <u>inflation rates</u> affect a country's purchase and sales of goods and services. As a country experiences relatively high inflation, its goods and services become more expensive than their foreign counterparts. This condition tends both to reduce the countrys's exports and to encourage imports, resulting in an increased outflow of foreign exchange. Hence, the country's balance of payments worsens (becomes more deficient).

2. Relative <u>interest rates</u> affect foreign exchange flows related to a country's long-term investments and its short-term investments. For this reason, a country with higher interest rates than other countries usually experiences a foreign exchange inflow as foreign investors take advantage of the country's higher-yielding investment opportunities.

3. Relative <u>economic growth</u> influences the imports and exports of a country's goods and services. If a country is enjoying greater economic prosperity than other countries with which it trades, its imports have a tendency to increase faster than its exports. As a result, the more prosperous country experiences an increased outflow of foreign exchange that causes its balance of payments to become more deficient.

4. <u>Political stability</u> in a country provides a business environment that promotes the export of goods and services and stimulates domestic investments by foreigners. Consequently, political stability favors greater foreign exchange inflows, thereby improving the country's balance of payments.

E. Balance of payments and exchange rates.

1. Net foreign exchange outflows associated with a deficit in a country's balance of payments reduce the country's supply of foreign exchange. Such a reduction in the country's foreign exchange supply exerts <u>devaluation</u> pressures on the deficit country's currency. A surplus in a country's balance of payments increases the country's foreign exchange supply, which tends to cause a <u>revaluation</u> of the currency of the country with a surplus in its balance of payments.

2. A deficit country's government may attempt to support its devaluing currency in foreign exchange markets by selling foreign exchange to foreigners who have accumulated its currency. However, such governmental support operations are limited by the intervening government's supply of foreign exchange.

V. International cash management

   A. The remittance policy of a multinational firm involves the transfer of both foreign profits and idle working-capital balances of the firm's foreign subsidiaries to the parent firm. A firm's remittance policy should be designed to maximize the parent firm's overall profitability and to satisfy its international liquidity requirements.

   B. Transfer mechanics.

      1. Cash dividends are the most direct method of transferring profits from foreign subsidiaries to the parent company.

      2. However, foreign governments sometimes discourage the remittance of cash dividends to parent companies by either taxing or blocking such dividend payments. In these situations, royalties, management fees, technical service fees, and licensing fees are often more readily transferable than cash dividends.

   C. If a multinational firm has various phases of a product's production and distribution chain in different countries, the firm can maximize its after-tax global profits associated with the product by setting prices for sales between its foreign subsidiaries within the chain in such a way as to minimize taxes on profits in each country involved. Thus the firm would attempt to minimize taxable income associated with its subsidiary in any country that has high tax rates. This can be accomplished by having the subsidiary either pay high prices for the product it purchases from the firm's subsidiaries in other countries or sell the product at low prices to the firm's other international subsidiaries. This type of pricing system between subsidiaries of a multinational firm is known as transfer pricing.

   D. Obstacles to a multinational firm's remittance policy.

      1. Foreign governments (particularly in countries that have a limited supply of foreign exchange due to balance-of-payments deficits) can inhibit remittance payments by imposing exchange controls, taxes, or limits on profits, fees, royalties, and interest that can be remitted to the parent firm (or its other international subsidiaries).

      2. Weak foreign exchange markets for currencies that are seldom purchased or sold create problems in the conversion of those less actively traded currencies into the parent firm's domestic currency.

      3. Exchange rate fluctuations also make a firm's remittance policy more difficult to implement in that they increase the firm's foreign exchange risk.

VI. Alternative types of international operations

   A. A firm that wants to expand its international sales can produce goods domestically and directly export them abroad. Obstacles to direct exports include foreign import restrictions and protective tariffs.

B. As an alternative to direct exports, a domestic firm can <u>license</u> other firms (usually foreign) to produce and market its products in other countries. With licensing, the domestic firm may be able to avoid many of the problems associated with direct exports. However, the licensing firm must be sure that the firms it licenses maintain both the quality and the reputation of the firm's products.

C. Both wholly owned <u>foreign subsidiaries</u> and <u>joint ventures</u> with other firms are other means by which a multinational firm can produce and/or sell its products in foreign countries. A foreign subsidiary is often preferred to a joint venture, because the firm's control of its foreign subsidiary's operations is not shared with other firms. (Neither, of course, are the risks the firm incurs through the subsidiary.)

VII. International capital budgeting

A. All foreign-denominated cash flows to be considered for international capital-budgeting purposes must be (1) converted into the multinational firm's <u>domestic currency</u> at exchange rates in effect at the time of their conversion and (2) adjusted for actual <u>cash remittances</u> to the multinational firm.

B. The firm's <u>cost of capital</u> (required rate of return) that is used to evaluate a foreign project should be adjusted in accordance with the project's riskiness relative to the risks associated with the firm's domestic projects. Among the factors that affect a foreign project's riskiness are possible <u>exchange rate fluctuations</u> and <u>controls</u> on the firm's remittance policy that may be levied by foreign governments.

C. After determining a foreign project's cost of capital and its expected cash remittances to the firm in the firm's domestic currency, financial officers can evaluate the project using the capital-budgeting methods (<u>internal rate of return</u>, <u>net present value</u>, <u>payback</u>, and so on) presented in Chapter 6.

VIII. Sources of international funds

A. Numerous government-sponsored agencies (for example, the <u>World Bank</u>, the <u>International Finance Corporation</u>, the <u>Internation Development Association</u>, and the <u>Inter-American Development Bank</u>) encourage foreign investment projects (usually in developing countries) by providing foreign exchange loans to governments, by guaranteeing loans made by private lenders, or by directly making loans to finance high-risk projects. The <u>Export-Import Bank</u>, on the other hand, grants credit to foreign importers in an attempt to stimulate U.S. exports.

B. Nongovernmental sources of international funds include swaps, Eurobonds, composite currency loans, Eurodollar loans, and Edge Act banks.

1. In a currency <u>swap</u>, a multinational firm can obtain foreign exchange by swapping its domestic currency with a foreign bank (or firm) in return for the foreign currency it needs. The parties engaging in the swap negotiate both the swap's duration and the exchange rate to be used for the swap. At end of the swap's duration, the firm and its foreign swapping partner reverse their original swap

transaction. Thus swaps offer multinational firms a means of obtaining foreign currencies without exposure to foreign exchange risk.

2. <u>Eurobonds</u> are long-term bonds issued by a multinational firm in a foreign capital market. Eurobonds can be denominated in either the borrowing firm's domestic currency or a foreign currency. If they are denominated in a foreign currency, the borrowing firm's value in domestic currency of the liability that Eurobonds represent fluctuates with changes in exchange rates. Specifically, if the foreign currency in which Eurobonds are denominated revalues against the firm's domestic currency, the firm's value in domestic currency of its Eurobonds' liability increases.

3. As an alternative to obtaining long-term financing with Eurobonds, a multinational firm can arrange a long-term <u>composite currency loan</u> denominated in <u>eurco</u> (that is, several foreign currencies). By diversifying the foreign currencies in which a composite currency loan is denominated, the firm can reduce the effects on its domestic-currency-denominated liability associated with the loan that result from a revaluation (against the firm's domestic currency) of any one of the currencies making up eurco.

4. A <u>Eurodollar</u> loan is a loan made to a multinational firm by a foreign lender (usually a bank) and denominated in the firm's domestic currency.

5. <u>Edge Act banks</u> are American bank subsidiaries that receive special federal charters to engage in banking activities that promote international trade (particularly U.S. exports).

IX. Accounting considerations

A. All U.S. firms with international operations are required to translate foreign-currency-denominated revenues, expenses, certain assets, and certain liabilities into dollars when they prepare their financial statements. Hence, exchange rate fluctuations can affect both the firm's income statement and its balance sheet.

B. The following table depicts the impact of exchange rate fluctuation on the dollar value of a U.S. firm's foreign-currency-denominated income and balance sheet accounts.

	Foreign-Currency-Denominated Accounts			
Event	Revenues	Expenses	Assets	Liabilities
Dollar devaluation	increase	increase	increase	increase
Dollar revaluation	decrease	decrease	decrease	decrease

C. The effects of currency translations on a U.S. multinational firm's financial statements have implications for the firm's international financial management. If the dollar were devaluing, for example, the firm might want to reduce its foreign-currency-denominated liabilities and to increase its holdings in foreign-currency-denominated assets. The opposite strategy would be advisable if the dollar were strengthening (revaluing) against foreign currencies.

367

CHAPTER 22

STUDY PROBLEMS

22.1. Consider the following transactions between the United States and France (FF denotes French francs).

a. An American travels to Paris and spends FF 12,000.

b. A French firm invests $70,000 in U.S. government securities.

c. W. T. Grents (an American firm) buys a French subsidiary for FF 240,000.

d. The French government purchases $200,000 of military arms from an American firm.

e. The American Red Cross gives a $150,000 gift to French flood victims.

If these transactions occurred when the exchange rate was $.25/FF, what were their effects on both the U.S. balance of payments with France and the U.S. supply of French francs? Would these transactions put revaluation or devaluation pressures on the dollar against the French franc?

Solution

Based on an exchange rate of $.25/FF (or FF 4/$ from the French viewpoint), the following table illustrates the impact of these transactions on both the U.S. balance of payments (BOP) with France and the U.S. supply of French francs.

Transaction	BOP Effect in $	U.S. Supply of FF
a	($ 3,000)	(FF 12,000)
b	$ 70,000	FF 280,000
c	($ 60,000)	(FF 240,000)
d	$200,000	FF 800,000
e	($150,000)	(FF 600,000)
Totals	$ 57,000	FF 228,000

The United States had a $57,000 surplus in its BOP with France as a result of these five transactions. In addition, the U.S. experienced a net inflow of FF 228,000 due to this BOP surplus. Thus the increased U.S. supply of French francs would cause the dollar to revalue against France's currency. Note: The French supply of foreign exchange (in this case U.S. dollars) decreased by $57,000.

22.2. Raynolds Paper (an American firm) is considering a $95,000 investment in its Swiss pulp mill. The new investment is expected to both have a 4-year life and to generate after-tax cash flows of 40,000 Swiss francs (SF) during each year of its duration. Raynolds plans to remit 75 percent of each year's cash flow in the form of cash dividends. At the end of the fourth year, the firm estimates that the investment in the pulp mill will have a salvage value (SV) of SF 25,000 (all of which will be remitted to the U.S.). Currently, the exchange rate between dollars and Swiss francs is $.60/SF, but Raynolds expects the dollar to devalue against the Swiss franc by 8 percent per year over the next 4 years. Raynolds's required return on this Swiss investment is 12 percent. Determine the investment's net present value (NPV), internal rate of return (IRR), and payback. Should Raynolds proceed with this investment? Why?

<u>Solution</u>

Year (1)	Cash Flow in SF (2)	Exchange Rate ($/SF) (3)	Proportion Remitted (4)	$ Cash Flow Remitted [(5) = (2) * (3) * (4)]
1	SF 40,000	$.648/SF	.75	$19,440
2	SF 40,000	$.700/SF	.75	$21,000
3	SF 40,000	$.756/SF	.75	$22,680
4	SF 40,000	$.816/SF	.75	$24,480
4th year SV	SF 25,000	$.816/SF	1.00	$20,400

Solving for the investment's NPV yields

$$NPV = -\$95,000 + \frac{\$19,440}{(1.12)} + \frac{\$21,000}{(1.12)^2} + \frac{\$22,680}{(1.12)^3} + \frac{(\$24,480 + \$20,400)}{(1.12)^4}$$

$$= -\$95,000 + \$78,763 = \underline{-\$16,237}$$

To determine the IRR on the Swiss investment,

$$\$95,000 = \frac{\$19,440}{(1 + IRR)} + \frac{\$21,000}{(1 + IRR)^2} + \frac{\$22,680}{(1 + IRR)^3} + \frac{(\$24,480 + \$20,400)}{(1 + IRR)^4}$$

The IRR that this equation yields is approximately <u>4.6 percent</u>. From the following table, Raynolds's dollar investment has a payback at the end of the <u>fourth year</u>.

Year	Cumulative Payback
1	$ 19,440
2	$ 40,440
3	$ 63,120
4	$108,000

Since the Swiss investment has both a negative NPV (-$16,237) and an IRR (4.6 percent) that is less than Raynolds's required return (12 percent), the investment should <u>not</u> be made.

<u>22.3</u>. A U.S. firm has $300,000 in idle cash balances that it wants to invest for the next 90 days. The firm has limited its investment choices to either American T bills yielding 8 percent per year or British T bills yielding 12 percent per year. The spot and the 90-day forward rates for British pounds (£) are $2.36/£ and $2.31/£, respectively. Further, in order to reduce its foreign exchange risk, the firm plans to use the forward market if it invests in the British securities. Given these circumstances, and assuming a 360-day year, determine which investment the firm should make to maximize the yield on its $300,000.

<u>Solution</u>

If the firm invests in British T bills, its pound-denominated investment would be

$300,000 * the reciprocal of $2.36/£ = <u>£127,119</u>

At 3 percent (12 percent * 90 days/360 days) for 90 days, the firm's interest income on this £127,119 investment would be £3,814 (£127,119 * .03). In 90 days, the firm would convert £130,933 (the sum of the investment's £127,119 principal and its £3,814 interest income) back into dollars at the 90-day forward rate ($2.31/£). Thus the firm's total dollar return in 90 days would equal

£130,933 * $2.31/£ = $302,455

Consequently, the dollar return on the investment in British T bills would be $2,455, and the firm's annualized yield associated with this investment would equal

($2,455/$300,000) * (360 days/90 days) = .0327 = 3.27%

Since the firm's yield on domestic T bills is 8 percent (versus 3.27 percent on British T bills), the firm should invest in U.S. T bills rather than British T bills.

22.4. Ella-Barnes Company (an American multinational manufacturer of chewing tobacco) has borrowed $800,000 (denominated in eurco) with a composite currency loan to finance improvements at one of its plants located in Scotland. The following table indicates the amounts of the various foreign currencies that make up a eurco (E), the exchanges in effect when the loan was made, and the exchange rates six months later.

Foreign Currency	Currencies in a Eurco	Initial Exchange Rate	Exchange Rate Six Months Later
German marks (DM)	DM 2.5/E	$ .50/DM	$ .60/DM
French francs (FF)	FF 6.5/E	$ .25/FF	$ .20/FF
British pounds (£)	£.3/E	$2.40/£	$2.20/£
Swiss francs (SF)	SF .7/E	$ .60/SF	$ .70/SF

a. How many eurcos did Ella-Barnes borrow?

b. What was Ella-Barnes's dollar-denominated liability related to the loan six months after the loan originated?

c. What would the loan's dollar-denominated liability have been in six months had the loan been in the form of Eurobonds denominated in German marks? French francs? British pounds? Swiss francs?

Solution

a. The original dollar-eurco exchange rate equals [(DM 2.5/E) * ($.50/DM)] + [(FF 6.5/E) * ($.25/FF)] + [(£.3/E) * ($2.40/£)] + [(SF .7/E) * ($.60/SF] = $4.015/E. Therefore, eurcos borrowed by Ella-Barnes equal $800,000 * the reciprocal of $4.015/E = E 199,253.

b. Six months later, the dollar value of a eurco equals [(DM 2.5/E) * ($.60/DM)] + [(FF 6.5/E) * ($.20/FF)] + [(£.3/E) * ($2.20/£)] + [(SF .7/E) * ($.70/SF)] = $3.950/E. Because the eurco value of the loan is fixed at E 199,253, the firm's dollar-denominated loan liability in six month equals

E 199,253 * $3.95/E = $787,049

The dollar value of the loan's liability decreased, because the eurco devalued against the dollar during the six-month period.

c. Assuming single-currency loans, Ella-Barnes's dollar-denominated loan liabilities associated with each loan would have been as follows:

Denomination	Dollar Liability
DM	$800,000 * ($.60/DM)/($.50/DM) = $960,000
FF	$800,000 * ($.20/FF)/($.25/FF) = $640,000
£	$800,000 * ($2.20/£)/($2.40/£) = $733,333
SF	$800,000 * ($.70/SF)/($.60/SF) = $933,333

Note that the dollar-denominated liability of the composite currency loan is much less subject to exchange rate fluctuations than the dollar-denominated liabilities associated with single-currency loans.

REVIEW QUESTIONS

1. Official shipping receipts that are used in international trade are referred to as
   a. banker's acceptances.
   b. sight drafts.
   c. time drafts.
   d. bills of lading.
   e. letters of credit.

2. A country with a balance-of-payments surplus is likely to have its
   a. currency revalue against other currencies.
   b. currency devalue against other currencies.
   c. imports exceed its exports.
   d. foreign exchange reserves decline as a result of the surplus.
   e. both b and d.

3. Rather than borrow short-term funds from its U.S. bank at 20 percent per year, Wyler Office Furniture borrowed 750,000 German marks (DM) for one year at 9 percent. Wyler immediately converted the German borrowings into U.S. dollars at an exchange rate of $.65/DM. When the loan came due, the dollar had devalued against the German mark to $.69/DM. The total dollar expense of the German loan is
   a. $32,700.
   b. $36,000.
   c. $49,825.
   d. $67,500.
   e. $76,575.

4. In Question 3, the effective annual interest rate on the dollar-denominated funds made available to Wyler by the German loan was approximately
   a. 2.7 percent.
   b. 9.0 percent.
   c. 15.7 percent.
   d. 20.0 percent.
   e. 26.4 percent.

5. One year ago, an American auto dealer paid 1,500,000 yen (Y) for a Japanese sports car when the exchange rate was $.004/Y. During the year the dollar devalued against the yen by 8 percent. However, the yen price of the sports car

decreased by Y 100,000. During this period, the dollar price of the Japanese car has
a. increased by $48.
b. increased by $480.
c. decreased by $264.
d. decreased by $848.
e. remained the same.

6. A German auto maker obtained a composite currency loan for 300,000 eurcos (E) through a London investment banking firm. A eurco is made up of 1.75 U.S. dollars ($), 2 British pounds (£), 1.50 French francs (FF), and 4 Dutch guilders (G). When the loan was made, the German mark (DM) had the following exchange rates: DM 1.6/$, DM 3.8/£, DM .4/FF, and DM .8/G. At these exchange rates, the mark-denominated value of the auto maker's loan was
a. DM 300,000.
b. DM 1,980,000.
c. DM 2,775,000.
d. DM 4,260,000.
e. DM 4,755,000.

7. In Question 6, the loan's exchange rate between German marks (DM) and eurcos (E) was
a. DM 4.4/E.
b. DM 6.6/E.
c. DM 8.6/E.
d. DM 10.8/E.
e. DM 14.2/E.

8. A French firm invested 480,000 French francs (FF) in a one-year certificate of deposit (CD) at a Swiss bank. The CD had a 4 percent annual yield. When the Swiss CD was purchased, the exchange rate between French francs and Swiss francs (SF) was FF 2.4/SF. By the CD's maturity, however, the French franc had devalued to FF 2.5/SF. Taking into account this devaluation, we can de-termine that the French firm's annual yield on the Swiss CD was approximately
a. -.16 percent (a loss).
b. 4.16 percent.
c. 8.33 percent.
d. 10.67 percent.
e. 12.33 percent.

9. If the U.S. economy were experiencing both higher inflation and greater eco-nomic growth than the British economy, which of the following statements would probably be true?
a. U.S. exports to Britain would grow faster than U.S. imports from Britain.
b. The British supply of U.S. dollars would increase.
c. The U.S. balance of payments with Britain would reflect more surplus.
d. The U.S. dollar would revalue against the British pound.
e. The American supply of British pounds would increase.

10. Suppose an Italian firm borrows funds for six months from an American bank. If both the loan's principal and its interest are payable in Italian currency (lira), the loan is known as a
a. Eurodollar loan.
b. currency swap.

   c. composite currency loan.
   d. Eurobond.
   e. loan denominated in eurco.

Use the following information to answer Questions 11 and 12.

An American firm is planning to expand its Venezuelan oil refinery. The expansion will require an investment of 850,000 Venezuelan bolivars (B), but it will increase the refinery's after-tax cash flows by B 400,000 per year for the next 5 years. The current exchange rate between U.S. dollars and Venezuelan bolivars is $.22/B, but the American firm estimates that the following exchange rates will be in effect over the project's life: $.21/B in the first year, $.21/B in the second year, $.20/B in the third year, $.18/B in the fourth year, and $.17/B in the fifth year. Due to exchange controls imposed by the Venezuelan government, the American firm will remit only 70 percent of the project's annual cash flows to the United States each year, but the rest of the funds will be remitted at the end of the fifth year. The firm's required rate of return on the expansion is 20 percent.

11. If the project's cash flows occur uniformly throughout the year, the firm will recover its dollar investment in about
   a. 2.1 years.
   b. 2.7 years.
   c. 3.3 years.
   d. 4.2 years.
   e. 5.0 years.

12. The project's net present value in terms of the American firm's dollar cash flow is
   a. $16,362.
   b. $19,667.
   c. $22,849.
   d. $28,834.
   e. $58,862.

KEY DEFINITIONS

Balance of payments: a measurement of a country's net flow of foreign exchange resulting from its imports and its exports of goods, services, travel, financial instruments, military assistance, and foreign aid. When foreign exchange inflows exceed outflows, the country has a surplus in its balance of payments. The opposite situation reflects a deficit in the country's balance of payments.

Banker's acceptance: a bank-guaranteed time draft (check) that is used to pay an exporter for goods sold to an importer.

Bill of exchange: a draft (check) used in international trade that is drawn on an importer's bank and made payable to an exporter. If the bill of exchange cannot be cashed or deposited by the exporter until a later date, it is called a time draft.

Bill of lading: an exporter's official shipping receipt for goods shipped to an importer (or another party designated by the importer).

Composite currency loan: a loan denominated in several foreign currencies that is used to reduce a borrower's exposure to foreign exchange risk. The multicurrency unit in which the loan is denominated is referred to as a eurco.

Edge Act bank: a specially chartered U.S. subsidiary of an American bank that finances international trade.

Eurodollar loan: a loan made by a foreign lender that is denominated in the borrower's currency. For example, a loan by a British bank to a Spanish firm that is denominated in Spanish pesetas rather than in British pounds would be considered a Eurodollar loan.

Exchange rate: the per-unit domestic currency price of another country's currency (or foreign exchange). A domestic currency devalues against a foreign currency whenever its exchange rate with the foreign currency increases. When the exchange rate decreases, the domestic currency revalues against the foreign currency. Deficits in a country's balance of payments tend to cause the country's currency to devalue.

Foreign exchange: the currencies of other countries.

Letter of credit: a written acknowledgement by an importer's bank assuring exporters that the bank has advanced the importer a line of credit to finance its import purchases.

Swap: an agreement between a multinational firm and a foreign bank (or firm) to exchange their respective currencies at a specific exchange rate and for a predetermined period of time. At the end of the swap's duration, the swap transaction is reversed. Swaps are used to reduce a firm's foreign exchange risk.

Transfer pricing: a multinational firm's pricing policy for products sold between its foreign subsidiaries that is designed to increase the firm's global after-tax profitability by reducing the taxes that each foreign subsidiary pays.

ANSWERS TO REVIEW QUESTIONS

1.	d	4.	c	7.	e	10.	a
2.	a	5.	a	8.	c	11.	c
3.	e	6.	d	9.	b	12.	b

Review Tests

REVIEW TEST FOR PART I (CHAPTERS 1 - 5)

THE NATURE AND SCOPE OF FINANCE

_____ 1. A primary difference between the proprietorship and the corporate form
of organization is
a. size.
b. U.S. partnership tax schedules.
c. personal liability.
d. all of the above.
e. none of the above.

_____ 2. Partnership agreements can be used to
a. determine the annual dividend payments.
b. calculate the tax liability of the total firm.
c. fix income distributions.
d. prearrange the continuity of the firm.
e. c and d

_____ 3. Owners of common stock are sometimes known as
a. residual owners.
b. preferred owners.
c. constant owners.
d. owners in perpetuity.
e. none of the above.

_____ 4. The financial operation of a firm is the responsibility of the
a. finance officer.
b. president.
c. treasurer.
d. banking officer.
e. none of the above.

_____ 5. The best measure of the success of a firm's decision-making processes,
according to most theorists, is
a. profit maximization.
b. maximization of managerial returns.
c. maximization of shareholder wealth.
d. maximization of dividends.
e. satisfaction of as many interests as possible.

_____ 6. When a company attempts to satisfy minimally everyone associated with the firm, it is said to be
a. maximizing shareholder wealth.
b. satisficing.
c. maximizing profits.
d. minimizing competition.
e. skirting the law.

_____ 7. When a firm attempts to absorb the costs of its detrimental effects on society, it reflects the viewpoint of
a. corporate social responsibility.
b. satisficing.
c. managerial reward maximization.
d. ignoring social responsibility.
e. shareholder wealth maximization.

_____ 8. What is the breakeven point in units for a firm with fixed costs of $200,000, variable costs of $6 per unit, and a per unit sales price of $10?
a. 33,333
b. 20,000
c. 50,000
d. 60,000
e. None of the above

_____ 9. What is the breakeven point in dollars for a firm with fixed costs of $180,000, variable costs of $12 per unit, and a per unit sales price of $21?
a. $180,000
b. $420,000
c. $210,000
d. $ 20,000
e. $250,000

_____ 10. What is the degree of operating leverage for sales of 6,000 units if a firm has fixed costs of $220,000, variable costs of $20 per unit, and a per unit sales price of $140?
a. 1.50
b. 1.20
c. 1.05
d. 2.00
e. 1.44

_____ 11. What would be the breakeven point for the firm discussed in Question 10?
a. 1,833.33 units
b. 2,000.00 units
c. 3,833.33 units
d. 2,200,000 units
e. None of the above

_____ 12. The degree of operating leverage for a firm with $120,000 in fixed costs and $600,000 in operating profit would be
a. 1.20.
b. 1.50.

     c. 6.00.
     d. 1.00.
     e. none of the above.

_____ 13. The Federal Reserve System uses _____ to achieve macroeconomic objectives.
     a. executive policy
     b. commercial policy
     c. monetary policy
     d. fiscal policy
     e. none of the above

_____ 14. Continuing _____ forces operating costs and operating revenues to go up over a project's life.
     a. interest cost
     b. inflation
     c. monetary policy
     d. decreases in the money supply
     e. none of the above

_____ 15. When a firm uses much more debt than equity, it is said to be
     a. highly unleveraged.
     b. highly leveraged.
     c. using high coverage ratios.
     d. unbalanced.
     e. none of the above.

_____ 16. A project's breakeven point occurs when total revenues equal _____.
     a. total cost.
     b. fixed cost.
     c. variable cost.
     d. mixed cost.
     e. none of the above.

_____ 17. We can use the technique of _____ analysis to evaluate various selling prices.
     a. leverage
     b. ratio
     c. breakeven point
     d. earnings per share
     e. none of the above

_____ 18. For a firm to be able to respond quickly to changes in the business cycle, it should have
     a. low fixed costs.
     b. low equity balances.
     c. high fixed costs.
     d. a low DOL.
     e. none of the above.

_____ 19. The balance sheet represents _____, whereas the income statement represents _____.
     a. one point in time; the accounting period performance
     b. the accounting period performance; one point in time
     c. several accounting periods; a single accounting period

d. a single accounting period; several accounting periods
e. none of the above

_____ 20. If a company has a current ratio of 3 to 1, the current liabilities of
the firm are _____ if current assets are $9,000,000.
a. $3,300,000
b. $2,500,000
c. $3,000,000
d. $3,500,000
e. none of the above

_____ 21. If a firm has an acid-test ratio of 3.5 and a current ratio of 4.0,
then inventories are _____ if current liabilities are $1,000.
a. $4,000
b. $3,800
c. $3,600
d. $500
e. none of the above

_____ 22. If we were interested in determining a firm's ability to pay short-
term obligations, we would investigate
a. profitability ratios.
b. liquidity ratios.
c. activity ratios.
d. leverage ratios.
e. none of the above.

_____ 23. A very high accounts-receivable turnover ratio would indicate
a. a slow and ineffective collection policy.
b. a fast and very effective collection policy.
c. a collection policy that may be too restrictive.
d. b and c.
e. none of the above.

_____ 24. A common stock shareholder who is living on fixed income would be
especially interested in a firm's
a. interest coverage ratios.
b. current ratio.
c. debt to equity ratio.
d. payout ratio.
e. none of the above

_____ 25. What is the P/E ratio of a firm that sells for $28 per share and has
earnings per share of $7.00?
a. .25
b. 2
c. 4
d. 8
e. None of the above

_____ 26. Common-size financial statements can express each item on the income
statement as a percentage of _____, and each item on the balance
sheet as a percentage of _____.
a. total assets; total sales
b. total sales; total assets

        c. total profit; total liabilities
        d. total liabilities; net sales
        e. none of the above

_____ 27. The use of interim reports to calculate ratios can lead to
        a. highly efficient comparative ratio values.
        b. misleading ratio values when seasonality in sales occurs.
        c. an abbreviated form of analysis.
        d. improved analytical data.
        e. none of the above.

_____ 28. Historical data are actually _____ in ratio analysis and planning
     unless the firm expects these values and relationships to continue.
        a. irrelevant
        b. very relevant
        c. too small
        d. essential
        e. none of the above

_____ 29. The basis of the budgeting process is the forecast of
        a. purchases.
        b. sales.
        c. capital expenditures.
        d. employee requirements.
        e. none of the above.

_____ 30. We coordinate the firm's cash inflows and outflows through use of a
        a. cash budget.
        b. accounts receivable budget.
        c. bank management program.
        d. accounts receivable schedule.
        e. none of the above.

_____ 31. Contingency budgets reflect
        a. alternatives to be used when estimates are inaccurate.
        b. failure to forecast accurately.
        c. changes that occur historically.
        d. changes in historical estimates.
        e. shifts in the operating environment.

_____ 32. A major concern of the budgeting process is
        a. motivating employees.
        b. driving employees toward a stated goal.
        c. pointing out production failures.
        d. assigning blame for errors.
        e. none of the above.

_____ 33. Selling and administrative budgets are developed by departments that
     are _____ involved with the production process.
        a. directly
        b. indirectly
        c. always
        d. never
        e. none of the above

_____ 34. Retry, Inc., collects its sales dollars as follows: 10 percent in cash, 40 percent in 30 days, and 50 percent in 60 days. What is the cash inflow for March, given the following sales amounts?

January	$100,000
February	$200,000
March	$300,000

a. $30,000
b. $130,000
c. $110,000
d. $160,000
e. None of the above

_____ 35. Retry, Inc., pays for 50 percent of its purchases in 30 days and 50 percent in 60 days. What is the expected cash outflow for March if the company makes the following purchases?

January	$150,000
February	$200,000
March	$350,000

a. $525,000
b. $150,000
c. $175,000
d. $160,000
e. None of the above

_____ 36. What would be the net cash flow position of Retry, Inc., in March? (Note: combine information in Questions 34 and 35.)
a. $20,000
b. $30,000
c. ($15,000)
d. ($10,000)
e. None of the above

_____ 37. If Retry, Inc., wants to maintain a minimum cash balance of $10,000 each month, how much (if any) would it need to borrow in March, if it started the month with a zero cash balance?
a. none
b. $25,000
c. $20,000
d. $30,000
e. None of the above

_____ 38. Control interval techniques can be used in budgets to
a. indicate success of production controls.
b. develop incentives.
c. easily identify significant deviations from the budget.
d. minimize cyclical variations.
e. none of the above.

_____ 39. Compound value refers to
a. the ending amount to which an original deposit grows.
b. the present value of future benefits.
c. the rate of return on an investment.
d. the process of accumulation of interest.
e. none of the above.

_____ 40. The median price of a house is currently $60,000. If the house will
increase in value 10 percent (compounded) each year, what will it sell
for in eight years?
a. $129,534
b. $155,622
c. $108,000
d. $128,616
e. None of the above

_____ 41. What is the compound value of a $10,500 investment that earns 20 percent
(compounded annually) for twenty-five years?
a. $63,000
b. $402,549
c. $1,001,658
d. $1,402,549
e. None of the above

_____ 42. What is the compound value of $1,000 invested in a project that pays
8 percent, compounded semiannually over a three-year period?
a. $1,240
b. $1,601
c. $1,265
d. $1,300
e. None of the above

_____ 43. What is the interest rate being earned on an investment of $1,000 that
grows to a compound value of $1,828 in seven years?
a. 7 percent
b. 9 percent
c. 2.6 percent
d. 5 percent
e. None of the above

_____ 44. The Rule of 72 indicates that it would take approximately _____
years for a $5,000 investment to double if the annual compound rate of
interest is 6 percent.
a. 7.2
b. 10
c. 6
d. 12
e. None of the above

_____ 45. An annuity is a series of flows that occur at regular intervals and
a. increase at a constant rate each period.
b. decrease at a constant rate each period.
c. only apply to a single period.
d. never change in amount.
e. none of the above.

_____ 46. If we place $10,000 in a savings account at the beginning of each year
for the next eight years, what will be the accumulated sum if the
account pays 12 percent compounded annually?
a. $24,760
b. $137,760

c. $104,760
d. $89,600
e. None of the above

_____ 47. If we require a minimum return of 14 percent on our investments, how
much should we be willing to pay today for $100,000 to be received ten
years from now?
a. $26,974
b. $32,197
c. $26,333
d. $40,000
e. None of the above

_____ 48. Which would you prefer: $1,000 received today or $1,200 to be received
one year from now (assume you can earn exactly 10 percent on your investments)?
a. $1,000 today
b. $1,200 received in one year
c. Neither of the above

_____ 49. The discount rate is the
a. interest rate used to restate future values in current value terms.
b. interest rate used to determine the future value of a current investment.
c. rate at which investors make risky investments.
d. rate that banks charge their most creditworthy customers.
e. none of the above.

_____ 50. If your company wants to save enough each year to purchase a new machine
(in three years) that will cost $90,000, how much must it save each year
if it can earn 10 percent on the savings account?
a. $30,000
b. $24,718.48
c. $21,000
d. $26,482.91
e. None of the above

_____ 51. What would the annual payments be to pay off a loan of $50,000 in equal
installments over a four-year period when the interest rate is 14 percent on the remaining balance?
a. $19,500
b. $12,500
c. $15,000
d. $17,160.31
e. None of the above

REVIEW TEST FOR PART II (CHAPTERS 6 - 7)

CAPITAL BUDGETING

_____ 1. Basic factors of capital budgeting decisions include
  a. net cash flows projected.
  b. initial outlay costs.
  c. the cost of capital.
  d. all of the above.
  e. a and b only.

_____ 2. The present value of a project is defined as the
  a. discounted cash flow.
  b. internal rate of return.
  c. net present value.
  d. initial outlay costs.
  e. none of the above.

_____ 3. Projected cash flows are defined as
  a. net profit after taxes.
  b. net profit after taxes minus depreciation.
  c. net profit after taxes plus depreciation.
  d. net profit before taxes.
  e. none of the above.

_____ 4. The year's final net cash flow must consider
  a. after-tax salvage values.
  b. net cash flows.
  c. released working capital.
  d. all of the above.
  e. a and b only.

_____ 5. The difference between a project's discounted cash flow and its original outlay is its
  a. cash flow.
  b. net present value.
  c. internal rate of return.
  d. cost of capital.
  e. a and b

_____ 6. When the net present value of a project is a positive number, we
            _____ the project.
            a. accept
            b. reject
            c. delay
            d. re-evaluate
            e. none of the above

_____ 7. The profitability index of a project compares the
            a. discounted cash flows with original outlay.
            b. internal rate of return with discounted flows.
            c. net present value with original outlay.
            d. net cash flows with net profit after taxes.
            e. none of the above.

_____ 8. The discount rate that equates the original outlay of a project with
            its discounted cash flows is called the
            a. net discount value.
            b. internal rate of return.
            c. profitability index value.
            d. net present value.
            e. none of the above.

_____ 9. When the internal rate of return on a project exceeds the cost of
            capital, we _____ the project.
            a. accept
            b. reject
            c. re-evaluate
            d. delay
            e. none of the above

_____ 10. Different reinvestment rate assumptions can result in internal rate of
            return and net present value decisions that
            a. require new discount rates.
            b. change the internal rate of return results.
            c. differ in terms of rankings.
            d. slow the firm's growth.
            e. none of the above.

_____ 11. Both the average rate of return method and the payback method ignore
            a. cash flows.
            b. the time value of money.
            c. interest costs.
            d. the cost of capital.
            e. none of the above.

_____ 12. Ranking techniques in the areas of NPV and IRR are used for
            a. net cash flows.
            b. capital rationing.
            c. cost of capital differences.
            d. original outlay.
            e. all of the above.

Use the following data for Questions 13 through 16.

Year	Proposed Cash Flows	
	Project X	Project Y
0	($30,000)	($45,000)
1	6,000	10,000
2	10,000	15,000
3	15,000	18,000
4	22,000	24,000

The cost of capital is 12 percent. No salvage value exists for either project.

_____ 13. Project X has a net present value of _____, and project Y has a
net present value of _____.
   a. $37,987.20; $48,950.97
   b. $11,201.40; $8,772.27
   c. $7,987.20; $3,950.97
   d. $67,981.20; $93,950.97
   e. None of the above

_____ 14. The profitability index for project X is _____, and the profitability index for Y is _____.
   a. 1.27; 1.09
   b. 2.27; 3.09
   c. 1.81; 1.94
   d. 1.94; 1.81
   e. None of the above

_____ 15. Project X has an internal rate of return of approximately _____,
whereas project Y has an internal rate of return of approximately

_____.
   a. 19 percent; 12 percent
   b. 14 percent; 17 percent
   c. 17 percent; 14 percent
   d. 12 percent; 19 percent
   e. None of the above

_____ 16. Given a cost of capital of 12 percent, which would you select?
   a. Project X
   b. Project Y
   c. Both projects
   d. Neither project

_____ 17. What is the internal rate of return on a project that has an initial
outlay of $204,014 and expected cash flows of $20,000 per year for the
next twenty-two years?
   a. 14 percent
   b. 10 percent
   c. 4 percent
   d. 8 percent
   e. None of the above

_____ 18. What is the net present value of a project with an initial investment of $200,000 that will return net cash flows of $50,000 per year over the next ten years? (Assume a cost of capital of 16 percent and no salvage value.)
   a. $300,000
   b. $41,660
   c. $500,000
   d. $46,221
   e. None of the above

_____ 19. What is the payback period for the investment outlined in Question 18?
   a. 10 years
   b. 4 years
   c. 2 years
   d. 7.5 years
   e. none of the above

_____ 20. The profitability index for Project X is 2.30. Project Y has a profitability index value of 1.80. What is the net present value of each project? (Assume that Project X costs $100,000 and Project Y costs $150,000.)
   a. $125,000 for X; $115,000 for Y
   b. $180,000 for X; $210,000 for Y
   c. $130,000 for X; $120,000 for Y
   d. $230,000 for X; $270,000 for Y
   e. None of the above

_____ 21. We can adjust capital budgeting decisions to reflect uncertainty by
   a. combining subjective probabilities with associated annual cash flows.
   b. ignoring the uncertainty factor.
   c. eliminating the use of event matrices.
   d. depending on contingency budgets.
   e. none of the above.

_____ 22. The _____ is considered to be the best measure of relative dispersion.
   a. standard deviation
   b. mean
   c. coefficient of variation
   d. mean absolute deviation
   e. range

_____ 23. The expected NPV can be used to reflect the
   a. expected dispersion of a project.
   b. expected net dollar return from the project.
   c. standard deviation of a project.
   d. coefficient of variation of the project.
   e. none of the above.

_____ 24. Techniques used to adjust capital budgeting problems for risk include
   a. the mean-standard deviation.
   b. risk-adjusted discount rates.
   c. the probability of acceptance errors.

388

> d. all of the above.
> e. none of the above.

_____ 25. When the risk-adjusted discount rate is used, cash flows are reduced to
   a. one-half their original values.
   b. certainty.
   c. risk alternatives.
   d. the original outlay.
   e. none of the above.

_____ 26. Portfolio effects occur to reduce overall risk when
   a. several assets are combined that are less than perfectly positively correlated.
   b. a single asset is volatile.
   c. assets do not change in value.
   d. diversification is held within a single industry.
   e. none of the above.

Use the following data for Questions 27 through 30.

Project A		Project B	
Cash Flow	Probability	Cash Flow	Probability
$400	.20	$300	.20
$500	.60	$500	.60
$600	.20	$700	.20

_____ 27. What is the expected cash flow of each project?
   a. $300 for A; $300 for B
   b. $500 for A; $500 for B
   c. $600 for A; $700 for B
   d. $400 for A; $300 for B
   e. None of the above

_____ 28. What is the standard deviation of each project?
   a. $4,000 for A; $16,000 for B
   b. $44.72 for A; $63.25 for B
   c. $63.25 for A; $126.49 for B
   d. $163.27 for A; $163.25 for B
   e. None of the above

_____ 29. What is the cash flow coefficient of variation of each project?
   a. .1265 for A; .2530 for B
   b. .0894 for A; .1265 for B
   c. .3274 for A; .3265 for B
   d. .1250 for A; .1250 for B
   e. None of the above

_____ 30. Which project would be selected if only one could be acquired?
   a. Project A
   b. Project B

_____   31.   What is the expected net present value of a project with the following
              data? (Assume a 14 percent cost of capital, ten-year life, and $70,000
              initial cash outlay.)

              Cash Flow   Probability

              $10,000   .30
              $14,000   .40
              $20,000   .30

              a. $76,000
              b. $12,231
              c. $6,155
              d. $16,155
              e. None of the above

_____   32.   What is the coefficient of variation for the project outlined in
              Question 31?
              a. .2000
              b. .3903
              c. .2764
              d. .2674
              e. None of the above

_____   33.   Your firm has determined that a project has an expected net present
              value of $600,000, with a standard deviation of $250,000. What is the
              firm's probability of realizing a negative NPV?
              a. .0019
              b. .0026
              c. .0082
              d. .4207
              e. None of the above

REVIEW TEST FOR PART III (CHAPTERS 8 - 11)

COST OF CAPITAL AND CAPITAL STRUCTURE

_____ 1. The term used to indicate the funds supplied by investors when they buy
            securities from a firm is
            a. cash.
            b. liabilities.
            c. capital.
            d. long-term debt.
            e. all of the above.

_____ 2. The rate of return required by investors to purchase the securities of
            a firm is called the
            a. internal rate of return.
            b. cost of capital.
            c. cost of fixed funding.
            d. external financing cost.
            e. none of the above.

_____ 3. Part of a firm's cost of capital reflects the _____ interest rate
            expected by suppliers of capital.
            a. short-term
            b. default-free
            c. long-term
            d. prime
            e. none of the above

_____ 4. A firm with a high probability of not being able to meet interest pay-
            ments or return of principal has great
            a. liquidity risk.
            b. default risk.
            c. market risk.
            d. transactions risk.
            e. none of the above.

_____ 5. The higher the default risk image of the firm, the _____ the cost
            of capital.
            a. lower
            b. less volatile
            c. higher

d. more constant
e. none of the above

_____ 6. Yield curves that slope upward suggest that investors
a. anticipate a recovery ahead.
b. anticipate a downturn ahead.
c. expected stable interest rates.
d. expect interest rates to increase.
e. none of the above.

_____ 7. The cost of capital for the most risky bonds has typically been
_____ the cost of capital for lower-risk bonds.
a. higher than
b. lower than
c. about the same as
d. none of the above

_____ 8. The matching maturities approach suggests the need to
a. match cost and expense of funds.
b. match maturities of assets with funds.
c. match short-term assets with long-term bonds.
d. ignore the use of short-term funds.
e. none of the above.

_____ 9. The financial officer attempts to monitor the _____ of funds as
well as their costs.
a. maturity
b. yield
c. availability
d. transaction costs
e. none of the above

_____ 10. If Treasury bonds pay 14 percent and corporate bonds pay 18 percent,
the risk compensation being required by the purchaser of the corporate
bond is
a. 18 percent.
b. 14 percent.
c. 4 percent.
d. 10 percent
e. none of the above.

_____ 11. The cost of capital increases with increases in
a. funds available.
b. inflation.
c. suppliers of funds.
d. the firm's liquidity position.
e. the firm's debt/equity ratio.

_____ 12. The present value of the expected cash flows from a security represents
a. the interest charge.
b. the yield to maturity.
c. the most an investor is willing to pay.
d. the coupon rate.
e. none of the above.

_____ 13. When a bond is sold by the original purchaser to another individual, the coupon rate on the bond
   a. changes to reflect the new value of the bond.
   b. changes to reflect the new interest rate.
   c. stays the same as the original issue.
   d. increases to reflect a shorter maturity.
   e. increases with the rate of inflation.

_____ 14. Preferred shareholders have a claim on earnings prior to
   a. bondholders.
   b. common stockholders.
   c. rights offerings.
   d. bank loans.
   e. none of the above.

_____ 15. Common stock value reflects
   a. the present value of expected dividends.
   b. the anticipated growth rate of the firm.
   c. the cost of debt.
   d. the cost of preferred stock.
   e. a and b.

_____ 16. The cost of retained earnings is often considered to be the same as the cost of
   a. existing common stock.
   b. debt.
   c. preferred stock.
   d. external equity.
   e. all of the above.

_____ 17. If a firm wishes to satisfy the expectations of its investors, it must equal or exceed the _____ on its existing securities.
   a. debt
   b. internal rate of return
   c. weighted average cost of capital
   d. discount rate
   e. none of the above

_____ 18. The weighted average cost of new capital can be used to
   a. analyze trends in past securities.
   b. evaluate returns on existing assets.
   c. select new projects.
   d. evaluate risk.
   e. none of the above.

_____ 19. What is the after-tax cost of new debt for a firm with the following issue? Maturity of twenty years; face value of $1,000; sale price of $900; flotation charges of $50 per bond; annual coupon interest rate of 10 percent; and a marginal tax rate of 40 percent. (Use the approximation formula.)
   a. 10 percent
   b. 6 percent
   c. 6.97 percent
   d. 8.24 percent
   e. None of the above

_____ 20. What is the cost of the following preferred stock? Market price of
$65; flotation charge of $5 per share; and annual dividend of $8 per
share.
a. 12.31 percent
b. 12.90 percent
c. 11.43 percent
d. 13.33 percent
e. None of the above

_____ 21. JV, Inc., expects to pay dividends of $4 per share on common stock next
year. The current market price of common stock is $25, and dividends
are expected to grow at 6 percent annually. What is the cost of common
stock capital?
a. 14 percent
b. 6 percent
c. 16 percent
d. 22 percent
e. None of the above

_____ 22. Xcan, Inc., has a historical growth rate of 6 percent that it expects
to continue. The previous dividend on common stock was $2 per share.
What is the weighted average cost of capital, given the following information?

Bonds: Before-tax cost of 10 percent (tax rate of 50 percent);
        30 percent of the current, optimal capital structure

Preferred Stock: Dividend yield of 8 percent;
                  20 percent of the current, optimal capital structure

Common Stock: Current market price of $20 per share;
               50 percent of the current, optimal capital structure

a. 12.00 percent
b. 14.10 percent
c. 11.40 percent
d. 18.90 percent
e. None of the above

_____ 23. A firm whose total capital structure is dominated by long-term debt is
said to have the greatest
a. capital position.
b. financial leverage.
c. operating leverage.
d. combined leverage.
e. none of the above.

_____ 24. Earnings per share will vary more for a firm with _____ financial
leverage.
a. higher
b. lower
c. combined
d. stable
e. none of the above

_____ 25. The _____ approach to capital structure management assumes that the firm's value will be affected by its capital structure.
a. traditional
b. Modigliani and Miller
c. Gorden Model
d. conservative
e. none of the above

_____ 26. The firm's capital structure cannot affect its cost of capital under the _____ approach.
a. conservative
b. aggressive
c. Modigliani and Miller
d. market value of equity
e. traditional

_____ 27. The firm with the largest difference between operating profits and interest expense has the greatest
a. leverage position.
b. bankruptcy cushion.
c. financial risk.
d. market risk.
e. none of the above.

_____ 28. ABC, Inc., has net operating income of $500,000, net income after taxes (50 percent) of $250,000, and earnings per share of $2.50. What would be the earnings per share if the firm financed growth by selling $1,000,000 in bonds that yield 10 percent? Assume that net operating income is unchanged.
a. $2.50
b. $3.00
c. $2.00
d. $1.50
e. None of the above

_____ 29. What would be the earnings per share in Question 28 if new equity were issued at $100 per share instead of selling bonds to finance $1,000,000?
a. $1.10
b. $2.10
c. $2.50
d. $2.27
e. None of the above

Use the following data to answer Questions 30 through 32.

Two firms are in the same business environment. Firm X has a 90 percent debt-to-capital ratio, and Firm Y has a 10 percent debt-to-capital ratio. Total capital structure for each is $2,000,000. All bonds outstanding have an 8 percent yield to maturity. Common stock of each firm sells for $20 per share. The tax rate is 50 percent for each firm, and net operating income is $400,000 for each.

_____ 30. What is the earnings per share for each firm?
  a. $11.80 for X; $2.02 for Y
  b. $12.80 for X; $2.13 for Y
  c. $11.40 for X; $9.20 for Y
  d. $11.30 for X; $5.60 for Y
  e. none of the above

_____ 31. What is the operating profit return of each company?
  a. 20 percent for X; 20 percent for Y
  b. 20 percent for X; 40 percent for Y
  c. 40 percent for X; 20 percent for Y
  d. 40 percent for X; 40 percent Y
  e. None of the above

_____ 32. At what point in interest costs would the leverage effect for X become
  negative?
  a. Where interest costs exceed 40 percent
  b. Where interest costs exceed 20 percent
  c. Where interest costs exceed 30 percent
  d. Where interest costs exceed 25 percent
  e. None of the above

_____ 33. What is the theoretical market price for common stock with the following
  characteristics? (Assume a minimum acceptable rate of return of 18
  percent.) Constant growth rate in dividends of 10 percent; previous
  dividend of $1.80.
  a. $11.00
  b. $1.80
  c. $18.00
  d. $24.75
  e. $17.50

_____ 34. As the firm moves away from its optimal debt-to-capital ratio,
  a. debt costs increase.
  b. equity costs increase.
  c. both debt and equity costs increase.
  d. financial risk is constant.
  e. none of the above.

_____ 35. When a stock sells ex-dividend, it sells _____ benefit of the
  dividend declared.
  a. with
  b. without
  c. with the same aggregate
  d. none of the above

_____ 36. Using the stable payout ratio approach to dividend management, the firm
  will
  a. retain the same percentage of net profits and vary the dividends.
  b. vary the percentage of net profits retained and pay a constant
     dividend.
  c. show continuous growth in dividends.
  d. pay only the residual in dividends.
  e. none of the above.

_____ 37. Dividend payout policies can be influenced by
     a. loan restrictions.
     b. state regulations.
     c. capital budget opportunities.
     d. liquidity positions.
     e. all of the above.

_____ 38. Inflation has the effect of _____ dividends by encouraging the
     _____ use of retained earnings.
     a. increasing; decreased
     b. increasing; increased
     c. decreasing; increased
     d. decreasing; decreased
     e. none of the above

_____ 39. Retained earnings provide the source from which _____ must be paid.
     a. cash dividends
     b. stock
     c. both cash and stock dividends
     d. debt
     e. taxes

_____ 40. The net effect on the dollar amount of a stockholder's equity after a
     stock dividend is
     a. increased ownership.
     b. decreased treasury stock.
     c. zero.
     d. increased taxes.
     e. none of the above.

_____ 41. The residual dividend policy
     a. pays bonus dividends in good years.
     b. pays out whatever remains after the firm's capital needs are satis-
        fied.
     c. always pays the same dividend.
     d. pays a constant payout ratio amount.
     e. invests dividends for the stockholders.

_____ 42. In 1979 a firm reported earnings per share of $8 and a stock dividend
     of 20 percent. What is the adjusted earnings per share?
     a. $9.60
     b. $6.90
     c. $7.50
     d. $6.67
     e. None of the above

_____ 43. Dividends per share were $2 _prior_ to a 20 percent stock dividend. If
     you owned 100 shares prior to the stock dividend, what would be the
     total dollar amount of dividend income after the stock dividend?
     a. $240
     b. $200
     c. $167
     d. $220
     e. None of the above

_____   44.   You own 4,000 shares of J-Bar, Inc. A 30 percent stock dividend has been declared. What percentage do you own of the firm before and after the dividend? (Assume that 10,000 shares were outstanding prior to the dividend.)
a. 40 percent before; 52 percent after
b. 52 percent before; 52 percent after
c. 40 percent before; 40 percent after
d. 52 percent before; 40 percent after
e. None of the above

WORKING CAPITAL MANAGEMENT

_____ 1. A factor is a company that specializes in
   a. insuring other firms' inventories against fire and theft losses.
   b. managing the cash balances of other firms.
   c. underwriting new issues of either stocks or bonds.
   d. both buying and managing the accounts receivable of other firms.
   e. providing short-term financing for other firms' inventory investments.

_____ 2. A firm has a credit policy of 1/15, net 20. Typically, the firm receives its payments from customers according to the following schedule: 25 percent of sales are collected on the last available day of the discount; 60 percent of sales are collected on the last day before the accounts become delinquent; and the remaining 15 percent of sales are collected 40 days after the accounts become delinquent. The firm's average collection period is approximately
   a. 8 days.
   b. 14 days.
   c. 22 days.
   d. 25 days
   e. 31 days.

_____ 3. A banker's acceptance ($100,000 par value) matures in 110 days and sells for $97,800. If an investor were to purchase this acceptance, the investor's annual yield (based on a 360-day year) would be about
   a. 2.25 percent.
   b. 5.44 percent.
   c. 7.36 percent.
   d. 9.00 percent.
   e. 11.68 percent.

_____ 4. Money market instruments
   a. have maturities in excess of one year.
   b. include mortgages and corporate bonds.
   c. are seldom traded in secondary markets.
   d. offer high yields due to their default risk.
   e. generally have good liquidity.

_____ 5. Raft River Boat Works has annual sales of $12 million and a gross profit margin equal to 24 percent of sales. Further, Raft River's average collection period (based on a 360-day year) is 40 days, and its cost of capital is 14 percent. Presently, the company's annual operating expenses associated with its credit department are $60,000 plus 1.5 percent of sales. Raft River's annual investment costs related to its investment in accounts receivable are approximately
   a. $141,867.
   b. $154,920.
   c. $161,333.
   d. $186,667.
   e. $240,000.

_____ 6. In Question 5, if Raft River has no shortfall costs related to its present policy, the current total costs of its investment in accounts receivable are
   a. $314,467.
   b. $358,767.
   c. $381,867.
   d. $399,867.
   e. $426,667.

_____ 7. Raft River (from the previous two questions) is considering a tighter credit policy that would: reduce annual sales to $11.6 million; decrease the average collection period to 34 days; and increase the fixed costs component of the credit department's operating expenses by $18,000 per year. The shortfall costs related to the tighter credit policy would be
   a. $56,000.
   b. $96,000.
   c. $136,000.
   d. $252,000.
   e. $304,000.

_____ 8. Considering the information given in Questions 5-7, if Raft River were to change to the tighter credit policy being considered, its annual before-tax profitability would be
   a. increased by $12,000.
   b. increased by $25,300.
   c. left unchanged.
   d. reduced by $41,400.
   e. reduced by $82,700.

_____ 9. The firm's optimal investment in working capital involves a trade-off between
   a. inventory and accounts receivable.
   b. current assets and fixed assets.
   c. the cost of capital and higher investment risks.
   d. using a factor on either a recourse or a nonrecourse basis.
   e. profitability and liquidity.

_____ 10. Value Auto Parts sells 2 million spark plugs per year. When Value
orders spark plugs from its supplier, the ordering costs are $150 per
order. If carrying costs are $.10/spark plug, Value's economic order
quantity (EOQ) associated with spark plugs is
a. 77,460 plugs.
b. 94,296 plugs.
c. 103,333 plugs.
d. 191,612 plugs.
e. 376,500 plugs.

_____ 11. Assuming uniform daily sales of spark plugs in the previous question,
if Value carries a safety stock of 75,000 spark plugs and orders new
spark plugs according to an EOQ criterion, Value's average spark plug
inventory is
a. 36,220 plugs.
b. 95,806 plugs.
c. 113,730 plugs.
d. 128,718 plugs.
e. 182,340 plugs.

_____ 12. Based on the information in Question 10, Value's minimum annual ordering
costs for its spark plug inventory would be approximately
a. $1,924.
b. $2,330.
c. $3,219.
d. $3,873.
e. $4,512.

_____ 13. When a delinquent account becomes uncollectible, the entire account is
written off as
a. an opportunity cost.
b. a default cost.
c. a shortfall cost.
d. a delinquency cost.
e. an investment cost.

_____ 14. Most short-term marketable securities (for example, commercial paper
and bankers' acceptances) are sold
a. for greater than their par values.
b. at their face values.
c. without any default risk.
d. on a discount basis.
e. without recourse.

_____ 15. Which of the following financial assets is the most liquid?
a. Commercial paper
b. Treasury bills
c. Common stock
d. Checking accounts
e. Eurodollar deposits

_____ 16. All of the following, except _____, are methods a firm can utilize
to minimize its cash needs.
a. less frequent payrolls
b. lock box systems

     c. advance payments to suppliers
     d. discounts to customers who pay their bills promptly
     e. delayed payments to creditors

_____ 17. Negotiable certificates of deposit
     a. have maturities in excess of one year.
     b. are issued by large, creditworthy corporations.
     c. have no secondary markets.
     d. possess no default risk.
     e. have minimum denominations of $100,000.

_____ 18. The following account balances appeared on Piper Corporation's most recent balance sheet:

Inventory	$ 29,000
Net worth	123,000
Notes payable	13,000
Cash & marketable securities	26,000
Wages, taxes, and accounts payable	46,000
Capital lease obligations	37,000
Net fixed assets	181,000
Accounts receivable	34,000
Long-term debt	51,000

     Determine Piper's working capital investment.
     a. $26,000
     b. $55,000
     c. $64,000
     d. $89,000
     e. $149,000

_____ 19. From the balance sheet information in Question 18, Piper's ratio of net working capital to total assets is approximately
     a. -54 percent.
     b. 11 percent.
     c. 33 percent.
     d. 49 percent.
     e. 72 percent.

_____ 20. A tractor dealer in Austin, Texas, bought four tractors from a manufacturer in Madison, Wisconsin. If the trucking company that delivered the tractors to the Austin dealer was paid by the Madison manufacturer for all insurance and transportation charges, terms of the tractors' sale were most likely
     a. Sight draft--bill of lading.
     b. C.O.D.
     c. C.B.D.
     d. Free on board.
     e. C.I.F.

_____ 21. Which one of the traditional "five Cs" of credit attempts to assess a potential credit customer's liquidity?
     a. Capacity
     b. Conditions
     c. Capital

    d. Character
    e. Collateral

_____ 22. A company requires a 15.66 percent annual yield on an investment in
T-bills that mature in 30 days. Assuming both a 360-day year and a
$10,000 par value for the T-bills, determine the maximum price the
company would pay for the T-bills to assure its required 15.66 percent
return.
    a. $8,646
    b. $9,568
    c. $9,871
    d. $9,927
    e. $10,117

_____ 23. A factor has offered to collect, on a 25 percent recourse basis, all
Budge Marine's accounts receivable for a fee equal to 5 percent of
credit sales. Budge Marine has $6 million/year in credit sales, a
15 percent cost of capital, and a 22 percent gross profit margin. The
company estimates annual savings in administrative costs would amount
to $120,000 from eliminating its credit department if the factor's
offer was accepted. Presently, Budge Marine's average collection
period is 60 days (assuming a 360-day year), and its default costs are
.6 percent of credit sales. Determine Budge Marine's total annual
credit costs affiliated with the factoring alternative.
    a. $247,000
    b. $282,000
    c. $296,000
    d. $309,000
    e. $341,000

_____ 24. Should Budge Marine (from the previous question) decide to use the
factor, its annual credit costs would
    a. decrease by $6,000.
    b. decrease by $17,000.
    c. decrease by $47,000.
    d. increase by $3,000.
    e. increase by $36,000.

_____ 25. Which of the following money market instruments offers investors
interest income that is exempt from federal income taxes?
    a. Bankers' acceptances
    b. Commercial paper
    c. Repurchase agreements
    d. Tax anticipation bills
    e. Federal funds

REVIEW TEST FOR PART V (CHAPTERS 14 - 15)

SHORT- AND INTERMEDIATE-TERM SOURCES OF FUNDS

_____ 1. A firm borrows $300,000 with a 12 percent interest term loan that is to
be amortized over five years. If uniform installments on the loan are
to be paid at the end of each year, each installment payment would be
a. $67,200.
b. $76,617.
c. $83,223.
d. $96,000
e. $105,741.

_____ 2. For the loan mentioned in the previous question, how much total interest
would the firm pay on the loan over the five years?
a. $116,115
b. $129,772
c. $138,218
d. $163,424
e. $180,000

_____ 3. The annual percentage cost of forgoing the available discounts on goods
purchased under 3/5, net 40 credit terms is
a. 3.09 percent.
b. 9.63 percent.
c. 18.51 percent.
d. 31.81 percent.
e. 55.67 percent.

_____ 4. Intermediate-term financing in the form of conditional sales contracts
is often available from
a. pension funds.
b. life insurance companies.
c. business finance companies.
d. equipment manufacturers.
e. commercial banks.

_____ 5. The legal document that entitles the lender to possession of an asset
pledged against a loan in event of default is known as a
a. consignment.
b. lien.

    c. recourse provision.
    d. security agreement.
    e. factoring covenant.

6. Inter-City Beverage has negotiated a $700,000 revolving credit agreement for one year with its local bank. The agreement with the bank requires Inter-City to maintain a $90,000 compensating balance throughout the year in a checking account that pays no interest. Normally, Inter-City carries a $40,000 average balance in its checking account at the bank. Additionally, Inter-City must pay nominal interest of 16 percent per year on any take downs plus a one-time commitment fee of $24,000 (to be paid at the beginning of the year). If Inter-City borrowed all the $700,000 for the entire year, the loan's effective annual interest rate would be
    a. 17.89 percent.
    b. 19.57 percent.
    c. 21.73 percent.
    d. 23.21 percent.
    e. 25.66 percent.

7. In the previous question, recalculate the loan's effective annual interest rate if Inter-City were to have a $475,000 average loan balance throughout the year rather than $700,000.
    a. 18.95 percent.
    b. 24.94 percent.
    c. 26.72 percent.
    d. 27.70 percent.
    e. 29.86 percent.

8. Which one of the following does not affect the classification of a lease as either an operating or a capital lease?
    a. The lease's duration in relation to the leased asset's economic life
    b. The present value of the minimum lease payments compared to the leased asset's market value at the lease's inception
    c. The transfer of asset ownership to the lessee at the lease's termination
    d. An option clause permitting the lessee to purchase the leased asset for a bargain price at the end of the lease
    e. The obligation of either the lessee or the lessor to be responsible for property taxes and maintenance associated with the leased asset during the lease's term.

9. Assuming a 360-day year, calculate the effective annual interest rate on a 240-day discount loan for $175,000 that has an 11 percent nominal interest rate.
    a. 11.87 percent
    b. 12.59 percent
    c. 13.26 percent
    d. 14.41 percent
    e. 16.50 percent

_____ 10. A small retail firm borrows $60,000 for seven months on an installment loan arranged at the bank. Payments of $9,300 each are to be made at the end of each month during the loan's term. The loan's effective annual interest rate is approximately
a. 15.5 percent.
b. 17.9 percent.
c. 21.3 percent.
d. 25.5 percent.
e. 26.6 percent.

_____ 11. A lease that requires the lessee to pay both insurance and maintenance expenses affiliated with the leased asset is referred to as a
a. capital lease.
b. leveraged lease.
c. double-net lease.
d. operating lease.
e. gross lease.

_____ 12. Inventory financing under a trust receipt arrangement is also referred to as
a. field warehousing.
b. factoring.
c. financing with a chattel mortgage.
d. terminal warehousing.
e. floor planning.

_____ 13. Short-term unsecured promissory notes issued by large corporations with good credit ratings are called
a. equipment financing loans.
b. commercial paper.
c. eurodollar loans.
d. conditional sales contracts.
e. bankers' acceptances.

_____ 14. Baxer Transfer and Storage has four new trucks leased under a ten-year capital lease from Elko Leasing, Inc. When the lease was negotiated, the trucks could have been purchased by Baxer for $32,500 each, and Baxer could have financed the purchase with a ten-year installment loan at 14 percent per year. Baxer's end-of-year lease payments to Elko Leasing are $24,000 per year during the lease's term. The imputed interest component of Baxer's second-year lease payment on the trucks can be used to reduce Baxer's taxable income during that year by
a. $8,500.
b. $16,620.
c. $18,200.
d. $19,780.
e. $24,000.

_____ 15. After Baxer has made its second annual payment on the lease described in Question 14, the amount on the asset side of Baxer's balance sheet indicated as "Leased Property Under Capital Leases" that reflects the trucks' lease would be
a. $77,187.
b. $102,919.
c. $111,333.

    d. $118,420.
    e. $150,763.

16. With operating leases,
    a. the term of the lease cannot exceed twelve years.
    b. the present value of the lease payments is capitalized as a liability on the lessee's balance sheet.
    c. title to the leased asset is transferred to the lessee at the end of the lease's term.
    d. annual lease payments are expenses in their entirety on the lessee's income statement.
    e. escalation clauses are prohibited.

17. Advances against a line of credit are commonly referred to as
    a. overdrafts.
    b. take downs.
    c. consignments.
    d. balloon payments.
    e. up tricks.

18. A leasing arrangement in which a third-party creditor finances the lessor's purchase of the leased asset is called a
    a. capital lease.
    b. triple net lease.
    c. term lease.
    d. leveraged lease.
    e. operating lease.

19. Which of the following credit terms reflects an annual percentage rate equal to 36.36 percent?
    a. 1/20, net 30.
    b. 2/15, net 35.
    c. 2/20, net 40.
    d. 2/30, net 60.
    e. 3/15, net 45.

20. Which one of the following statements is incorrect concerning commercial paper?
    a. Maturities are usually less than 270 days.
    b. Most issues are in excess of $10 million.
    c. Old issues are often rolled over.
    d. New issues can be either direct or dealer placed.
    e. Interest rates on commercial paper are usually above the prime rate.

21. Which of the following would not be expected to serve as lessors in leasing agreements?
    a. Insurance companies.
    b. Pension funds.
    c. Specialized leasing companies.
    d. Investment bankers.
    e. Subsidiaries of commercial banks

_____ 22. Rochelle Sporting Goods borrows $650,000 from its bank with a four-year installment loan that requires equal end-of-year payments during the loan's life. If the loan's annual interest rate is 18 percent, determine the loan's interest expense to Rochelle during the second year of the loan.
a. $68,095
b. $94,567
c. $117,000
d. $147,064
e. $241,631

_____ 23. For the loan described in Question 22, Rochelle made the first two annual payments and then decided to completely repay the loan's remaining principal (and accumulated interest) with one balloon payment at the end of the third year. Calculate the size of the third year's payment.
a. $166,740
b. $446,401
c. $650,000
d. $724,890
e. $767,000

_____ 24. A bank's prime rate is the
a. effective interest rate the bank charges on discount loans.
b. interest rate the bank pays on its negotiable certificates of deposit.
c. maximum interest rate an FDIC-insured bank can charge on business loans.
d. same as its federal funds rate.
e. nominal interest rate the bank charges its most creditworthy borrowers.

_____ 25. A company has a 120-day discount loan with an effective annual interest rate equal to 16.33 percent. Assuming both a 360-day year and a $140,000 loan principal, what is the loan's nominal interest rate?
a. 14.0 percent
b. 14.5 percent
c. 15.0 percent
d. 15.5 percent
e. 16.0 percent

LONG-TERM SOURCES OF FUNDS

_____ 1. When warrants are exercised,
   a. the firm's equity base increases but its debt structure remains unchanged.
   b. the firm is not provided with new funds even though its equity base increases.
   c. the firm's debt capital is reduced by the dollar amount of the warrants exercised.
   d. the firm's debt capital increases, and new funds are provided to the firm.
   e. the firm's debt-to-equity ratio is unaffected.

_____ 2. Institutional investors most likely to be involved in private placements of new securities include
   a. commercial banks and life insurance companies.
   b. investment bankers and business finance companies.
   c. casualty insurance companies and mutual funds.
   d. business finance companies and commercial banks.
   e. pension funds and life insurance companies.

_____ 3. State laws that govern public offerings within each state are referred to as
   a. wash sale restrictions.
   b. red herring regulations.
   c. protective covenants.
   d. blue sky laws.
   e. SEC codes.

_____ 4. A corporate bond has both an 8 percent coupon rate and a $1,000 par value. When originally issued 12 years ago, the bond had a 25-year maturity. If the bond is priced to yield 11 percent to maturity, the bond's current market value is
   a. $798.
   b. $824.
   c. $1,000.
   d. $1,237.
   e. $1,320.

_____ 5. If the bond described in Question 4 was callable in three more years at a call price of $1,080, which one of the following sets of information would be correct concerning both the bond's approximate yield to first call (YTFC) and its current yield (CY)?
  a. YTFC = 11.0 percent and CY = 8.0 percent.
  b. YTFC = 16.0 percent and CY = 8.0 percent.
  c. YTFC = 16.6 percent and CY = 10.0 percent.
  d. YTFC = 18.5 percent and CY = 10.0 percent.
  e. YTFC = 18.5 percent and CY = 13.8 percent.

_____ 6. Burrows Publishing House has 3,400,000 shares of common stock outstanding, with a market value of $7.25 per share. Burrows plans to raise $6,000,000 in new common equity capital via a rights offering that has a subscription price of $6.00/share. If the Hatch Trust Fund owns 2,000 shares of Burrows common stock on the stock's ex-rights date, approximately how many new shares of Burrows common stock would the Hatch Fund be entitled to purchase as a result of the rights offering?
  a. 367 shares.
  b. 487 shares.
  c. 588 shares.
  d. 714 shares.
  e. 2000 shares.

_____ 7. For the rights offering in Question 6, the theoretical value of a share of Burrows common stock on the ex-rights date would be
  a. $5.62.
  b. $6.00.
  c. $6.28.
  d. $6.97.
  e. $7.53.

_____ 8. Letter stock is
  a. preferred stock that has cumulative voting rights.
  b. common stock that has not been registered with the SEC.
  c. common stock issued through a rights offering.
  d. common stock without a par value.
  e. preferred stock that can be converted (at the holder's option) into a fixed number of common stock shares.

_____ 9. Harper Steel has convertible debentures ($1,000 par value) outstanding; the coupon rate is 9-1/2 percent, and the remaining maturity is seventeen years. The conversion ratio of each debenture is 30 shares, and Harper's common stock sells for $28/share. Bonds in the same risk class as the Harper convertible debentures have an 11 percent yield to maturity. If each Harper convertible bond has an 8 percent conversion premium, which one of the following sets of statements is correct?
  a. Conversion value is $840, and bond value is $958.
  b. Market value is $1,095, and current yield is 11.48 percent.
  c. Bond value is $950, and conversion value is $700.
  d. Price floor is $840, and bond value is $887.
  e. Current yield is 9.92 percent, and price floor is $887.

_____ 10. Suppose that the convertible debentures discussed in Question 9 had antidilution provisions and that Harper's common stock increased in value to $32/share and then had a three-for-one stock split. Under these conditions, each convertible debenture's
a. conversion ratio would be reduced to 10 shares.
b. conversion value would be increased to $960.
c. bond value would be reduced to $840.
d. floor price would remain unchanged.
e. associated conversion price would be increased to $33.33/share.

_____ 11. Dispatch Express has 8.5 million authorized shares of common stock, but only 5.8 million shares have been issued. Over the years, Dispatch has acquired 700,000 shares of treasury stock. If Dispatch announces a five-for-six reserve stock split and has after-tax earnings of $16 million prior to the reverse split, approximate earnings per share following the reverse split will be
a. $2.46/share.
b. $2.61/share.
c. $3.13/share.
d. $3.31/share.
e. $3.76/share.

_____ 12. In terms of cash flows, which one of the following methods of issuing new common stock is most distinct from the other four methods?
a. A rights offering
b. A conversion of warrants
c. A conversion of convertible bonds
d. A public offering
e. A private placement

_____ 13. The selling of borrowed common stock by an investor who anticipates a decline in the common stock's market price is an example of a
a. wash sale.
b. deferred conversion sale.
c. short sale.
d. best efforts sale.
e. red herring sale.

_____ 14. Seminole Power Company attached warrants with its recently issued new debentures. Each warrant allows its holder to buy two shares of Seminole common stock at $18.75/share for the next five years. Currently, each share of Seminole common stock sells for $20.50/share, and each Seminole warrant has a market value of $4.25. The premium affiliated with each warrant is
a. $.75.
b. $1.25.
c. $2.50.
d. $2.75.
e. $3.50.

_____ 15. Timberline Plastics is considering refunding $8 million of 12 percent debentures ($1,000 par value) that were issued five years ago. The old debentures originally had a 25-year maturity, and their flotation costs were $200,000. Should refunding occur, the 12 percent debentures would be replaced with new 20-year second mortgage bonds that could be sold at par ($1,000/bond) with a 9.5 percent coupon rate. Additionally, Timberline estimates it would pay overlapping interest on the old debentures for about two months during the flotation of the new mortgage bonds. The old debentures are currently callable at a call price of $1,130 each, and flotation costs on the new mortgage bonds would be $260,000. If Timberline's cost of capital is 13 percent and its tax rate is 46 percent, the refunding alternative's net present value is
   a. -$59,570; therefore, do not refund.
   b. -$21,202; therefore, do not refund.
   c. $18,117; therefore, refund.
   d. $43,955; therefore, refund.
   e. $97,638; therefore, refund.

_____ 16. Which one of the following statements is incorrect?
   a. A bond without a conversion feature will sell at a discount whenever its yield to maturity exceeds its coupon rate.
   b. Unsecured long-term bonds backed only by the borrowing firm's credit-worthiness are known as debentures.
   c. Corporate investors owning preferred stock receive an 85 percent tax exemption on dividends obtained from their preferred stock investment.
   d. Warrants have no effect on a firm's stated earnings per share until they are exercised.
   e. Convertible bonds are sometimes used as a means of delayed equity financing.

_____ 17. The economic purpose of secondary markets is to
   a. bring together both investors and issuers of new securities.
   b. lower investors' risks against default on corporate bonds.
   c. enhance the liquidity of securities issued in the primary markets.
   d. facilitate the placement of money market instruments.
   e. provide a place where companies can issue either stocks or bonds.

_____ 18. With a negotiated underwriting, after the SEC approves the sale of new securities in a public offering,
   a. pre-underwriting conferences between the issuing firm and its investment banker can commence.
   b. a final prospectus must be distributed to all investors who purchase the new securities.
   c. the underwriting syndicate is formed.
   d. a red herring can be issued to the SEC.
   e. investment bankers must complete the sale within 30 days.

_____ 19. A firm issuing bonds may be required to make periodic payments into an escrow account if the bonds' indenture requires the bonds to
   a. have a call feature.
   b. be registered in the bonds' registry.
   c. have warrants attached to them.
   d. be convertible into either common or preferred stock.
   e. have a sinking fund.

_____ 20. A second mortgage is an example of a
a.   junior mortgage.
b.   open-end mortgage.
c.   collateral trust bond.
d.   blanket mortgage.
e.   debenture.

_____ 21. If a callable bond is selling at a discount, its yield to first call will
a.   be less than its yield to maturity.
b.   equal its coupon rate.
c.   exceed its current yield.
d.   be less than its coupon rate.
e.   equal the difference between its current yield and its yield to maturity.

_____ 22. If a firm's convertible bond issue is overhung,
a.   a forced conversion is doubtful.
b.   outstanding warrants of the firm cannot legally be exercised.
c.   the SEC could require the firm to call the issue.
d.   the bonds' conversion ratio can be lowered to eliminate the overhang.
e.   the price of the firm's common stock has probably risen significantly since the convertible bonds were issued.

_____ 23. Warrants
a.   often offer investors higher dividend yields than common stock investments.
b.   reduce the firm's outstanding debt when they are exercised.
c.   can occasionally trade for less than their theoretical value.
d.   are sometimes used to make a new debt issue more attractive to investors.
e.   seldom have antidilution provisions.

_____ 24. General Semiconductors, Inc., recently bought 1,000 shares of Raflin preferred stock ($100 par value) for $76/share. The stock pays a $2/ share quarterly dividend, and General Semiconductors is subject to a 40 percent federal tax rate. General Semiconductors's annual after-tax dividend yield affiliated with its preferred stock investment is approximately
a.   6.32 percent.
b.   6.95 percent.
c.   8.00 percent.
d.   9.89 percent.
e.   10.53 percent.

_____ 25. The major advantage that common stock financing has over debt financing with long-term bonds is
a.   the lower cost of capital associated with common stock.
b.   the tax deductibility of dividends on common stock.
c.   the lack of restrictions and lack of fixed financial obligations that are inherent with bonds.
d.   the relatively low flotation costs related to issuing common stock.
e.   the positive effects that increased financial leverage, due to equity financing, could have on the firm's earnings.

REVIEW TEST FOR PART VII (CHAPTERS 20 - 22)

SPECIAL SITUATIONS IN FINANCIAL MANAGEMENT

_____ 1. A firm that does not have sufficient liquid assets to fulfill its current financial obligations is referred to as
a. bankrupt.
b. legally insolvent.
c. in a reorganization.
d. technically insolvent.
e. a financial failure.

_____ 2. The purchase by a commercial bank holding company of a finance company is an example of a
a. product extension.
b. horizontal merger.
c. vertical merger.
d. market extension.
e. pure conglomerate merger.

_____ 3. If, due to tight monetary policy in the United States, the yield on American T-bills rose significantly above the yields on similar money market instruments in France, this differential in short-term interest rates would tend to
a. worsen the U.S. balance of payments with France.
b. strengthen the U.S. dollar against the French franc.
c. cause the French franc to revalue against the U.S. dollar.
d. cause the U.S. dollar to devalue against the French franc.
e. increase France's supply of U.S. dollars.

_____ 4. One of the requirements that must be satisfied for a merger to qualify as a pooling of interest is that
a. the acquiring firm cannot dispose of a significant portion of the acquired firm's assets for at least five years after the merger.
b. the merging firms must be independent of each other and autonomous for at least three years prior to the merger.
c. after the merger, the accounting basis for the acquired firm's assets must be changed to coincide with the accounting basis used by the acquiring firm for its assets.

_____
d. the merger must be finalized either in a single transaction or within one year according to a prenegotiated plan.

e. the stockholders of the acquired firm must be paid in cash by the acquiring firm for their stock in the acquired firm.

_____ 5. A Swiss chemical company is planning to build a sulfuric acid plant in Galena Park, Texas, to supply its American customers along the Houston Ship Channel. After an initial outlay of $15 million, the plant will generate after-tax cash flows of $4 million/year for the next five years. After the fifth year of operation, the Swiss firm estimates that is can sell the sulfuric acid plant for $10 million. All annual cash flows associated with the Texas project will be converted into Swiss francs (SF) at prevailing exchange rates and then remitted to the Swiss firm's home office. Presently, the franc's exchange rate for U.S. dollars ($) is SF 1.6/$; during each of the next five years the exchange rate is expected to vary as shown in the table below.

Year	Exchange Rate (SF/$)
1	1.55
2	1.45
3	1.40
4	1.50
5	1.58

If the Swiss firm's cost of capital for this project is 15 percent, the sulfuric acid plant's expected net present value to the Swiss firm is approximately

a. SF 1.8 million.
b. SF 3.4 million.
c. SF 3.9 million.
d. SF 5.1 million.
e. SF 5.4 million.

_____ 6. In Question 5, suppose that the Swiss firm changes its remittance policy such that all annual cash flows are invested in American T-bills during the five years. Then, after the fifth year, all dollar balances will be converted into Swiss francs at the fifth year exchange rate and subsequently remitted to the Swiss firm. If the Swiss firm anticipates the annual yield on American T-bills to be 10 percent over the five years, the plant's expected net present value with such a remittance policy would be approximately

a. -SF 1.3 million.
b. SF 3.0 million.
c. SF 3.7 million.
d. SF 4.3 million.
e. SF 5.1 million.

_____ 7. An agreement with creditors that allows a financially troubled firm to lengthen the maturity of its past due debt is known as

a. an order of relief.
b. a composition.
c. an informal bankruptcy petition.
d. a conversion.
e. an extension.

_____ 8. Susank Finance is planning to acquire Godfrey Computer Services through an exchange of common stock. The following premerger information is known about both firms.

	Susank	Godfrey
After-tax earnings	$6,440,000	$2,250,000
Common stock outstanding	2,000,000 shares	600,000 shares
Price-to-earnings ratio	7.3X	9.0X

For accounting purposes, the proposed merger would be considered a pooling of interest. Further, Susank's management estimates that synergistic effects from the merger will enhance Susank's postmerger after-tax earnings by $150,000. In the exchange of common stock between the two firms, Godfrey's stock was valued at $40/share, and Susank's stock was valued at its premerger market value. Given this information about the proposed merger, determine Susank's postmerger earnings per share.
a. $2.93/share
b. $3.22/share
c. $3.46/share
d. $3.75/share
e. $4.19/share

_____ 9. In the previous problem, it is expected that the merger with Godfrey will increase Susank's postmerger price-earnings ratio to 8.0 times Susank's postmerger earnings per share. With this expectation, what is the maximum price at which Godfrey's common stock could be valued in the exchange if Susank's management wanted Susank's common stock to have a market value of $24/share after the merger?
a. $23.50/share
b. $33.75/share
c. $37.08/share
d. $39.21/share
e. $42.37/share

_____ 10.   Martin Furniture had the following liabilities immediately prior to
its court-supervised liquidation.

Wages payable	$ 75,000
Taxes payable	18,500
Trade credit	164,000
Bank loan due	220,000
Morgage bonds	193,500
Subordinated debentures	335,000
Total liabilities	$1,006,000

The debentures were subordinated to Martin's bank loan, and the
mortgage bonds were collateralized by Martin's building. Further,
Martin's bank had a floating collateral lien on 100 percent of Martin's
inventory. The book and liquidation values of Martin's assets are
shown below.

	Book Value	Liquidation Value
Liquid assets	$ 19,000	$ 19,000
Accounts receivable	235,000	165,800
Inventory	386,000	180,300
Machinery and equipment	257,000	132,400
Trucks and autos	97,000	55,100
Building	295,000	340,000
Furniture	28,000	6,000
Total	$1,317,000	$898,600

The court ruled that 80 percent of Martin's wages payable must be
paid, with the remaining 20 percent being discharged by the court. If
the court's costs and legal fees associated with the liquidation were
$78,700, determine the total dollar distribution made to the holders of
Martin's subordinated debentures.
a. $216,000
b. $228,600
c. $287,900
d. $306,400
e. $335,000

_____ 11.   From the information provided in Question 10, what approximate percentage of Martin's trade creditors' original claims was paid in the liquidation?
a. 61 percent
b. 68 percent
c. 76 percent
d. 91 percent
e. 100 percent

_____ 12. An American bank made a simple interest loan having a 16 percent annual interest rate to a Mexican firm. The loan was denominated in pesos and had a 180-day maturity. Further, the amount of the loan was 800,000 pesos. When the loan was made, the exchange rate between dollars and pesos was $.046/peso. If, six months later when the loan came due, the dollar had revalued against the peso to $.045/peso, calculate the bank's effective annual yield on the loan (taking into account the dollar's revaluation). Assume a 360-day year.
a. 7.5 percent
b. 9.7 percent
c. 11.3 percent
d. 16.0 percent
e. 20.8 percent

_____ 13. Right-Taste Cola acquired Supreme Bottlers by paying cash to Supreme's stockholders for their common stock. Prior to the acquisition, the annual before-tax earnings of Right-Taste and Supreme were $13 million and $8 million, respectively. Even though the book value of Supreme's common stock was $22/share, Right-Taste paid Supreme's stockholders $25/share for the two million outstanding shares of Supreme's common stock. To finance the acquisition of Supreme, Right-Taste issued 9 percent subordinated debentures having a 20-year maturity. Further, Right-Taste has a policy of amortizing goodwill over five years. If Right-Taste has 4.5 million shares of common stock outstanding before the acquisition and its marginal tax rate is 44 percent, what are Right-Taste's postmerger earnings per share, assuming that (due to synergy) the acquisition would reduce Right-Taste's pretax operating expenses by $190,000?
a. $1.62
b. $1.81
c. $1.93
d. $2.08
e. $2.37

_____ 14. A bill of exchange that can immediately be cashed by an exporter is also known as a
a. bill of lading.
b. banker's acceptance.
c. time draft.
d. letter of credit.
e. sight draft.

_____ 15. All the following, except _____, are types of mergers classified according to their legal status.
a. sale of assets
b. consolidation
c. holding company
d. pure conglomerate
e. statutory merger

_____ 16. A French firm borrowed 200,000 thousand eurcos for one year via a composite currency loan from a U.S. bank. The annual interest rate on the eurco-denominated loan was 14 percent. For purposes of the loan, one eurco (E) equaled 20 French francs (FF), 10 German marks (DM), and 5 U.S. dollars ($). When the loan originated, exchange rates were FF 4/$ and FF 2.22/DM; however, when the loan's principal and interest came due at the end of one year, exchange rates were FF 4.3/$ and FF 2.15/DM. In terms of French francs made available by the eurco loan, the French firm's effective annual interest rate associated with the loan was
   a. 12.32 percent.
   b. 14.00 percent.
   c. 15.47 percent.
   d. 16.07 percent.
   e. 17.61 percent.

_____ 17. A legal declaration of a firm's insolvency is known as
   a. technical insolvency.
   b. bankruptcy.
   c. an order of relief.
   d. a reorganization plan.
   e. conversion

_____ 18. When the purchase method is used to account for a merger,
   a. some goodwill is always created.
   b. negative goodwill could appear on the acquiring firm's balance sheet after the merger.
   c. the postmerger income statement of the acquiring firm is the combined premerger income statements of both the acquiring and the acquired firms.
   d. the accounting basis of the acquired firm's assets must remain unchanged following the merger.
   e. goodwill will result from the merger if an upward adjustment is necessary to the acquiring firm's balance sheet as a result of the merger.

_____ 19. If the United States had a balance of payments deficit with Britain, which one of the following pairs of possible outcomes would be likely?
   a. The U.S. supply of pounds would increase, and the dollar should devalue against the pound.
   b. The pound should revalue against the dollar, and the British supply of dollars would increase.
   c. The dollar should devalue against the dollar, and the British supply of dollars would increase.
   d. The dollar should revalue against the pound, and the U.S. supply of pounds would increase.
   e. The U.S. supply of pounds would remain unchanged, but the pound should devalue against the dollar.

_____ 20. With the exception of _____, all the following may provide a motive for a merger.
   a. lowering of the acquiring firm's business risk
   b. expanding the acquiring firm's customer base
   c. increasing the acquiring firm's cost of capital

d. stabilizing the acquiring firm's sales
e. synergistic earnings

_____ 21. The purpose of the Export-Import Bank is to
a. provide foreign exchange loans to governments of countries ex-
    periencing balance of payments deficits.
b. insure composite currency loans.
c. make loans to finance high-risk projects in developing countries.
d. arrange currency swaps.
e. stimulate U.S. exports by extending credit to foreign importers.

_____ 22. The possible outcomes of a court-attempted reorganization of a financially distressed firm include
a. an informal bankruptcy, a conversion, or a voluntary agreement.
b. a discharge, a legal declaration of insolvency, or a conversion.
c. an extension, a recapitalization, or a composition.
d. a conversion, a dismissal, or a discharge.
e. a dismissal, a voluntary agreement, or an upward revaluation of the
    firm's fixed assets.

_____ 23. Which pair of mergers below reflects classification by economic impact?
a. Product extensions and holding companies
b. Statutory mergers and market extensions
c. Pure conglomerates and horizontal mergers
d. Vertical mergers and consolidations
e. Both a and c

_____ 24. An involuntary petition of bankruptcy can be filed by three or more unsecured creditors of the firm if their aggregate claims against the
firm exceed
a. $3,000.
b. $5,000.
c. $7,500.
d. $9,000.
e. $12,000.

_____ 25. A banker's acceptance is a bank-guaranteed
a. time draft.
b. bill of lading.
c. terminal warehouse receipt.
d. lien against a firm's inventory.
e. letter of credit.

ANSWERS TO REVIEW TEST QUESTIONS

PART I

1. c	6. b	11. a	16. a	21. d
2. e	7. a	12. a	17. c	22. b
3. a	8. c	13. c	18. a	23. d
4. b	9. b	14. b	19. a	24. d
5. c	10. e	15. b	20. c	25. c

26. b	31. a	36. c	41. c	46. b
27. b	32. a	37. b	42. c	47. a
28. a	33. b	38. c	43. b	48. b
29. b	34. d	39. a	44. c	49. a
30. a	35. c	40. d	45. d	50. b
				51. d

PART II

1. d	6. a	11. b	16. c	21. a
2. a	7. a	12. b	17. d	22. c
3. c	8. b	13. c	18. b	23. b
4. d	9. a	14. a	19. b	24. d
5. b	10. c	15. c	20. c	25. d

26. a	31. c
27. b	32. d
28. c	33. c
29. a	
30. a	

REVIEW TEST ANSWERS

PART III

1.	c	6.	a	11.	b	16.	a	21.	d
2.	b	7.	a	12.	e	17.	c	22.	c
3.	b	8.	b	13.	c	18.	c	23.	b
4.	b	9.	c	14.	b	19.	c	24.	a
5.	c	10.	c	15.	e	20.	d	25.	a

26.	c	31.	a	36.	a	41.	b
27.	b	32.	b	37.	e	42.	d
28.	c	33.	d	38.	c	43.	b
29.	d	34.	c	39.	c	44.	c
30.	b	35.	b	40.	c	

PART IV

1.	d	6.	c	11.	c	16.	c	21.	a
2.	d	7.	b	12.	d	17.	e	22.	c
3.	c	8.	e	13.	b	18.	d	23.	d
4.	e	9.	e	14.	d	19.	b	24.	e
5.	a	10.	a	15.	d	20.	e	25.	d

PART V

1.	c	6.	c	11.	c	16.	d	21.	d
2.	a	7.	b	12.	e	17.	b	22.	b
3.	d	8.	e	13.	b	18.	d	23.	b
4.	d	9.	a	14.	b	19.	a	24.	e
5.	b	10.	d	15.	c	20.	e	25.	d

PART VI

1.	a	6.	c	11.	e	16.	d	21.	c
2.	e	7.	d	12.	c	17.	c	22.	a
3.	d	8.	b	13.	c	18.	b	23.	d
4.	a	9.	e	14.	a	19.	e	24.	d
5.	d	10.	b	15.	a	20.	a	25.	c

PART VII

1.	d	6.	b	11.	b	16.	c	21.	e
2.	a	7.	e	12.	c	17.	b	22.	d
3.	b	8.	a	13.	b	18.	e	23.	c
4.	d	9.	c	14.	e	19.	b	24.	b
5.	c	10.	a	15.	d	20.	c	25.	a